HOLY DIGITAL GRAIL

STANFORD
TEXT TECHNOLOGIES

Series Editors
Ruth Ahnert
Elaine Treharne

Editorial Board
Benjamin Albritton
Lori Emerson
Alan Liu
Elena Pierazzo
Andrew Prescott
Matthew Rubery
Kate Sweetapple
Heather Wolfe

Holy Digital Grail

A Medieval Book on the Internet

MICHELLE R. WARREN

Stanford University Press
Stanford, California

STANFORD UNIVERSITY PRESS
Stanford, California

© 2022 by the Board of Trustees of the Leland Stanford Junior University.
All rights reserved.

No part of this book may be reproduced or transmitted in any form or by any means, electronic or mechanical, including photocopying and recording, or in any information storage or retrieval system without the prior written permission of Stanford University Press.

Printed in the United States of America on acid-free, archival-quality paper
Library of Congress Cataloging-in-Publication Data
Names: Warren, Michelle R., 1967- author.
Title: Holy digital grail : a medieval book on the internet / Michelle R. Warren.
Other titles: Text technologies.
Description: Stanford, California : Stanford University Press, 2022. |
    Series: Stanford text technologies | Includes bibliographical references
    and index.
Identifiers: LCCN 2021050032 (print) | LCCN 2021050033 (ebook) |
    ISBN 9781503608009 (cloth) | ISBN 9781503631168 (paperback) |
    ISBN 9781503631175 (epub)
Subjects: LCSH: Manuscripts, Medieval—Digitization. | Arthurian romances—
    Manuscripts—Digitization. | Codicology—Technological innovations. |
    Literature and technology. | Digital humanities.
Classification: LCC Z110.R4 W37 2022 (print) | LCC Z110.R4 (ebook) |
    DDC 091.0285—dc23/eng/20211109
LC record available at https://lccn.loc.gov/2021050032
LC ebook record available at https://lccn.loc.gov/2021050033

Cover design: Kevin Barrett Kane

Typeset by Kevin Barrett Kane in 10/15 Spectral

CONTENTS

ILLUSTRATIONS

BL	British Library
BNF	Bibliothèque Nationale de France
CCCA	Corpus Christi College Archives, Location OA 6E
CCCC	Corpus Christi College, Cambridge: Parker Library
EEBO	Early English Books Online, Chadwyck-Healey and Proquest.com
EETS ES	Early English Text Society, Extra Series
EETS OS	Early English Text Society, Original Series
f.	folio
Grail	Lovelich 1874–78. Note: *Grail* references have Roman numeral chapters (I to LVI) followed by Arabic numeral lines.
JSTOR	Journal Storage Project, ITHAKA.org
LMA	London Metropolitan Archives
MED	*Middle English Dictionary*, https://quod.lib.umich.edu/m/middle-english-dictionary
Merlin	Lovelich 1904–32. Note: *Merlin* references have continuous Arabic numeral lines (1–27852).
NA	National Archives, United Kingdom

I've written this book both very quickly and very slowly. Almost every word published here was typed over the past two years, yet I also started way back in 1996. Along the way, I almost abandoned this project more than once, as it became more and more difficult to reconcile the original research methods with the growing number of databases, digital image collections, and other networked resources. Once I brought the tension between old archives and new archives into the research, I had the opposite problem: how to stop when the digital landscape keeps changing so rapidly.

This book represents an extended "user journey" through the infrastructure of medieval studies in the early twenty-first century. For those who study medieval literature, it exposes how various modern interventions have influenced our access to texts and thus how we perceive medieval creations. For those who manage collections and libraries, it looks closely at how institutional practices filter back into literary history. And for those who make and study digital culture, it connects today's objects to the long history of making and saving books. This book bears witness to a particular moment in the history of digital infrastructure—the lifespan of Parker Library on the Web 2.0, which began on January 10, 2018, and ended on March 3, 2021. Historical research is always bounded by specific modern frameworks to some degree, though rarely with such identifiable precision.

As I worked on this book, I wondered if I could write in a way that recognized that it would have multiple formats, just like the books I study here. This book is at once a bound book made of paper, a collection of digital files in PDF (Portable Document Format), a scrolling digital text-block, and probably some other formats as well. The digital versions can be accessed through devices with varied screen sizes. They might be processed through text-to-speech software. With these formats in mind, I adopted the author-date style of in-text references (*Chicago Manual of Style*, 17th edition). I appreciate how this style keeps the apparatus of scholarship exposed across all formats, and I hope readers will too. This style also helped me write without footnotes, a decision I made in the interests of accessibility and in the spirit of storytelling.

I wondered, too, how this book would appear on digital platforms. In the library catalogue at Dartmouth College, I found that Stanford University Press books appeared with ProQuest Ebooks identified as an "alternate author." This metadata quirk seems to misinterpret ProQuest's role while also revealing a truth about how infrastructure creates meaning for texts and books. Platforms do have some of the functions of authorship in that they "authorize" access and structure relationships that condition interpretation. At Dartmouth College, the library catalogue interface is itself a ProQuest product—Ex Libris Alma—which is notorious for listing databases by ProQuest as more "relevant" in search results than books on the library's own shelves. Here, in the cataloguing of my book about a book, I found yet more evidence of how infrastructure coauthors literary history.

Ironically, printed copies of this book that end up on library shelves have the best chance of long-term preservation—and the best chance of being incomplete. In the interest of longevity, libraries typically purchase hardcover copies and discard the dustjackets. Here, however, the cover design by Kevin Barrett Kane of Stanford University Press is integral to the meaning of the book. Every detail interprets some aspect of the stories I tell here, as Kevin so generously explained when I inquired (personal email, August 9, 2021). The background reproduces a piece of paper from the Special Collections Library at Stanford, rich in texture and unfolded with the faint suggestion of a cross in the creases, resonant with the theme of the Holy Grail. The distinctive red accents reflect the color branding of both Stanford and Corpus Christi College, Cambridge, custodians of the materials I study here. The main title is set in a font, Trade Gothic, of nineteenth-century fame, the era when editing and cataloguing created canons of medieval English literature. The subtitle is set in a font, Adobe Caslon Pro, that is the perfect amalgam of English print history and digital design: it is a "revival" of an eighteenth-century typeface by William Caslon designed by Carol Twombly at Adobe in the very era when digital manuscripts were first reaching the internet. Those reading this description in a coverless book might find a cover image in various online places, including the Dartmouth Digital Commons: digitalcommons.dartmouth.edu/faculty_other/9.

The stories I tell about medieval literature in this book range across centuries and through many fields of specialization. That breadth has brought many rewards as I've made connections that otherwise would have remained hidden. At the same time, the venture has brought the risk of making mistakes in unfamiliar subfields. I've spent years becoming an expert amateur in many different areas: learning new things is, after all, the essence of research. If I've made errors, I hope I've left readers enough clues to find ways to correct them.

HOLY DIGITAL GRAIL

MEDIEVAL LITERATURE IN THE DIGITAL DARK AGES

MEDIEVAL BOOKS THAT SURVIVE today have been through a lot. Some have had the good fortune to spend centuries protected by people who care. Others have been singed by fire, mottled by mold, or eaten by insects. Some have been annotated by thoughtful readers; others have been treated as scrap paper. Some have been dismantled for sale as fragments or cut up to extract illustrations. Still others have suffered from repairs, like stiff glue, that inadvertently caused further harm. Less invasive forms of preservation have also left their marks, such as cataloguers penciling in shelf marks (call numbers) or conservators flattening out pages to produce more consistent digital photographs. Surviving books have thus been shaped by many intentions and accidents over the centuries. Today, all these factors contribute to the meaning of texts and the materials that preserve them. In this book, I tell the story of one such book—from its textual origins in twelfth-century England to its twenty-first-century diffusion across the internet. This trajectory has been propelled by a succession of technologies—from paper manufacture to printing to computers. In the process, literary history, too, became a cultural technology.

The book in question currently lies on a metal shelf in a vault at Parker Library, Corpus Christi College, Cambridge, where it is known simply as "MS 80." This shelf mark is stamped in crisp gold characters on the spine. Inside, the text tells how Joseph of Arimathea, a secret disciple of Jesus Christ, used a cup from the Last Supper to collect some of Christ's blood and later brought this Holy Grail from Jerusalem to Britain. After the colonization and Christianization of Britain, the story continues with the birth of the magical Merlin and the reign of the legendary King Arthur. MS 80 ends in the midst of Arthur's first year as king, but the narrative arc continues in other books with the amorous adventures of Lancelot, the quest for the Holy Grail by various Arthurian knights, and ultimately the collapse of Arthur's kingdom and his uncertain death. These stories are still famous, having been told and retold across medieval Europe and eventually throughout the world. They are still being repeated in many languages and in nearly every popular media. This popularity has made King Arthur and the Holy Grail widely recognized symbols in many different contexts.

Among the many medieval texts about Arthur, MS 80 is unique. It was created, moreover, in unlikely circumstances: in the early fifteenth century, a craftsman of the London fur trade, Henry Lovelich, translated archaic French prose into more than fifty thousand lines of English rhyming couplets. The book was meant to be illustrated but remained incomplete and possibly unread for a number of years. MS 80 may be obscure, but six centuries later it isn't hard to find if you know where to look. I first found it as a graduate student while combing through Robert Ackerman's *Index of the Arthurian Names in Middle English* (1952c). I was looking for texts that mention King Arthur's sword Excalibur and was struck by one text that used a French word as the sword's name, *Trenchefust* (cut wood) (Ackerman 1952c, 232). This detail sent me searching for the edition, where I learned that the author was a "skinner and citizen of London" and that there was a manuscript in Cambridge (Kock 1904–32). I wasn't sure if I'd ever visit Cambridge, but I knew how to find the library's address thanks to a required course in bibliography (Williams 1985). I took note of Corpus Christi College just in case. Several years later, I had my first chance to travel to Europe for academic conferences, and, somewhat on a lark, I decided to try to see MS 80. The library didn't yet have a website or email, so I pulled out the paper folder with the postal address and sent off a letter requesting an appointment. It seemed almost miraculous to receive an affirmative reply a few weeks later. Librarian Gillian Cannell had reserved one of the four seats at Parker Library for me on August 8 and 9, 1996.

I was a careful researcher, but I wasn't prepared for what I saw in Cambridge—a large, beautiful paper manuscript designed for extensive illustration. Throughout the book, periodic blank spaces had been left for drawings that should have been completed after the text was written. Questions flooded my mind: What was supposed to appear in the blanks? Who had designed the format? Which episodes had been selected as worthy of illustration? Who had paid for this unique book, and why wasn't it finished? How had it ended up at Corpus Christi College? The library's catalogue didn't answer any of these questions nor any of the others I developed later: Which French sources had Lovelich used? How did the guild context affect his translation strategies? The manuscript, despite being incomplete, had attracted some readers over the years, and some had written notes in the margins. They were hard to decipher at a glance: some seemed like commentary, others merely pointed to a line or two, and some had nothing to do with the text at all. How many annotators were there? What had they written and why? Further research revealed that twentieth-century literary historians had deemed the text wholly uninteresting: how had this fascinating book become a boring text?

By the end of my first day in Cambridge, I already had more questions than I could possibly answer even if I stayed for several weeks. I was therefore delighted to learn that I could purchase a microfilm of MS 80. Thus, even before I left the reading room, modern technologies were revising my relationship with the manuscript and my approach to literary history. Similarly, back in the United States, the process of procuring a printed check in British pounds brought me into relations with the international banking system that I now see as an integral part of manuscript preservation. When the microfilm finally arrived, I headed straight to the university library to find a microfilm machine and continue studying MS 80's illustration patterns and annotations—all the features not well documented in the editions (Furnivall 1874–78; Kock 1904–32). Over the next several years, I stayed engaged with MS 80 through the microfilm, using it regularly as I developed research connecting Lovelich's text to literary history in fifteenth-century London (Warren 2007, 2008). A presentation about MS 80 eventually helped me land a new job at Dartmouth College—a location that came to play a pivotal role in the stories I now have to tell about MS 80. At the time, though, my research was headed in other directions (Warren 2011). I wasn't sure how much more I had to say about Lovelich or his book.

Then, late in 2009, an email arrived from a Dartmouth librarian, Francis X. Oscadal, announcing a one-month trial subscription to Parker Library on the Web. Could it really be that MS 80 was now just a click away? My curiosity renewed, I copied as many digital images as I could, unsure if the library would pay the $3,500 annual subscription fee (Harrassowitz 2009). Before long, the library did subscribe, and I settled in to continue my research. In 2012, I returned to Cambridge to discuss born-digital research projects under way with Parker Library on the Web (Gillespie and Horobin 2015). There, in the newly renovated reading room, I started to see digital images as more than a convenience. Just as the manuscripts had been moved into a new vault for better protection, the website required attention and updating to remain accessible. The digital images and their associated data were more fragile in some ways than the oldest book in the vault. The website was a new material object that had become part of book history.

My journey to digital studies was sealed in 2015 when I first read about the idea of "digital vellum" (Lepore 2015). This term is a metaphor that refers to a digital preservation system as durable as the refined animal skin used for many medieval books—some more than a thousand years old and counting (*vellum* serves here, and throughout this book, as a generic synonym for parchment). The rapid pace of digital obsolescence is old news by now: new operating systems won't run on hardware more than just a few years old; old file formats won't open in new software. As a result, digital objects disappear on a regular basis. "Digital vellum" would provide a solution to this problem of digital preservation. Until that solution is invented, we operate in what has been called the "digital Dark Ages"—another medieval metaphor. This term correlates information depravation with the state of Europe after the Roman Empire. The rhetorical "Dark Ages" serves as a shorthand for ignorance, social chaos, economic failure, and all bad things that should be left behind. In digital discourse, then, medieval metaphors point to both the problem of preservation (a looming "Dark Ages") and the solution (a "vellum" that will rescue precious objects). This solution, however, remains elusive, a "holy grail" as it turns out. These three medieval metaphors bring the internet to the heart of manuscript studies and literary history in the twenty-first century. And they make medieval studies integral to understanding the deep histories of modern computing.

This book about MS 80, then, is about more than another book. It's about how we research now. It's about how digital infrastructure is changing the nature of books, even very old books. In retrospect, my path to MS 80 was laid out by modern infrastructures long before I reached Cambridge in 1996: a university in California founded at the latter end of North American colonization, an index gathering words from editions produced in their own nationalist circumstances, communication systems transporting people and paper around the world. Information tools had shaped both my curiosity and my ignorance: at first, I could only know what others had already found important. Working backward through layers of infrastructure, I found that the specificity of MS 80 was often essential: a book containing an English text about the Holy Grail and King Arthur attracted certain kinds of attention; it promised certain kinds of value to collectors, editors, and readers. At other times, MS 80 is somewhat incidental to this story: it has been produced, collected, recorded, classified, preserved, accessed, edited, and copied in the same ways as many other books. MS 80's trajectory exemplifies how books persist through time as part of complex economies that continually shape and reshape their meaning. Their existence on a shelf and their distribution online rest on a bedrock of capital accumulation via global imperialism. As I followed MS 80's movements across these many platforms, the platforms themselves came into focus as meaning makers. Throughout this book, I will argue that literary history is coauthored by the technology platforms that produce and preserve texts.

The primary platform is Parker Library itself. MS 80 exists today because it was collected by Matthew Parker (1504–75)—the first Anglican Archbishop of Canterbury, charged by Queen Elizabeth I to find proof of England's independence from the Roman Catholic Church. A well-practiced antiquarian and collector, Parker searched far and wide for materials. Among the many manuscripts that he and his associates consulted, MS 80 was among the hundreds selected for Parker's personal collection. In 1574, Parker bequeathed most of his books to Corpus Christi College, where he had been Master (1544–53). He provided detailed instructions for the collection's preservation, establishing a library that became a "national heritage treasure" ("Parker Library" 2019). The collection's fame has endured for five centuries. Its celebrity justified the construction of a new state-of-the-art vault in 2006 and a multiyear project to photograph the medieval manuscripts for a digital platform. To produce Parker Library on the Web, Corpus Christi College partnered with Stanford University—a move facilitated by the twists and turns of the global market for European cultural heritage. The project received significant financing from the Andrew W. Mellon Foundation—a major source of grant funding for scholarly infrastructure in the humanities, among other cultural priorities. The first Parker Library on the Web opened in 2009 to great acclaim (Parker 1.0); in January 2018, the platform relaunched as a free resource with an entirely new format, garnering even more public attention (Parker 2.0). MS 80 thus owes its digital visibility not to its literary reputation but to its perhaps accidental arrival in Parker's hands in the sixteenth century.

Parker's collection is famous in part because it is full of celebrities—manuscripts of remarkable beauty, age, or both. Christopher De Hamel—former Parker Librarian—fully embraces the celebrity metaphor in *Meetings with Remarkable Manuscripts*. He compares encounters with famous manuscripts to interviews with famous people, complete with all the emotions of anticipation, awe, and sometimes disappointment when reality fails to match reputation. He notes that some books are harder to meet than "the Pope or the President of the United States" (De Hamel 2016, 1–2). On my first visit to Parker Library, I certainly felt the anticipation and awe that De Hamel describes. I had expected my request to be denied. I felt even more special when I found out that the library had only four seats. And then there was the pleasure of finding a book designed for illustration, something no one seemed to have studied. But I would also like to resist the starstruck approach that leads De Hamel to focus on "celebrated manuscripts" that are "dazzlingly illuminated" and that lend their "glamor" to their readers, to the envy of those studying "more modest books" (De Hamel 2016, 4). MS 80 is generally considered one of those lesser lights. Yet, as De Hamel also notes, "The life of every manuscript, like that of every person, is different, and all have stories to divulge" (De Hamel 2016, 3). In the following chapters, I take this premise to heart, delving into the vagaries of celebrity across the centuries as stars rise and fall according to cultural changes, find second and third careers, and gather new entourages that rebrand their reputation.

The rhetoric of celebrity has not diminished with digitization. Although the internet has been heralded as a democratizing force, various forms of elitism and restriction persist. Even digital resources that are open access have often had to rely on the glamour of celebrity to garner the funding that brought them into existence. In medieval studies, the expense of production labor has often meant promoting already canonized texts and already famous books (Prescott and Hughes 2018). In English studies, digital projects have leveraged the most famous medieval authors—Geoffrey Chaucer first and foremost—to draw attention and resources to new styles of digital research (e.g., Mooney, Horobin, and Stubbs 2011; Minnis 2012). Parker Library, too, has traded on its most dazzling documents to promote fundraising efforts for the collection as a whole. Until quite recently, the library's website celebrated the collection as "a jewel in the Corpus crown" ("Parker Library" 2018)—a royalist image that defines value with exclusivity. These kinds of approaches have indeed helped maintain valuable cultural heritage and generated important new research. The expansion of access to digital images has undeniably transformed scholarship, teaching, and public access to cultural heritage in many positive ways. At the same time, digitization has left the literary canon largely intact—along with the nationalist values that built the canon. Meanwhile, projects that promise "newer and better" technologies reinforce ideas about progress that are equally indebted to nationalist legacies. The very vocabulary of digital technology obscures the realities of infrastructure: "home" pages make novelty seem familiar, while the "cloud" covers the cables that make electronic display possible. The interactions among books, texts, software, hardware, aesthetics, and capitalism have become so complex that they are harder and harder to grasp.

What is a medievalist—or anyone—to do in the face of these tensions? How can literary history account for this complex inheritance? Throughout this book, I give several answers by investigating long histories of preservation and access. These histories of one text in one book expose institutional and infrastructural drivers of aesthetic value, capital investment, and editorial labor that also shape many other texts and books. My analysis encompasses vast interconnected networks in order to catch infrastructure in the act of turning fiction into facts, text into poetry, documents into art, and speculation into scholarship. As Whitney Trettien has put it: "Only in acknowledging and historicizing how media technologies remediate, disseminate, and store scholarship in the humanities and its subject matter can we begin to rework these networked technologies in ways that challenge a hegemonic, market-driven notion of what contemporary techne is, or could be" (Trettien 2018, 56). The value of a text or book is not as a fixed commodity but a fluctuating index of social and technological forces. MS 80, on its own, might have been left to rot. As part of Parker's collection, it was swept up in the political and aesthetic legacy of the library itself, which now extends to the internet.

By focusing intently on one object in its many forms, my multimedia history of MS 80 seeks to grasp how the knowledge economy operates over time. Medieval literature is only a small part of the traffic in knowledge, but it is revelatory because it takes so many different forms—manuscripts, printed books, microfilms, born-digital media. The Arthurian narrative in MS 80 is distinctly revelatory for similar reasons: a unique version of a much-told story, it illustrates the many ways in which texts are preserved and valued—translation, adaptation, annotation, genre classification, cataloguing, editing. The origins of the grail myth, moreover, are shrouded in mystery, lending the story a sense of timelessness even as each transmission takes a specific form at a specific time. Arthurian literature is itself a platform that has hosted a myriad of values across the centuries. The Holy Grail and King Arthur have a "celebrity" that exceeds any particular version of their story: they are recognizable on their own, even wildly out of context. They are part of the broader appropriation of the "medieval" as a projection of modern ideals and prejudices. Some of those projections are quite specifically about technology. By connecting medieval metaphors in computing with medieval books reproduced on computers, I open the study of books toward the study of the infrastructures that sustain books—as objects, on shelves, in communities.

MS 80 is, all by itself, the very definition of an "unfinished book," in the phrase of Alexandra Gillespie and Deirdre Lynch (2021). The section titles of their new history of the book pose the questions that I answer in various ways in the following chapters: What is a book? Where is a book? When is a book? These questions align with an infrastructural approach to book history: the answers are not single or fixed but infinitely variable. One task, then, of literary history is to answer these questions with many stories about how texts and books endure—from collecting to cataloguing to editing to financing. Integrating literary history with infrastructure studies expands the relevant "plot points" in these stories. For MS 80, I've organized my answers in chapters with overlapping chronologies rather than as a single progression from manuscript to print to digital. Today, each technology informs the others. I argue that there is no getting around the digital knowledge economy, even while holding the manuscript in the Parker Library reading room.

This introduction lays out my framework for understanding MS 80 across the centuries—from its French sources to its creation in London and eventually to its diffusion over the internet. I look first to the history of computing and digital preservation since the 1960s, when the internet and the first graphical interfaces were being developed. Since that time, medieval metaphors have been part of how technologists convey their goals and aspirations. Drawing on the established popularity of Arthurian images, what I call "tech medievalism" extends the deep web of storytelling that also produced MS 80. The aura of legendary prestige that animated the design of MS 80 has also animated and distributed the value of new technologies. This story culminates when Vint Cerf—coinventor of the protocols that power the internet—draws medieval manuscripts into the "digital Dark Ages" to illustrate the durable properties of "digital vellum." Here, book history and digital infrastructure fuse, both literally and figuratively. This fusion broadens the very idea of "book" to include properties shared by computers and the internet. This expansive notion of book history has reached new levels of refinement as manuscript scholars have turned to the digital and media scholars have turned to the material. From this framework, I draw out six stories about MS 80, each a distinct approach to reading and accessing books. Together, these six chapters integrate the social functions of literature with the political functions of technology. MS 80 serves as a catalyst for an approach to literary history that accounts for preservation and access alongside production and aesthetics.

Computing with Medieval Metaphors

The story of MS 80 on the internet begins with the history of computing itself—specifically, with the medieval metaphors that stretch from the first graphical interface to the most recent preservation protocols. Tech medievalism rests on popular stereotypes about the European Middle Ages as either a depraved time ended by modernity or an idealized time that modernity should recover. This duality makes medieval metaphors particularly useful for technologists, since it positions invention as a comprehensive solution to past and future problems. In tech medievalism, *medieval* means "outdated," even as certain medieval icons align with futuristic perfection. On the positive side of this calculus, the "Holy Grail" is among the most recognizable tools. The phrase—with or without the *holy*—can be found everywhere, from casual conversation to specialized academic publications across many fields. It readily invokes goals that are highly desirable yet possibly unattainable. Technologists will go to truly astonishing lengths to devise GRAIL acronyms: Graphical Reality Augmentation Interface Language, Graphics and Imaging Laboratory, GALEN Representation and Integration Language, Gravity Recovery and Interior Laboratory, Gene Relationships across Implicated Loci, Gene Recognition and Analysis Internet Link, and General Real-time Adaptable Indoor Localization (Google search, October 2018). By aligning complex science with the grail's simplified message of perfection, these acronyms smooth the way for public acceptance of new ideas. Time and again, "grail" has proven an irresistible image for heroic innovation. This phenomenon makes MS 80 part of the long transmission of Arthurian legend from the "Dark Ages" to the "digital Dark Ages."

In medieval literature, the Holy Grail is a sorting technology: it separates the ignorant and impure from the genuine Christian knight. The sacred object, famously, can be found only by one pure knight, Galahad. His reward is full knowledge of divine secrets. A few other knights achieve partial glimpses, but the mass of collaborators who set out on the quest either die or return to Camelot defeated. They never find the grail because it hides itself from them. In computing, then, grail metaphors shore up the romantic idea that invention is driven by individual geniuses endowed with innate superiority, with the mass of collaborators consigned to defeat even before they begin. The inventors themselves can become objects of desire: notably, Steve Jobs—the legendary founder of Apple—has been described as a "holy grail," that is, a unique and irreplaceable genius who attracts questers (Bayers 2013; Palmer 2015). This ideology occludes computing practices that value communitarian and democratic networking, such as those documented by Joy Lisi Rankin in *A People's History of Computing in the United States* (2018) or Charlton McIlwain in *Black Software* (2020). The cult of individualism has also erased the contributions of the human "computers," often women, who contributed both intellectual and physical labor to major scientific achievements, such as the Black women mathematicians profiled by Margot Lee Shetterly in *Hidden Figures* (2016). Computing innovations of the 1960s, moreover, profited from what Lisa Nakamura (2014) has called the "racialization of early electronic manufacture" on the lands of the Navajo Nation. Grail metaphors, like interface itself, mask these operations of power.

The first technology grail was the interface to one of the first personal computers. In the 1960s, researchers at the RAND Corporation—with funding from the US Department of Defense—developed the first working prototype of a tablet with a stylus. And they called their interface GRAIL: Graphical Input Language. The explicit purpose was to "shield" the user from "systems functions"—that is, the raw code running machine processes (Ellis, Heafner, and Sibley 1969, v). Instead of programming the machine directly, the GRAIL interface made computing more like handwriting directly on a page: the user "constructs and manipulates the display contents directly and naturally without the need to instruct an intermediary (the machine)" (Ellis, Heafner, and Sibley 1969, 3). The graphics become a new kind of intermediary that obscures the mechanisms of machine processing. What better image than the grail to convey the ineffable, elusive fusion of thought, representation, and code? The grail metaphor mystifies computing—and defines computing as a mystification. With the GRAIL project, digital interface entered the world as a medieval metaphor that taught users not to ask too many questions about machines or their makers.

The GRAIL interface crystallizes two enduring aspects of digital infrastructure: metaphor as a device and singular solutions as an ideology. Metaphors influence how people define problems and develop answers. In the 1990s at Apple—where the graphical user interface came to commercial fruition—metaphor itself was once called the "holy grail" of design: good metaphors guide users subliminally whereas bad ones create confusion (Erickson 1990, 65). Metaphors rely on users' ability to transfer a familiar idea to a new context; if the existing associations and the new ones are mismatched, the transfer fails. Computers in general are "metaphor machines" (Chun 2011, 55–66), since their internal processes are invisible to the human eye: layers, desktops, files, and clouds are all metaphors for electronic functions. The metaphors condition how people relate to computers and networks (Blanchette 2011; Emerson 2014; Hu 2015). Among recent digital grails, the "GraalVM" software by Oracle (another mystifying metaphor) takes mystical abstraction to a new level: the software distances users from direct instructions by creating a virtual environment where several programming languages can be used simultaneously; a plugin, "Galaaz," even translates so that programmers only have to know one language (https://graalvm.org; https://github.com/rbotafogo/galaaz). With GraalVM, the whole environment becomes an interface where differences are reduced to a single solution. This style of reduction again links the grail to interfaces that direct users away from knowledge about system infrastructure.

All the technologies that sustain MS 80's multimedia history have been associated with the Holy Grail at some point. The first technology of mass photographic copying, microfilm, was developed commercially by Eugene Power, founder of University Microfilms, Inc. (UMI)—the ultimate source for some of today's most significant digital resources on ProQuest, such as "Dissertations and Theses" and "Early English Books Online" (EEBO). Power attributed his idea for "editions of one" printed from microfilm rolls to a 1931 meeting with John Marshall, secretary of the Medieval Academy of America, and Robert Binkley, chair of the Joint Committee on Materials for Research of the American Council of Learned Societies and the Social Science Research Council (1930–40). Binkley went on to envision the "scholar's workstation," a personalized machine of interactive microfilm (1934)—the predecessor to the more famous Memex described by Vannevar Bush (Bush 1945; Cady 1990, 377). When Power later recalled Binkley's 1931 presentation, he described "the concept of somehow being able to produce copies of academic material in small quantities or one at a time, on demand" as his "personal holy grail" (Power 1990, 16). Here, the grail represents profitable academic publishing—small quantities for specialized audiences, essential to a healthy knowledge economy but elusive under industrial capitalism.

Today, MS 80 is also a digital artifact reproduced on Parker Library on the Web. It is thus subject to all the challenges of digital preservation amid ever-changing software and hardware. Unlike microfilm, which is estimated to last five hundred years, digital objects expire within a decade or so if not migrated, updated, or otherwise transformed. Durable solutions to digital preservation remain elusive. Librarian Margaret Hedstrom (1999) has argued that instead of one, comprehensive solution, libraries should adopt multiple strategies for different types of materials: "the search for the Holy Grail of digital archiving is premature, unrealistic, and possibly counter-productive." Even now, digital archivist William Kilbride notes that intervening in "document life cycles" remains "the holy grail among archivists and records managers—alluring but always just out of reach" (Kilbride 2016, 416). It seems almost inevitable, then, that someone would ask, "Is the Cloud the Holy Grail for long-term image storage?" (Shipton 2015). Most recently, the Schoenberg Institute for Manuscript Studies cast "linked open data"—the principle behind the protocols that drive Parker 2.0—as "the holy grail of the digital humanities" ("Hooking Up" 2019). That is, the mass linking of resources through interoperable standards remains a highly desirable yet elusive goal for digital research in the humanities. Across digital discourse, the grail conveys the idea of a complete solution to multifaceted problems.

In medieval texts, the Holy Grail first appears at Camelot, where King Arthur holds court. Like the Holy Grail, Camelot serves as a romanticized symbol of perfection, associated with social harmony and good governance. In 1990, it became the symbol of a new file format—now known as PDF (Portable Document Format). The file specification was first described by Adobe Systems cofounder John Warnock as "The Camelot Project" (Warnock 1990; Gitelman 2014a, 123). This metaphor expressed the technical function of gathering a document's specifications into one, sovereign place so that it could be reprinted with the same format on any printer. Recent commentators have embellished the idea by connecting the PDF's capacity to "view-and-print-anywhere" to Camelot's magical capacity to appear anywhere—a mythical city with no fixed geographical location (Willinsky, Garnett, and Wong 2012). The PDF facilitates "editions of one" beyond Power's wildest dreams. Power and Warnock both faced technical challenges with the reproduction of documents. And both turned to colloquial Arthurianism to make their solutions feel like magic. Today, PDF-enabled print-on-demand publishing is itself regularly described as the "holy grail" of profitable workflow (Google search results for "grail print-on-demand," May 2020). The allure of Arthurian magic keeps generating promises that technology will solve every problem.

The counterpoint to these aspirational images comes from the "digital Dark Ages," which invokes the ignorance and social chaos that might ensue from the loss of digital information. The first to medievalize digital preservation seems to have been librarian Terry Kuny in "A Digital Dark Ages? Challenges in the Preservation of Electronic Information" (1997). Under this provocative title, Kuny developed an extended metaphor that began with medieval Christian monks as analogues for modern librarians: both are faithful guardians of knowledge, preserving and distributing books (Kuny 1997, 1). This image incorporates another neomedieval preservation trope—monks as the first copyists. In the 1960s, the head of the Manuscripts Division at the Library of Congress, Lester Born, aligned the "wonders of the medieval scriptoria" with those of the microfilm lab (Born 1960, 348). Around the same time, a journalist for *Business Week* celebrated Eugene Power of UMI by describing his microfilm business as "a modern version of a medieval monastery" with "monkish work cells" (cited in Power 1990, 233). UMI was later sold to Xerox, which in the 1970s marketed the photocopy machine as a major advance on monks' copying techniques (Foys 2018). Recent work in media studies also evokes monks as the first copyists (Mattern 2017, xiii; Smithies 2017, 10–11). While medieval Christian monks certainly do belong to the long history of media production, they are hardly the *first* copyists: their persistent image in preservation discourse is yet another component of tech medievalism that draws on reductive stereotypes.

According to Kuny, librarians in the 1990s were already working in the "digital Dark Ages"; their collections were gradually being destroyed by various "barbarians" such as intractable quantities of information, rapid obsolescence of storage media, the proliferation of complex formats, financial constraints, restrictions on intellectual property, and commodified information (Kuny 1997, 2–4). To defend against these incursions, Kuny proposed several tactics: standardization, migration, limiting the scope of what gets saved, keeping nonelectronic formats, managing intellectual property rights, and collaborating (1997, 6–7). These strategies recognize the limits of digital materials: "Digital collections facilitate access, but do not facilitate preservation. Being digital means being ephemeral" (1997, 10). Nonetheless, librarians could ensure at least partial transmission with carefully crafted preservation plans: "The traces of information that we are able to save from our digital vellum will be valuable sources of information to the future" (1997, 10). With vellum as the metaphor for durable digital storage, Kuny completes the medieval image. Kuny was hardly the first to identify the challenges of digital preservation (Cloonan 1993; Rothenberg 1995; Conway 1996). But his pithy formulation—archived in a well-preserved networked repository—has indelibly linked data loss to a neomedieval future.

The "digital Dark Ages" are simultaneously a fact of the past (many things have already been lost), a condition of the present (new things are lost every day), and a projected future event (when more things will have been lost). The phrase gained popular traction following a 1998 conference at the Getty Center in Los Angeles, "Time & Bits: Managing Digital Continuity" (MacLean and Davis 1998). The Getty partnered with the Long Now Foundation (LNF), founded by Danny Hillis and Stewart Brand in 1996 to counteract tendencies toward short-term thinking—exemplified at the time by the so-called "Y2K problem" of computers not designed for dates beyond 1999. LNF is preparing for the "Y10K problem" of the year 9999. Hillis and Brand are both eclectic serial entrepreneurs—with Hillis best known for inventing parallel computing and Brand for embodying the convergence of "counterculture and cyberculture" (Turner 2006; Lambert 2005, 39–45; "Danny Hillis" 2019). In the wake of the Getty conference, they both used the phrase "digital Dark Ages" to refer to the period "from the widespread use of the computer up till the time we've solved this problem [of preservation]" (MacLean and Davis 1998, 33, 42). Brand quoted Hillis in a book chapter, "Ending the Digital Dark Age" (Brand 1999a), and in a *Library Journal* article, "Escaping the Digital Dark Age" (Brand 1999b). These titles reveal Brand's optimistic focus on solutions. Not surprisingly, he had earlier expressed his view of the positive impacts of computing as a "renaissance" (Brand 1987, 252). Almost predictably, Getty conference participants also invoked monk copyists (MacLean and Davis 1998, 25, 37).

Once preservation is framed in "dark age" terms, the metaphor extends to frame an entire ideology of progress.

Another Getty conference participant, Brewster Kahle, amplified the "digital Dark Ages" on a digital preservation project launched around the same time: the Internet Archive (Kahle 1997; Lyman and Kahle 1998). The phrase, attributed to Hillis, was featured on the Internet Archive's "About" page from the time the site went public in 2001 until February 2017: "Without cultural artifacts, civilization has no memory and no mechanism to learn from its successes and failures. And paradoxically, with the explosion of the Internet, we live in what Danny Hillis has referred to as our 'digital dark age'" ("About the Archive" 2001–17; cited in Chun 2008, 168; De Kosnik 2016, 46–51). Kahle's imagination of digital preservation was further fed by the loss and preservation of ancient manuscripts. In fact, the first word of his article announcing the Internet Archive is *manuscripts*—referring to the ones that burned in the ancient library of Alexandria (Kahle 1997, 82). The article appeared as part of a special report in *Scientific American* on "civilizing" the internet. Another contribution held up the famous, partly burnt, manuscript containing the Old English *Beowulf* as an example of how digital imaging could rescue damaged texts (Lesk 1997; Kiernan 1991). In both these examples, the destruction of manuscripts points to the scale of loss that awaits digital culture.

Since the 1990s, the "digital Dark Ages" has continued to designate the fragility of digital materials. The phrase has been consecrated as a synonym for data loss by dedicated pages on the Library and Information Science Wiki ("Digital Dark Ages" 2005) and Wikipedia ("Digital Dark Age" 2006). One frequently cited loss concerns a project inspired by a medieval book—the 1086 census of Britain known as the *Domesday Book*, a collection of records for taxation. To celebrate the nine-hundredth anniversary in 1986, the British Broadcasting Company created a massive digital snapshot of Britain. The BBC adopted the latest laser disc technology—with the result that fifteen years later the content was largely inaccessible because disc readers were no longer widely available. The technical failure of the BBC Digital Domesday has been widely reported as a "digital Dark Ages" event; it remains a cautionary example for scholars, librarians, businesses, and the general public of how unstable digital storage really is (O'Donnell 2004; Harvey and Weatherburn 2018, 120–21). Over the last twenty years, Digital Domesday has gone through several recoveries, migrations, and relapses into the dark. The latest public website was taken down as recently as June 2018 (Finney 1986–2006; "BBC Domesday Project" 2018). News reports about Digital Domesday frequently convey the significance of the "digital Dark Ages" with the heart-tugging example of future grandchildren deprived of today's family photos. Manuscript photos—and other digital resources—risk the same fate unless they receive regular care.

Preservation is a matter not only of technology but economics (Kilbride 2016, 414). Here, too, the "digital Dark Ages" provide the metaphor. In fact, the very first reference to the phrase indexed on Google.com is a 1996 article about the global political economy in *Wired* magazine (whose editor, Kevin Kelly, also attended the Getty conference). In this article, David Kline characterizes increasing global inequality as the dark side of the digital: "How do we ensure that the future does not become a wonderland of opportunity for the minority among us who are affluent, mobile, and highly educated and, at the same time, a digital dark age for the majority of citizens—the poor, the non-college-educated—who are not?" (Kline 1996). Kline concludes that governments, far from obsolete, are sorely needed to safeguard social and economic health by ensuring a stable digital infrastructure. This formulation of the "digital Dark Ages" makes time a state of being that is unevenly distributed across the world. The "Dark Ages" happen anywhere that lacks technology—whether in the past, like the 1970s (Plotnikoff 1997), or the present, like rural areas without high-speed internet access (Fildes et al. 2018). The "Dark Ages" also threaten wherever digital property might be damaged (Ja 2015; Schmitt 2018). As the internet has become infrastructure, lack of secure access both reflects and creates other forms of inequality. This global dynamic includes historical archives and scholarly resources, as institutional wealth also shapes what gets published and who can access it.

And once a problem is defined in medieval terms, the solution becomes a "renaissance." The starkest formulation may be the European Union's official definition of digital strategy, entitled *The New Renaissance*: "Our goal is to ensure that Europe experiences a digital Renaissance instead of entering into a digital Dark Age"; all stakeholders must "take up their responsibilities in order to ensure that Europe's citizens and economy fully benefit from the potential of bringing Europe's cultural heritage online" (Niggemann, Decker, and Lévy 2011, 12). This goal requires coordinated public and private funding across numerous institutions. It suggests that economic benefit will be one criterion for bringing materials online. The corpus of digitized materials—including medieval manuscripts— constitutes a new "canon" of items deemed worthy of investment. Even as this corpus grows, online availability will always be limited by selections that reflect a host of technical, social, and financial arrangements. The digital capitalism of cultural heritage conjoins public service and profit. These arrangements illustrate the flip side of Brand's famous quote about free information, rarely cited in full: "Information wants to be free because it has become so cheap to distribute, copy, and recombine—too cheap to meter. It wants to be expensive because it can be immeasurably valuable to the recipient" (Brand 1987, 202). In cultural heritage, the calculation of value has many dimensions, from aesthetics to nationalism to tourism. With the profitable future framed in historic metaphors, the economy depends on not looking too closely at history.

Parker Library on the Web and MS 80 exemplify all these "digital Dark Age" issues. In the 1990s, medieval manuscripts headed online along with everything else. By 1996, when curators at Parker Library first considered digitizing the manuscript collection (CCCA, Box 5), numerous other projects were already under way at other institutions (replies to Warren 2018b). The British Library opened its first website in 1993 with an image of the Magna Carta, which was soon joined by images from the *Beowulf* manuscript (Prescott 1998). Concerns about how to maintain these new artifacts emerged gradually, as the earliest projects started to break. When Parker Library on the Web opened in 2009, sustainability was addressed in part by the subscription fee. Ten years later, when the site migrated to a new interface with open access, preservation costs were absorbed in new infrastructure arrangements at Stanford Libraries. The transformation of Parker 1.0 into Parker 2.0, however, brought significant changes to the manuscript descriptions and other features. These changes have rewritten the pathways of discovery for historical data. The effects are profound yet fleeting: Parker 1.0 lasted ten years, and Parker 2.0 lasted three (version 2.1 was released in March 2021). Each new iteration can expose how digital infrastructures affect knowledge systems. Parker 1.0 is now evidence of an important historical moment in the practice of medieval studies, library science, and internet publishing. It reveals the current arrangements to be *arrangements*—not natural, inevitable, or "better" but rather the temporary products of complex interactions among communities, protocols, machines, and capital. These arrangements are not obstacles to overcome but infrastructures to understand. In a very real sense, they are writing the future of medieval studies.

Medieval Manuscripts with Digital Infrastructure

The "digital Dark Ages" and "digital vellum" have received a boost in visibility in recent years thanks to a series of pronouncements by Vint Cerf, a Google.com executive. Cerf is a coinventor, with Robert Kahn, of the Transmission Control Protocol (TCP) and Internet Protocol (IP) that structure networked communications (Abbate 1999, 122–31). Cerf's "digital vellum" would be a self-contained format that would include its own virtual operating system and hardware specifications, enabling digital objects to function long after the conditions of their creation have disappeared. This solution requires not only standardized descriptions for all the elements of hardware and software but the secure communication of those standards into the future (no small hurdle). Cerf, however, is relentlessly optimistic, as befits his title of Chief Internet Evangelist at Google. His promotion of "digital vellum" in numerous interviews and lectures led to a spike in "digital Dark Age" warnings about the fragility of digital storage ("Digital Dark Ages" 2004–21; Kosciejew 2015). The "vellum" metaphor focuses on the material aspects of digital preservation by alluding to a medieval material that combines storage, interface, and format. In this imagined archival future, entire computing systems function as self-contained "books" on digital shelves. They could be moved to new environments without losing their functions; they could last for years even if no one opens them.

For Cerf, though, vellum isn't only a metaphor. He refers regularly to his experiences handling actual medieval books, contrasting their longevity with the short lifespans of magnetic media. At one event, he mentioned a particular manuscript that happens to be particularly famous—the Archimedes Palimpsest, from which texts by the Greek mathematician Archimedes were "rediscovered" and "correctly interpreted" despite having been rubbed away and written over (Cerf 2015, min. 5:13–17). In another lecture, he described his own encounter with the book in an aside during his usual survey of storage media: he noted that he had just had dinner at a restaurant whose owner, Rick Adams, is an avid collector of ancient writings. Cerf recalled spending several hours "crawling around" looking at Adams's manuscripts—including the Archimedes Palimpsest (Cerf 2016, min. 12:20). At first, the anecdote seems anodyne: any manuscript will do. The Archimedes Palimpsest, however, has made a centuries-long journey through manuscript, print, and digital formats before crossing paths with Cerf. This remarkable story neatly illustrate the multimedia and infrastructural approaches to book history that I develop for MS 80 throughout this book.

The story of the Archimedes Palimpsest, or Codex, has been told by Reviel Netz and William Noel (2007) in the style of a detective novel. The manuscript contains a Byzantine prayer book from the 1200s made of seven booklets from the 900s; the earlier texts have been partially rubbed away and written over. Long held in the library of the Greek Orthodox Patriarchate in Constantinople, the codex was identified as a palimpsest in 1906 by the Danish scholar Johan Ludwig Heiberg: he discerned a text by the ancient Greek mathematician Archimedes underneath the medieval prayers (Peterson 2011). The book then disappeared in the 1920s, during the brutal establishment of the Turkish nation-state under Atatürk. It reappeared in Paris in the hands of a Jewish bookseller, Salomon Guerson, who sold it in 1942 to a French civil servant, Marie Louis Sirieix, in exchange for safe passage out of Nazi-occupied France. By that time, the book had acquired forged medieval-style images in gold leaf. It remained with Sirieix's daughter and Guerson's daughter-in-law, Anne Guerson, until 1998, when she sold it at a Christie's auction for $2 million (Lowden 2011). Almost immediately, the new anonymous owner turned the moldy, damaged book over to the Walters Art Museum and began funding a comprehensive conservation project (Netz and Noel 2007, 7–20). After five years of meticulous physical repairs, the leaves were photographed for digital analysis (Quandt 2011). Sophisticated computational processing revealed almost all the underlying text, including a previously unknown text by Archimedes and several other new texts (Netz et al. 2011, 1:174–239). At the end of the project, the book moved to the owner's private library while the digital files were made available in open access formats (Noel 2011, 14; *Archimedes Palimpsest* 2008–11). This whole story reached a broader audience through Noel's 2012 TEDx talk, which has been viewed more than a million times and translated into thirty languages (as of November 8, 2019). The fame of the Archimedes Palimpsest helped promote the principle of "open data" for cultural heritage, now increasingly adopted as the norm for medieval manuscript repositories.

Cerf's naming of Adams as the book owner adds another chapter to this already rich story. Adams's identity had previously been inferred but removed from Wikipedia as "speculation" (Shermer 2010; "Archimedes Palimpsest" 2018). Cerf has ended the speculation. Adams, it turns out, is an internet innovator in his own right. Cerf's calling him a "restaurant owner" is practically a misnomer, even if it's also true. In 1984, Adams devised the Serial Line Internet Protocol (SLIP), which enabled the network protocols TCP/IP to work with serial ports: with SLIP, personal computers could connect to the internet via modem (Romkey 1988). Adams went on to found UUNet in 1987, the first commercial Internet Service Provider (Swisher 1996; Malik 2003, 9–15). He sold UUNet at an enormous profit in 1995 and ended up connected to Cerf through a tangle of corporate relationships (Malik 2003, 17–23; Lambert 2005, 59–64). Adams turned part of his wealth to book collecting—including the Archimedes Palimpsest. When the codex sold at Christie's, the purchaser was identified only as "not Bill Gates," fueling rumors of tech industry connections (Netz and Noel 2007, 7). The book's current fame thus rests on internet profits and protocols.

Palimpsests and the internet present similar challenges for information preservation. How do you keep the bits that belong together from mixing with the bits from other messages? For the internet, this question is answered by the transfer protocols devised by Adams (SLIP) and Cerf (TCP/IP). For the palimpsest, highly processed digital images provided the answer. Those images, in turn, became new units of information, themselves transmitted over the internet from an open access repository. According to Noel, the data are available online because the owner "understands data as well as books. . . . The thing to do with data, if you want it to survive, is to let it out and have everybody have it with as little control on that data as possible" (Noel 2012, min 11:38). Noel presents the desire to "democratize" information as the owner's motivation for purchasing the book in the first place: "Why did he buy this book? Because he wanted to make that which was fragile safe. He wanted to make that which was unique ubiquitous. He wanted to make that which was expensive free. And he wanted to do this as a matter of principle" (Noel 2012, min 2:48). The Archimedes Codex became what it is today, then, as a result of Adams's view of the internet as durable, secure, and free. The data, however, will not take care of themselves. They rely on the digital preservation commitments of their host institutions—which aren't entirely free.

The Archimedes Codex also became what it is today because of Adams's patronage—first acquiring the book and then funding all the digital research (Netz and Noel 2007, 277). It thus embodies another dimension of tech medievalism—in this case, turning tech profits toward cultural heritage preservation. Financial resources are of course always integral to the making and saving of books, whether by individuals or institutions. Capital curates. The names in the shelf marks of medieval manuscripts—such as Robert Cotton (d. 1631), Francis Douce (d. 1834), or Thomas Phillips (d. 1872)—attest to the flow of British imperial profits into book collecting. A further set of shelf-mark names—J. P. Morgan (d. 1913), Henry Huntington (d. 1927)—track the passage of both books and empire to the United States. The twentieth-century history of the Archimedes Codex testifies starkly to the geopolitics of survival: someone in Turkey needed money and sold the book; Guerson needed money to enable his own survival and sold the book again; for lack of a buyer, the book stayed in a basement and got moldy; in the hands of a new owner, it became an international superstar, propelled to celebrity by substantial investments in new technologies. While few books have had histories this dramatic, many have passed through more modest cycles of care and neglect. All share in the geopolitical circuits that commodify books and information.

At the end of the Archimedes Codex's first decade online, the obvious question is, How well is it preserved? On the "vellum" side, the data files are doing quite well. The internet addresses printed in 2011 still work even though the files have moved to a new repository at the University of Pennsylvania (*Archimedes Palimpsest* 2008–11). Like good digital vellum, the OPenn repository includes detailed instructions for making a complete copy of OPenn, including the Archimedes files (http://openn.library.upenn.edu). Even more promising, text from the palimpsest has been selected for a DNA experiment that might encode digital information for thousands of years—a selection linked to medieval models of preservation, including (once again) monks who copy books (Aron 2015; Cottingham 2015). On the "Dark Age" side, the website "ArchimedesPalimpsest.org" has lost some functions owing to broken links and defunct browser plugins (accessed December 18, 2018). And what was once touted as "the oldest Google Book in existence" (Noel 2011, 13) has disappeared, leaving only its cover page—quite unexpected for a file made of open data (*Archimedes Palimpsest* 2019). The Google Book User Reviews track the slide from enthusiastic praise to disgruntled critique as access ended first outside the United States and then altogether (reviews aren't dated, but new complaints have appeared since 2018). So much for Cerf's "digital vellum" at Google. In between these poles, OPenn preserves a crucial reminder that some originals were never complete: the well-curated data files on OPenn include a text file entitled "How to Use This Data Set," with several instructions labeled "forthcoming" and "TBD" (*Archimedes Palimpsest* 2008–11). These notes are unlikely to come forth: gaps in the record are always part of the record, even under the best preservation circumstances.

The Archimedes Codex provides a revelatory parable for book history in the "digital Dark Ages"—not because it is typical but because it is exceptional, representing nearly every possibility. A Christian monk did preserve Archimedes's texts (just as Kuny and many others imagine) but only by trying to erase them. Some aspects of the book are completely accessible (on the internet) and others hardly accessible at all (in Adams's private library). Indeed, the book now has many distinct forms, each with different access modes and each sustained by different infrastructures: tenth-century vellum (supporting text and images from the tenth, thirteenth, and twentieth centuries); twentieth-century photographs (and their digitized copies); twentieth- and twenty-first-century print editions; twenty-first-century digital images (in multiple color-processed versions). Every effort to preserve the codex has been partly destructive; some destructive actions have enabled preservation (Lowden 2011, 213). Digitization has done the same: in order to image the pages and read the book, the book had to be taken apart and made largely unreadable. Now, each leaf is encased in an individual frame, all housed in a custom-made cabinet (Quandt 2011, 156–61). Is this format still a book? At some point, we may know which lasted longer—the pages in boxes or the related bits now scattered across multiple servers and personal computers. The fate of the codex is bound up with the fate of the internet.

The internet story of the Archimedes Codex encapsulates my approach to MS 80. First, the Codex's disparate forms call for a multimedia approach to book history: it is at once a filing cabinet, several printed editions, hundreds of photographs, and thousands of digital files. The material history of a book includes all its forms across the centuries—manuscript, photographs, editions, translations, storage boxes, microfilms, photocopies, and digital files. And all the people involved with these formats are bookmakers: artisans, scribes, editors, patrons, translators, conservators, collectors, photographers, programmers, librarians, and many other cultural laborers. Their collective actions—and inactions—create and conserve the artifact and its perceived significance. In this frame, my account of MS 80 shares the multidimensional approach to book history of Martin Foys (2007), Siân Echard (2008), Bonnie Mak (2011), David McKitterick (2013), Alan Galey (2014), Sarah Werner (2018), and Zachary Lesser (2019).

Second, the reproduction of the Archimedes Codex in multispectral digital images points to the role of technology in constructing material history. For the palimpsest, numerous computational interventions revealed previously unreadable text. This result rests on layers of hardware engineering, software design, and scientific research into the nature of reflective light and X-rays. The networked distribution of the digital files adds more layers of infrastructure. Photographing manuscripts isn't at all new, but networked images—especially those made to represent what humans cannot otherwise see—materialize new ways of knowing. These technologies draw book history into the field of critical infrastructure studies. In this frame, my stories about MS 80 rely on insights from information and media studies developed by Susan Leigh Star (1999), Sheila Anderson (2013), Lisa Parks and Nicole Starosielski (2015), Deb Verhoeven (2016), Ingrid Burrington (2016), Shannon Mattern (2017), and Safiya Noble (2018).

Finally, all these forms and materials constitute "the text." The Archimedes Codex represents an extreme case (discovery of previously unknown texts) of the general situation (knowing about texts at all). The fact that MS 80 was once highly valued and later denigrated as a waste of time provides its own extreme case for literary history. MS 80's preservation in the sixteenth century intersects with accounts of early modern English medievalism by Alexandra Gillespie (2006), Jennifer Summit (2008), and Megan Cook (2019). MS 80's printing in the nineteenth century makes it part of the "multistranded" history of Middle English told by David Matthews (1999, xiv). Similar styles of literary history have been written for modern texts by Alan Liu (2018), Peter Murphy (2019), Jonathan Senchyne (2019), and Joshua Calhoun (2020). These modern textual histories overlap with the print histories of MS 80 in modern catalogues and editions. Precisely because MS 80 did not come into the twentieth century as one of those "celebrated manuscripts" that lends its "glamor" to readers (De Hamel 2016, 4), it prompts serious study of how reputations get formed and modified over time. What we think we know about the past emerges over and over again from an ever-shifting interplay of preservation, obsolescence, adaptation, and destruction.

Medieval books accessible on the internet thus have all the components of the internet itself. They require electricity, cables, hardware devices, software applications, transfer protocols, file format standards, markup standards, and so forth. Their many different iterations—codex, PDF, JPEG, and more—manifest remarkable continuities as well as numerous salient distinctions. From different vantage points, a book is at once storage device, format, interface, platform, and infrastructure itself. Every change in these technologies changes the nature of books. The global infrastructure of the internet impinges directly on the material remains of medieval Europe.

The model for this kind of capacious book history has actually been in place for some time. Donald F. McKenzie, in his remarkably prescient 1985 Panizzi Lectures at the British Library, proposed what would now be called a transmedial and transhistorical practice that enfolds medieval manuscripts into a book history that extends to electronic media such as computers, magnetic tape, and databases (McKenzie 1986, 39–60). McKenzie anticipated studies of infrastructure by referring to the library as "a text or meta-text" (51), wondering how subscription databases would affect the concept of book ownership (60) and describing in detail issues of digital longevity that were only just emerging (62–63). McKenzie demonstrated that medieval manuscripts, printed books, and digital media belong together. His "sociology of texts" doesn't even require a codex. Instead, it rests on a sociological understanding of the entire infrastructure that makes and maintains media.

From a multimedia perspective, McKenzie's most important sentence compares a computer to a book: "Only as its memory systems have grown has the computer changed its nature from blackboard to book" (61). In this formulation, blackboards represent temporary writing surfaces while books provide long-term storage. McKenzie draws medieval manuscripts into this analogy by noting the shared properties of vellum and magnetic tape: "Just as vellum manuscripts were scraped clean for re-use, so too are magnetic tapes vulnerable to re-use, with the destruction of the texts already on them" (62). This view of media—different formats, similar functions—leads McKenzie to historicize print as "only a phase in the history of textual transmission" (52). This view has shaped many scholars' approach to print (e.g., Johns 1998; McKitterick 2003). But McKenzie's flexible approach to form has also been taken up in all the areas he drafted into bibliography: medieval manuscripts (Echard 2000; Gillespie 2007; Brantley 2009; Lerer 2015), media studies (Hayles 2003, 277; Kirschenbaum 2008, 42–43; Gitelman 2014a, 7), and information science (Blanchette 2011; Buckland 2017, 44–45). Digital images derived from medieval manuscripts are yet another form on this continuum from books to bits.

Form, of course, is the subject of McKenzie's most cited sentence: "Forms effect meaning" (McKenzie 1986, 4). This pithy formulation has been explicated many times, most cogently for medieval manuscripts by Alexandra Gillespie: "Books have form; this form has the potential to produce meaning; this meaning is not unified or essential or separable from the conditions of its production and utilization, but nor is it exhausted by those conditions" (Gillespie 2007, 273). Books have varied forms, just as computer files have varied formats. Formats also effect meaning. Jonathan Sterne's analysis of the mp3 format for audio files, for example, parallels McKenzie's analysis of form: "Studying formats highlights smaller registers like software, operating standards, and codes, as well as larger registers like infrastructures, international corporate consortia, and whole technical systems" (Sterne 2012, 11). The primary format for networked digital images is the JPEG (Joint Photographic Experts Group). Like the mp3, the JPEG compresses data for efficient transmission and storage: "compression is the process that renders a mode of representation adequate to its infrastructures" (Sterne 2015, 35). Sterne furthers McKenzie's multimedia book history by describing the codex as a "form of compression" "compared with the scroll" (Sterne 2015, 42). Another format that effects meaning for digital books is the PDF. In Lisa Gitelman's account, PDFs incorporate two distinctions crucial to book history: between image and text and between reading and authoring (Gitelman 2014a, 124–34). Since so many printed books have been turned into PDFs—and since a PDF can be reprinted as a codex—the format binds together otherwise irreconcilable objects.

Form and format are both sometimes treated as synonyms for interface. At one point, Gitelman calls the PDF an interface (2014a, 119); Meredith

McGill has described format in terms that sound like interface: "the complex middle ground between production and reception" (McGill 2018, 674). These conflations arise in part because PDFs and JPEGs can appear in many different ways on a screen: a digital book is a combination of file format and interface. Johanna Drucker's comparison of a codex with interface pinpoints their convergence: "A book is an interface. . . . We are aware that digital interface seems more mutable and flexible than that of a book, but is this really true? The interface is not an object. Interface is a space of affordances and possibilities structured into organization for use. An interface is a set of conditions, structured relations, that allow certain behaviors, actions, readings, events to occur. This generalized theory of interface applies to any technological device created with certain assumptions about the body, hand, eye, coordination, and other capabilities" (Drucker 2013, par 31). In this definition, a book, like a keyboard or software, structures certain behaviors. A digital book, moreover, can be structured in multiple ways—as a list of file names, as a semblance of a codex (simulating page turning), as a semblance of a scroll, and so forth (Porter 2018c). Every interface orients users in particular ways, structuring the very possibilities of thought.

Books are also platforms—structures that make meaning out of other components and can themselves become components of other structures. Indeed, the printed paperback codex exemplifies the platform concept in Nick Montfort and Ian Bogost's influential definition: "a mass-market paperback is made cheaply and at low quality to be able to sell long novels on thin paper to a large audience at limited cost. Understanding the qualities of different media and formats has been essential to both the practice and study of the arts. Platform studies extends these sorts of insights into digital art, literature, and media, by considering the importance of a work's platform" (Montfort and Bogost 2014, 393). If a platform is something on which something else is built, then a certain kind of paper is analogous to a certain kind of software. Indeed, from the perspective of a multimedia history of text technologies, Whitney Trettien describes "the book" as a platform whose predigital history is entwined with today's networked platforms (Trettien 2018, 52–53). The platform concept casts all book forms as ways of knowing rather than ways of being: from different vantage points, a book is a platform, a product of other platforms, and a component of still other platforms. Platforms gather points of history and then scatter, flatten, and fuse them.

At the broadest scale, books manifest the very infrastructure that sustains them—from bindings shaped by shelf placement to the processing load required to visualize an image. Whether one starts from vellum, paper, or software, a book becomes "the endpoint of a latticework of complex infrastructure" (Mod 2018). In digital environments, "the economic logics typical of platforms" and "the public interests and quasi-universal services formerly characteristic of many infrastructures" become inseparable: "The question is not only who profits and controls, but who, and what, is cast aside along the way" (Plantin et al. 2018, 306). The very properties of infrastructure—as services and materials that fade from view so long as they are functioning—make this question difficult to answer. The effort, though, is book history for the digital era. As Sterne notes of file formats, "content and infrastructure exist in a relation of circular causality" (Sterne 2015, 42). Book history thus becomes what Geoffrey Bowker and Susan Leigh Star have called "infrastructural inversion": "recognizing the depths of interdependence of technical networks and standards, on the one hand, and the real work of politics and knowledge production on the other" (Bowker and Star 1999, 34). This method addresses ubiquity (classification and standards are everywhere), materiality, temporal multiplicity (pathways are always being revised), and the practical politics of decision-making (Bowker and Star 1999, 37–46). Today's medieval books—digital or not—carry traces of these infrastructural dynamics. They store, format, and interface with every element that sustains them. From the perspective of infrastructure, the question is not only "what" is a medieval book but "when" (Star and Ruhleder 1996) and "how" (Drucker 2008). That is, infrastructure isn't a fixed kind of material (a cable, a website) but a way of relating with that material that begins at a certain point in time—and may end at another. A book is a moment in time as much as a thing in space; it changes with each style of engagement.

Ultimately, a medieval manuscript that has been photographed is a hybrid book-form. "MS 80" refers at once to 100 sheets of paper bound as a codex, 199 exposures on a microfilm, 414 archival TIFF files, innumerable TIFF derivatives, and several internet addresses. Each of these formats is itself a more complex amalgam of materials, processes, protocols, and social interactions. Like every manuscript that has been reproduced in one format or another, "MS 80" has become what Bonnie Mak has called a conceptual palimpsest—"a single object that can concurrently sustain several referents" (Mak 2014, 1519). Similarly, it calls for what Sarah Werner and Matthew Kirschenbaum have termed a "transmedia" approach in which "the digital is also historical" (Kirschenbaum and Werner 2014, 452). Although they don't refer to McKenzie—or to manuscripts—they describe a "materialist turn" in digital studies that draws software, platforms, and media archaeology into book history (Kirschenbaum and Werner 2014, 430–37). Even medieval manuscripts that have not been digitized partake of digital infrastructure: "How many of us encounter the objects of our study unmediated through subsequent technologies? Even in special collections, what we find is presented to us through the thresholds of catalogs, phase boxes, and call slips. We all experience this, even if we do not always theorize it. But what might we learn if we do think about the entrance of old media into the platforms of new media?" (Kirschenbaum and Werner 2014, 451). My book answers this question for medieval manuscripts and the many materials derived from them.

If digital images are part of a hybrid book-form, what kind of part are they? The question of how to name the relationship between an image and a codex is itself an element of infrastructure. Terminology reveals a "way of knowing" a copy that becomes "what it is": terminology is epistemology that slips into ontology. Uncertainty about terminology arises from the "dubious ontology" of digital objects themselves (Allison et al. 2005, 367): they are "both data in their own right and metadata that describe other objects" (Owens 2018, 157). In medieval studies, terms used as near synonyms include *facsimile, surrogate, version, edition, simulacrum*, and *avatar* (all in Echard 2008, 198–216; most in Treharne 2013). Some terms underscore continuities between hand copying and machine copying (*exemplar, witness, copy*). Others draw out what Bonnie Mak has called the "ontological rift" (Mak 2011, 66) between a codex and an interface that looks like a codex:

avatar (Tarte 2011b), *marionette* (De Kosnik 2016, 227–61), and *skeuomorph* (Hayles 1999, 17). Rather than choose a single term, we might contribute to what Bridget Whearty has called a "rigorous codicology" of images (2018, 197) by drawing distinctions that name the variable functions of images in hybrid book-forms. For example, as Dot Porter has summarized, *facsimile* emphasizes faithful copying, *surrogate* invites replacement, and *avatar* points to the distinctive qualities of digital representation (Porter 2018a). In the language of infrastructure, an image is a facsimile "when" it is treated as a faithful copy, a surrogate "when" it is used as a replacement, and an avatar "when" its distinctive digital qualities come into focus. At different moments throughout this book, MS 80 on Parker Library on the Web is all those things and more.

Six Arthurian Stories about One Book

MS 80 fuses six centuries of existence—online, in print, and on the shelf. The rendering of the first folio on Parker 2.0 neatly illustrates almost every point on the book's time line (fig. 1). On very close inspection, chain lines from the manufacture of the paper are visible, as are faint reddish lines marking out a grid for two columns of text. At the top of the page, a title has been added in sixteenth-century italic. On the upper right corner, two shelf marks reflect eighteenth-century catalogues. By the mid-nineteenth century, the top of the page included a folio number and the bottom a hypothesis about the leaf's place in the book's quire structure (B xii). At some unknown dates, someone drew a line through the illustration space, and insect larvae chewed holes. Early in the twenty-first century, photographers used white-tipped page holders to secure the page for digitizing. All these features are visible in the Parker 2.0 image viewer, Mirador (https://projectmirador.org). The digital frame includes various navigation structures, as well as a slightly different shelf mark (080), Lovelich's name, and the titles of the printed editions (*The History of the Holy Grail, Merlin*). This interface has been rendered via a unique internet address (not pictured), in a web browser (not pictured), on a hardware device with a screen (not pictured), through the machine processing of HTML (Hypertext Markup Language) (not pictured)—and

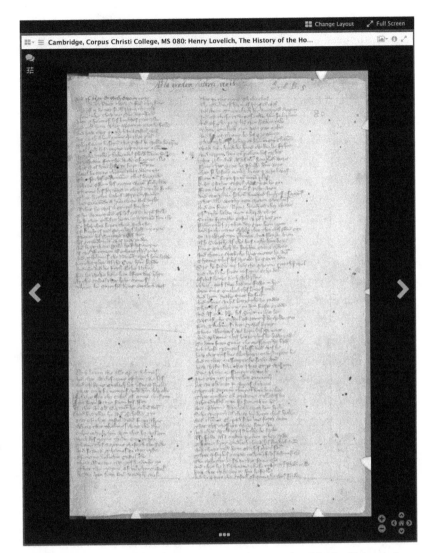

Figure 1 Screen image of MS 80, folio 1r, on Parker Library on the Web 2.0, with image viewer Mirador 2.0 (2018–21).

SOURCE: https://parker.stanford.edu/parker/catalog/xd494bt3141. Courtesy of Parker Library, Corpus Christi College, Cambridge. Licensed under a Creative Commons Attribution-NonCommercial 4.0 International License.

a myriad of other networked protocols and hardware. This image is itself now reproduced in this book in both print and digital editions, rendered in grayscale rather than color. Each copy will have its own unpredictable future. MS 80 is still gathering time and multiplying forms.

MS 80 shows how infrastructures coauthor literary history. In the chapters that follow, I tell six stories that are particular to MS 80 as the basis for broader conclusions about the interactions among books, literature, and the systems that sustain them. Each chapter illustrates a different "way of knowing" a book that contains a literary text. Each method applies equally to medieval production, modern print, and today's internet. Throughout, I expand familiar and common concepts in some unconventional ways in order to shed light on how digital systems build on other technologies. My comparative approach identifies both consistencies and distinctions across varied book formats and representations of text—from the fifteenth-century paper manuscript to early modern catalogues to printed editions to microfilms to websites.

The first three chapters address three familiar ways of making literary meaning: through the study of sources, the study of context, and the study of readers. These chapters begin in medieval England and move through various modern moments to arrive in the digital present. The second trio of chapters addresses common ways of accessing texts: through catalogues, editions, and reproductions. These chapters begin in modern England and encompass the global dimensions of book collecting and publishing. Together, the six chapters form an overlapping sequence that illustrates the recursive entanglements of text and technology. Their starting dates stretch from 1135 to 1956; they all end punctually in 2018. This method of dating acknowledges that any discussion of technology is immediately "dated"—but not obsolete. Today's conditions are the defining conditions of every other moment: everything takes place in the "digital Dark Ages."

I begin with what might be called the oldest technology for transmitting and preserving stories—translation. This chapter, "Translating Arthur: Books, Texts, Machines," answers some of the first questions I had about MS 80: what were Lovelich's sources for the English text, and why was the manuscript designed for illustrations? The answer to both questions is, in part, a French book about the Holy Grail and King Arthur made sometime after 1235. This French story, though, incorporates a longer tradition that begins in the twelfth century with Geoffrey of Monmouth's *History of the Kings of Britain*, completed in Latin around 1135. Geoffrey, moreover, claimed to translate from yet another source in "British." From Geoffrey to Lovelich, then, any number of translators presented themselves as mere conduits for someone else's information. Of course, each was much more than that. They created new meanings and new formats out of old materials. In recent times, Lovelich's own text has been translated into Dutch in this same spirit—as evidence of the "true secrets" of the Holy Grail. This theory of translation as information transfer has reached its apotheosis with machine translation (MT), which I used to access the Dutch texts in 2018. My experiences with MT led eventually to yet another "holy grail" in the history of computing—automated translation with the nuance of human translation. The whole history of translation around MS 80—from Geoffrey's British to Google's English—is traversed by myths about translation itself.

Reading Lovelich's text today presents its own challenges of translation. Fifteenth-century English differs enough from modern English that it can't be read easily without practice and the aid of the *Middle English Dictionary* (https://quod.lib.umich.edu/m/middle-english-dictionary). Printed editions make reading easier, but they are uncertain guides to "Lovelich's text" because the editors' methods were inconsistent and even obscure. Given these circumstances, and my hope that this book will reach many readers not habituated to Middle English, I have adopted Lovelich's own guiding principle for citations: to make the story "more clear to your understanding" (*Grail*, LVI:528). I thus use paraphrase liberally and turn Middle English into modern English. The syntax of these translations is sometimes a bit awkward by today's standards, reflecting the tenor of Lovelich's style. I have embraced what Ardis Butterfield (2012) calls "rough translation"—supple, halting, good for some purposes. When a Middle English word or phrase includes nuances of particular significance to my interpretations, I include it in parentheses so that readers can investigate further. Likewise, I refer to folios in the manuscript when the text's representation there is uniquely meaningful. I have also translated or modernized citations for other medieval and early modern English texts; readers can find their way to the originals through the bibliography. I personally enjoy reading Lovelich's text: I hope to have transmitted some sense of why.

Chapter 2 turns to the context in which Lovelich translated—the London Skinners' Guild in the early fifteenth century. This chapter, like chapter 1, answers some of my earliest questions about MS 80. "Performing Community: Merchants, Chivalry, Data" shows how texts both reflect and influence their social context. The Skinners' story begins in 1327, when the guild received its first royal charter. Since the fur trade deals in skins for basic warmth, as well as rarified royal symbolism, the Skinners were involved with a broad spectrum of social classes. Lovelich's exact role in the trade is unclear, but he was connected somehow to one of the most prominent merchants in the guild's history, Henry Barton (d. 1435). I argue that Barton and Lovelich produced MS 80 to provide their fellow guildsmen with a book that promoted civic and national belonging. Lovelich's translation infuses an urban perspective into a story about pious and valorous knights, making chivalry a value that even a craftsman could embrace. MS 80 is one of several texts in the Skinners' corporate bibliography: these texts express some of the guild's social, religious, and political practices from the fifteenth century to the seventeenth.

All the information that contextualizes MS 80 derives from dense configurations of data curation. The records begin with handwritten documents of medieval governance: Letter Books, Journals of the Aldermen's Court, Court of Hustings, Court of Common Pleas, Close Rolls, Issue Rolls, Patent Rolls, and Parliament Rolls. They continue with printed indexes, digitized books, and electronic databases. Since the 1990s, the interfaces for accessing these historical data have changed more than once, including the very buildings that house the oldest formats. When I started researching MS 80's context, the first place I went was the Skinners' Hall in London. The caretaker cheerfully showed me the medieval records of the guild's religious fraternities—and served me tea right there in the vault. On a later trip, I saw the same books at the central Guildhall Library, under more formal arrangements (MSS 31692, 31693). Most recently, I looked for these books in the database of the London Metropolitan Archives—where they have new, longer shelf marks. Each time, the conditions of access shaped my understanding of the books. Similar changes have affected almost every archive and library I've visited throughout my research. The Public Record Office in central London became part of the National Archives in the distant suburbs. The British Library left the British Museum. Indeed, the last words of McKenzie's Panizzi lecture anticipated that move as an epistemological one in which books would become texts, requiring "a new concept of the text in history" (McKenzie 1986, 66). The fact that almost none of the historical data sources have "stayed put"—including MS 80 itself—reflects a combination of economic, political, and technological pressures that have directly influenced the stories that can be told about the past.

Data curation shapes every chapter, of course. Metadata practices, the presence or absence of full-text search, the accuracy of OCR, and subscription financing have all determined the stories I can tell. As databases have become larger and more complex, the interfaces for "search" and "browse" have become more simplified. This conjunction is changing how people access and understand information—and thus history itself (Gitelman 2014b; Putnam 2016; Schneier, Stinson, and Davis 2018). When Early English Books Online changed its interface on July 7, 2020, for example, the nature of early modern books changed, too. In an instant, EEBO became less visible as a collection with a complex multimedia history of cataloguing, microfilming, digitizing, and transcribing (Pollard and Redgrave 1926; Wing 1945–51; Power 1990; Gadd 2009). At the same time, individual items became more discoverable from searches started elsewhere. Those results, though, will favor the 40 percent of the EEBO collection with full-text transcription ("Early English" 2020; https://textcreationpartnership.org, 1999–2015). Meanwhile, the compound effects of digital surrogacy will be harder to identify amid the aggregated results of dozens of separate databases (Mak 2014; Blaney and Siefring 2017). With this kind of data integration, obsolete spellings and historical errors become current and accurate. Lovelich's name, for example, also appears as *Lonelich* and *Louelich*; his first name might be Henry, Herry, or even Thomas. These variations are pointed reminders that search carries history and that platform integration can fragment data rather than consolidating them. These contingencies run through all the stories I tell about MS 80; the more dramatic examples structure the plots.

Chapter 3 addresses the reception of MS 80 by those who have left marks in and around the book. Here, too, I return to some of my earliest questions about the annotations written in the margins. This chapter, though, is about much more than readers of Lovelich's text. "Marking Books: Makers, Users, Coders" takes up "marking" in the broadest sense— from the book's production to readers' commentary to the "markup" that structures the book's display on websites. This story begins in 1435, the year of Barton's death, which stands for the making of MS 80. Scribal notes show that the book was made to guide readers' attentions toward certain passages, while readers' own notes show how they guided themselves—or even ignored the text entirely. One particularly avid reader, John Cok (d. 1468), focused on religious themes; he also penned the note about Barton's involvement with the book. In the modern era, notes in MS 80 show how the book was collected, catalogued, and edited—most crucially by Archbishop Parker. In the internet era, annotation is part of interface: HTML, TEI (Text Encoding Initiative), and IIIF (International Image Interoperability Framework) all incorporate different functions of annotation. Collectively, they define how texts and images appear on Parker Library on the Web. The results extend the functions of handwriting on paper while also creating entirely new types of books.

Chapter 4 analyzes how cataloguers at Parker Library have represented MS 80's place in literary history. Over the centuries, the genre of Lovelich's text and its relations with other texts have been reevaluated several times. "Cataloguing Libraries: History, Romance, Website" begins in 1574, when Archbishop Parker drew up an inventory for the collection he intended to bequeath to Corpus Christi College. Since then, the book now called "MS 80" has had a variety of different titles and shelf marks, each aligned with shifting interpretations of genre. Each catalogue has built on its predecessors, according to the infrastructure principle of "path dependency"—that is, the "layering of an emergent system upon an existing one" (Parks and Starosielski 2015, 2). Each catalogue's relationship with its "inherited data" (Fyfe 2016, 569) crystallizes in how it represents MS 80. For Parker and the Protestant cataloguers who followed him, Lovelich's translation was "history" that supported Anglican independence from the Roman Catholic Church. In the eighteenth century, a new cataloguer called the text "romance"—a classification that continues to reverberate through literary history even though later cataloguers discarded it. Parker Library on the Web has reconfigured this inheritance in several ways—recycling older classifications but networking them in ways that open new perspectives on literary history. Taken together, the catalogues prescribe as much as they describe: they reproduce books as projections that become as real as the books on the shelves.

Chapter 5 tracks how editions make literary history. This chapter delves into the values that brought Lovelich's text into print as an exemplary romance and then into the English curriculum as "bad poetry" and finally back into print as a literary treasure. "Editing Romance: Poetry, Print, Platform" begins in 1861, when part of MS 80 was published as *The History of the Holy Graal* for the exclusive Roxburghe Club. The editor, Frederick J. Furnivall, was immersed in romantic projections of the Middle Ages—inspired largely by the popular Arthurian poetry of Alfred Tennyson. Furnivall, like many since, couldn't resist the grail. To further promote Arthurian romance, he founded a publishing platform that became essential infrastructure for medieval English literature—the Early English Text Society (EETS). All of MS 80's text eventually appeared in the series (Furnivall 1874–78; Kock 1904–32). By the early twentieth century, however, medieval romance was falling out of academic favor, so guides for students introduced Lovelich as one of the dullest poets of the English tradition—a reputation that began to fade only when scholars looked past the editions and returned to the Parker Library shelves.

This aesthetic trajectory unfolds through the editions' publishing formats: the deluxe Roxburghe volumes, the cheap EETS volumes, and the digitized editions of both. All these formats are entangled with the *Oxford English Dictionary* (*OED*)—the authoritative repository of the English language that Furnivall also helped found and edit. MS 80 thus intersects with the basic infrastructure that defined "English" in nationalist and imperialist terms in the nineteenth century. These data—and the values that produced them—still circulate through digital platforms. The transmission of Lovelich's text from printed editions into the *OED* and onto the subscription platform Literature Online illustrates what I call "platform philology"—turning poetry into data and back again. Simultaneously, each format distributes the text through what I call "platform codicology"— imparting literary value through publishing formats and protocols. In a final twist, public domain PDFs have brought Lovelich's editions back into print by "print-on-demand" publishers who profit from Google's mass digitation of library books. It turns out that people will still pay for the codex format—and for romantic notions of literary history.

Finally, chapter 6 evaluates the most recent changes to MS 80 for their impact on future histories of literature. In this chapter, "Reproducing Books: Binding, Microfilm, Digital," I tell the story of MS 80's reproduction since the mid-twentieth century—a new binding in 1956, a microfilm copy, and digital images for Parker Library on the Web. In each case, the value of Parker Library as a collection brought attention to a book that otherwise might not have been selected for special investments. As such, MS 80's reproductions exemplify the conditions of other Parker manuscripts—which in turn illuminate the preservation and distribution of cultural heritage materials more broadly. On one level, the implications are epistemological: each form defines how the book can be known; reproductions point to the interpretive work of copying and of the interfaces that structure access to copies, whether on shelves or on websites. On another level, reproductions are deeply political: the patronage arrangements at Parker Library have been persistently national, connecting book history to specific legacies of colonial capitalism. These same legacies are sustaining digital infrastructure with implications far beyond medieval studies.

I conclude by returning to the Holy Grail and to romance—both popular mechanisms for deflecting the power plays of technology. "Indexing the Grail, Romancing the Internet" revisits some of the starting points for this book and connects them with some of the most recent end points.

These lessons concern not only book historians and medievalists but all kinds of readers and users of all kinds of books. In retrospect, MS 80 has taken me on a decades-long journey through some of the defining myths of our times. With any luck, readers will pick up some of the plots where I've left off. I can only hope that readers will also form new questions that lead somewhere else entirely.

CHAPTER 1

TRANSLATING ARTHUR

Books, Texts, Machines

ARTHURIAN STORIES ORIGINATE IN TRANSLATION. The first extended narrative of King Arthur's reign appears in Geoffrey of Monmouth's *History of the Kings of Britain* (completed around 1135). Geoffrey claimed to translate into Latin from a single source—a "very old book in the British tongue" (Geoffrey 2007, 4–5). This claim, true or not, lends legitimacy to Geoffrey's far-flung narrative, which stretches from the Trojan War to the seventh century AD. Along the way, Geoffrey combines verifiable events (generally called "history") with invented episodes (generally called "romance"). This mixture proved irresistible to generations of audiences, inspiring numerous copies, adaptations, and translations over the following centuries. By the fifteenth century, "King Arthur" had generated a vast interrelated corpus of texts in many languages and forms. From beginning to end, translation casts new inventions as old traditions. These tropes transmit authenticity from language to language and culture to culture. In this way, every writer, reader, patron, and collector borrows prestige from their predecessors.

Geoffrey's *History* illustrates another defining characteristic of medieval translation: its inseparability from empire, codified in the phrase *translatio studii et imperii* (translation of learning and empire). Geoffrey's narrative begins with the settlement of Britain by Trojans, who embody the westward movement of culture and empire. The Trojans anchor a genealogy that legitimizes one empire after another—from Greece to Rome to Britain and eventually on to the Americas. Along the way, *translatio* refers equally to the movements of objects, bodies, knowledge, and power. Transfer from one language to another is just one part of these processes. The idea that knowledge and power move in a linear, westerly direction, however, is a myth told by Western powers themselves: neither knowledge nor imperial sovereignty are as hegemonic or sequential as the myth suggests. Instead, *translatio* creates and destroys in spiraling cycles of partial preservation and fragmented loss. Translation thus encodes the demise of the empires it seems to sustain.

MS 80 preserves a unique moment in the long and continuing process of Arthurian *translatio*. The book contains English verses translated from French prose by Henry Lovelich in the early fifteenth century. Lovelich's source, dubbed the "Vulgate Cycle" by its first modern editor (Sommer 1908–16), takes up several volumes even in its most compact forms. The cycle, developed in the early thirteenth century, covers some of the same time line and even some of the same events as Geoffrey's *History*. Lovelich's text corresponds to the part that recounts the migrations of Joseph of Arimathea after the Crucifixion, his conversion of Britain to Christianity, the birth of Merlin, Arthur's coronation, and his first travails as king. Arthur's court is eventually populated with knights who descend from both the first British Trojans and the first British Christians. Their genealogies mingle ("medlyth" [*Grail*, LVI:518]) the Holy Grail with a much longer story arc that includes Lancelot (famous for his affair with Arthur's queen, Guinevere), Galahad (famous for questing after the Holy Grail), Mordred (famous for betraying Arthur), and ultimately the death of Arthur (famous for not really dying). These multiple story lines crisscross each other, forming intricate patterns of foreshadowing and repetition. This recursive structure undermines the linear myth of empire even as it promotes lineage as the guarantor of truth and transcendence. In this narrative, *translatio* reveals the fragility of its own myth.

This plot features translation itself as a powerful form of authorship. Readers are told that 717 years after Christ's passion, a hermit copied the story of the Holy Grail's transfer (*translatio*) from Jerusalem to Britain out of a book written by the hand of God. Later, so the story says, a man named Robert de Boron translated that text from Latin into French. When Merlin arrives, he tells the entire story of the Holy Grail and his own birth to a priest named Blaise, seeming to create a second copy of the book that God gave the hermit. Blaise adds new episodes based on Merlin's reports of past and future events at Arthur's court. Eventually, the relationship between Blaise's book and Robert's becomes unclear. Through overlapping and contradictory claims about translation, the French narrative confounds the very notion of singular authorship. In MS 80, by contrast, Lovelich gathers the tangled translation plot into a single authoritative voice. He presents himself as a reliable guide to Britain's treasured Arthurian memories.

Even as Lovelich emphasizes that nothing changes from translation to translation, he produces an entirely novel text. His undertaking, though unusual, draws on practices that were common in early fifteenth-century London. MS 80 represents the kind of text sought out by many at the time: "English romances on the model of the French" (Coleman 1981, 41). Such books helped broaden shared cultural knowledge across increasingly blurry differences of class and lineage: books of English romance were made for merchants, nobles, and royals alike (Henry 1983; Lawton 1983; Drimmer 2018). MS 80's intended audience was mercantile: an annotation states that Lovelich was a skinner who translated at the request of another man, Henry Barton (f. 127r; see chap. 3). Beyond this brief note and a few mentions in legal transactions, Lovelich's biography is largely unknown. He could have been exposed to various kinds of French as a fur trader (Jefferson 2000; Butterfield 2009, 328–35; Sutton 2013, 95). The language of fifteenth-century commerce, though, was quite distant from thirteenth-century literary prose. It is remotely possible that Lovelich was called a "skinner" because he provided the guild with textual services, akin to the "mercer" Robert Bale, who translated French for the Mercers'

Guild c. 1440 (Davies 2016, 32–35; Erler 2016). Indeed, some clerks were directly involved in connecting Arthurian heroism to civic governance (Davies 2011). Some decades after Lovelich's time, the Skinners' religious fraternities did include several members called "clerk of the craft" (Lambert 1934, 56–57, 82). Whether or not Lovelich should be counted among the "craftsmen-turned-scribe" (Davies 2016, 32), somehow he had the skills and resources to produce a lengthy and complex text.

MS 80 transfers (*translatio*) the prestige of French aristocratic legacies to a new urban environment. It brings new audiences into the English *imperium*. The paper book, designed for illustration, performs a multifaceted *translatio* of language, form, culture, and social class. My approach to the book builds on the work of manuscript scholars who integrate textual, visual, and material analysis (Busby 2002; Meuwese 2007; Drimmer 2018), particularly those who have studied MS 80 (Meale 1994; Eddy 2012). I also expand on medieval translation theories that foreground relationships between knowledge and power (Stahuljak 2004; Rikhardsdottir 2012; Campbell and Mills 2012). The result recuperates a sense of MS 80 as a single text, contrary to literary histories that have treated Lovelich as the translator of two separate works—a Christian lesson in moral conduct (*Grail*) and a romance of Arthurian knights (*Merlin*) (Wells 1916; Ackerman 1959; Hodder 1999a, 1999b). Indeed, almost every scholar who has engaged Lovelich—beginning with the editor Frederick Furnivall in the 1850s—has focused on either the *Grail* (Lagorio 1971; Radulescu 2013; Malo 2013) or the *Merlin* (Ackerman 1952b; Dalrymple 2000; Boboc 2006; Finotello 2014; Griffith 2017). This division of the single book into two texts obscures the relationship between Christian themes and chivalric ones; it also obscures Lovelich's accomplishments as a translator.

Translation reorients Lovelich's place in literary history. Medieval writers treated translation as a preservation technology that "carried over" the authority of ancient sources into new texts. Yet modern scholars have often treated translation as a sign that medieval writers lacked imagination. In fact, the idea that Lovelich was a "bad translator" partly explains how "MS 80" the interesting book became "MS 80" the boring text. The very same scholar who first brought Lovelich to my attention by indexing the

proper names—Robert Ackerman—deemed the text riddled with translation errors that proved Lovelich's "carelessness and incompetence" (Ackerman 1952b, 483; 1952c). The text does include words that might mystify
any monolingual English audience, as well as several characters invented
out of misinterpreted phrases. Today, though, new theories of translation
support quite different assessments of these features. Roger Dalrymple,
for example, concluded that Lovelich used a range of "newish" words
and that "poor translation" could be understood instead as "a sustained
practice of word-borrowing" (Dalrymple 2000, 161–62). French words like
occisiown ("slaughter," *Merlin* 8517) or *chawd-melle* ("heated battle," *Merlin*
13384) might serve to expand the English lexicon. Notably, the grail names
are never translated and form an oft-repeated rhyming pair: "Seint Graal"
and "Sank Ryal" (Royal Blood). These strategies add up to what Ardis Butterfield has called "rough translation"—practiced by some of the most
highly praised English writers who combine variable competencies in
French with "experimental English" (Butterfield 2012, 210, 223). From this
perspective, there is an "uncertain boundary between halting literary and
fluent colloquial English" (Butterfield 2012, 218). Whether by accident or
creative improvisation, then, MS 80's linguistic enigmas enhance a story
that teaches the value of mystery.

The translation story of MS 80 has three parts: the book, the text, and the
modern reception. I begin by elucidating the properties of MS 80 as a copy
of a French book: the codex heightens the status of the new English text by
translating the layout of a French illustrated manuscript. The exact source
is unknown, but the closest analogue is Oxford, Bodleian Library, Douce
MS 178 (https://digital.bodleian.ox.ac.uk/objects/d94075ee-c3d3-4f88-bb72-
33c2f9fd5c4a). Second, I turn to Lovelich's craft as a translator. As he negotiates his place in a chain of textual transmission that begins with God, he
writes in an accessible English style attuned to fifteenth-century literary
norms yet adapted to the particularities of his merchant community. His
strategies repatriate the Arthurian story, making it newly available for civic
and national purposes. MS 80 would have brought to the Skinners' Guild
a luxury book that preserved the story of Britain's Christian origins, offered didactic lessons on the Trinity, and dramatized chivalric valor. These

themes resonate directly with the Skinners' role in civic performance and with Barton's role in politics (see chap. 2).

Finally, I turn to the latest twist on MS 80's history—the translation of the *Grail* and *Merlin* editions into modern Dutch. These are the only known translations of Lovelich's English text. I encountered them on a particularly deep Google search for "Lovelich" on September 28, 2018. They were posted on the blog of the Rob Scholte Museum by folklorist Cor Hendriks as part of a series called "Secrets of the Grail"—twelve posts of commentary and source translations. In this context, Lovelich's text is but one fragment of a mystical whole. Rather like Lovelich's own approach, translation here appears to merely transfer valuable information from one context to another. I adopted this approach myself when I used Google Translate to produce "rough translations" of the Dutch Lovelich. Reading Lovelich in machine-authored English brought out a new truth about *translatio studii et imperii*: literary history relies on contradictory theories of translation, in which language change is simultaneously meaningful and meaningless. Eventually, my engagement with machine translation uncovered yet another example of tech medievalism—the "Holy Grail" of a machine translation that replicates the suppleness of human authorship. Translation, in all its guises, continues to rewrite the history of medieval books.

French Books for England

MS 80 was designed to be a grand book. It was made c. 1435 from large sheets of paper, a relatively expensive imported material (Da Rold 2020b, 58–90, 172). It has all the marks of high-quality commercial production (Meale 1994, 217–19). Each page features two neat columns of text, with generous margins and blank spaces for illustrations at irregular intervals—101 spaces across the surviving two hundred folios (at least twenty-five folios have been lost from the beginning, maybe more from the end). The spaces define episodes of varying lengths, from dozens of lines to dozens of pages. Even blank, such spaces signal narrative structure to readers (Hardman 1994). Images in the spaces would have made the book even easier to navigate for the kind of episodic reading and listening that was typical for long narrative. Illustrated paper manuscripts, however, are relatively rare owing in part to the porosity of paper (Da Rold 2020b, 177–78). Perhaps MS 80's patrons chose paper because it was a familiar material, widely adopted in guild record-keeping (Da Rold 2020b, 48–49). Or perhaps vellum would have put a book of this size just out of financial reach. Whatever the reason, MS 80 translates a deluxe French book into a rare paper format.

The illustration pattern in MS 80 suggests that it was modeled on a specific copy of the Arthurian French prose cycle. Versions of the cycle survive in many manuscripts, with a wide variety of formats and textual variations. Lovelich's text corresponds to the portions usually called *Estoire del saint graal*, *Estoire du Merlin*, and *Suite-Vulgate du Merlin* (Walter 2001–9). Like MS 80, these "three" French texts are often preserved as a single codex, copied as a single unit. They have varying lengths and mixes of idiosyncratic details, broadly classified as "long" and "short" versions. MS 80 is associated with the "long" versions, interspersed with abridgments (Ponceau 1983, 212–13; Micha 1980, 32–48, 224). Comparisons between MS 80 and "short" French versions are thus misleading (e.g., Furnivall 1861, 1863; Sommer 1908–16, 1:2, 2:2). In fact, MS 80 features a detail shared by only a handful of French texts: references to a "book of Brutus"—that is, a French text derived from Geoffrey of Monmouth's *History*. In French, this "book" might refer to the verse translation of Geoffrey by Wace, *Le Roman de Brut* (c. 1155). In English, a "book of Brutus" brings to mind an English prose *Brut* chronicle, readily available in fifteenth-century London (Matheson 1998). Lovelich, then, is the London translator of a French text that has already incorporated sources that can be traced back to Britain. These interpolations narrow the range of possible models for MS 80.

The first allusion to the "book of Brutus" in MS 80 occurs during the reign of King Lucius, the first British king to convert to Christianity. When Lovelich reaches this passage, he follows a French text whose narrator tries to account for the fact that the *Brut* doesn't mention the Holy Grail as part of the conversion story nor the essential role of one "Sir Piers" (Ponceau 1997, 2:546):

And yet nevertheless Brutus's story
Doesn't make any mention [*memorye*] of Sir Piers,
Because it is fully true [*ful syker*] without a doubt
That he who into French [*romaunce*] this story drew out,
He knew full little of the Holy Grail [*Seynt Graal*],
Or of the story of Royal Blood [*Sank Ryal*],
And therefore no one should marvel here
That he doesn't speak of Sir Piers there,
But even so (Sir Piers) cannot be excused,
Nor ever refused, from this story.
(*Grail*, LII:1061–70)

Piers was a member of Joseph of Arimathea's retinue, first introduced alongside the grail-keepers Alain the Fisher King and Bron (*Grail*, L:233–34). Piers becomes king of Orkney and progenitor of Gawain and his four brothers, some of Arthur's most famous knights. The French narrator thus insists on including Piers, despite the *Brut* translator's ignorance, in order to connect Arthur's court to one of the founding lines of British Christianity. In English, this passage further explains why English *Brut* chronicles lack information that MS 80 includes.

The second *Brut* reference in MS 80 also concerns Piers. It occurs when Merlin meets up with his scribe, Blaise. In some French texts—and in Lovelich's translation—Joseph's companions are named here as Alain and Piers (*Perron* in French) (*Merlin*, 1625). At the end of Merlin's session with Blaise, Lovelich directs readers who want to know more about early British Christianity to find "Brutus's book," which has been "translated from Latin into romance [French] by Martin de Beure" (1667–76). A number of French manuscripts refer here to a French *Brut* (while others declare that there is no need to speak of the pre-Christian kings) (Micha 1979, 76). Only two French texts, however, locate the translator in Bièvre, name his language as "romance" (rather than "French"), and also refer to Alain and Perron. They are Oxford, Bodleian, Douce MS 178 (f. 156r) and Chantilly, Musée Condé, MS 643 (Micha 1979, xxi–xxviii). These two manuscripts are part of a larger group that shortens certain passages while retaining others at full length (Micha 1980, 224), but only Douce MS 178 has been edited in this way throughout (Ponceau 1983, 29–33, 654–67). The specific terms of Lovelich's *Brut* passage are thus found in only one surviving French manuscript, Douce MS 178.

The third and final *Brut* allusion in MS 80 occurs after Arthur's election to the throne. Various barons refuse to recognize his kingship, and numerous battles ensue. Merlin goes to Brittany to raise additional troops; as he returns, the narrator pauses to explain the etymologies of Britain, London, and Cornwall. This passage of about sixty lines summarizes information found in *Brut* chronicles, beginning with two Trojan kings who fled the Greeks (*Merlin*, 10183–244). King Brutus named Britain after himself and called the city he built New Troy; later King Logrius rebuilt the city and renamed it "Logres" after himself; that name lasted until after the death of both Arthur and Lancelot, when there was a great pestilence during which many "barons and common people also" lost their friends and so started calling the country "Blue Britain . . . for their hearts were blue and black" (10220–23; also used 15515, 21840). The second Trojan king, Corineus, defeated the island's indigenous giants and named Cornwall after himself (10227–44). This lengthy passage doesn't name "Brutus's book" but instead summarizes a good portion of it, addressing the origin of the British dynasty as well as the island's "blue" nickname, which readers might recall from the beginning of the book (Ponceau 1997, 1:2, 23; these pages are now missing from MS 80). This passage, like the explicit *Brut* references, witnesses someone's prior effort to align the French narrative with the *Brut*'s historical time line.

The *Brut* passages in MS 80 point to Douce MS 178 as the closest surviving analogue (Douce MS 178, ff. 139r, 156r, 195r-v; MS 80, ff. 81v, 95r, 127r). The illustration patterns reinforce the connection. Douce MS 178 is one of nearly twenty illustrated manuscripts that include the *Estoire-Merlin-Suite* sequence—beginning with the hermit who writes about the grail and ending with an embattled Arthur (Fabry-Tehranchi 2014, 495–503; Moran 2014, 659–62). Some manuscripts have two columns of text per page, some three; some have illustrated initials and some column-width panels. Both Douce MS 178 and MS 80 have two columns of text, but Douce MS 178 has illustrated initials whereas MS 80 has column-width panels. For the most part, the illustration spaces in MS 80 track very closely with the illustrated initials in Douce MS 178. Even though the two manuscripts don't match precisely in every respect, their filiation is closer than any other surviving model. Copyists and book designers freely modified their models in idiosyncratic ways, even when producing several copies from one model; they might even swap illustrated panels for illustrated initials and vice versa (Stones 2003, 2005). MS 80 and Douce MS 178 thus probably share a common source—although they may not have the same direct source, and Douce MS 178 was not the direct source of MS 80 (the French manuscript came to England through the modern collector Francis Douce, 1757–1834 [Middleton 2006, 73–75]). Nonetheless, the correspondences between the two manuscripts strongly suggest that MS 80 represents the comprehensive *translatio* of a French book into an English one. MS 80 translates the language and transfers the layout as part of acquiring knowledge (*translatio studii*) and solidifying power (*translatio imperii*).

Two marginal rubrics in MS 80 describe a specific illustration plan that reinforces the link with Douce MS 178 at a crucial narrative juncture— Arthur's coronation. This thematic focus further underscores how the practical components of translation and bookmaking also perform the myth of *translatio studii et imperii*. Both rubrics are in the same quire: the first refers to Arthur's coronation—*coronacō arthu'* (f. 117v, after *Merlin*, 7784)—and the second to a "meeting of kings" as Ban and Bors arrive from Brittany to assist Arthur against the rebel barons—*obviacō regium* (f. 123r, after *Merlin*, 9218). These two rubrics, both transcribed by the editor Ernst Kock, describe a sequenced pair of illustrated initials in Douce MS 178 (ff. 181v, 189v) (see figs. 2 and 3). These are the first illustrations after twenty-five pages of continuous text leading up to Arthur's coronation. Of the thirty-six manuscripts that narrate both Arthur's election and its aftermath, only seven depict the coronation (Fabry-Tehranchi 2014, 91, 103–11)—and only one other is part of the same text group as Douce MS 178 (private collection, ex-Bodmer, ex-Newcastle 937). These are the only two descriptive rubrics in the entirety of MS 80: they focus attention on Arthur's accession to power—a king crowned by kings—and the beginning of Britain's most illustrious empire.

Figure 2   Comparison of MS 80, folio 117v with Bodleian, Douce MS 178, folio 181v.

SOURCES: https://parker.stanford.edu/parker/catalog/xd494bt3141 (courtesy of Parker Library, Corpus Christi College, Cambridge); and https://digital.bodleian.ox.ac.uk (photo: © Bodleian Libraries, University of Oxford). Licensed under a Creative Commons Attribution-NonCommercial 4.0 International License.

Figure 3   Comparison of MS 80, folio 123r with Bodleian, Douce MS 178, folio 189v.

SOURCES: https://parker.stanford.edu/parker/catalog/xd494bt3141 (courtesy of Parker Library, Corpus Christi College, Cambridge); and https://digital.bodleian.ox.ac.uk (photo: © Bodleian Libraries, University of Oxford). Licensed under a Creative Commons Attribution-NonCommercial 4.0 International License.

A little farther on, another quire has several generic rubrics that suggest a plan to furnish the book with vivid imagery. This quire has more spaces than any other surviving quire—fifteen in all. And one opening has more than any other—four, each annotated with various forms of the word *pageant* (ff. 153v–154r; see fig. 4); another "pageant" follows a few folios later after three spaces without rubrics (f. 159r; all noted in Kock 1904–32, 462). *Pageant* is used in other manuscripts to denote "picture"; the word can also refer to plays, props in plays, and processions (Driver 2014). In MS 80, the rubricated spaces punctuate a battle scene and so might refer to the "procession" of troops into battle (Eddy 2012, 366). Together, these five "pageants," along with the two Latin rubrics, suggest that the book's production was interrupted in the midst of planning for the illustrations. They, along with the generous spaces, document the vision to create an English book that would transfer French prestige to ambitious Londoners.

MS 80 is part of broader English interests in French books. The French prose cycle was part of the "ready cross-Channel permeability of French texts in the later Middle Ages" (Wogan-Browne, Fenster, and Russell 2016, 369). Some of the Arthurian manuscripts were originally copied on the Continent and then brought to England; more than a dozen others were copied by English scribes, in England or on the Continent (Middleton 2003; Stones 2010, 2016). Wills and inventories suggest some of the circulation patterns. In 1305, Guy de Beauchamps donated to Bordesley Abbey what sounds like a copy of the full French cycle (Blaess 1957, 512–13). Thomas Woodstock, Duke of Gloucester (d. 1397), had several large books in French telling the stories of Merlin, Lancelot, and Arthur (Middleton 2003, 221). The poet Thomas Hoccleve recommended reading "the storie of Lancelot de lake" to learn about chivalry (Warren 2007). Later in the fifteenth century, Richard Roos bequeathed a "great book called Saint Grail" (Meale 1985, 103). Among the merchant classes, a bankrupt grocer in the 1390s is said to have had four "books of romance" (possibly French) (Scott 2014, 169). Much later, another grocer, Thomas Crull, bequeathed in 1540 "my two French books of the life of King Arthur printed on paper and covered in boards and red leather" (Scott 2014, 168). These disparate examples suggest some of the ways that Lovelich might have come to own

Figure 4   MS 80, folios 153v–54r, with spaces for illustrations and three "pageant" rubrics.

SOURCE: https://parker.stanford.edu/parker/catalog/xd494bt3141. Courtesy of Parker Library, Corpus Christi College, Cambridge. Licensed under a Creative Commons Attribution-NonCommercial 4.0 International License.

or borrow a book to translate. They also show that Arthurian books were one of the ways in which merchants adopted aristocratic habits in their quest for social and economic success.

Lovelich's English book would have broadened the audience for the mysteries of the Holy Grail, the magic of Merlin, and the kingship of Arthur. The project was unique in scale. MS 80 has only one near-corollary in English, the prose *Merlin* completed a few decades later. That text survives in one nearly complete copy (Cambridge University Library, MS Ff.3.11, 245 folios) and one leaf from an otherwise lost copy (Bodleian, MS Rawlinson D. 913, f. 43) (Wheatley 1865–69; Meale 1986). Plenty of other texts engage with the French prose cycle in ways that suggest widespread knowledge among English writers—from Geoffrey Chaucer's allusion to the "book of Launcelot de Lake" (Warren 2007) to Thomas Malory's *Morte*

Darthur (c. 1485)—a full-scale reworking of the cycle with no prior model as "book." And some chroniclers did reconcile Joseph of Arimathea's grail story with the time lines of the *Brut* (Matheson 1985; Moll 2003; Carlton and Moll 2018). Other writers took inspiration from particular episodes to craft short metrical texts, such as the alliterative *Morte Arthure* and the stanzaic *Morte Arthur* (Benson and Foster 1994). Like MS 80, most of these Arthurian texts survive in single copies and may have had limited audiences. Nonetheless, they are part of a large and influential narrative network pinned to the French prose cycle. In this broader context, MS 80 is both an anomaly and a paradigm of literary practice.

MS 80 stands out as an unusually ambitious project. The translation itself was an enormous undertaking. And the book's luxury aspirations contrast markedly with the most commonly available French manuscripts, which were relatively plain and undecorated (Middleton 2003, 224). If the purpose was only to inform a new community about Britain's remarkable origins, a simpler book would have sufficed. Instead, Lovelich and his fellow guildsman Barton initiated a project that would make the story accessible in English while also reproducing the prestige that accrued to deluxe illustrated manuscripts. The book could then symbolize the guild's aspiration to increase its social standing and exert influence over civic affairs. The book was meant to be seen as much as heard. While it probably never reached its destination, the material format points to this visionary intent.

English Style for Merchants

Translation mediates MS 80's dual status as both unique and paradigmatic. This combination made the book valuable, as well as accessible, to new audiences in fifteenth-century London. In line with the practice exemplified by Geoffrey's *History*, Lovelich uses translation to establish his legitimacy as author. At the same time, he inherits from the French cycle a complex and ingenious scheme of *translatio* that further elevates his English style. Lovelich's literary practice is thus bound up with the French cycle's portrayal of translation as the foundation of authorship.

By following the "plot" of translation in the English text, the persona "Lovelich-translator" comes into focus as a master of precious Arthurian memories that belong to all who can understand English.

Lovelich manufactures an authoritative English style out of the French cycle's spectacles of *translatio*. The French text, for example, is well known for its self-conscious narration of its own transmission. The technique known as interlace plaits together story lines such that they take place both simultaneously and sequentially: a thread may be dropped for many pages before the narrator takes it up again, noting that it occurred at the same time as episodes that seemed to come before or after (Chase 2003; Brandsma 2010). This weave of interconnections is modulated at the sentence level by self-reflexive syntax in which the "story" talks to itself about itself (Warren 2000, 174–76; Combes 2003). Along the way, genealogies and prophecies draw future events into earlier time frames. The era of Joseph of Arimathea precedes, but also coincides with, the Arthurian future; the dramas of Christian conversion sow the British landscape with marvels that will come to fruition much later with Lancelot and Galahad. These resolutions take place well after the *Estoire-Merlin-Suite*, in the portions of the cycle called *Lancelot* and *Queste del Saint Graal*. Some passages allude to the very end of the cycle, *La Mort le roi Artu*, and even to times beyond Arthur's life. The frequency of these allusions accommodates modes of reading and listening that are "tabular" (in order or not) and "modular" (complete or not) (Moran 2014, 336–38). Even a short engagement with the text can encompass a broad sweep of narrative time.

Lovelich adapts these French structures in ways that amplify the legitimacy of translation. He repeatedly claims to know the truth about everything, promising that the audience will eventually share in his own omniscience, if he can finish translating the book. Throughout, the spectacle of translation is represented through the making, copying, and reading of books. By drawing attention to the material forms of books, Lovelich reinforces the idea that the story has been securely transmitted from its first author to its most recent reader. The story's transmission appears unbroken from God to Robert to Merlin to Blaise to Lovelich and into readers' memory. The story line itself flashes forward and backward at regular intervals, underscoring the narrator's comprehensive knowledge of the whole story. From the beginning, readers await the end of the British marvels, anticipate the end of Arthur, remember Joseph of Arimathea, and recall British lineage from the Trojans down to the present. MS 80 thus encompasses the whole story, even if not the whole narrative.

The ultimate source is Christ's own writing, followed by the hermit's translation of this sacred text. Although the beginning pages of MS 80 are now missing, the story of these sacred origins comes across in later passages. As Joseph establishes Christian worship around the grail, his first conversion case is King Evalach, baptized with the new name Mordreins. Over many pages, Mordreins has his new faith tested by several perilous adventures. Along the way he is attacked by a phoenix: while explaining the nature of this rare bird, the narrator refers to the "divine story" that has put these facts "in our memory" (XXIII:465–66). Evalach's brother-in-law Seraphe, who takes the Christian name Nasciens after meeting Joseph, also has his new faith tested through a series of mysterious adventures. In the middle, the narrator gives a lengthy exposition of why even the most incredible events—such as a large turning island—must be believed: the story never lies—even if "all the certainty of the Sank Ryal is hard to find"—because it comes from "the mouth of truth," which is Jesus Christ, who wrote the story "with his own hand" (XXVII:264–78). The narrator goes on to summarize at some length the two instances when Christ wrote before his passion, affirming "full boldly" that the grail story is the only thing that Christ wrote after his passion: anyone who says otherwise is lying (XXVII:346–67). These passages underscore that the grail story originates with the hand of God and thus is thoroughly unimpeachable even when translated into English.

The next book portrayed in MS 80 is written by the biblical King Solomon. Nasciens discovers it aboard a beautiful ship while exiled on the aforesaid turning island. This encounter, narrated in detail across nearly eight folios (almost two thousand lines, XXVIII–XXXI), is full of Christian exegesis from divine voices, a "good man," and the narrator. Indeed, the rhetoric of revelation merges the narrator's voice with divine speech: they use the same phrasing to affirm the truth of their explanations. The narrator even tells the biblical story of Genesis as an explanation for three wooden spindles found on the ship. Nested within this story is Solomon's book, which also explains the ship. This book is destined for the "best knight," who will be the last of Solomon's lineage (XXX:505)—that is, Galahad. Solomon, though, learned this future from another book (XXX:140, 426). He is rightfully confused about how he has knowledge of an heir who won't be born for two thousand years. The tangle of prophecy and retrospection is truly mysterious. Solomon's book provides "remembraunce" (XXX:525) of the oldest events in the story (how Solomon's wife designed the ship), but it will only be read at the end of the grail quest (hundreds of years after Nasciens). Solomon's book thus stands apart from all the others in the story, destined to eventually subsume them. Not even Solomon's great "konnenge" (skill, wisdom) can explain this conundrum. Meanwhile, back on the ship, Nasciens's faulty "memory" causes him doubts that land him in the cold water of unbelievers, ejected from the ship (XXXI:21). The episode ends with Nasciens alone, talking to himself, having forgotten "in all degree" everything about the ship (XXXI:470-71). Readers, however, have the omniscient privilege to turn back the page and remember. They can piece together the lineage that begins with Solomon, passes through Nasciens, and ends with Galahad. MS 80 itself thus serves the august function of Solomon's book. "We" are already privy to what no one else knows, thanks to Lovelich's translation.

The next book conflates MS 80 even more powerfully with divine writing. After Nasciens's son Celidoine converts Label, king of Persia, the narrator pauses to justify the detour through Label's story. Here, the original book by Christ and the English book by Lovelich converge to make durable and comprehensive memories:

> And although this matter and others do not belong to this story,
> Yet he that made this book has put it into memory
> In order to make a clear noticing,
> And in order to declare everything
> More openly to men's mind,
> All the matter, the better to bring the story to an end.
> Thus he puts all things into memory,

He that first made this holy story.
(*Grail*, XXXIII:540–48)

Then the story passes forth,
That is called by some men Seynt Graal
And it is also called Sank Ryal
By many people, without a doubt.
(*Grail*, XXXIV:1–4)

The reference here to "he that made this book" is ambiguous: it could mean Christ, the holy hermit, or the maker of the English book we're reading. The goals of "clear noticing" and "declaring everything more openly" align with the narrator's statements elsewhere, as does the idea of "bringing the matter to an end" and putting "all things in memory." Indeed, a narrator comment in an earlier passage links memory directly to books (XIV:4–9). Yet in the end the syntax folds back on itself, with a further modifying clause, "that first made this holy story." Christ, the hermit, or the English translator? It all depends on the referent of "this." Whatever the case, the vocabulary of making and of memory echoes contemporary ideas of authorship (Ebin 1988, 38–42; Sponsler 2014, 25–27). "Making memory" describes both storytelling and bookmaking. In this gesture, Lovelich's translation of the "holy story" merges his own authorship with the sacred history of Christian conversion.

This passage extends the elevating power of translation to the grail itself. "Men's minds" are divided over the name of the story—Holy Grail or Royal Blood. This doubling reflects ambiguities in the definition of Joseph's holy relic: is it the vessel that he used to capture Christ's blood or the blood itself? This confusion derives from the opening scenes of the grail story (now lost in MS 80): on the day of the Crucifixion, Joseph retrieves from Jesus's house "a vessel [*escüele*] from which the Son of God had eaten" and then gathers from his body "a drop of blood" into the same vessel (Ponceau 1997, 1:24–25). The equivocation between vessel and blood is amplified in Britain by the grail's association with a blood relic at Glastonbury (Lagorio 1971). In Lovelich's translation, the double name emphasizes a totalizing memory, conveyed by "this book" that leaves nothing out, even alternate titles. In this passage about "this book," then, "this story" reverts to the very first book—the one written by Christ and given to the hermit to copy. The English book and the divine book become simultaneously distinct and indistinguishable. Translation, conversion, and the grail itself transmit a single transcendent truth that passes unchanged through every transfer.

As Nasciens's temptations continue, we finally meet the French translator, Robert de Boron. His book represents the principle of secure, linear transmission from God to the current page. It counteracts the potentially troubling effects of detours and inconsistencies. Robert's book appears first when the story crosses paths again with Label, "who doesn't belong to the story," because his daughter will marry Celidoine, who does belong. We then learn that the "matter" of this story has been translated by "my master Robert Boron" from Latin to French "next after that holy hermit, who had taken it from God Himself" (XXXVIII:218–22). This explanation describes a clearly linear transmission from God to the hermit to Robert. Yet matters are soon confused by another document written by God—a genealogy in Hebrew and Latin given to Nasciens to reward his faith. It reveals the nine generations of his progeny down to Lancelot and Galahad (XXXIX:157–298). Lovelich gives this document three different names— *wryt*, *lyveret*, and *rolette* (XXXIX:205, 267, 297). Form thus becomes a divine mystery: how can it be both a booklet and a roll? In any case, this "book" containing Nasciens's genealogy must also be part of every other book; otherwise, the story of Nasciens's genealogy couldn't be told. Robert's book thus serves to recuperate all the potentially troubling and mysterious strands of transmission into a single source. Lovelich-narrator, in turn, provides the unified English version.

Robert's book returns several more times, each time promising that translation has faithfully preserved God's word. After various further temptations and violent conversions, Nasciens, Celidoine, Mordreins, Joseph, and his son Josephes are finally reunited in North Wales. To celebrate their victories, they pray around the grail and Josephes performs a mass. Mordreins, ever literal in his faith, desires to see the grail "openly" and defies God's warning not to approach too near: he is immediately struck blind and infirm (XLVI:239–58). A believer at last, he prays to live long enough to meet Nasciens's ninth descendant, as foretold in the genealogy (XLVI:272–78). After Celidoine finally marries Label's daughter, Mordreins retires to an abbey to await Galahad, "of whom we spoke before, who should come ninth of Nasciens's line, as you heard told before" (XLVI:490–92). Lovelich-narrator affirms that Galahad will indeed visit Mordreins:

> as it says here,
> in the story of Sank Ryal in this manner,
> and also as my sire Robert of Boron,
> who this story all and some
> turned out of Latin into French,
> by holy Church's commandment, truly.
> (*Grail*, XLVI:495–500)

The affirmations of divine truth pile on even as the sources multiply: the story of Sank Ryal (which one?), Robert's translation, and ecclesiastical authority. The story has been faithfully and authoritatively translated yet also seems to exist in more than one version. Somewhere along the way, God's Hebrew-Latin genealogy of Nasciens joined the plot. The message—in English—seems to be that true memories can be found in every version. Lovelich-translator thus acquires an omniscience that derives straight from God. In this performance, translation faithfully transmits both knowledge and power (*translatio studii et imperii*).

As marvels related to the grail multiply, Robert's book reinforces Lovelich-narrator's omniscience. Even when Robert's book fails, it enhances the narrator's authority: Robert may not know where the sinful Symeon went, but the narrator does: "when the time and place both come, you shall hear more of this case openly declared to your ear, so that you shall understand it more clearly" (L:775–84). Later, Lovelich-narrator uses Robert's book to contradict the *Brut*. The occasion is the conversion of King Lucius: Robert, who "translated this matter from Latin to French," provides the authoritative "witness" to the fact that Lucius was converted by Piers—even though "Brutus's story makes no memory of Sir Piers"

(LII:1057–62). The narrator then follows the life of Piers and his progeny down to King Lot, introducing a genealogy on the model of Nasciens's. Lot married Arthur's sister and had four sons, one of whom, Mordred, was actually Arthur's son born of unwitting incest, "as many books tell in rhyme" (LII:1150). All this goes to show that Gawain was actually descended from the line of Joseph of Arimathea (LII:1117–64). This is a somewhat belabored way of connecting Joseph's kin to the knights of Arthur's court—but pointedly not to Arthur, whose incest is an affront to the divine logic of both genealogy and translation. Through Piers, Robert's book encompasses the whole of the Arthurian cycle as told in the *Estoire-Merlin-Suite*, *Lancelot*, *Queste*, and *Mort*. Since the narrator knows Robert's book, the narrator knows everything.

The final and most ambitious passage of translation drama involving Robert comes as Lovelich names himself as author for the first time. Here, Robert is credited with a second story, called "Prophet Merlin," also translated from Latin into French: "he joins together Merlin with Sank Ryal because the one story is mingled with the other" (LVI:512–20). Only now do we learn how Robert's French book became the English book we've been following:

> And I, as an ignorant [*vnkonneng*] man truly,
> Into English have drawn this story.
> And though it may not be pleasing to you,
> Would that you excuse me
> Of my negligence and ignorance [*unkonnenge*]
> In having taken on such a thing,
> Into our mother tongue to write [*endite*],
> The sweeter and lighter to sound,
> And more clear to your understanding
> Than either French or Latin, to my supposing.
> And therefore at the end of this story,
> Would you pray a "pater noster" [Our Father] for me,
> For me who is called Henry Lovelich,
> And greet Our Lady full of might

Heartily with an Ave, that you bid to her,
That I might better proceed with this process
And bring this book to a good end.
Now, Jesus Christ, send me grace,
That there might be an end to all this.
Now, good Lord, grant me charity.
(*Grail*, LVI:521–40)

Taking Robert's place, Lovelich-narrator writes himself into the succession of translators as an "unknowing" conduit for the divinely sanctioned story. His self-deprecating excuses for "negligence" echo well-worn author tropes that stretch back to Geoffrey's *History* and beyond. Reliability comes precisely from not deforming the truth with extraneous rhetorical flourishes. As translator, Lovelich's "ignorant" performance increases understanding and knowledge by "enditing" (composing, writing) in the familiar idiom of English—"our sweet, light, and clear mother tongue." His closing request for prayers is another established trope. In the grail context, however, a prayer to Jesus Christ to bring "the process of the book to a good end" calls for intercession from the text's original author— the hermit's book written by God. Lovelich's self-portrait as translator thus aligns MS 80—the text and the book—with established traditions of authorship.

Just a few pages later, Merlin's arrival introduces a new book—the one dictated by Merlin to his scribe, Blaise. As Merlin takes command, he links knowledge and memory to metrical style in ways that counteract Lovelich-narrator's "uncunning." Before the book can begin, Merlin has to convince Blaise that a devil's son can be a reliable narrator. At two-and-a-half years old, Merlin has already defended his mother in court and outwitted the judge. He tells Blaise that his extraordinary gifts come from God, whose "secrets" [*prevyte*] (line 1592) devils could not know:

You say that I am the devil's son:
You may as well have said that I came from God
And that He granted me both wisdom [*wit*] and memory:
What harm would it have done you to say it?

> For it is God's will that I know
> Things to come, all in a row.
> (*Merlin*, 1577–82)

Merlin mischievously equates the devil's paternity with God's: either could grant unnatural powers. Merlin's "divine gift" includes knowledge of all past and all future events—"things to come all in a row," which is to say in order, one after another. Merlin repeats this description of linear time in later statements about the future (3976, 25164). The narrator also uses the phrase to explain the ordering of events: "Now further this lettering does show us here all the process upon a row" (15921–22; also XLV:90). The connotation includes the literal shape of text on the page: "as the story hereafter shall make you know all the substance, row by row" (22281–82). In this way, the stable structure of metrical form—one line after another—complements the divinely sanctioned truth of Merlin's knowledge.

As Merlin outlines the plan for his book, he brings every book that preserves this story—including MS 80—into the succession of books and translations that began with Christ. Addressing Blaise, Merlin promises a story full of marvels:

> Now I shall tell you such marvels, so plainly,
> That you will marvel
> At how such wisdom [*wyttes*] might sink into any man.
> Blaise, now make a book
> So that hereafter many men shall look upon it.
> (*Merlin*, 1596–1600)

Anyone reading MS 80, at any time, numbers among the "many" who look on a book of marvels told by Merlin. Blaise immediately gathers "pen, ink, and parchment" to write; Merlin proceeds to summarize the whole of the grail story, including "all that happened" with Joseph of Arimathea, Alain, and Piers. Merlin then continues with the most recent events: the devils' plot to impregnate his mother and their failure to control him (1613–38). Blaise fulfills the role of copyist, like the hermit of 717. He even recalls the lesson in the Trinity, which the hermit had doubted: before Blaise begins writing, he asks Merlin to swear on the Trinity to tell the truth. In a truly devilish move, Merlin enjoins Blaise to correct him if he does anything against God's will (1602–12). In this clever feint, Merlin grants Blaise even more perfect knowledge of God than Merlin himself has just claimed. From this point forward in MS 80, "this book" refers simultaneously to Christ's, the hermit's, Robert's, Blaise's, and Lovelich's.

In the description of the writing process, Lovelich-narrator becomes the coauthor of Merlin's knowledge. To begin, Lovelich-narrator swears to the truth of the writing process, "so God save me" (line 1617). This claim aligns him with Merlin, who has just attributed his wisdom to "God's will." Soon, Blaise's agency also merges with Merlin's:

> Thus Merlin began all this work,
> And Blaise brought it to a good ending [fine].
> And the longer that Blaise was writing,
> The better he thought he could write [endite]
> And the more that he worked on the story,
> The more he saw like Merlin.
> (Merlin, 1639–44)

As Blaise fuses his perspective with Merlin's, the prospect that Blaise would ever "correct" anything dissipates. At the same time, Blaise and Lovelich-narrator are made similar. Both are "enditing" (composing) (LVI:517, 1642); both are laboring to bring their stories to an end (LVI:537, 1649). And both have just written out "the story called Saint Graal." At this point, Lovelich-narrator takes over from Blaise and Merlin to complete Christian history with information about pre-Christian history, directing readers to "the story of Brutus's book" translated by Martin de Bièvre (1667–76). In this moment, Lovelich performs Merlin's omniscience: unlike Martin, he knows all about the grail. A little later, Merlin specifies that the whole book "shall be called Saint Graal, full truly" (2324–28). Merlin thus gives Blaise's book the same title as the hermit's, although it includes much more. Merlin promises that the grail will be "beloved in many countries" (1660–66) and that the book, likewise, "shall always be beloved and heard by the people full heartily" (2286–302). Lovelich proves these affirmations true when he translates these passages from French into English—and they are proven all over again whenever anyone reads MS 80. As the book that encompasses all the other books, MS 80 is the truest of all.

Repeated scenes of storytelling and book writing throughout the rest of MS 80 reiterate the secure transmission of true knowledge. Each time, Merlin leaves court to tell Blaise what has happened, which Blaise in turn writes in the book (3039–44). Each of Merlin's visits includes a comprehensive recap "of the adventures that already befell and also of the adventures that were coming" (17697–98). The repetition of the sessions, and their descriptions of totality, perform omniscient storytelling. They also remind us of the mechanism of our own knowledge, in phrasing repeated in various forms by Lovelich-narrator: "Blaise wrote all these things and into his book he wrote everything; thanks to him we now have knowledge of these things" (11462–64; also 3475–78, 5795–800, 6913–18, 11462–64, 14092, 17707–8, 20937–38). In fact, all the didactic storytellers use the same vocabulary of instruction. They assure their audiences of omniscient truth. Whether the authority is Christ, Joseph, Merlin, or Lovelich-narrator, the rhetoric is the same: we have been told the truth by someone who knows everything. All told, the Merlin-Blaise book project produces the entire story over and over again.

Lovelich-narrator underscores these omniscient powers when he inserts his name a second time. As Merlin travels to Brittany to elicit help from Kings Ban and Bors against the barons who refuse Arthur's accession, the narrator decides that "it is good reason" that we understand the origins of Britain's name (10183–84). He then summarizes the beginning of the *Brut*, recounting the story of the Trojans Brutus and Corineus. The narrator alludes to the harm wrought by Corineus's descendants and promises to tell more later if he can:

> Of the marvels that befell after,
> I hope to declare to you all,
> If God will grant me grace and might,
> Health of body and my eyesight.
> Out of French into English I will try

To draw it so that you may understand.
Therefore for Henry Lovelich, may you pray,
That until this be ended, he may not die,
But live in health and prosperity.
Now good lord, grant it to be so.
Forth to my matter now will I pass.
(*Merlin*, 10246–55)

By alluding to marvels in the distant future, Lovelich writes himself into the liminal time between knowledge and inscription. He underscores his authorial presence by expanding the French narrator's pithy appeal for "strength and power" ("force et pooir" [Douce 178, f. 195v]) into the emphatic plea for "grace, might, health, prosperity, and eyesight." He then draws the audience into responsibility for his health—and the book's completion—by rhyming *pray* with *die*. The book, if finished, would secure memory beyond his lifetime—"remembrance" without "variance" (10512–13). If translation and transcription don't happen in time, however, there will be no book and no memory. In these gestures, the book's disparate sources and time lines collapse into the hands of one guide—Lovelich.

Toward the end of MS 80 (f. 175v), Blaise's book appears one last time to reaffirm the authenticity of Lovelich's English text. In the midst of King Arthur's heated battle against King Rion, Lovelich-narrator pauses to call out the valor of a knight named Nasciens—namesake and heir to the original Nasciens who witnessed the grail (22567). Now we learn that this first Nasciens also wrote the first grail book, later incorporated into Blaise's book:

This same Nasciens had in his keeping
All the holy story up to the ending
Of all the story, great and small,
Which men call the Seint Graal.
First he wrote it with his own hand,
As these letters give us to understand,
By the commandment of his high sovereign
Who commanded him to write, full plainly.

> That story joins with the book of Blaise,
> That Merlin devised by his own ease.
> This Blaise was a holy hermit
> Who wrote according to Merlin in diverse places.
> Wherever Merlin met with Blaise,
> Into this book Blaise set his stories,
> By which book we now have knowledge
> Of many things that Merlin promised were coming.
> (*Merlin*, 22591–606)

Nasciens's biography parallels the hermit of 717: both wrote a book about the grail by divine commandment. This doubling seems to undermine the linear logic of transmission since it gives the "one true story" more than one origin. "Our knowledge" is further mediated by Blaise's book, which incorporates Nasciens's and also has the same title, "Seint Graal." Blaise's book thus overwrites and overrides all the prior sources—Nasciens, the hermit of 717, Robert of Boron, and the others. The lesson, once again, is that no amount of translation can compromise the truth. And repetition makes the story more true, not more doubtful. In MS 80, Lovelich-narrator becomes only the latest conduit for the "holy story."

From beginning to end, Lovelich-translator masters this whole apparatus of overlapping sources as a first-person protagonist. Across the entirety of MS 80, the portrayal of prior books, scribes, and translators is subsumed within Lovelich-translator's ubiquitous voice. He makes his presence felt at nearly every turn. As we read in English, he reminds us that we are reading in English (XXVIII:239–40, 9331–32, 25806). As we hear rhymes, he reminds us that we are hearing rhymes (LII:1148, 14525–26). He replaces the reflexive French syntax (the story that talks to itself) with an English narrator who guides readers and listeners with a directive tone. He often draws "us" into the story with first- and second-person plurals, drawing our attention to the action ("as you may see"). In one revelatory case, he turns third-person French into second-person English: "so lay people can understand" (Douce MS 178, f. 195v) becomes "that you may understand" (10251). All of these translation strategies underscore the cohesive truth of the whole story, which rests on the combined authority of the immediate source, its transcendent origin, and its projection into prophecies that have already come true. The process of storytelling is thus consistently on display. By repeatedly "ensuring" us that our "knowledge" will eventually be complete, Lovelich affirms that nothing has been lost in translation.

Transitions between episodes are Lovelich's most dramatic accomplishment as translator. He turns the relatively repetitive French formulas into a diversified vocabulary that creates suspense and movement. As Dalrymple first pointed out, these transitions "cast the reader as mobile in the Arthurian landscape" (Dalrymple 2000, 158). The narrator of the story tells, declares, records, rehearses, and proceeds with the urgency of a messenger on a vital errand. The narrator, the story, and "we" ourselves cease, stop, "blynne" (desist), "twynne" (part), leave, turn, and forsake. "We" must proceed, speak, "spelle" (speak), talk, see, look, begin, bring, and "fonge" (undertake). Sometimes we "must hye" (hurry), "go ful snelle" (swiftly), or "rake" (hasten). Other times, we rest, dwell, abide, renew, return, and "pere" (return, 10546). The story sometimes leads (LIII:2), other times wends. The occasionally novel idiom heightens the drama: several times, we are invited to "walk further" toward the next "matter" (XV:2, 17429, 19194), another time to "pace" (13619); once, the story speaks of Merlin for as long as "the space of a mile" (17556); elsewhere, we "glide forth" toward Arthur (11468). The sense of motion is palpable from page to page. The narrative—along with the narrator and the audience—is mapped onto a landscape where one moves from place to place, "proceeding" step-by-step toward true understanding. Everything happens in the present tense, as "we" follow along in real time.

As we rush along, the narrator is always at the center of the action. He enjoins us repeatedly to listen and learn, harken and hear. We are assured—and even "certified" (XXV:457, 21687)—of the truth of his every word: "I you plyht" (promise, swear); "I shall teach you" (XXX:592); "I shall tell you with good will" (LVI:281); "This is the truth, as I tell you" (14403). The story has no "guise" to lie (XXVII:264–65) and there is always a "good reason" for what it says. Lovelich reinforces these affirmations with a rich variety of adverbs: everything will be shown or told openly, plainly, clearly, certainly, properly, truly, "verament" (truly), "sekerle" (truthfully, assuredly), "without variance," and without any "lette" (delay). Once in a while, Lovelich-narrator asks us a direct question: "Now what do you think of this city that I have told you about?" (17355–56). Only rarely does he express doubt: "Now I shall rehearse all the process of this matter as closely as I can guess" (25173–74). The narrator keeps us in the "here and now" of the story (or, *ci* in French), such that time telescopes across the millennia: "Now of this story listen now here" (19087). There will be an "end" but only once everything has been revealed: "of each thing that is in doubt, the story rehearses it before passing out [of the scene] and brings it to clear understanding" (XXVII:21–23). Over and over, the narrator intervenes to remind us that he is narrating, even if all he has to say is "I tell it thee."

Lovelich's narrative style resonates with some of the most popular poetry of his day, notably the prolific John Lydgate (fl. 1400–50), commissioned by merchants and kings alike. Each of the characteristics that modern critics have criticized in Lovelich's style had rather different connotations in the fifteenth century (see chap. 5). Variable meter, for example, approximates the fluidity of oral speech (Hardman 2006). Lovelich's lines vary in length from seven to twelve syllables, with frequent alliterating phrases and consistent rhyming couplets (Dalrymple 2000, 159). This "rough meter" is not a perfect four-stress line but a perfectly enjoyable rhythm with clear poetic features. Lydgate describes his own style—when writing for the king no less—in these very terms: his *Troy Book* includes lines of varying lengths, "both short and long" (Lydgate 1906–35; V:3484). Lydgate's syntax is also paralleled in Lovelich's style: sentences that start with conjunctions, continue for multiple lines with diffuse subordination, and end in the first line of a couplet (such that the rhyme sutures two sentences together) (Hardman 2006, 23–25). This style propels continuous engagement, as there is almost always a reason to go on to the next line. Lydgate and Lovelich also share a preference for the "doublet couplet," in which the first line gives new information and the second expands or comments: the unit of a complete idea is often the quatrain (Dalrymple 2000, 160, 162). This cadenced repetition is well suited for reading aloud because it gives listeners time to process new ideas. These stylistic parallels between Lydgate and Lovelich—in conjunction with their overlapping social spheres (Warren 2008)—integrate MS 80 into the broader literary culture of early fifteenth-century London.

In this context, the very length of Lovelich's text becomes a poetic asset that further reinforces the truth of the story. Lydgate correlates length directly to the amount of truth an author has to share: in *Fall of Princes* he suggests that short texts are "constrained under words few for lack of truth"; telling sufficient truth requires a "long process" (Lydgate 1923–27, 1:92–97; Ebin 1988, 36–37). Indeed, *process* is one of the terms that Lovelich uses regularly to convey the truth of his narrative. From this perspective, one of the greatest truths that Lovelich has to tell is the name of King Arthur's sword—a double quatrain about translation that exhibits every feature of "good writing:"

> And about the sword was written full well
> "Escalabort," which was engraved in steel.
> A Hebrew name it was, certainly,
> That in French is called "Trawnchefyst,"
> That is in English, to tell you the truth,
> As trenchant, and sharp, and cutting very quickly [*ful snelle*].
> And that, forsooth, is fully true,
> As you shall hear hereafter, certainly.
> (*Merlin*, 8413–20)

This passage is full of repetition, amplification, and diffuse syntax. The name "Escalabort" is both "written" and "graven." It has three translations (Hebrew, French, English). The English translation is given in three synonyms (*trenchant, sharp, cutting*)—one of which is basically French (*trenchant*). The truth of the translation is declared no less than three times—forsooth, full true, as you're about to hear. Meanwhile, most of the lines begin with conjunctions (*as, and, that*), which blur the line between clause and sentence. In reading, it's easy to pause almost anywhere but also difficult to stop. In fact, these eight lines are part of a longer unit of sixteen lines (four quatrains, eight couplets), itself part of a series of units of roughly similar length marked by the conjunctions *when* or *then*. In the midst of

Arthur's battles, the naming of his sword thus stands out as a virtuoso performance of English style.

All in all, MS 80 performs an act, and a theory, of translation as something that should visibly display the absence of change. Lovelich's translation strategies turn narration away from self-reflexivity ("the story" that talks about itself in French) and toward an audience eager for truth. Along the way, his identity as author fuses with translation. Most pointedly, the third and final appearance of his name takes the cryptic form of a Latin-English pun. At the end of a passage where Lovelich implies that the book is being read at a feast, he asks for wine to slake his thirst (see chap. 2). He then asks to be remembered: "I pray, my lords, that you keep in mind this: Gallina Ciligo Amo Similis" (21595–96, f. 171v). Making sense of these words requires both semantic and phonetic translation: in English the Latin words are *hen*, *rye*, *love*, and *like*; strung together as sounds, they become "Henry Lovelich" (Ackerman 1952a, 532). This bilingual pun may not have been understood by all listeners or readers; it may even have been created by a scribe rather than by Lovelich (a squiggly line links the couplet, with the second line written below the ruling) (see fig. 5). Whatever the pun's origin, it uses translation to turn translation into authorship. This procedure echoes the myth of *translatio* that runs all through MS 80: the pun produces authority by replacing one language with another.

Dutch Grail for Machines

The translation theory manifested in MS 80 isn't distinctly English or even distinctly medieval. Lovelich inherited it from the long accretion of *translatio studii et imperii* that preceded him; many others have taken it up since. One spectacular manifestation involves the only known translation of Lovelich's own text—into Dutch by the folklorist Cor Hendriks. I have in turn used Google Translate to draw the Dutch into English. These digital texts show how the myth of translation *in* MS 80 permeates the translation *of* MS 80. Just as Lovelich-narrator repeatedly states that translation transmits information securely through time, Hendriks and machine translation rely on the idea that meaning remains unaltered in the passage from one language to another. This translation theory is

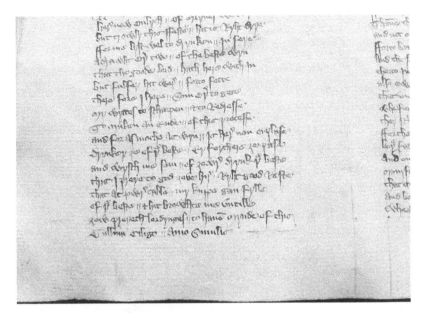

Figure 5 MS 80, folio 171v, with Henry Lovelich's name in a Latin cryptogram.

SOURCE: Photo by Michelle Warren (March 13, 2018). Reproduced courtesy of Parker Library, Corpus Christi College, Cambridge. Licensed under a Creative Commons Attribution-NonCommercial 4.0 International License.

fundamental to information security in the digital era—where it has been symbolized as yet another "Holy Grail." The machine translation of Lovelich's grail narrative, then, perfects the grail as the quintessential symbol of a secure knowledge economy. Yet like the myth of *translatio studii et imperii*, MT masks contradictions that would destabilize the transmission of knowledge and power.

The Dutch translations of Lovelich were posted as PDF files on Hendriks's blog in 2015 and 2017. They are part of a two-year series of twelve posts called "Secrets of the Grail" (De Geheimen van de Graal). Each post addresses different aspects of grail lore, with translated citations from primary sources; most of the posts have fuller translations attached as PDF files. The series begins with an explanation of the grail as the cup of the Last Supper, with a translation of the French verse *Joseph of Arimathea* attributed to Robert de Boron (November 3, 2015). The third post covers Joseph's time in prison after the Crucifixion—with Hendriks's "compressed translation" (gecomprimeerde vertaling) of the first half of Lovelich's text (Hendriks 2015, 171 pages; Furnivall 1874-78). The twelfth and final post covers "The Death of Merlin," with Hendriks's version of the second half of Lovelich's text (2017, 127 pages; Kock 1904-32). Elsewhere in the series, Hendriks translates at length from the French prose *Merlin* (Sommer 1908-16). All these files have footnotes and scholarly documentation. They represent, like Lovelich's own translation, an immense investment of time, labor, and skill.

The grail series exemplifies Hendriks's practice of what I would call extreme philology—source tracing of such detail and creativity that it resembles conspiracy theory. Hendriks applies this method rather indiscriminately to all manner of topics. He seems to have drifted from academic ethnology (Meder and Hendriks 2005) to popular myth (with blog series on "The Macaws" and "Cinderella's Slippers" in 2019) to actual conspiracy theories such as "The Climate Change Hoax" (eight blog posts, 2018-19). He is particularly adept at tracing internet hoaxes from social media platforms to mainstream news outlets, where repetition turns misinformation into facts. Hendriks's meticulous method parallels in many ways how textual scholars trace the transmission of narrative across medieval manuscripts—as I have done, for example, in assessing possible French models for MS 80. One scribe's error or idiosyncratic decision can become canonized in a sequence of copying that turns a spurious detail into the author's original words. "The Secrets of the Grail" series similarly seeks to document the relationships between disparate texts in order to uncover the truth. Hendriks's posts on conspiracy theories enact the method's logical conclusion: if you look long enough, even unconnected things seem connected. The use of extreme philology to prove conspiracies points to the speculative current that runs through all philology. The procedures that identify sources can just as easily turn against truth and manufacture doubt.

Hendriks's blog is part of an even larger project to destabilize our faith in the knowledge economy. It's part of the Rob Scholte Museum, opened by Scholte to showcase his personal art collection. Scholte is a well-known and controversial Dutch artist known for work that manipulates images and satirizes copyright. He is a prankster of authority structures. Since opening the museum in 2014, Scholte has been embroiled in an epic conflict with the building's owner, the town of Den Helder. As of December 2019, he had lost a court battle with the building's new private owner (who wanted to raze the building) (Weltevreden 2019). At most recent report, Scholte and the town are still in mediation, his art still in the town's custody (Weltevreden 2021). The convoluted case is made more so by Hendriks's blog. Each day, the blog reposts older materials with the current date: a letter protesting the museum's eviction (first posted April 15, 2015), an explanation of the letter (first posted April 15, 2015), and an ongoing count of the number of days since the town and the museum first agreed to terms (first posted December 9, 2015) (still the case as of this writing). "Yesterday's" posts no longer include these three items, only the day's "new" content—a mix of unsigned posts (local events, global conspiracy theories) and new folklore material signed by Hendriks. For the uninitiated, each day looks like the first day. In this digital performance, past, present, and future recede from each other in repetitions that can't be retrieved. By the time I figured out what was going on at the Rob Scholte Museum, I was almost convinced that the whole conflict was an elaborate art project in the form of a hoax: at the end, Scholte himself would demolish the building in the guise of the "new owner." Extreme philology can make the most far-fetched conclusions seem logical and ordinary.

Hendriks's grail translations are part of this aggressive play with information insecurity. He sifts through medieval literature for evidence the same way that he sifts through memes. With this method, the grail is a myth that more or less magically manifests in any number of otherwise unconnected texts. Any source—from any time and in any language—can be the source of a "true fact." In this framework, Lovelich's texts are just one more source of evidence. The length of the translations underscores their legitimacy as sources—not only cited but reproduced at length, and just as true when "compressed" in Dutch as in the Middle English editions. Translation combines the mechanics of transmission with the mysticism of the grail myth itself: information passes unchanged through many forms. With this method, one can always find the thread from a Dutch blog to

MS 80 to a hermit's book written in 717 to the Last Supper. The process is akin to reaching "Henry Lovelich" from "Gallina Ciligo Amo Similis." In this theory of transmission, translation is a cipher for information that remains stable so long as one applies the right key.

To access the Dutch "Secrets of the Grail," I signed on to this very same translation myth. Since I haven't studied the language, I turned to Google Translate to make my way through Hendriks's blog and various news articles about the Rob Scholte Museum. For a medievalist trained to weigh linguistic subtleties for cultural and historical meaning, this practice felt vaguely like cheating. Yet the "rough translations" that appeared in my web browser in the flash of a single click turned out to be quite "good enough." Machine translation functions by automated substitutions, much like the bilingual cipher of Lovelich's name. The fixed precision of the computational process relies on the flexible imprecision of human reading: the sense can come across even if the details are only approximate. The computational goal is "fully automatic useful translation" (FAUT): "no-cost public access to crude but functional web-based MT" (Lennon 2018, 78). At this relatively low standard, machines "translate the web for the entire world" (Knies 2008). This is exactly what Google Translate provided me for Hendriks's blog. In MT, I found the apotheosis of the translation myth at the heart of the grail myth itself.

When I looked further into the history of MT, I also found another Holy Grail—an even earlier origin for the tech medievalism now prevalent in digital preservation. The original goal of MT was "fully automatic high-quality translation" (FAHQT)—not just "useful" but of sufficient quality for sensitive military surveillance. Some of the earliest efforts were funded by governments and, in the United States, the Rockefeller Foundation (Lennon 2018, 55–61). FAHQT was highly desirable, yet it eluded many research teams. Almost predictably, then, it was called a grail: "from 1949 to 1966, both enthusiasts and skeptics described fully automated high-quality translation (FAHQT) in mythic terms, as a 'holy grail'" (Lennon 2018, 54). Like other tech grails, FAHQT would shield people from direct knowledge of complex systems by providing a more accessible intermediary—one so intuitive that it wouldn't seem like an intermediary. With FAHQT, a translation wouldn't seem like a translation at all. The quest for FAHQT rested on scientific faith in the power of computers to mediate universal knowledge.

The grail myth in MT is itself something of a myth. I searched for quite some time before finding any historical documentation. The one source I eventually found doesn't champion scientific solutions but instead exposes the fragility of the knowledge economy. Mortimer Taube's *Computers and Common Sense: The Myth of Thinking Machines* (1961) subjects MT to the same kinds of critique that Rob Scholte applies to copyright: the systems we rely on to produce truth rest on faith, not fact. Taube posits that MT lacks all basis as a scientific enterprise—and so resembles a romance myth: "nowhere in the literature of MT is there a systems engineering study of its feasibility or practicality. In the absence of such a study and in light of the known informality of language and meaning, research in MT takes on the character not of genuine scientific investigation, but of a romantic quest such as the search for the Holy Grail" (Taube 1961, 41). This "romantic quest" points to fundamental flaws with the system of scientific authority: research grants flow to projects justified by desire rather than by evidence.

In Taube's analysis, the quest for MT illustrates how research infrastructure itself becomes the author of research. The system authenticates projects rather than the other way around. Taube illustrates the point with a famous case of bibliographic fraud: nineteenth-century forgeries of printed pamphlets, authenticated by a succession of experts (Taube 1961, 118-20; Carter and Pollard 1934). As one curator's mistaken judgment became the basis of the next one's, the system of authentication took over as the source of authentication. The truth was eventually uncovered through forensic bibliography—another form of extreme philology similar to Hendriks's analysis of internet hoaxes. In both cases, spurious or impossible ideas gain credibility as they are taken up by people or institutions with credibility. Taube implies that much scientific research operates in the same way, with similarly fraudulent results.

In the long history of translation, "the Holy Grail of MT" exposes secure transmission as a myth. Lovelich, Hendriks, and Google all embrace the myth. Translation myths try to hide the fact that translation matters: it does effect meaning. Information does not pass unchanged through language. Information insecurity is thus built into every transmission system. But those systems are also built to hide this fact. It can take some extreme philology to uncover the myth and see how systems of authentication build trust in themselves. In literary history, this process operates through editions, catalogues, and reproductions. So it becomes the work of literary history to investigate myths of transmission and the workings of power that they mask.

MS 80—as book and text—has been the subject of *translatio* many times. One strand began with the "carrying over" of a French illustration format that connotes economic prosperity and social prestige. In an English book made of paper, however, this format is startlingly new. Another strand of *translatio* began much earlier—exactly when is unclear—with the very idea of the Holy Grail and King Arthur. The text in MS 80 repeats this established narrative in a unique performance of form, authorship, and language. And when Hendriks brought the text into Dutch, he made Lovelich as authoritative as any other source related to the grail in any way. The machine translation of the Dutch Lovelich reexposed Lovelich's own theory that information exists independently of language. Each translation implied that meaning never changes; each translation created new meanings. Together, these translated texts illustrate how translation both creates and destabilizes knowledge systems. Even now, every time some rendition of MS 80 appears on a screen, it has been translated, bit by bit, node to node, from electrical pulses into patterns of color that invite us to overlook exactly how they have been transmitted. Even now, MS 80 is on the move, somewhere, propelled by the myth that it makes.

CHAPTER 2

PERFORMING COMMUNITY

Merchants, Chivalry, Data

ARTHURIAN STORIES WERE BORN POPULAR. When Geoffrey of Monmouth devoted more words to King Arthur than to anyone else in his *History of the Kings of Britain* in the twelfth century, he was responding to Arthur's already attractive reputation. Arthur's appeal in turn made Geoffrey's *History* itself quite popular—copied, adapted, and translated countless times over the centuries. Arthur's story eventually reached many different communities, across disparate time periods, locations, social classes, ethnicities, races, and national identities. Many people know the most famous components of his reign—the sword in the stone, the Round Table, Camelot—even if they've never read any particular text. The result is a large and diverse "textual community" (Stock 1990) defined by shared knowledge of "the once and future king." Membership in this community can bring certain social and political advantages. The nature of those advantages, however, depends on the context. This very flexibility has sustained Arthurian popularity from language to language, place to place, format to format, and so on. Each version reflects what people already care about and also generates new investments. This chapter, then, constructs a social context for MS 80 in order to explain why people made this particular book and what it might have meant to them.

MS 80 was created by and for a specific community—the London Skinners' Guild—in the first decades of the fifteenth century. Henry Lovelich's English translation absorbs Arthurian tradition and then redirects it toward this social context. MS 80's connection to the Skinners is documented by a marginal note that identifies Lovelich as a "skynnere" who translated at the request of a man named Henry Barton (f. 127r). Barton was also a skinner, one of the most prominent—an alderman in royal service and two-time mayor who left an endowment large enough to pay for guild functions into the seventeenth century (see chap. 3). By translating the text and making the book, Lovelich and Barton participated in civic culture while also seeking to influence it. The Skinners, as purveyors of furs, were one of the wealthier guilds in fifteenth-century London (Veale 1966). In this context, MS 80 represents the strategic appropriation of an elite cultural form. The book tells the story of Christianity's arrival in Britain with Joseph of Arimathea and then King Arthur's accession to the throne followed by his lengthy wars against rebellious barons. By bringing the Holy Grail and King Arthur to the Skinners' Guild, MS 80 could forge a new textual community around knowledge of ancient British history, thereby increasing guild members' participation in civic and national culture.

The production of MS 80 within the orbit of the Skinners' Guild reflects emerging textual practices among the merchant elite. Evidence from wills, inventories, and surviving books documents about 160 London merchant book owners in the late Middle Ages (Scott 2014). Their books represent a whole range of genres, from business records to chronicles, romances, and books for pious study (Boffey 2010). Books themselves were a "recognized way of holding capital in a portable and negotiable form" (Mynors 1963, xi; cited in Lawton 1983, 42). Indeed, on one occasion a mayor received an illustrated "book of King Alexander" as payment for a debt (Busby 2002, 1:308). Through book ownership and textual patronage, merchants sought "to regulate behaviours, produce social distinctions and ensure the survival of oligarchic rule" (Lindenbaum 1999, 285). They even sought to influence behavior from beyond the grave with "common profit" books—books used to create a chain of prayers for someone's soul (Barron 2016, 50–51). MS 80 provides in one continuous narrative many common types of merchant books: a saint's life, moral lessons, feats of valor, and royal history.

In addition to MS 80, the Skinners accumulated a broad-ranging corporate bibliography of texts and materials directly or indirectly supported by their patronage. The guild was responsible for London's annual celebration of the Feast of Corpus Christi, a religious holiday that honors the "holy body and holy blood" of Christ in the bread and wine of communion. As sponsors, the Skinners commissioned the poet John Lydgate to write commemorative verses (c. 1420). Some decades later, the guild arranged for the records of its religious fraternities, Corpus Christi and Assumption of Our Lady, to be copied into large, illustrated volumes (c. 1440–90). In the late fifteenth century (1464 to be precise), a skinner named William Naseby purchased a Middle English prose *Brut* chronicle, which includes both Britain's conversion to Christianity and Arthur's reign. A hundred years later (1579–80), the Skinners' Guild paid twelve pence to a soldier "who made a book of war" (Lambert 1934, 376). Around the same time, they sponsored an inauguration pageant for one of their members who had been elected mayor (1585), the first of several such pageants commemorated with printed booklets (1619–89). Across more than two hundred years, these various commissions echo different aspects of MS 80 as both book and text. Together, they form the social and textual context for Lovelich and Barton's translation project.

In this chapter, I tell the story of MS 80 as a book in a particular community that also performs community in multiple ways over time. First, I assess the rhetoric of community that surrounds medieval guilds, including the Skinners' first royal charter in 1327. As fur traders, the Skinners had a specific role in the civic *commune* because different types of fur were associated with different social groups and civic functions. This context sheds light on how Lovelich represents social hierarchies in his translation. The text is also saturated with eucharistic symbolism, linking MS 80 to the guild's sponsorship of the Corpus Christi procession, its two religious fraternities, and eucharistic controversies of the early fifteenth century. Meanwhile, Joseph of Arimathea's role in fifteenth-century ecclesiastical debates echoes through MS 80. Finally, I turn to MS 80's civic lessons in chivalry as an ideology of social responsibility. The text's account of British foundations points forward to both Naseby's *Brut* and the mayor pageants of the 1600s. There, we find celebrations of the Skinners' value to the monarchy and—in one case—a reference to "Sir Henry Barton" as a famous medieval mayor. When Barton becomes a character in someone else's text, his enduring reputation echoes back to MS 80's original context.

This seventeenth-century Barton reveals the role of data curation in generating historical contexts. I found this Barton late in 2018 when I entered his name as a keyword in Early English Books Online. I was looking to confirm a reference to Barton in John Stow's *Survey of London* (c. 1600). The results included something I couldn't have known to look for: a mayor's pageant by the poet Thomas Middleton (1619). Middleton's pageant and others like it draw on the idiom of chivalry that Barton himself promoted with MS 80. And like MS 80, Middleton's pageant bears witness to the absorption of aristocratic forms into civic politics. "Sir Barton" on EEBO changed the context I could imagine for Barton, Lovelich, and MS 80. It was the kind of find that evokes the pleasure of "serendipity" yet is anything but accidental (Verhoeven 2016). Instead, "Sir Barton" on EEBO is infrastructure caught in the act of making history. The search results culminate centuries of labor and institutional arrangements often left out of literary history: archiving, cataloguing, microfilming, digitizing, metadata curation, transcription, subscription marketing, and library investments. All these histories are also part of MS 80's context. Implicitly, then, this chapter illustrates how networked data define our access to social and literary history.

Skinners' Guild and London Society

The guild context shapes how Lovelich translates social classes and civic themes in MS 80. Medieval guilds were communal organizations where craftspeople and merchants gathered for mutual economic, social, and political benefit. In the interests of community well-being, guilds sought to regulate both the commercial practices and the moral conduct of their members. Guilds encompassed business, religion, and leisure in ways that reinforced shared concerns, quelled social dissent, and enriched those who played along. Whether one emphasizes their role in governance (Wallace 1997), conflict management (Turner 2007), or collective solidarity (Rosser 2015), guilds were the heart of social life in late medieval London. Disputes over the very definition of the civic and national community thus centered on the guilds: merchants might go against the will of the common citizens, the commons might resist the king, the king might coerce the merchants, and so forth (Nightingale 1995; Barron 2004; Sutton 2005). The *commune* was hardly ever at peace for long.

When the Skinners petitioned for a royal charter in 1327, they deployed the rhetoric of *communitas* to justify their request for monopoly trade authority. They cast commercial regulation as beneficial to the "common profit of the greats and the community of the realm" ("comun profit des grantz et del communaute du Reaume," NA, SC 8/260/12977; *Calendar* 1891, 34). These terms make the interests of the powerful the basis of the common good. Edward III granted the Skinners' petition; its terms remained largely unchanged in later ordinances (1365, 1392, 1437). The guild had authority to punish those who mixed old and new furs, monitor "wild work" brought from the country into the city, control imports, ensure honest trade, and hold property in common (Sharpe 1899–1912, Letter Book G, ff. clxii, clxiv; *Calendar* 1905, 286; 1907, 190–91). Challenges to guild practices were also framed in communal terms: the charter of 1437 arose because the commons complained to the king that guilds were causing "commune damage" in pursuit of "singler proffit," undermining the king's own authority to make laws (Given-Wilson 2005, Henry VI, membrane 2, item 35). "Community," then, is a politicized concept that brought some people together by excluding others.

Thanks to the protections of the royal charters, the Skinners became one of the twelve "great companies" in London. Members of this urban elite led city government, collaborated with the king, and organized public ceremony (Lambert 1934). Yet among the twelve, the Skinners had an unstable place in the "middle." Hierarchical rank was jealously guarded, as it structured political and economic influence. In processions, the guilds that marched first were understood by all to have greater influence than those who marched last. In 1339, a riot was recorded between the Skinners and Fishmongers over the order of procession in civic ceremonies (Sharpe 1899–1912, Letter Book F, f. xlv). A similar dispute over sixth place kept the Skinners and Tailors in conflict until the end of the fifteenth century; the terms of their 1484 resolution were observed into the seventeenth century (Lambert 1934, 115–17; Veale 1966, 121–25). Processional order was a very public way of both confirming and conferring civic status.

The Skinners' commodity implicated them in social ranking well beyond corporate politics. The kinds of fur that people wore indicated their degree of wealth and status. Rules and customs concerning who was or wasn't supposed to wear what furs sought to align dress with social rank in the public sphere. These rules were set out periodically in sumptuary petitions that translated desirable social hierarchies into the shapes and textures of clothing. Not all petitions became statutes, and statutes were not always enforced; nonetheless, sumptuary language reflects concerns about the troublesome convergence of rank by lineage and rank by wealth. Beginning in the fourteenth century, the wealthiest merchants increasingly resembled the nobility in their social habits and dress (Thrupp 1948, 234–87; Phillips 2007). A regulation of 1363 calculated the collapse of class distinction with precision: a merchant worth £500 could dress like a gentleman worth £100 (Given-Wilson 2005, "Introduction 1363"). Petitions of 1402 and 1406 carefully matched different types of fur to different social identities (Given-Wilson 2005, Henry IV, membrane 6, item 76; membrane 7, item 110). These petitions define three grades of pelts that correspond to three levels of social hierarchy. This apparent clarity, however, is undermined by the many exceptions—for guildsmen, royal servants, civic officers, and sometimes specific individuals (Phillips 2007, 25–26). In both 1402 and 1406, the petitions recognize a blanket exception to all rules for men-at-arms when they are armed, who may dress however they wish ("q'ils purront user vesture ce qe lour plerra"). On the whole, petitions and statutes sought to use dress to define the parameters of social difference in a well-regulated community (Sponsler 1997, 1–23). Indeed, the 1406 petition envisioned excommunication for those contravening the law, the ultimate exclusion from Christian society.

Regulations within guilds also targeted clothing as a sign of both internal cohesion and external distinction. The Skinners were particularly concerned to convey internal order by dress codes, since their membership was socially stratified: "the prosperous, merchant, employer groups were distinguished from the lesser, younger, employee, artisan colleagues by the wearing of a distinctive livery" (Barron 2004, 214). The Skinners' regulations addressed the types of fur that should be worn by whom in the service of the mayor; they also imposed fines for wearing the wrong array at the wrong time, such as cloaks instead of gowns or improper colors for apprentices (Lambert 1934, 213, 214, 242, 245, 269). Eventually, the Skinners' younger members were defined as two groups by two types of fur—the "foynes bachelors" and the "budge bachelors" (Tatham 1663, 1). All these practices maintained distinctions within the guild while signaling their collective solidarity to outsiders.

In the interests of corporate cohesion, the Skinners and other guilds deployed a number of tactics beyond dress regulations. Social events such as feasting and drinking could smooth over tensions and deepen bonds across social differences (Karras 2003, 144; Turner 2007, 143–44). Such gatherings sometimes included plays or other types of performance that provided didactic lessons, as well as entertainment (Lancashire 2002, 69–117). Meanwhile, clerks and scribes produced written records that forged community identity by creating institutional memory (Davies 2011, 150); such books became part of "the inheritance of the guild passed on from generation to generation" (Davies 2016, 29). Group cohesion and friendship, however, were corporate ideals promulgated against a "background of persistent discord" (Rosser 2015, 105). In the course of the fifteenth century, such tensions increased among the Skinners, as a relatively small group controlled decisions that disadvantaged their less powerful brethren (Veale 1966, 114–15). In the process, various kinds of texts and text-based activities were integral to the oligarchs' efforts to create an ordered and durable community.

The Skinners' communal interests resonate with the stories told in MS 80 and with the book itself as a written record, or "remembrauncer"

(Jefferson 2000, 208). The one literal contextual reference occurs late in the manuscript after the story of Merlin's love for Nimiane. Lovelich-narrator declares that he has "made an end of this talking" (21579) and asks the audience for wine to quench his thirst:

> But truly this feast is right dry,
> For I really wish to drink, in truth,
> A drought or two of the best wine
> That the good lord has here within,
> But it's difficult to get (?) [*fulfey hit were forto fette*]
> Therefore I hope some other to get,
> My wits to sharpen and restore,
> To make an end of this process.
> And since wine is here now,
> Drink some of it, before you pass further,
> And then send me some of your best drink.
> This I pray to god: give the steward right good rest,
> At your table fill my cup
> With the best and bring it back to me!
> (*Merlin*, 21581–94, f. 171v)

This aside—marked off by a thin line through the text column—implies a performative scene, in which someone is reading aloud to a group gathered for feasting. MS 80 is well-suited for such recitation with its large pages, layout for illustration, and (in these later folios) marked half-lines to facilitate the rhythm of reading. Such an event could be relatively small or "a more lavish occasion" (Dalrymple 2000, 165). In Lovelich's depiction, the speaker's cup is passed from table to table in the hope that everyone will give a small portion of wine from their own cups. Following this request, Lovelich-narrator addresses the group with the cannily ambiguous "lordynges" (21595)—a conceit that humbles the poet before his audience by granting them "mastery" (*MED*). The flattery is complete with a bilingual Latin-English pun of his own name, an obscure expression that would create an "inside joke" for those who understood (21596; see chap. 1). This feast passage thus combines social hierarchy (the lord who hides his good wine, the overworked steward, the Latin literate) with the communal solidarity forged by feasting.

Beyond this feasting scene, Lovelich alludes regularly to a performance setting with references to reading, hearing, and listening. Early on, reading conveys the extreme prowess of the future convert Nasciens: "one of the most wondrous stories that ever was read in any book" (XIV:6-7). At the far end, just a few pages after the feasting aside, the narrator recalls this Nasciens, "of whom I read to you" (22567). The book itself is a performance to be read and seen: "Now here anon this book rehearses for whoever will read and look" (24850-51). Reading is connected to hearing and "saying" in a number of passages:

As here before you have heard me say. (XXXVI:646)

And in this manner Arthur was chosen king,
As you have heard me rehearse in this place. (7783-84)

As hereafter you shall hear and see. (10511)

As hereafter you shall hear said
In the story I read on this very same day. (12683-84)

Now, as you have heard me both read and say. (12999)

These interjections connect the narrator's speaking to the audience's hearing ("me" to "you"), expressed most densely in the rhyming of "your ear" and "more clear" (L:783-84). One of the more elaborate descriptions gathers all the narrator's authority around reading and listening to authenticate the marvelous properties of three spindles made by King Solomon's wife for Galahad:

And since some people have doubts,
All will be declared without variance,
And they will have more understanding,
Otherwise they would think this matter a lie [gabbing].
Therefore here the story turns

And of another thing makes memory,
Which is full sweet to hear,
Both to listen and also to learn [lere].
And in time coming, this story
Shall explain the three spindles openly,
And give all the knowledge of the ship.
All this you shall know in time coming.
(Grail, XXVIII:473–84)

The narrator here is concerned that people's doubts will cause them to treat the truth as a lie (gabbing): the solution is to "make memory" of the whole complicated event. The result will be an "open declaration" that gives listeners ("you") "more understanding" of "all the knowledge." The mechanism for transmitting this true knowledge is a tight configuration of hearing rhymed with reading (here/lere) and reading alliterated with listening (lestene/lere). Through these and many similar passages, Lovelich keeps his audience at their tables.

Throughout MS 80, Lovelich reminds his audience regularly that they are participating in a communal performance. The story is a "process" that reports, rehearses, and records memorable events (e.g., 20259, 27575, 25985). "Showing," meanwhile, puts the story into memory (remembrance, XXXIX:490–91; LVI:1–2); it rhymes with "knowing" (22931–32). Both these terms are associated with performed storytelling, including plays, pageants, and processions (proces, sheuen [MED]). The term pageant itself is used once: "now rehearses here this pageant" (19391). This term casts the narrative into the language of urban performance, where pageants were plays, episodes in plays, props, images on props, and wagons for carrying players and their props (Dalrymple 2000, 158; Driver 2014). All three of these terms are associated with public spectacle, particularly those organized by guilds (Dalrymple 2000, 165; Warren 2008). Each term, moreover, has a tinge of mercantile connotation: craft production requires correct process or procedure; showing one's wares is part of selling them; banners and tapestries called pageants were part of guild décor and ceremony. In all, Lovelich's use of these terms creates familiarity for his audience, suggesting that the ancient acts of Joseph of Arimathea, Merlin, and Arthur are displayed for their collective consumption so that they, too, can participate in national history.

A variety of rhetorical strategies further binds the audience to the performance. Throughout, Lovelich uses *we* and *you* to construct solidarity, assuring "us"—"both old and young" (XXVII:24)—of his careful and truthful guidance through a memorable story. From time to time, as with the feasting passage, he reminds us of his bodily presence: "As you have heard rehearsed here by me" (XXVI:28). He makes sure that we know how hard storytelling is: he says that he'll make a short description because he doesn't have the strength for a long one (XII:373–78; XIII:648). Later, he prays for the strength to finish the book (LVI:511–40); further along, he prays again for "health of body and my eyesight" and that he not die before the end (10246–55). He brings us close to the performance with promises to tell more "before you go" or "before I go" (20266, 24976) and with occasional rhetorical questions (9982, 10221, 17355–56). He fabricates further intimacies by treating the narrative itself as a space of action that "we" share: the chivalry of Seraphe (Nasciens) is so great that "into this time of him we may speak" and praise him like "a herald" (XIII:675–78); he promises to describe Merlin's disguise "so well as if I had been there" (11574). Most dramatically, he narrates battle scenes as if "we" are eyewitnesses: "There might you hear noise full great" (16185); "But now of all this chasing let us now rest" (23539); "Now leave we here of this carping" (25983). All in all, Lovelich's tone implies a unified audience whose bond strengthens as we/they share more and more knowledge of the story.

Descriptions of characters' social classes, however, would also have reminded a fifteenth-century audience that they are a stratified community invested in hierarchies. When a devil comes to tempt Christian converts, the power he offers is in fact the overturning of hierarchies—"foul" to beautiful, fool to wise, poor to rich, low to high (XXI:73–77). Social mobility is literally the devil's work. In the early battle scenes, Lovelich names a number of social ranks that characterized his own society, covering the gamut of the nobility and their servants: earl, baron, duke, knight, bachelor, yeoman, page, and swain (XIII:103, 254, 501; XIV:254, 885–87; XXVI:265; XXVII:353, 513; XXXIII:386; XLIV:129). Two of these terms—*bachelor* and *yeoman*—would also designate younger and less prosperous guildsmen.

This ambiguity invites a broader audience to see themselves reflected in the narrative. At the same time, the sheer quantity of distinct terms emphasizes social differences. Lovelich uses this strategy of inclusion by divisive enumeration repeatedly—for example, "both knight and squire, both rich and poor" (LVI:453–54). This social vocabulary accommodates the text to its new context while infusing that context back into the text.

The most revealing translation of social terms surrounds Arthur's selection as king via a sword pulled from a stone. The succession is contested because everyone believes that Uther died without an heir. The archbishop who oversees the election stages a social drama by presenting the idea that anyone could be king. He repeatedly reminds everyone of their duty to submit to the will of God, who outranks them all as "king of kings" (6983–7058). He ingeniously appeals to everyone's sense of proper hierarchy as the basis for accepting a king from any rank: the "high, proud, or rich" should bend to God's will; the poor shouldn't be angry regardless of the outcome because the rich are "more worthy" (7117–24); no one knows whom God has chosen—lord, knight, or squire; poor, commoner, or bachelor (7127–28). This final list covers the gamut of rank, wealth, and age. Of course, "we" know all along that Arthur is the royal heir by blood, a secret revealed by Merlin only after the election (7967–8046). The archbishop's rhetoric thus uses the idea of social mobility to reinforce the immovable order of divinely sanctioned inheritance.

In the end, everyone tries the sword, and everyone fails—first 250 of the "worthiest lords" and then the "commons" and "poor men" (7144, 7150). When Arthur inadvertently succeeds—a mere child who believes himself of low degree—reactions split along class lines, with the barons opposed and the commons in favor (7427–28). The barons consider Arthur's election socially inappropriate: a "knave" of such "low degree" should not have sovereignty over them (7461–62, 7573–74, 7821, 7865–66). Meanwhile, the archbishop continues to set "lower men of good life" on the same level as clerks and "worthy men" (7529–30). Arthur's distinction thus arises from his role as the "people's king." The people, though, approve of social hierarchies, praising Arthur after he is crowned because "he rewarded every man after his degree" (7679). These socially calibrated gifts earn Arthur the loyalty of nearly 7,000 "commons" but only 350 knights (8060–104, 8489–99). After the election, Arthur convenes a parliament where he makes new knights and again distributes gifts, making himself loved not only by knights and squires but also by the "comunaulte" (8566)—that is, the commonwealth of citizens. Arthur thus becomes the hero of an urban social order that benefits from the prestige of the monarchy while generating new privileges outside the logic of lineage.

Throughout the prolonged debates over what to do about the contested election, Lovelich characterizes social groups in several ways. In some cases, they are divided by wealth: "rich and poor" (6902, 7054). Other descriptions emphasize rank by lineage: every man or lord "after his degree" (6940, 7453, 7813); "commons, gentles, and lords" (7072). In some cases, lineage and wealth mix together: "neither gentry nor riches" (7084); barons are called "rich men" (7503). Finally, a number of ambiguous terms encompass either wealth or rank: "more and less" (6924, 6938, 7042, 7472), "great and small" (7670), "high or low" (7866). Most pointedly, Lovelich renders the aristocratic ideology of "the three orders"—laborers, knights, and clergy—simply as "governance" (7112; Douce MS 178, f. 179r; Micha 1980, 271). This translation echoes other writers who made civic governance—"common profit"—a chivalric value. Lovelich's contemporary Lydgate, for example, once described knights as champions of "common profit" (Lydgate 1911–34, 2:724–34). In *Fall of Princes*, Lydgate went further to present Arthur's knights as defenders of "common profit" who keep their statutes of "virtuous ordinance" in a "register" (Lydgate 1923–27, 3:900). A few decades later, the chronicler John Hardyng made "common profit" the principal responsibility of the grail knights (Simpson and Peverley 2015, 206). The slippage of "common profit" into chivalric discourse translates the gradual convergence of civic and aristocratic values in the fifteenth century.

Lovelich's translation of Arthur's election encapsulates MS 80's overall relationship with urban society. As an English narrative and an illustrated book, MS 80 broadened the potential audience for Arthurian romance without leaving behind the form's aristocratic dimensions. Lovelich's text portrays faithful and worthy action as a chivalric attribute that even the commons can embrace. Conversely, the text and the book could bolster the guild's self-image as a prestigious social organization. The whole undertaking—translating an important text, making a beautiful book—is consistent with other practices within guild culture, from community performance to record-keeping to reading practices. MS 80 was thus designed to both reflect and shape the culture of its intended audience.

Corporate Religion and the Grail

The Skinners' religious practices give MS 80's account of the Holy Grail both spiritual and political significance. Like many guilds, the Skinners began as a religious fraternity in a parish church. Since practitioners of particular trades tended to live in the same neighborhoods, the parish fraternities became identified with the neighborhood trade (Barron 2004, 206–11). These guilds provided their members with both spiritual and practical support, making financial contributions to the church and sponsoring liturgical celebrations (Duffy 2005, 131–54). Over time, devotional practice and commercial organization became inseparable, such that by 1437 the Skinners' charter treated the fraternity and the company as a single "guild" (*Calendar* 1907, 190–91). The fraternities, though, were not limited to Skinners: they strategically cultivated members beyond the trade. The fraternities thus became "potential means to negotiate integration into variously advantageous social groups" (Rosser 2015, 151–52). Through the fraternities, members from all backgrounds—up to and including kings and queens—bolstered their mutual commitments well beyond the church and well beyond the trade.

Like other major companies, the Skinners had two fraternities. In their case, the "greater" one was dedicated to Corpus Christi, and the "lesser" or "yeoman" one was dedicated to the Assumption of Our Lady. Corpus Christi began as something of a "political pressure group" led by prosperous merchants (Veale 1966, 106), while Assumption enabled lower ranked craftworkers to organize for their own benefit, sometimes in opposition to the more powerful merchants (Veale 1966, 112–13; Rosser 2015, 179–84). Both fraternities, however, had members from across the social spectrum—from apprentices to shopkeepers to wealthy merchants to nobles and royalty. The differences between the two fraternities may have varied through time in ways that are difficult to recover since the surviving records are retrospective constructions (Bolton 2019). The records are now preserved in two lavishly produced volumes, one "register" for each fraternity. In addition to lists of dues-paying members, these registers include copies of company charters, membership oaths, and rules for conducting trade (Wadmore 1902, 26–42). Members pledged their allegiance to the king while promising to produce "true work" according to the craft's ordinances; they swore to keep the "worship," or honor, of both the craft and the city (Lambert 1934, 52–53). The registers thus treat religion, citizenship, and trade regulation as inseparable practices.

The fraternity registers document the guild's symbolic negotiation of both internal and external governance (Davies 2012, 266–67). The books signify wealth and prestige in both their production and their illustrations (Meale 1989, 212–13). The register for Assumption is the more richly illustrated—material evidence of its aspirational functions and perhaps also "some measure of the prosperity of the small masters" (Veale 1966, 113). Commissioned c. 1441, the book represents some of the highest production values available in fifteenth-century London; new entries were added incrementally through 1689 (LMA, CLC/L/SE/A/004B/MS31692; Scott 1996, 2:342–44). Two late fifteenth-century portraits in the book advertise the Skinners' closeness to royalty: Elizabeth Woodville, wife of Edward IV, c. 1472 (f. 32v) and Margaret of Anjou, the widowed queen of Henry VI, c. 1475 (f. 34v). A later image of the Virgin Mary being crowned by the Trinity honors the fraternity's namesake (f. 41r). All three portraits feature opulent displays of white ermine fur to signify royalty (Meale 1989, 212–13; Laynesmith 2004, 33–34). The register for Corpus Christi shows a similar engagement with royal patronage, with members from Lovelich's era including Richard II and his queen, Anne; Henry V; Henry VI; and Humphrey Duke of Gloucester (LMA, CLC/L/SE/A/004B/MS31693, f. 12). The membership of rival aristocratic factions—Lancastrians and Yorkists—suggests that the guild sought to use the fraternity to protect its interests amid political turmoil (Lambert 1934, 55). The register itself was first commissioned c. 1485, with new entries added through 1734. Although less elaborately illustrated than Assumption, the Corpus Christi register is nonetheless a large, fine volume with decorated initials featuring chalices holding a "glowing" eucharist (symbol of Corpus Christi) and detailed border art. Both registers show how patronage—divine, royal, corporate—produced decorated books.

Together, the fraternity registers document the Skinners' use of book production as an aspirational social practice. Lovelich and Barton, more-over, were both members of Assumption (ff. 5v, 6, 6v), suggesting that their involvement with MS 80 expresses a similar impulse (Barton was also enrolled in Corpus Christi, f. 14v). Barton certainly had contacts with other textual patrons during his decades as an alderman (see chap. 3). It is thus tempting to connect MS 80 to the guildhall clerks who have been identified as copyists of other Middle English literary manuscripts. In-deed, Linne Mooney and Estelle Stubbs posit that a clerk of the Skinners' Guild copied both the beginning of the Assumption register (ff. 2r–19r) and a book of Chaucer's *Canterbury Tales* (Petworth House [UK], MS 7) (Mooney and Stubbs 2013, 5, 120). This idea is obviously attractive for my arguments about MS 80's role in civic culture, but I haven't been able to substantiate it. The sources cited by Mooney and Stubbs don't refer to the Skinners or the Assumption register (Griffiths 1995; Doyle 1997). A different note by Jeremy Griffiths does hypothesize that the same scribe copied the Petworth Chaucer, two copies of Nicholas Love's *Myrrour of the Blessed Lyf*, and "very possibly" the beginning of the Skinners' Assumption register (Griffiths 1985). Somehow, then, a tentative observation that the same scribe might have copied the Assumption register and the Petworth Chaucer became a certainty that a Skinners' company clerk copied Chau-cer (also in Horobin 2010). The Skinners did have a clerk of some kind in the 1440s, named John Pery (Lambert 1934, 93), but I have not seen him connected to any specific records. Instead, it seems that when the Skin-ners wanted a book to showcase their impressive membership roster, they turned to the high-end commercial trade—paying thirty shillings for the work (f. 19r; Robinson 2003, 1:67–68). The scribe who did the work likely copied other manuscripts under similar terms.

The Skinners' fraternities gave them a visible role in London public life. Their 1393 guild charter confirms their exclusive responsibility for the annual procession to celebrate the Feast of Corpus of Christi in early summer (*Calendar* 1905, 286). This was one of the most powerful community events of the year, combining joyous celebration with an affirmation of social and religious hierarchies. In London, the procession followed a route similar to royal processions, symbolically linking divine, royal, and corporate authority (Bowers 2001, 143–45). The day's symbolism emphasized the "harmony of the social 'body'" through shared communion (Rosser 2015, 104). At the same time, it "spoke the idiom of privilege and lordship" (Rubin 1991, 240). On a practical level, the procession reinforced social hierarchy because it separated people, such as masters and journeymen, who otherwise worked together (Rubin 1991, 265). The most politically important guild members, moreover, would have been in line closest to the eucharist, carried by a priest in an ornate vessel (Rubin 1991, 241, 247–71). Ultimately, the feast day didn't express "an underlying *communitas*" so much as assert a partisan ideal of community: it deployed a "rhetoric of inclusion" in the service of civic interests that were "highly exclusive" (Rubin 1991, 263–66). As sponsors, then, the Skinners had a regularly scheduled opportunity to perform their privileged role in civic power.

The Skinners' role in the Corpus Christi procession associates them with Lydgate, one of London's most prolific poets (Warren 2008). Lydgate wrote a verse "ordinance" for Corpus Christi, widely believed to have been commissioned by the Skinners (Lancashire 2002, 124–26). The ordinance presents a series of stanzas, each invoking a biblical or ecclesiastical figure and explaining their symbolic connection to the eucharist, much like a sermon (Lydgate 1911–34, 1:34–43; Rubin 1991, 229–32). The figures could very well have corresponded to "pageants" or props carried in the procession (Sponsler 2014, 101–14). Later records show the Skinners paying for the painting and repair of Corpus Christi pageants, including a "John the Evangelist"—one of the figures named in Lydgate's verses (Lambert 1934, 148–49; Lancashire 2002, 179–80). Overall, Lydgate's verses convey an orthodox sense of community well in accord with the Skinners' civic standing, reinforced by an unusual use of collective pronouns (Sponsler 2014, 101–9). The verses would have increased the symbolic charge of an event that placed the Skinners at the center of the "body politic."

The Skinners' affiliations with Corpus Christi and Mary's Assumption resonate very directly with MS 80. They may even explain why Lovelich and Barton invested so much in the translation. The grail narrative is nothing less than a "eucharistic romance" (Rubin 1991, 141). French illustrated manuscripts often depict the grail as a ciborium—the vessel that holds the consecrated bread (Stones 2000; Meuwese 2008). And the French narrative was influenced by a new emphasis on compulsory communion in the early thirteenth century; in the process, Mary's status was "augmented" since she was the "oven that baked the bread" (Rubin 1991, 64–66, 142–47). The Skinners' two fraternities are thus symbolically linked. In this context, commonplace prayers to "Our Lady" in Lovelich's translation intersect with his own fraternity affiliation. Throughout the conversion stories in the first half of MS 80, the virgin birth is one of the mysteries that prospective Christians have to accept (e.g., XLIII); converted Saracens regularly invoke Mary and "Our Lady" (e.g., XIX:13, XL:40, XLIV:242). And when Lovelich-narrator asks for prayers for his health, he asks that they be addressed to "Our Lady full of might" (LVI:534). These expressions, though formulaic, have special resonance in a community organized around Our Lady's Assumption and Corpus Christi.

MS 80 originally began with an extended lesson on the Trinity, the Virgin, and the eucharist. The first narrator is a hermit who recalls his former doubts about the Trinity and the explanations that God sent him in a vision. With his faith restored, he receives from Christ the book about the grail, which he duly copies. More lessons ensue as Joseph of Arimathea introduces Christianity to the Saracen Evalach. In the process, Joseph's son Josephes becomes the first bishop and performs the first sacrament with the "sainte escuele" (holy vessel) in which Joseph captured drops of Christ's blood (Ponceau 1997, 1:25–88; these pages are now lost from MS 80). Evalach's wife, Sarracynte, turns out to already be a Christian: she explains to Josephes how she converted with her mother and received the sacrament "in her mouth"; they kept "our holy savior both in flesh and bone in the form of bread" in a "holy box" (XV:481–82, 561). Later, Joseph is said to have a "holy dish" that contains "Sank Ryal" (XVII:17–18)—that is, the blood of Christ: it is a "glorious vessel" covered by a "plate" (*plateyne*) (XVII:49–50). Its mysteries will be revealed in the future: "And then shall you have knowledge of Sank Ryal and many other things, which are the secrets of the Seint Graal that some men call Sank Ryal" (XVII:168–72). This doubling of holy blood and holy grail elevates the eucharist by consolidating several traditions (see chap. 1).

The fusion of grail and eucharist traverses the whole of MS 80. When the early convert Nasciens encounters the Ship of Faith, he finds inside a bed said to signify "the holy table . . . where every day God's son of heaven is consecrated with full mild prayer, where the wine is turned blood red and the bread to true flesh" (XXXI:322–26). In due course, Galahad will bring the grail to this bed and sail for Sarras. Meanwhile, Joseph and his companions arrive in Britain, and the grail begins its eucharistic service at another table:

> That day they ate no meat
> But received the savior, as I understand,
> Upon the table of the Seynt Graal,
> Which is otherwise called Sank Ryal.
> (*Grail*, XLII:305-8)

Here, the vessel made holy by Christ's blood becomes in turn the source of Christ's body. This sanctified dish becomes the mysterious object of Arthurian desire, described repeatedly as the means by which all the adventures of Britain will end. The grail thus knits together apostolic and Arthurian time, passing from Joseph to Galahad. This eucharistic logic also legitimizes Arthur's reign: he begins his first parliament "in September upon Our Lady's day" (8558); Merlin swears "on the sacrament" that Arthur is truly Uther's son and rightful heir (9773). All these gestures make Lovelich's translation a blend of piety, chivalry, and national history.

In the decades when Lovelich was likely working—c. 1410 to c. 1430—eucharistic belief was at the center of religious controversy. This context deepens the significance of MS 80 as a community performance. In these years, the annual Corpus Christi procession took place in the context of heresy trials where the denial of transubstantiation brought a death sentence. The theological challenge began in the 1380s with the Oxford scholar John Wyclif (c. 1320–84) and became a popular movement referred to as "lollardy." The core beliefs undermined the legitimacy of the established church and thus its sacraments, most especially the eucharist. Wyclif and his followers produced an English translation of the Bible that became both extremely popular and extremely dangerous. In 1411, church authorities produced a posthumous list of Wyclif's heresies and burned his books (Hudson 1988, 82–85; Catto 1985). In 1414, the new archbishop Henry Chichele continued vigorous prosecution of heresy (Gillespie 2011). In this atmosphere, heresy charges could arise from conflicts that had little to do with theology (Strohm 1998). This prospect increased when the newly enthroned Henry V promulgated the "Statute of Leicester," making the secular government an arm of the church: civic officers were called on to identify heresy and prosecute offenses in their own courts or refer offenders to the ecclesiastical authorities (Wylie 1914, 282–83, 290; Sharpe 1899–1912, 1:130). This statute devolved immense power to the mayor and aldermen of London, who—like the king and archbishop—could wield religious conformity as a political and economic weapon.

Amid this tumult, a skinner named John Claydon was executed for possessing a book reputed to include the eucharistic heresy. Claydon's profession may be incidental to the case, but a trade rivalry may have contributed to his fate. In any event, his guild's allegiance to Corpus Christi makes his offense social as well as theological. His care in commissioning the book, moreover, further witnesses the role of material formats in religious culture. Claydon had a long-standing practice of having the book, *The Lanterne of Li3t*, read aloud in his household (he himself was illiterate). The tract was infamous for challenging the legitimacy of the established church (Swinburn 1917). Claydon became vulnerable to prosecution when his apprentice, Alexander Philip, left to join the household of Thomas Fauconer, mercer and mayor. Fauconer had taken the new oath of office stipulated by the Statute of Leicester, which brought even upstanding citizens to "the mercy of trade rivals and domestic spies" (Wylie 1914, 292). When Philip told Fauconer about Claydon's household practices, Fauconer seized the opportunity to remand both Claydon and his books to the archbishop for examination (Sharpe 1899–1912, 1:139; Wylie 1914, 285–92; Jacob 1947, 132–38; Hudson 1988, 211–14, 318–25). The trial record includes a meticulous description of how Claydon's copy of the *Lanterne* text was produced, as well as an analysis of its fifteen heresies—with denial of transubstantiation the most damning. The charge results from a rather creative interpretation of a passage that criticizes the church for letting sinners take communion (Hudson 1988, 211; Swinburn 1917, 60). Nonetheless, Claydon and his books were burned on September 10, 1415; another participant in Claydon's reading sessions had already been executed (Wylie 1914, 292; Jacob 1947, 138n1). By extending capital punishment to the books, the authorities sought to disrupt the transmission of both text and belief. A year later, Barton the skinner took office as mayor, a position of proven lethal power.

While Claydon's fate was unfolding in London, English prelates were using Joseph of Arimathea in their fight against heresy at the Council of Constance (1414–18). In defense of their national reputation, they sought the formal (posthumous) condemnation of Wyclif (Van Dussen 2012, 94–100). They also sought recognition as an independent "nation" within the council, casting their own vote alongside France, Germany, Spain, and Italy. To this end, they elevated none other than Joseph of Arimathea. In 1417, Thomas Polton argued that Joseph gave England apostolic priority since he established Christianity in Britain before St. Denis in France (Crowder 1977, 110–26; Genet 1984). A few years later, this claim was corroborated by the "discovery" of the bodies of Joseph and his companions at Glastonbury Abbey (Carley 1994). The abbey already had a thriving Arthurian cult, having "discovered" his grave in 1191 (Gerald 2018). By the 1420s, then, Glastonbury garnered ancient prestige through both Joseph and Arthur, the featured protagonists of MS 80.

Lovelich responds to these popular ideas with "the earliest truly literary use of the Glastonbury account of Joseph" (Lagorio 1971, 226–27). In MS 80, Joseph's grave is not in Scotland, as the French source says, but in England, at the "abbey of Glas . . . which is now called the abbey of Glastonbury" (LIV:9, 156). The French grail may have been "heterodox" in its origins (Lagorio 1971, 231), but in fifteenth-century England the grail-bearer,

Joseph of Arimathea, became the champion of orthodoxy, representative of the ancient rights and privileges of the English church. By producing MS 80, Lovelich and Barton brought this prestigious national myth to the eyes and ears of their fellow guildsmen, enhancing the civic significance of their own religious practices.

Civic Lessons and King Arthur

The grail myth is indelibly "mingled" (*Grail*, LVI:518) with chivalry. The grail's guardians are all knights of perfect Christian faith. MS 80 thus brings idealized chivalry to an urban, nonaristocratic audience. By the early fifteenth century, status by noble lineage was becoming more and more indistinguishable from status acquired by wealth, resulting in a "bourgeois-gentry cultural formation" (Riddy 2000, 237). Lovelich's translation both expresses and produces this formation. At the same time, the power to police civic belonging became more and more concentrated in the hands of the wealthiest members of the twelve wealthiest guilds. The city's royal charter of 1319 made guild membership a condition of citizenship: guilds thus became "incubators for citizenship," regulating conduct and fostering loyalty to craft, city, and crown (Hanawalt 2017, 106–33). And the guilds alone elected the aldermen and mayor. The mayor's inauguration became a carefully orchestrated demonstration of civic hierarchies, separating the commons at large from the ruling elites (Hanawalt 1998, 20–24). These city officers were responsible for "saving and keeping the king's peace," as chronicles record (e.g., Kingsford 1905, 76). In exchange, the king granted them the "freedom" to govern, a freedom he could also revoke (Barron 2004, 37–42, 204–6). MS 80—created at the request of a mayor—gives the Arthurian story a decidedly civic inflection while repurposing the trappings of aristocratic chivalry.

MS 80 is an artifact of the chivalric culture that emerged among London's corporate elite in the fifteenth century. This Arthurian project is analogous to other guild practices that adopted aristocratic forms in order to consolidate corporate identity and secure civic privileges, such as arms and other kinds of iconography (Davies 2012, 264). Imagery drawn from the Nine Worthies (famous kings who included Arthur) provided models of moral conduct for both elite merchants and their apprentices (Manley 1995, 273–74; Davies 2011, 155–60). And concepts such as "honor" or "worship" became as "crucial for artisanal [identity]" as they were "for knightly masculinity" (Karras 2003, 111). The flexibility of chivalric vocabulary is illustrated in a letter sent to the king by the mayor and aldermen (including Barton) in 1417: they call the king a "chivalrous person"; they support his "worship" (honor) and the realm's "profit"; they address their prayers to the "holy company of heavenly knighthood" (Chambers and Daunt 1931, 68–70). Elements of chivalric culture thus became "interwoven" with corporate life (Davies 2012, 263). Lovelich's translation, which combines the grail with Arthur's early reign, is an ambitious example of these practices. By bringing the story of pious and honorable knights to the Skinners' Guild, MS 80 could give merchants and tradesmen direct access to prestigious national heritage.

The slippage between chivalric and civic values occurs subtly through the ambiguous vocabulary of "worth." The grail itself is a mystical mechanism for conflating noble birth and noble action. It divides the worthy from the sinful, regardless of rank or status. When Nasciens looks into the grail, he reports having seen the defense against all wickedness, the founding of all knowledge, and the beginning of religion. The final profound truth, however, is "the points of all gentry" (XVII:93)—that is, a full accounting of virtue conveyed in terms of "gentility" or noble rank. In this expression, chivalry becomes a moral patrimony that doesn't require martial action. Instead, all it requires is honesty and social responsibility. Much later, Lovelich describes two evenly matched knights in a tournament, one motivated by desire for "worship" (honor), the other for "richness and lordship" (9375–76). Rather than distinguishing the two knights, these terms underscore their similarity: in the end, the tournament is declared a draw (9617). With honor, wealth, and lordship as synonyms, chivalric values can slip into the hands of even an artisan apprentice.

Lovelich's inflection of civic paradigms is evident in his translation of the devils' plot that leads to Merlin's birth. The demons are angry because Christ has rescued Adam, Eve, and others from hell. In response, the "master devils" "counsel" together and gather "in parliament" (10–12).

This familiar form of political assemblage is transposed here to Christian history, with the masters leading the way. They ask of Christ: "what master man is he" (13)—that is, who has taken leadership and dared to rescue the sinners. They are indignant that someone so lowborn has stolen their powers: "Say, how was this yeoman born by whom our right is thus forfeited?" (23-24). Lovelich's devils sound like a group of craftsmasters whose traditional influence has been usurped by a mere "yeoman." The devils go on to describe themselves as masters who have lost their servants:

> For they have been our servants by right,
> Yet he has over them such great might
> That they forsake our service
> And only to Jesus do they take.
> All our power is done
> And thus we lose them, each and every one.
> (*Merlin*, 57–62)

The devils' sense of commercial threat echoes an earlier description of Christ's redemption: "man's soul to buy from hell, the devil's power to strike down [*felle*]" (XXXI:333-34). To counteract this decline in power, and avenge their property losses, the devils decide to engender a child on a human woman. They imagine that if they have someone in their thrall with the same prophetic powers as Christ, they will regain followers and "profit" (101). One of the devils approaches a woman with a rich husband, described as a "worthy" and "rich" man who has many "worldly goods"— livestock, camels, jewels, and "other worthiness" (131-36). The devil ensnares the man by making him angry: he kills his cattle and horses and then his son; his wife kills herself in despair, and the man dies of grief. The devil then turns to the three daughters, turning two to "adultery" (240) and ultimately raping the most resistant one when she accidentally falls asleep angry (584-96). Thus is Merlin conceived. He will embody the hazy moral of this story: the devils are wrong but they also win, at least for the moment. This contest plays out in materialist terms familiar to those who have servants and worldly goods.

The urban context is further highlighted when Lovelich emphasizes the role of cities in Christian history. In the mythic Mediterranean East, the story moves from city to city. When Josephes finally arrives in Britain, he reaches Camelot—the city with the most "worship" (XLVII:18-25). Much later, the generic French "land" (*terre*) becomes "city, borough, and town" (Douce MS 178, f. 235r; *Merlin*, 17320). Throughout, the most prominent city is London—site of the "parliament" and judicial duel that lead to the conversion of Lucius, Britain's first Christian king (LII:290, 853-55). And London, not Camelot, becomes "king Arthur's chief city" (12995, 20822). As soon as Arthur wins his first battle against the barons who resist his election, he goes to London to begin a "parliament" (8555). After creating new knights and distributing gifts, he sets up defenses around Britain in "cities, towns, and castles" (8575). In an unnamed city, Arthur learns that he has a half-sister who is at "school" in London (8621-22). The "worthy burgers" of London celebrate Arthur by hosting an eight-day festival (8748-54). Following the festivities, Arthur returns to London to organize a "merry procession" to welcome Kings Ban and Bors "full worshipfully" (9252-54): the streets are cleaned, silk banners hung, festive dances prepared, and lanterns lit; the weather is fair and clear (9303-16). The scene fairly resembles a royal entry in fifteenth-century London (Dalrymple 2000, 164). Throughout the ensuing battles against the rebel barons, the citizens of London become Arthur's most loyal and effective supporters (Dalrymple 2000, 163-66; Finotello 2014, 134-49). Even the "peasants" support the cause, bringing war booty to London's citizens who are defending the city (13317-76).

Lovelich's emphasis on London citizenry derives in part from the word *Logres*, which designates both London and the realm as a whole. This doubling also occurs in the French prose text, but the effect is decidedly partisan in English for a London audience. Lovelich makes the equivalence explicit by stating that *Logres* is now called *London* (Dalrymple 2000, 163; *Merlin*, 8554, 9218, 25528). The etymology of *Logres*, moreover, derives from a *Brut* chronicle (*Merlin*, 10183-244). Lovelich translated from a French source that already included these British enhancements (see chap. 1). In English, these interpolations fully "repatriate" the Holy Grail and King Arthur. The city's Trojan origins, as recorded in the *Brut* and summarized in MS 80's *Logres* etymology, were treated as the source of its special privileges and the cornerstone of civic pedagogy (Lindenbaum 1999, 298–99). In part for these reasons, Middle English prose *Brut* chronicles and their adaptations were among the most common nondevotional books used by London citizens (Barron 2016, 44–53). The many surviving *Brut* manuscripts include one purchased in the late fifteenth century by a skinner named William Naseby; the book was so valued that Robert Naseby wrote a note in it threatening any would-be thief with hanging (Yale, Beinecke MS 494, f. iv, 102v; Shailor 1992, 2:478–80). The value that the Nasebys placed in their chronicle is emblematic of the sense of civic ownership over national history that solidified among London elites in the course of the fifteenth century. MS 80 arises from and conveys these same values. Each time the text refers to the "realm of Logres" (e.g., 17922), London accedes to dominion of the whole island, conflating city and nation.

The *Logres* etymology draws attention to Lovelich's broader alignment with chronicle writing, perhaps the most popular genre of English writing in the early fifteenth century. Stylistically, Lovelich's translation shares various traits with London chronicles, from vocabulary to eyewitness reporting to comments on weather (Dalrymple 2000, 164–66; Radulescu 2013, 97–110). His regular references to "memory" and specifically to "remembrance" (e.g., 10515) echo the vocabulary of record-keeping as practiced in government, guilds, and households (Davies 2016, 27). Lovelich may have drawn inspiration from chronicles just as London chroniclers drew inspiration from romances (McLaren 2002, 142–43). Indeed, toward the end of MS 80, Lovelich explicitly calls his narrative a "chronicle" (*Merlin*, 23443). In fifteenth-century London, chronicles were part of "a new kind of literary experience" that fostered "a communal sense of identity" (Sponsler 2014, 145). MS 80 participates in this trend, turning Arthur's story into a text that echoes civic chronicles and places citizen heroes alongside chivalric ones.

The civic and chivalric themes that traverse MS 80 came to full fruition in the Skinners' later textual commissions. About two hundred years after Lovelich and Barton, the Skinners participated in several scripted inauguration pageants for mayors. From the 1580s to 1702, these annual processions drew on the syntax of royal entries to make partisan arguments about civic community in favor of the merchant elite (Manley 1995, 212–93; McLaren 2002, 51–63). Organized by the guild of each year's new mayor, the pageants addressed the perpetual rivalry between city and crown over legal and economic jurisdiction. In some cases, commemorative booklets were printed that describe the event and showcase the speeches (Hill 2011, 218–30). The Skinners may have been at the vanguard of this practice, with the oldest surviving booklet dating from the inauguration of their mayor Wolstan Dixie (Peele 1585). They may also have been especially eager to capitalize on civic ceremonial, since the Corpus Christi procession had been outlawed at the beginning of the Reformation (Lancashire 2002, 60). Over the course of the seventeenth century, the Skinners produced at least six pageant booklets (Middleton 1619; Dekker 1628; Bulteel 1656; Tatham 1663; Jordan 1671; Taubman 1689). Each time, they commissioned the most favored civic poets, who in turn drew on a consistent set of tropes to inspire the mayor and ennoble the guild. Some strategies are relatively generic, such as vaunting the city itself, while others play to the Skinners' special status as furriers in order to emphasize their special closeness to the monarchy.

The mayor pageants recontextualize both MS 80 the book and Barton the patron-mayor. The mayor's office had a long association with royal sovereignty, since the mayor served as the king's representative in the city and the city as the king's royal seat (Barron 2004, 147–58). For a 1415 meeting in Guildhall, the mayor sat literally in the king's place between the archbishop and the princes (Riley 1868, 603–5); two years later, Barton himself became mayor. In the course of the fifteenth century, it became more and more common to address the mayor as "Worshipful Lord Mayor" and even to refer to his "sovereign discretion" (Barron 2004, 156). This elevation is stated clearly in a London chronicle from the 1460s, perhaps written by a former mayor: "within London he is next unto the king in all manner of things," responsible to keep the city's "worship" (Gairdner 1876, 222; McLaren 2002, 29–33; London, British Library, MS Egerton 1995). The early modern inauguration pageants continue this tradition of treating the mayor as the "king's substitute" (Bergeron 1993). They also respond to new frictions between city and crown: the mayor's "cultic elevation" resists royal incursions into civic freedoms, including trade monopolies (Manley 1995, 266–70). These relationships took a special symbolic twist whenever a skinner was mayor because of fur's role in royal ceremony and social ranking: skinners provided the rarified materials, such as white ermine, that signified royalty. Fur also conveyed the mayor's own elevated status: he could wear the same furs as a knight, and his wife could even wear ermine (Given-Wilson 2005, Henry IV, membrane 6, item 76; membrane 7, item 110; Edward IV, membrane 6–7, item 20). The Skinners' mayor pageants thus all play on the sovereign's dependence on their trade.

The pageant of 1619 by the popular writer Thomas Middleton (c. 1580–1627) features none other than "Sir Henry Barton" as the Skinners' most famous medieval mayor. The booklet published to commemorate the event displays the entanglements of the mayor's office, the monarchy, the Skinners' craft, and textual patronage that stretch all the way back to Barton's era. The booklet is a punctual echo of the conditions that motivated Barton and Lovelich to produce MS 80. The pageant commission was awarded following a guild-sponsored poetry competition at Skinners' Hall (O'Callaghan 2009, 90–103; Hill 2011, 59–60). The booklet commemorates this corporate patronage, with Middleton submitting both his service and "the book" to "your Lordships Command" (Middleton 1619, A3r). These "lords" are "The Noble Fraternity of Skinners" who have dedicated "their loves and costly triumphs" to their brother, the mayor-elect Sir William Cockayne. The mayor himself is associated with royalty: "his Majesty's Lieutenant, the Lord Mayor of the Famous City London." Cockayne later receives the same imperial fealty as the king from the English, Scot, Welsh, French, Irish, and "that kind Savage, the Virginian" (B3v). Together, these presentation formulas tout the universal fame of London, the Skinners, and now the Lord Mayor Cockayne.

Middleton's pageant adapted various conventional elements to the particularities of the Skinners trade. It features prose descriptions of the procession, verse speeches by allegorical figures, and theatrical scenes or "triumphs" as backdrops for the speeches. The first "triumph" that Cockayne encountered was a wilderness scene—a trope representing the challenges of good governance used as far back as 1392 in a royal entry by

Richard II (Carlson 2003, lines 359–70, 535–36). The scene represents the sovereign's power to tame civic unrest. For the Skinners, the wilderness trope symbolizes both the disorder that threatens the city and the diversity of animals used in the fur trade—all "harvested" by the mayor. For Cockayne, a speech by the figure Orpheus explains the mayor's power to bring "harmonious government" to the "rude and thorny ways" that have grown up in the "unpruned commonwealth" (B2v–B3r). The wilderness scene makes the Skinners' trade the visible result of good governance—unruly nature turned to profitable social symbol.

At the next "triumph," Cockayne and his retinue encountered solutions to the "rough wilderness" of governance—including the example of Barton's memorable leadership. Barton is one of eight former Skinner mayors featured in the "Sanctuary of Fame"—and the only one to receive a short prose biography in the booklet: "That Sir Henry Barton an Honor to Memory, was the first, that for the safety of Travelers, and strangers, by night through the City, caused lights to be hung out from All Hallows Eve to Candlemas; therefore in this Sanctuary of Fame, where the beauty of good actions shines, he is most properly and worthily recorded" (B4v). This public safety initiative is mentioned in the widely read *Survey of London* by John Stow (Stow 1598, 435). Indeed, a Guildhall proclamation from Barton's time as mayor charged "on behalf of the king and the city" that every "honest person" hang a lantern during Christmastimes—or pay a fine; the proclamation also forbade costumes and plays in the streets (Chambers and Daunt 1931, 96–97). These measures made it easier for the mayor to keep the "king's peace." The lighting itself symbolizes good governance: in Middleton's pageant, the Sanctuary of Fame is decorated with twenty-six burning lamps, which represent the twenty-six aldermen: "they being for their Justice, Government and Example, the Lights of the City" (B4r). Barton's winter lanterns thus brought both practical and symbolic justice.

In Middleton's account, all the mayors are knights, including Barton. There is no historical record of his elevation: "Sir Barton" is a retroactive title deemed proper to former mayors. According to the pageant of 1656, mayors "seldom leave their Office without the honor of Knighthood conferred upon them" (Bulteel 1656, 8). Over time, the honorific played to the development of "citizen romance," where a "neofeudal ethic of loyalty, chivalric service, and communal solidarity" provided a mythology that made mercantile wealth consistent with "the values of traditional English society" (Manley 1995, 274). The Tailors went so far as to turn Sir John Hawkwood into a full-blown chivalric hero (Webster 1624, B2r-v; Winstanley 1687; Davies 2011, 155–62). Even in Barton's day, though, the mayor's office brought chivalric associations. Barton's contemporary John Carpenter (d. 1442), the city clerk who compiled London's governance customs (1417–19), states that aldermen were treated with baronial rank (Riley 1859–61, 1:33). In 1503, the mayor joined a procession hooded "like a baron," and the aldermen were outfitted "like knights" (Kingsford 1905, 259). The burden of actual knighthood, however, could outweigh the honor, such that wealthy commoners resisted medieval kings' efforts to convert property rents into knighthoods (Thrupp 1948, 275–77). By the seventeenth century, however, knighthood no longer implied military service, so the honorific served as another dimension of civic chivalry. "Sir Barton" thus translates forward the chivalric ethos already on display in MS 80.

Middleton's next scene is the "Parliament of Honor," which celebrates the nobility by celebrating the Skinners' religious fraternity. The figure Antiquity promises "a Story, That shall to thy Fraternity add Glory" (Middleton 1619, B4v). Antiquity then enumerates the "Records of Fame," with the greatest fame going to the kings, queens, and nobles who were members of the Skinners' fraternity—which had more royal members than any other guild (Middleton 1619, C1r; same in Dekker 1628, C1r). Antiquity elaborates on the ennobling power of fur itself:

> And see with what propriety, the Fates
> Have to this Noble Brotherhood knit such States;
> For what Society, the whole City brings,
> Can with such Ornaments Adorn their Kings,
> Their only Robes of State, when they consent
> To ride most glorious, to High Parliament;
> And mark in this their Royal intent still,
> For when it pleased the Goodness of their Will,
> To put the richest Robes of their Loves on

To the whole City, the Most, ever came
To this Society, which Records here prove,
Adorning their Adorners, with their Love;
Which was a Kingly Equity:
Be careful then, Great Lord, to bring forth Deeds,
To match that Honor, that from hence proceeds.
(Middleton 1619, C1r–v)

In Middleton's verses, the Skinners are "knitted" to the whole social body through the garments they provide the monarchy and through the monarchy's membership in the guild's fraternity. These kings and queens "adorn their adorners"—that is, lend their royal reputation to the guild that in turn clothes them in the furs that signify royalty. The "knitted" connection runs in two directions, with the skinners as sole providers of the robes of state and the kings providing "the richest robes of their love" by joining the Skinners' fraternity. This royal weave increases the mayor's obligation to "match" the honor of "kingly equity" through his deeds in office.

Middleton's booklet extends these historical lessons with a brief prose chronicle "illustrating" the medieval royals and nobles alluded to in the verses. With these biographies, the booklet offers further lessons in national, civic, and corporate history. The account begins with Edward III—who authorized the Skinners' first charter in 1327—and extends through the fifteenth century, tallied at the end as a "Royal Sum" of "24 Skinners." Along the way, Middleton calls attention to events of particular significance to London and the Skinners. Middleton's impulse is taken up in later Skinner pageants as well. Ten years later, Dekker considered Middleton's lessons so effective that he declines to name the historical figures "because they have in former years been fully expressed" (Dekker 1628, C1r). Some thirty years later, Bulteel treated his whole booklet as a chronicle, beginning with "our own Historians" for the story of "Brute," founder of "New Troy"; he interspersed London's timeless virtues with a review of civic history since the time of Edward the Confessor (d. 1066) (Bulteel 1656). All these gestures toward chronicle writing reflect the Skinners' long-standing claim to a special place at the heart of the nation. They echo back to the Skinners' earlier engagements with *Brut* chronicles, including MS 80.

The pageant of 1619 ends with a speech by the figure Love, who also gave the first speech. All along, Love has accompanied the mayor in a chariot drawn by two "luzarns" (lynx), which, by established convention, represent the Skinners' arms and their far-flung trade (Lambert 1934, 209, 270, 266; Peele 1585). Love reminds Cockayne that "there's no free gift" and that his guild "expects some fair Requital" for its investment in the pageant: justice, care, and "zeal to right wrongs" (Middleton 1619, C4v). In this way, good governance is expressed in the language of fair trade. Good governance also elevates the mayor to "brotherhood" with royalty: the mayor's acts will "crown" him like a king in royal fur: justice "will become thy Soul (whence Virtue springs) / As those rich Ornaments thy Brother Kings" (C4v). So adorned, the mayor becomes the city's "bridegroom . . . A Careful Husband, to a Loving Spouse" (D1r). This mutual adoration is mutually enriching in every sense. Love's promotion of "parity and reciprocity," however, masks an undercurrent of "exclusive privileges" that the mayor is meant to defend in favor of the merchant elite (Manley 1995, 262). The pageant, then, sutures community bonds but also seeks to control dissident behavior. It thus carries forward the ideologies that motivated guilds as social organizations in the first place. Much like the Skinners' medieval performances—feasts in their Hall, dress regulations, Corpus Christi processions, the illustrated Fraternity registers—Middleton's pageant performs community by demanding a compliant performance of community values. MS 80 also translated these values into the idiom of Middle English poetry and vaunted national origins.

After Love's speech, Middleton inserts a poem that celebrates the Skinners' wares (perhaps performed in the pageant, perhaps not). The verses enumerate "those Beasts, bearing Fur, and now *in use, with the Bountiful Society of Skinners*," which were presented in the Wilderness scene at the beginning of the pageant. The furred animals witness the Skinners' particular skill in taming wild things and turning them into social symbols:

Ermine, Foine, Sables, Martin, Badger, Bear,
Luzerne, Budge, Otter, Hipponesse *and* Hare,
Lamb, Wolf, Fox, Leopard, Mink, Stoat, Miniver,

Raccoon, Moashy, Wolverine, Caliber,
Squirrel, Mole, Cat, Musk, Civet, Wild & Tame,
Cony *white*, Yellow, *Black must have a Name*;
The Ounce, Rose-Gray, Jennet, Pampilion,
Of Birds, the Vulture, Bitter, Ostridge, Swan;
Some worn for Ornament, and some for Health,
All to the Skinners' Art bring Fame and Wealth.
(Middleton 1619, D1r)

This list follows the social hierarchy of furs (and feathers), from the rarified to the practical. These verses join with earlier speeches by Love and the other figures to encourage the mayor to live up to the high honor of both his office and his trade. As Lord Mayor and a furrier, he holds the health of the community in his hands on every level. The final rhyme of "health" and "wealth" emphasizes again the close bond between good governance and commercial success. Careful cultivation of this bond brings "Fame"— that is, lasting memory to be celebrated perhaps in a future "Sanctuary of Fame" alongside "Sir Barton" (B4v). In Middleton's pageant, the Skinners' furs civilize the city, the nation, and the world. This power stretches back to Barton, who also requested a lavish textual performance that also lay claim to powerful forms for civic and national belonging.

MS 80 exemplifies how the merchant classes gradually embraced chivalry as a social ideology. In this way, London elites renegotiated their place in the national *communitas*. Their strategies included ostentatious textuality—illustrated manuscripts and public performances. The Skinners were particularly visible in their production of books (MS 80, the Fraternity Registers) and processions (Corpus Christi, mayor pageants). In this context, MS 80 proffered an innovative path toward tradition, with a fabulous fusion of chivalry and piety. As an English book, it broadened the range of social groups who could join the textual community defined by Arthurian knowledge. At the same time, the book projected narrowly elitist aspirations. Like furs themselves, MS 80 engages royalty while also courting anyone of sufficient means. This style of populist elitism runs through the Skinners' textual projects into the seventeenth century: in the name of the commons and the commonwealth, mayors were likened to kings. The Skinners were not alone in this vision, but they developed it with particular panache.

However valuable MS 80 was to Lovelich, Barton, and possibly others in their community, modern ideas about poetry turned Lovelich into one of the most denigrated authors of English literary history (as I show in chap. 5). Similar aesthetic views have shaped the development of digital resources—with works from the established canon often receiving the most attention. The representations of the Skinners' pageants on EEBO show that even a database shaped by catalogues can also be shaped by unspoken assumptions about poetry. Middleton's booklet, for example, has been transcribed in full—verses and descriptive prose alike. Other pageants, though, have only their verses transcribed, even though the prose is also authored by the poets (Jordan 1671; Taubman 1689). Images of the complete text are only a click away, but the text itself is not machine searchable (nor are the texts of the 60 percent of items that are not transcribed at all). EEBO thus encodes someone's twenty-first-century definition of literature onto these seventeenth-century texts. Perhaps only Middleton's relatively more canonical status made it possible for me to find "Sir Barton." In the gaps between search and discovery, literary history emerges from data curation.

CHAPTER 3

MARKING MANUSCRIPTS

Makers, Users, Coders

THE PAGES OF A MEDIEVAL MANUSCRIPT have never been blank. Whether made of vellum or paper, each leaf bears the marks of its manufacture. Once the pages are ready for writing, they are further marked by pricks and lines that guide scribes to format the text in columns and rows. In addition to writing out the text, scribes might add marks to make the text more accessible to its eventual readers, such as paragraph symbols or scansion lines for rhythm. These codes convey a maker's conception of the text to users, who in turn might express their own conceptions by adding yet more marks—underlines, symbols, signatures, comments, and so forth. Some marks, though, have nothing to do with the text: doodles and other unrelated matter turn pages back into raw material—convenient spaces ready for writing. The digital reproduction of medieval manuscripts has brought these historical marking practices into dialogue with the networked "markup" that defines how texts and images appear on websites and how users can interact with them. Marks in the margin are thus far from marginal: they point to entire systems of social relations, textual interpretation, cultural classification, and technological infrastructure.

MS 80 is a prime example of the many functions of annotations, notes, and other marks in manuscripts. The large sheets of paper bear clear traces of their production, such as watermarks and other impressions from the mold. These sheets have been folded in half, in groups of four to form quires of eight folios (sixteen pages). Each page has been prepared for writing with faint red lines defining text columns and generous margins all around. The text is presented with readers in mind—and some readers have responded with attentive interpretation. MS 80 has also been used as scrap paper: the wide margins offered ample room for personal lists and signatures. Some handlers, though, were rather neglectful: they let pages get burned, ripped, or lost entirely. Even though one might usually distinguish between, say, an accidental smudge and intentional verbal commentary, in this chapter I treat marks, notes, and annotations of all kinds somewhat interchangeably. They are all part of the infrastructure that produces meaning in and around books. All these marks arise from accessing the book; they all require interpretation. From the perspective of infrastructure—in which a book is also a storage device, format, interface, and platform (see my introduction)—all kinds of marks participate equally in making the book. Whether in manuscript or online, annotations are part of the infrastructure that sustains books. Their varied functions illustrate how infrastructure is a "when" instead of a "what" (Star and Ruhleder 1996, 113; Anderson 2013, 18): one moment the mark is on the book, then in the book, and later perhaps even the book itself. Annotations are both components and products of the systems that produce, preserve, and distribute books and texts—such as catalogues, editions, and reproductions. They define—and create—MS 80's passage from codex to edition to website.

The pivotal moment in MS 80's trajectory was its arrival in the hands of Archbishop Matthew Parker in the late sixteenth century. Parker collected books in part to defend the Anglican Church from papal oversight. To this end, Parker and his associates searched manuscripts and printed books for precedents that would justify British royal and ecclesiastical autonomy.

Along the way, they underlined, commented, and even reconfigured the books to better serve their interests (Sherman 2008; Knight 2013). They turned medieval manuscripts into a sixteenth-century archive (Page 1993, 43–61; Graham 2006; Grafton 2017). Annotated books are thus a defining feature of Parker's collection and part of what makes it such a valuable record of Reformation thought. Some annotations can be attributed to specific individuals—Parker himself, his secretary John Joscelyn, Stephen Batman, and others (Graham and Watson 1998; Horobin and Nafde 2015). Other marks, such as red underlining or italic lettering, are more difficult to pinpoint but can be broadly characterized as "Parkerian"—that is, reflecting Parker's purposes, whether made by him personally or not (McKisack 1971, 37–39). Together, these marks are part of the "curatorial substructure" that shapes access to the collection in general and to literary history in particular (Knight 2013, 13). In the long history of media, Parker Library exemplifies how annotations consolidate cultural authority (Straw 2007, 12). The right to make annotations is actually one way of asserting cultural authority. Indeed, when Parker decided to bequeath the bulk of his collection to Corpus Christi College, he forbade anyone to write in the books (Page 1993, 45; CCCC MS 575). In point of fact, librarians and conservators (and even some readers) have continued writing in the books—adding shelf marks, folio numbers, and other apparatus like titles and chapter numbers. In this way, MS 80 has become a modern book located in modern knowledge systems—catalogues, editions, and digital platforms.

The marks in MS 80 span the book's entire history, from papermaking to the internet. At least fifteen, and perhaps more than thirty, different people have written on the paper. The earliest marks indicate careful professional production and the aspiration to create a deluxe illustrated volume, c. 1435 (see chap. 1). Later, a scribe and former goldsmith apprentice, John Cok (d. 1468), read the text carefully for its religious symbolism. He also penned an annotation that identifies the translator Henry Lovelich as a skinner and Henry Barton, another skinner, as his patron (f. 127r). This note conjures a constellation of social contexts: the Skinners' Guild, Barton's political career, and merchant culture in London (see chap. 2). As the only evidence of Barton's connection to MS 80, the annotation on folio

127r is the hinge between the text and its context. About a hundred years later, in Parker's collection, MS 80 acquired more marks: a title, a flyleaf comment, some red underlining, and possibly some marginal notes. These annotations draw the Holy Grail and King Arthur into sixteenth-century debates over English national memory.

Along the way, a number of other people had their pens in the book. Some took advantage of the wide margins to personalize the book with signatures: Anne Hampton (f. 39r; Meale 1993, 141), Ana (f. 45r), and several others scattered across the later quires (ff. 74r, 76r, 108r, 113r, 134r, 162v, 200v). Others wrote personal notes: something in English (f. 150r); something smudged out in a center margin (f. 163r); something "theological" written upside down (f. 192r; James 1912, 1:164); an alphabetical list of Latin conjugations on the verso of eight folios in a row (ff. 191v–200v; James 1912, 1:164). Some handlers were more careless than others, leaving stains (f. 11r) and even burning small holes (ff. 101, 200); one left an inky fingerprint (f. 1v). By the end of the sixteenth century, the beginning of the book was lost (about twenty-five leaves) and the first two surviving leaves bound at the end (which is also missing an unknown number of leaves). These material changes have been noted in the margins by modern cataloguers, along with shelf marks, folio numbers, quire signatures, and conservation notes (discussed in chap. 4). Apparatus from printed editions, such as titles and chapter numbers, has also been penciled into MS 80's margins. Most recently, a curator has noted on a flyleaf that MS 80 was rebound in 1956 (discussed in chap. 6). These modern marks extend earlier practices of making and using the book. They show how libraries themselves mark books in the course of cataloguing and preservation. Modern annotations guide users in the same way that medieval scribes do.

Perhaps surprisingly, digital annotations replicate many of the same functions as handwritten marks. For MS 80, Parker Library on the Web structures a continuum from manuscript to print to the internet, drawing attention to the relationship between annotations *in* the books and annotations *of* the books. In a web browser, HTML syntax functions like production annotations: it instructs processing so that texts, images, and other features appear on screens in a certain way. Specialized markup standards, such as the Text Encoding Initiative (TEI, https://tei-c.org), classify text elements to facilitate machine-processing. Annotations are also central to the syntax of the International Image Interoperability Framework (http://iiif.io). In IIIF, "annotations" define how digital objects (text, image, video, etc.) appear on a viewing "canvas." In this digital space, annotations define the relationships between objects (Crane 2017). Those relationships have "motivations"—that is, definitions of their purpose (such as "comment" or "paint"). In IIIF syntax, motivations make explicit what is usually implicit in handwritten annotations: why did someone make a mark in a certain place, in a certain way? The answers produce literary history that attributes meaning-making to many people besides canonical authors.

Annotations, then, plait together literary history and book history. In this chapter I tell the story of MS 80 from the perspective of its makers, users, and coders. All three of these functions extend across the book's entire history: the earliest makers marked the text with code for readers; the most recent computer coders have remade the book; everyone who touches the book or accesses Parker Library on the Web is a user. From start to finish, annotations make networks, whether in the shelf-book or the digital book. Nonetheless, I proceed here more or less in chronological order. First, I address the book's production, beginning with the relationship between Lovelich the translator and Barton the patron. The earliest marks on the paper are consistent with their ambition to produce a deluxe manuscript for a mercantile audience. Later annotations point to very different readers later in the fifteenth and sixteenth centuries: Cok and the Parkerian annotator(s) read the text for Christian history and Arthurian genealogies. Other early users (or perhaps some of the same users in a different frame of mind) ignored the narrative, leaving drawings, lists, and signatures whose motivations may never be known. Finally, I turn to the modern annotations that have remade MS 80 as a networked object. The manuscript itself bears marks from the catalogues and printed editions that first distributed the text beyond Cambridge as part of the English literary canon. Most recently, the digital editions of MS 80 on Parker Library on the Web rely on markup that replicates some common functions of marginalia, such as instructions and commentary.

Simultaneously, the digital editions have entirely new properties built into their code. Throughout this chapter, I show how, in every format and on every platform, annotations and other marks are part of the infrastructure that creates the meaning of books and texts.

Making a Merchants' Book

MS 80's earliest history is documented by one of its later annotations. A note on the outer margin of folio 127r, by someone other than the text copyist, states, "Henry Lovelich, skinner, that translated this book out of French into English at the request of Henry Barton" ("henre louelich skynnere þt translated þs boke oute of ffrensshe in to englysshe at þe instaunce of harry barton") (see fig. 7). This note sits alongside a passage where Lovelich names himself and asks the community to pray that he stay healthy long enough to complete the translation "out of French into English" (*Merlin*, 10246–55). The annotator, though, knows more than the text reveals: that Lovelich was a skinner and that he undertook his textual labors at Barton's "instaunce"—a term that implies a paid commission (Doyle 1961, 99n44; Meale 1994, 219; Connolly 1998, 160; Warren 2008). Barton's patronage illustrates the increasingly common practice of merchants adopting aristocratic values and "desiring books that would affirm their social status" (Lerer 1993, 60). The Lovelich-Barton annotation thus identifies MS 80 as a merchants' book embedded in the social context of the Skinners' Guild (see chap. 2). The note connects this social context to the material conditions of bookmaking.

Barton's career illustrates how merchants might access royal and aristocratic models of textual patronage—and decide to bolster their sense of social status by commissioning books like MS 80. As a purveyor of furs, Barton traded at the upper echelons of London society, crossing from the royal household to the aristocracy to the merchant elite of every profession. He began in the service of Queen Anne (d. 1394), who granted him an annuity, later confirmed by Richard II (1394) and reconfirmed by Henry IV (1399). King Henry made Barton a yeoman of the royal chamber and then elevated him to the newly created post of King's Skinner (1405–35). In this capacity, Barton spent the next thirty years attending to all the details of producing and caring for the royal furs—from acquiring skins to arranging for the transport of furred garments (Veale 1966, 81, 206-7). Barton was thus responsible for the furs of Henry IV, Henry V, and Henry VI. Although the royal Wardrobe did not always pay its bills, Barton grew relatively wealthy, with property in London and estates in Buckinghamshire, Hertfordshire, Berkshire, and East Anglia (Rawcliffe 1993). He exemplifies the gradual erosion of social distinctions between the rural gentry and the urban elite that began in the fourteenth century. The annotation thus points to a world in which different social classes were making and using books in increasingly similar ways (Doyle 1983; Horrox 1988; Meale 1989; Parkes 1991).

Alongside his royal service, Barton had a sustained career in city government. He held multiple offices over three decades: sheriff (1405-6), alderman (1406-35), collector of the tonnage and poundage (1408-10), collector of the wool custom (1410-16), mayor (1416-17, the first skinner since 1374), member of parliament (1419-20), and mayor again (1428-29) (Rawcliffe 1993). The mayor's office represented a rather significant financial obligation, given the mayor's responsibility to clothe his retinue and personally host civic events. The weight of expense led to a 1424 regulation intended to protect aldermen's budgets by restricting reelection; nonetheless, a few years later Barton served a second term, clearly one of the few with the means to shoulder the burden. As mayor, Barton shared responsibility with the king for the peace of the city. According to John Stow, Barton established winter streetlighting ("Lanthornes with Lights")—an attribution perhaps corroborated in a Guildhall proclamation dated 1418 (Stow 1598, 435; Chambers and Daunt 1931, 96-97). The mayor's rolls from Barton's period haven't survived, but many other records show him active in civic affairs, from witness to arbitrator to defendant to plaintiff in property and trade disputes. Other merchants and gentry found that Barton's civic standing made him a desirable trustee in property conveyances and executor of wills. As a citizen and alderman throughout this extended period, Barton would have participated in a host of London events: Richard II's reconciliation with the city (1392), the celebration of Henry V's victory at Agincourt (1415), the coronation of his queen Catherine (1421), and the royal entry of Henry VI (1432). Barton was thus deeply involved in the city's political economy in the first decades of the fifteenth century.

Even in death, Barton sought influence over London affairs. In addition to typical provisions for prayers, his 1435 will set up durable endowments to support religious and corporate charity (LMA, CLC/L/SE/A/006/ MS31301/189; Lambert 1934, 120–26; Thrupp 1948, 177–80). He thus followed the model of "good civic death" set in extravagant fashion by his fellow mayor and alderman, the mercer Richard Whittington (d. 1423) (Appleford 2015, 55–65). Barton's lengthy will included a substantial bequest of vestments, linen, and plate to the Guildhall, helping to spur the construction of a central chapel. He gave his business assets entirely to the Skinners, turning the rents into a source of corporate wealth. He also endowed a full-time "priest of Corpus Christi" to pray and conduct services for the guild. To perpetuate his civic standing, he had his tomb built in a chapel at St. Paul's Cathedral, with an alabaster effigy (Stow 1633, 356). He also endowed a chantry there, stipulating an annual obituary celebration and offering payment for members of the city administration to attend. Barton's burial arrangements expressed a symbolic closeness between city government and St. Paul's. The Skinners kept up the provisions attached to "Henry Barton's lands" into the seventeenth century (*Calendar of Records of the Skinners' Company* 1965). The chapel, though, was torn down in 1549 during a Reformation attack on the cathedral (Stow 1633, 356; Lambert 1934, 166, 171). Ironically, a decade or two later, Protestant interests would motivate Archbishop Parker to conserve the book that Barton started when he asked Lovelich to translate a French romance into English.

Lovelich, meanwhile, had a less public and less prosperous career. He never held any of the civic offices typical for prominent guildsmen (sheriff, alderman) and did not record a will. Historical records do confirm his identity as "civis et pelliparius" (citizen and skinner). They also substantiate his association with Barton: in 1409, he served as Barton's representative in a property transfer involving other skinners; in 1411 he transferred his own property to Barton (LMA, CLC/L/SE/A/006/MS31302/135, 198). Lovelich and Barton also appear together as dues-paying members of the Skinners' Fraternity of the Assumption of Our Lady, with Lovelich listed as a warden in 1401 (LMA, CLC/L/SE/A/006/MS31692, ff. 5v, 6, 6v). Perhaps Lovelich was among the independent masters sometimes "forced by altered circumstances to give up his shop" (Rosser 2015, 166). Whatever the case, archival records suggest that Lovelich had a relatively moderate status within the guild.

The exact nature of Lovelich's relationship with Barton is unclear. In the early debate about Lovelich's identity, Walter Skeat posited a "close friendship"—on the assumption that Lovelich himself had written the patronage annotation and used the familiar "Harry" to refer to Barton (Skeat 1902b). It's possible that Lovelich was a "retired businessman" using his "ample leisure" to write for his friend (Ackerman 1952b, 474, 484). This idea of friendship has been used to characterize the translation as a relatively insignificant private matter between two individuals (Pearsall 1976, 71; Gray 2008, 386–87). In the guild context, however, friendship was freighted with social and spiritual significance. Gervase Rosser has shown how "the art of solidarity" in guilds—both corporate and religious—rested on a concept of friendship that decentered the individual in favor of the community (Rosser 2015, 89–117). As members of the same religious fraternity, Lovelich and Barton would have been sworn "brothers" bound in mutual charity (Rosser 2015, 109). Within this frame, a book made for a friend would contribute to a multifaceted relationship with financial, spiritual, political, and social dimensions (see chap. 2).

Barton had several models for textual patronage in his immediate vicinity. His own guild probably commissioned the monk John Lydgate to compose verses for the annual Corpus Christi procession (see chap 2). Other guilds also commissioned Lydgate for verses and performance texts (Cooper and Denny-Brown 2008). Some aldermen are known to have engaged in direct patronage, as Barton may have done: John Welles, grocer and mayor, paid Lydgate for verses describing Henry VI's 1432 royal entry (Sponsler 2014, 115–38); Robert Chichele, grocer and two-time mayor, asked the clerk Thomas Hoccleve to translate a ballad (Nightingale 1995, 375). Other aldermen in Barton's time owned many different kinds of books (Barron 2016, 60–63). Most significantly perhaps, Barton served in city government alongside Richard Whittington—mercer, three-time mayor, royal creditor, and innovative philanthropist. Among Whittington's many bequests was the Guildhall's "common library" for the instruction of local clergy, built between 1423 and 1425 by his executor, John Carpenter, London's common clerk during Barton's most active years (1417–38) (Barron 1969; 1974; 2016, 66–69). Carpenter himself commissioned Lydgate to write verses for the "Dance of Death" painted at St. Paul's (Sponsler 2014, 75–82; Appleford 2015, 65–97). Although the existence of something like a literary library at Guildhall is disputed (Roberts 2011; Mooney and Stubbs 2013; Warner 2018), Barton certainly worked with clerks who mixed government business with literary production.

Textual patronage later in the fifteenth century also illuminates the making of MS 80. Around the time of Barton's death, the Skinners commissioned a decorated, large format book to display the membership of their Fraternity of Our Lady's Assumption (c. 1440); much later, a similar book was begun for the Fraternity of Corpus Christi (c. 1485) (see chap. 2). A more direct parallel with MS 80 appears in a copy of Lydgate's *Troy Book*, in which members of the Vintners Guild had their arms painted (three barrels of wine, c. 1442; Bodleian Library, Digby MS 232; Lydgate 1906–35). The manuscript is formally quite similar to MS 80 (double columns, column-width illustrations): it might represent the kind of book that MS 80 was meant to become. In the 1470s, the draper Thomas Kippyng commissioned an illustrated copy of Stephen Scrope's translation *Mirroure of the Worlde* and possibly the translation itself (Bodleian Library, MS Bodley 283; Scott 1980). Similarly, William Caxton describes his translation of the French *Somme le Roi* into English in terms similar to the Lovelich-Barton annotation: Caxton states that he has "reduced [the Royal Book] into English at the request and special desire of a singular friend of mine a mercer of London" (Caxton 1485, a.ii verso). And the first English translation of Thomas More's Latin *Utopia* sounds like a business affair: "translated into English by Ralph Robynson citizen and goldsmith of London, at the procurement and earnest request of George Tadlowe citizen and haberdasher of the same city" (Robynson 1551, title page). These translation "requests" echo Barton's "instaunce." They show how commissioned books and commissioned translations were tools of cultural negotiation, particularly among the merchant classes.

The mercantile context implied in the Lovelich-Barton annotation shaped not only the text but the codex. The properties of the paper, for example, are as much a part of the book's social significance as the properties of the text: "Every sheet of paper tells a story" (Bower 2001, 5). The story told through MS 80's pages is one of civic ambition. First, paper is an import commodity, like the most favored furs at the high end of the Skinners' trade. Merchants, particularly grocers and mercers, were both early adopters of paper for record-keeping and champions of expanding the market for their products (Da Rold 2020b, 48–49, 63, 79–87). The paper used for MS 80 was from the more expensive end of the paper market—a large format called "royal," commanding higher prices owing to the difficulty of its manufacture (Da Rold 2020b, 58–90; Gordon and Noel 2017). Skilled commercial artisans folded these large sheets in half (creating two folios or four pages), gathered them into quires of eight sheets, and eventually sewed the quires together into a book. The pattern of watermarks across the sheets provides further evidence of professional production: their consistency points to stacks of paper used in sequence. The book begins with about thirty sheets with a unicorn head followed by about seventy sheets with an "R" topped by a cross (with some mixing of the two stocks in the middle of the book) (Doyle 1961, 99n44; Bernstein 2019). One sheet has a third watermark, balancing scales; perhaps it replaced a damaged sheet (one folio is written in lighter ink, f. 149) or was simply at hand when stocks ran out. These commercial conditions corroborate recent work by Orietta Da Rold showing that paper should be understood as a technology that brings specific connotations and affordances—not as a "cheaper" alternative to vellum (Da Rold 2020b). For MS 80, paper associates a familiar corporate practice (record-keeping) with a new kind of text (verse narrative). For a lengthy text like Lovelich's translation, paper made the book more accessible in every sense—but not cheap in any sense. MS 80's paper format contributes to the patron's aspirations for a status-enhancing book that would bring a new kind of text to a new kind of audience.

The first set of written marks on the paper further substantiate high-quality production. The pages feature a grid marked out in reddish lines to form two columns with generous margins. The columns are filled with "the work of a neat and careful copyist who writes an upright, if somewhat awkward, anglicana [script]" (Meale 1994, 219). To aid in assembling the book, the bottom right corner of the first folio of each sheet is labeled with letters and numbers that define quires of eight sheets each (C.i. through P.ii. survive, with D.iv. missing). In most cases, the back of the last sheet of each quire has a catch phrase that matches the first line of text on the next quire. Starting part way through the book (f. 60v, in the middle of a quire), the top line of each column has decorative ascenders on certain letters, which add a note of elegance to the page. Some of the flourishes have been embellished with patterns, solid ink, and faces. Throughout the book, the scribe left spaces for illustrations, likely following the model of a French book similar to—or the same as—the one that Lovelich used for his translation. Annotations next to several of the spaces describe plans for even greater elegance: two describe scenes related to Arthur's accession to the throne; five others call generically for "pageants"—that is, pictures (Driver 2014, 34). Together, these production marks show a remarkable ambition to produce an English illustrated manuscript on paper, a quite rare format (Meale 2013, 15). MS 80 thus combines the most elevated literary format (illustrated books on vellum) with the relatively new style of large format paper books, innovating within tradition.

Other scribal marks show concern for the experiences of future readers. They make it easy to imagine the book being read aloud, perhaps even at a feast in Skinners' Hall (see chap. 2). While the illustration spaces define large sections of text, marginal paragraph symbols mark subsections, making it easier to find one's place in the lengthy narrative. The scribe further attended to readers by carefully correcting transcription errors—adding letters, words, and entire lines in the margins. Across the last two surviving quires, the middle of most lines is marked with two diagonal slashes—caesurae to guide the rhythm of reading aloud (starting on f. 165v). Other scribal notes point readers to specific themes. Twelve passages are marked by several different styles of note: six lowercase abbreviations of "nota" ("note this," ff. 2v, 29v, 30r, 39v; *Grail*, XIII:420, XXVII:329, XXVIII:115, 369, 465, 515); three capitalized abbreviations of "Nota" (ff. 103v, 105r; *Merlin*, 3959, 4277, 4313); and three descriptive phrases (two formal, one less formal) (ff. 54r, 87r, 135r; *Grail*, XXXIX:205, LVI:215; *Merlin*, 12267). Nicole Eddy has shown in detail how these notes trace the arc of the Arthurian story, focusing on genealogy and the narrative's (fictional) sources (Eddy 2012, 336–61). Even with many caveats as to the notes' source(s) and the possibility that some have been trimmed away, the notes clearly underscore the narrative's "apocalyptic foreshadowing" of Arthur's destruction even as Britain's defining miracles are being established (Eddy 2012, 345; see chap. 1). The descriptive phrases are particularly revealing, as they all address lineage: Nasciens (whose genealogy leads to Lancelot and Galahad, f. 54r), Lancelot (whose genealogy starts with Nasciens, f. 87r), and finally Mordred (the child of incest, blamed for Arthur's downfall, f. 135r). These annotations echo the narrator's insistence on the continuity of lineage from Joseph of Arimathea to the Arthurian era. The book was made, then, to guide readers' engagements with the text and to assist them in untangling the twists and turns of British history.

The making of MS 80 exemplifies the confluence of material and social contexts in book history. The Lovelich-Barton annotation on folio 127r is central to this story. It has had its own uneven path through literary history. The patronage annotation was very important to the eighteenth-century cataloguer James Nasmith, who transcribed it as part of his elevation of Lovelich's authorial reputation (discussed in chap. 4). The nineteenth-century editor Frederick Furnivall, however, was too in thrall to romantic medievalism to care about anything except the grail story; he never mentioned annotations at all (discussed in chap. 5). At the turn of the twentieth century, a different editorial spirit valued annotations as historical evidence. Henry Bradley, editor of the *Oxford English Dictionary*, noticed MS 80's annotation while editing "L" for the dictionary: his query eventually established that the translator was "Lovelich" rather than "Lonelich" (Bradley 1902a, 1902b; Skeat 1902b; Furnivall 1903). The *Merlin* editor Ernst Kock transcribed all the annotations he noticed in the second half of MS 80, including the Lovelich-Barton note (Kock 1904–32, 273). More or less at the same time, however, the influential cataloguer M. R. James excluded annotations from his descriptive model altogether but still took the time to reduce all the interesting marks in MS 80 to "marginal scribbles" (James 1912, 1:xxxii, 164). Despite this discouragement, scholars went on to make the Lovelich-Barton annotation central to new literary histories: Ian Doyle (1961, 98–99) linked MS 80 to the literary collections of John Shirley; Carol Meale (1994, 217) included MS 80 in the broader practice of romance reading among the merchant classes; Nicole Eddy (2012) used annotations to reevaluate the romance genre. Today, most of the information that describes MS 80 on Parker Library on the Web can be traced to the Lovelich-Barton annotation. The inconsistent history of MS 80's patronage annotation indexes the fluctuating value of annotations in general to literary history.

Using Arthurian Narrative

The Lovelich-Barton annotation marks the pivot point between MS 80's makers and its eventual users. Two sets of annotations suggest that some attentive readers were indeed focused on figuring out the twisted lines of British history, just as the makers envisioned. One of those readers, in fact, was the author of the Lovelich-Barton annotation—identified as John Cok (Doyle 1961, 98–99). For five decades, until his death in 1468, Cok served St. Bartholomew's Hospital on the outskirts of London: he became deacon, keeper of rents, and scribe of the hospital's cartulary (which includes an abbreviated English chronicle and two deeds witnessed by Henry Barton) (Kerling 1973, 105, 106; Etherton 2004). In addition to MS 80, Cok annotated a handful of other texts; in each case, he provided apparatus while also expressing personal interests (Doyle 1961, 99; Eddy 2012, 216–72; Horobin 2013). He was connected to London literary circles through John Shirley, who rented a tenement and shops from St. Bartholomew's; Cok became Shirley's executor (Connolly 1998, 164–65). Shirley lavished his scribal attentions on Chaucer and Lydgate, becoming one of the "makers" of their reputations (Lerer 1993, 117–46). Similarly, Cok's annotation on MS 80's folio 127r "makes" Lovelich a commissioned poet: Cok has the kind of information about Lovelich that Shirley had so often about Lydgate. Indeed, Cok may have received the book from Shirley, whose social networks in London overlapped with Barton's (Meale

1994, 217–19; Warren 2008; Veeman 2016). For whatever reason, Cok ended up with close knowledge of MS 80's production and the inclination to read the book carefully.

When Cok opened MS 80, he would have encountered a text resonant with his religious vocation. His annotations, unsurprisingly, track the progress of Christianity from the mythical Mediterranean city Sarras to North Wales (Eddy 2012, 212–369, 473–77; Radulescu 2013, 95–148). Along the way, he marked specific lines for emphasis using a clef symbol, drawings of a pointing finger (manicules), his signature, and short emphatic phrases (e.g., "per totum quod cok"). He also devised periodic plot summaries. The first group of marks engages the adventures of the first Christian converts from Sarras ("Saracens") (ff. 21r–30v, twenty-eight marks). These knights connect the apostle Joseph of Arimathea to King Arthur's reign. Mordreins (formerly Evalach) is the first to dream the Arthurian future: he sees nine streams flowing from the belly of his brother-in-law Nasciens (formerly Seraphe). These streams symbolize the nine generations that culminate with Galahad (*Grail*, XVIII:89–114). Mordreins has this dream while learning about the "limbs of the soul" from a "Good Man." Next to this passage, Cok inserts a manicule that points to the beginning of the theological lesson; a few lines later he summarizes "vii membra anime" (seven limbs of the soul) and signs his name; between the lines, he adds numbers to count the limbs (f. 21r, XXII:284–91). Over the next several pages, Cok's notes track Mordreins's temptation and resistance, pointing to lines of particular drama (e.g., "cok bene"). Some notes also interpret, naming various visitors "dominus" (lord) or "diabolus" (devil): unlike Mordreins, readers do not have to wait in doubt for explanations from the Good Man. Meanwhile, Nasciens's faith is also tested at length. Among the many marvels, Cok notes only the magical properties of the sword aboard the Ship of Faith: he marks two clef symbols and "nota" (ff. 30r–30v; XXVIII:225, 244, 254). The sword, we eventually learn, was made by King Solomon and his wife as a message to their last descendant, Galahad (XXX:273–386). Collectively, these notes point to ancient marvels that will culminate in Arthur's reign and the recovery of the Holy Grail by Galahad.

The second group of Cok's notes tracks the challenges of converting Britain to Christianity (ff. 56v–69r, fifteen marks). Cok signs his name to the date of Joseph's arrival in Britain with the Holy Grail—a Saturday before Easter (f. 56v, XLI:217–18). Skipping past the first conversions and battles, he marks up the events surrounding the imprisonment of Joseph, his son Josephes, and their companions by King Crudelx in North Wales. Two of Cok's detailed Latin summaries correspond to the scribe's paragraph marks (f. 64r, XLV:1, 57). Meanwhile, back in Sarras, Mordreins has a vision in which a crucified Christ commands him to go to Britain to rescue Joseph (XLV:91–117). Mordreins complies, joining with Nasciens to defeat Crudelx and liberate the Christians. During the ensuing celebration, Mordreins—ever flawed in his faith—goes too close to the grail and is blinded. Recognizing his sin, he prays to Christ that he live to greet Nasciens's ninth descendant, "who will do the marvels of the Holy Grail" (XLVI:275)—the fulfillment of his earlier genealogical vision. Mordreins then plays matchmaker to this lineage by arranging the marriage of Nasciens's son Celidoine (XLVI:327–38, 376). Across these events, Cok's marks call attention to Joseph, the grail, and Mordreins. Once again, he attends to connections between early British Christianity and the Arthurian future.

Cok's annotations pick up on the next opening as Mordreins prepares for his new life as a blind hermit, awaiting Galahad. Cok summarizes: "how King Mordreins, when he was made blind, commended the keeping of his wife and his shield to Nasciens his brother" (f. 68v). This summary runs alongside Mordreins's address to his barons; above, Cok brackets off his signature; below, he signs again to point to the lines addressed to Nasciens (XLVI:437–87). This is another passage that ties Joseph's apostolic history to the Arthurian future: the shield that hangs on Nasciens's grave originated in Sarras and will return there with Galahad (XII:255–98; LIV:75–130). At the bottom of the column, Cok marks emphatically the lines that identify Robert de Boron as the translator: on the left Cok points a manicule at a clef next to Robert's name; he brackets the line with another clef on the right, signing his name; underneath, he repeats in English more or less what the text already says in English: "Sir Robert of Boron that turned this out of Latin into French" (f. 68v, XLVI:497; see fig. 6). This note

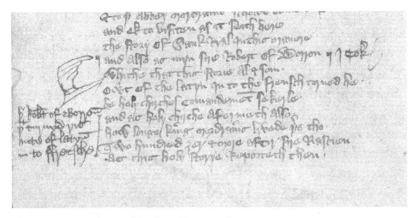

Figure 6   MS 80, folio 68v, with John Cok's annotations.

SOURCE: https://parker.stanford.edu/parker/catalog/xd494bt3141. Courtesy of Parker Library, Corpus Christi College, Cambridge. Licensed under a Creative Commons Attribution-NonCommercial 4.0 International License.

about the text's source pairs with the later annotation identifying Lovelich as the next translator (f. 127r). Together, these annotations secure the text's own lineage as a trustworthy document.

Across the next three columns, Cok's annotations follow the conversion of Camelot. Three Latin summaries describe the evil actions of the Saracen king: he is "false King Agrestes," who "simulated Christianity" and "killed twelve good men, relatives of Joseph of Arimathea" (ff. 68v–69r, XLVII:47–196). Additional notes underscore the horrors of martyrdom: the seeds of Agrestes's destruction are sown by his false conversion (line 75, "Cok per totum"), driven by envy (line 104, indexed with a delicate manicule); the treachery is facilitated by an accomplice named Landoyne (line 117, "bene"; line 147, "bene Cok"); the murderers attack "the sisters as well as the brothers" (line 156, "per totum"); Joseph's kin are beaten to death on a cross (line 187, "Cok per totum"). At the end, Josephes returns to avenge the martyrs, reconvert the Saracens, and found the church of St. Stephens. This story is particularly significant for the Arthurian future, since Camelot is where both the grail and Galahad make their entrance.

Cok's final set of annotations underscores the miracle of conversion through Joseph's misadventures with a Saracen named Mathegrans (ff.

72v–73r, twenty marks). First, Joseph's prayers set the Saracen idols on fire (XLIX:245); Joseph then identifies himself as a Christian (line 277, "declaration of the faith by Joseph") and Cok counterpoints with the Latin note "of the Saracen Mathegrans" (line 299). Next, Joseph raises Mathegrans's brother from the dead—a miracle marked by Cok's signature on the left and his Latin summary on the right (line 323). Cok dwells on the miracle by noting that the Saracen converted "post mortem" (line 330) and marking "bene Cok" where Joseph sees the man rise up (line 337). After this resurrection, the Saracens convert (line 353, two clefs by Cok) and are baptized (line 363, "baptismo sarazenorum," writes Cok). Cok continues to draw out miracles by adding "bene" where Mathegrans looks for a piece of sword lodged in Joseph's thigh (line 373) and "bene miraculum" when Joseph draws out the broken piece, clean and bloodless (line 384). The annotations continue as Joseph christens the Saracens (line 403, "bene Cok") and Mathegrans dies (line 405, "of the death of Mathegrans"). The scene then shifts to Joseph's reunion with his companions in "the forest of Darnauntys"—an English annotation that repeats the text exactly (L:6). Cok's next "per totum" is in the center column—likely marking the exact moment when Joseph meets his fellows (L:10). Cok's final four notations follow Joseph through several more obstacles. He explains to his companions how they can pass over a deep and perilous lake (L:31, "de concilio Iosephi"); they follow his instructions (L:39, a clef). As they pray, a white hart surrounded by four lions passes by, a marvel that prompts Cok to add a Latin summary, itself annotated "per totum" (L:51). Finally, everyone passes across the water except one unrepentant sinner—a final miracle summarized in Latin (L:77). All told, Cok's notes across these two action-packed pages lavish attention on the miracle of Christian faith.

A hundred years or so after Cok, Reformation readers opened MS 80 to find an equally resonant text—but for different reasons. It's unclear how the book passed from Cok to Archbishop Parker, but Parker and his associates had many reasons to value the book once it reached their hands. Joseph of Arimathea, for example, had become a symbol of the ancient autonomy of the English church. When Catholic bishops urged the new Queen Elizabeth to keep faith with Rome, she reportedly rejected them by noting that Joseph was "the first preacher of the word of God within our realms" (December 6, 1559, cited in Carley 2008, 169). Elizabeth revived arguments first used in the fifteenth century to give England an independent voice in ecclesiastical affairs (Lagorio 1971; Carley 1994; Magennis 2015). From this perspective, MS 80 looked like an English-language Acts of the Apostles—in the lineage of John Bale's *Actes of Englysh Votaryes* (1546). There, Bale had already asserted Britain's primacy in Christian history through Joseph: "Britons took the Christian faith at the very spring or first going forth of the Gospel, when the Church was most perfect and had the most strength of the Holy Ghost" (Bale 1546, 14). Elsewhere, Bale described Joseph as one of the earliest British authors, crediting him with several epistles (Bale 1557–59, 1:15–16). Parker himself summarized Joseph's evangelization of Britain in his *De antiquitate Brittanicae ecclesiae* (Parker 1572, 3–5; Knight 2013, 47–51). In this context, an English book with the name "Josephes" on the very first page—and annotations with the same name (ff. 64r–73r)—probably looked quite useful.

MS 80 also responds to Reformation interests in King Arthur. Under Henry VIII (1509–47), Arthur served as precedent for England's rejection of papal authority. The same year of Henry's Act of Supremacy (1534), John Leland published editions of the historians Gildas (d. 570) and Nennius (c. 800), using Arthur to argue for Henry's independent "imperium" (Carley 2011, 152–53). Arthur's historicity became an urgent cause for English Protestantism when the Italian Catholic Polydore Vergil treated Arthur as an outlandish fabrication (Vergil 1534, revised 1555). Leland responded with vigorous defenses (Leland 1544; Carley 1996). In the words of James Carley: "Silence about Arthur the Briton could . . . ultimately be interpreted as part of a campaign of repression on the part of the papacy and Leland's recovery of this hero was, among other things, a vindication of Henry's break with Rome" (Carley 2011, 162). During Elizabeth's reign, John Prise (an associate of Parker's) followed Leland's example in defending Arthur (Prise 1573; Summit 2008, 119–21). And John Dee invoked "That Triumphant BRYTISH ARTHVR"—alongside Joseph of Arimathea—to justify Elizabeth's dominion in North America (Dee 1577, 56; Carley 2011, 163–65). Finally, when Richard Robinson translated Leland's Arthurian defense, he inserted a note of new information from Parker's associate Stephen Batman, purporting to prove that Arthur descended from "the stock of Joseph" (Robinson 1582, B3; Summit 2008, 122). A book about Arthur that begins with Joseph, then, had many reasons to be chosen for Parker's collection.

Once in Parker's hands, MS 80 was annotated, in keeping with Parkerian practices. For these Anglican readers, medieval books brought the authority of ancient history along with the danger of Catholic origins. Parkerian annotations across many manuscripts bear witness to readers' efforts to draw valuable evidence out of somewhat suspect sources (Summit 2008, 113–21). Earlier in the sixteenth century, for example, Bale expressed the wish that, at the Dissolution of the monasteries, "profitable corn had not so unadvisedly and ungoodly perished with the unprofitable chaff"; he even recommended printing antiquities, "lies and all," so that their potential truth would not be lost (Bale 1549, B.v, B.iii.r). In Parker's time, Batman advised: "Much good matter will you find indeed / Though some be ill, do not the rest despise" (cited in Summit 2008, 117). Elsewhere, Batman cautioned against "frantic brains" who too quickly judged old books "papistical" (cited in Horobin and Nafde 2015, 570). Parker's selection of MS 80 for his collection aligns with this broader Reformation approach to medieval sources.

The first sixteenth-century note in MS 80 illustrates well the challenges of using medieval texts for Reformation purposes. The note has been written in a neat italic script on the verso of a recycled vellum flyleaf, perhaps added to protect the paper manuscript when it came to Parker's collection (the other side is covered with sixteenth-century writing concerning the legal affairs of one Elizabeth Chapman). The flyleaf note records a seemingly harsh judgment against the book: "Oh quantos labores insumpserit hic Author in rebus non ita probabilibus" (Oh such great labors this Author expended on things not very probable). Since the book has in fact been carefully protected by the flyleaf itself, this note suggests that the presence of "improbable things" is not in itself a reason to discard a book. Instead, the text will require careful parsing to extract its kernels of truth. By the time MS 80 reached Parker, many people had doubts about Arthur's historicity, Leland's and Prise's defenses notwithstanding. Dee described the difficulties eloquently in 1577: "overbold writers . . . both confounded the truth with their untruths and also have made the truth itself to be doubted of or the less regarded for the abundance of their fables, glosses, untruths, and impossibilities inserted in the true history of King Arthur, his life and acts" (Dee 2004, 53; Carley 2011, 175n92). MS 80 illustrates this "confounding" situation. The flyleaf note reminds readers to proceed with caution, interpretive skills at the ready.

On the first page of text, another sixteenth-century addition also interprets the book—a title in neat italic: "Acta quaedam Arthuri .regis." (with "regis" added less neatly, perhaps much later). The writing style resembles titles in other Parker manuscripts (e.g., CCCC MS 64). The phrase "Certain Acts of [King] Arthur" seems to point to the book's historical value, but it actually confounds truth and fable, just as the flyleaf comment warns. Bale's catalogue of British authors illustrates the problem. On the one hand, *acta* are clearly historical works, such as the *Acta quaedam Thomae Becketi* by Thomas Soulemont (d. 1541) and Bale's own *Acta Romanorum Pontificum* and *Acta coelibum Anglicorum* (Bale 1557–59, 1:713, 703, 704). On the other hand, Bale lists as *Acta Arthuri Regis* a book immediately recognizable as more "fabulous" than historical—Thomas Malory's *Morte Darthur* (Bale 1557–59, 1:628–29). The title *Acta* thus refers to both factual history and fictional romance. Bale's assessment of Malory, moreover, suggests one way that Lovelich might have been read in Parker's circle. Bale describes Malory as a reader of "historias" (stories or histories) who translated Latin and French into English. He praises Malory's preparation and enduring good reputation but also notes that his book is full of "fabulas" (fables or inventions) that should be eradicated in the service of "true history" ("ut ueritas in historia seruetur") (Bale 1557–59, 1:628–29). Relatedly, Bale notes the mixing of truth and fable in a book he calls the *Sanctum Graal* (Bale 1557–59, 2:31). "Certain Acts of Arthur," then, is an ambiguous title for a text that includes both useful history and "improbable things."

The remainder of MS 80's Parkerian annotations show the line-by-line search for Arthurian facts. They build on the previous marks made by Cok and the scribe, clustering in two sections: the transition from the grail story to Merlin's birth and Arthur's accession to the throne. The first

marks follow the (probably) scribal marginal note, "genalagie" (f. 87r). Someone (Parkerian?) added Roman numerals counting the generations, and
someone (else?) made four red underlines: Lancelot's name, that he wed
the daughter of the King of Ireland, and then his name two more times
(ff. 87r-v; LVI:253–59, 283). These underlines may single out Lancelot as
nonhistorical, or they may underscore, literally, his connection to history.
Parker did also collect a manuscript of the French prose *Lancelot*, now part
of CCCC MS 45. That text also attracted Parkerian annotations: one notes
that William Copland printed twenty-one books of King Arthur in English
(likely his edition of Malory, 1557); the other casts aspersions on the *Lancelot*'s "grandes et fictitias historias" (long and fictitious stories, f. 84v). The
negative judgment is hardly surprising, especially given that Henry VIII's
1539 "Declaration of Faith" had proscribed *Launcelot du Lake* as "impure
Filth and vain Fabulosity" (cited in Carley 2008, 156n2). The Parkerian annotations in CCCC MS 45 thus send mixed messages: one shows how to
find more Arthurian narrative; the other suggests that such books are a
waste of time. Similarly, the annotation of Lancelot's genealogy in MS 80
does double duty as warning and confirmation of Arthurian value.

Lancelot's lineage is intertwined with the lineage of the text itself,
which holds Parkerian attention onto the next folio, where "another
branch" of the story is announced, called "Merlin's" by "Master Robert."
These three phrases are underlined and then further emphasized by a
red hash mark in the margin (two horizontal lines crossed by two vertical lines, on a slight slant) (f. 88r; LVI:511–13; similar in CCCC MS 7, f.
106r). Overleaf, "Herry Lovelich" receives the final underlining at the end
of this passage about translation and authorship (f. 88v, LVI:533). These
annotations reinforce Cok's emphasis on Robert de Boron's authority (f.
68v), providing a fuller apparatus for identifying sources—the same kind
of reading applied to books throughout Parker's collection. These annotations make it easier to find sources of ancient British history that could
support contemporary political arguments.

While reading with this heightened focus, the Parkerian annotator
underlined several words and phrases in passing, seemingly for linguistic interest. Still on folio 88v, the new branch of the story begins with a

"parliament" of devils who lament the power they have lost to Christ, whose "ministers" (underlined) continue his work on Earth (f. 88v; *Merlin*, 54; see chap. 2). On the opposite page, three words are underlined: *gynneng*, *lyhtleche*, and the untranslated French phrase "petyt & graunt" (f. 89r, lines 118, 151, 186). Overleaf, the underlining continues: the common word *thussone* ("thus," perhaps in an unusual spelling) and then several words in a passage that describes the custom of stoning adulterers, along with the "judgment" (underlined) for adultery passed on Merlin's mother (f. 89v, lines 234, 240-41, 248). This cluster of underlinings mixes Christian history and linguistic curiosity. Their scattered and inconsistent nature suggests no particular plan. Nonetheless, they register a practice of active reading, confirming that the book was carefully "searched" for various kinds of evidence.

The second series of Parkerian annotations cluster around the episode with the sword in the stone (see chap. 2). The first mark underlines Arthur's name as Merlin assures the dying Uther that his son will reign after him (f. 114r, line 6799). In the confusion after Uther's death, the barons beg Merlin to choose their new lord, their "salvation" (underlined); Merlin replies that he is "not at all" (underlined) worthy but proceeds to describe how the new king will be selected (f. 114r, lines 6845, 6847). The process requires the lords to pray at "Noel" (underlined) for the Lord to give them a king (f. 114r, line 6870). When the sword in the stone appears, the name of the presiding archbishop, "Orbice" (Dubricius), attracts further underlining (114v, line 7019). Finally, several pages later, "Arthur kyng chosen was" (f. 114v, line 7783) (this momentous conclusion is followed by an illustration space with the scribal rubric "coronacō arthu'" [Arthur's coronation]). Still reading attentively, the annotator underlines the word *thussone* again (f. 114v, line 7843). This second underlining of a common word suggests that linguistic notes occur sporadically in conjunction with thematic attention. The spelling *thussone* for "thus" may be unusual for the Parkerian reader, as the only example of this form in the *Middle English Dictionary* comes from Lovelich. All in all, the red underlining shows a reader attentive to certain themes (genealogy, translation, Arthur's election) who also noticed certain words or phrases for possibly unrelated reasons. This method of annotating can be found elsewhere in Parkerian books (Bryan 2016). MS 80's annotations are thus once again typical of Parkerian practice.

Two additional notes in MS 80 could be Parkerian, although they could also have been added earlier or later. On the same page as Cok's Lovelich-Barton annotation, a seemingly sixteenth-century hand has used the illustration space to add the header "why it is callyd bryt"—just above a detailed explanation of how "Britain" is named after the Trojan settler "Brutus" (f. 127r, lines 10175–226). Elsewhere on the same page, in similar style, someone has written "Bredygam forest" next to Merlin's reunion with Arthur in "the forest of Bredygam" (line 10272; see fig. 7). These notes summarize factual information. On this same page, Lovelich expresses similar values when he declares his intent to provide a full account of every Arthurian event if he lives long enough (lines 10245–54; see chap. 1). Whenever these annotations were made, they echo the spirit of the previous Parkerian marks. They are among the last traces left by MS 80's earliest readers. They witness once again a focused effort to sift "profitable corn" from "unprofitable chaff." They draw out "true history" from among the "not very probable things." All these readers—Cok, Parker, and possibly others—use annotation to make the text more reliable and more accessible. As users, they also become makers.

Networking the Manuscript

Since Parker's time, MS 80's annotations have shifted from textual interpretation to cataloguing, editing, and reproduction. These newer marks locate the book in larger networks of books, both within and beyond Parker Library. Whether on the pages of the shelf-book or in the code of the digital book, annotations reflect and create networks. Networking, though, is not unique to modern marking. Folio 127r is once again exemplary. It gives a succinct view of how annotations can turn any page into a network of historical, textual, and social relationships. As marks accumulate over time, they form a "community on the page" (Bryan 1999, 181). For folio 127r as reproduced here, this community stretches from the book's beginning as an idea shared by Lovelich and Barton sometime

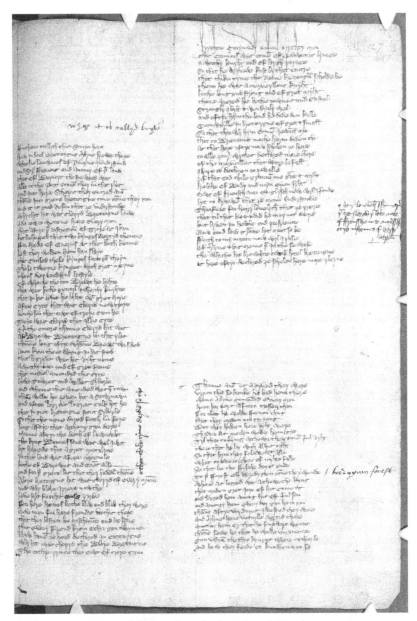

Figure 7 MS 80, folio 127r on Parker Library on the Web 2.0 (2018–21).

SOURCE: https://parker.stanford.edu/parker/catalog/xd494bt3141. Courtesy of Parker Library, Corpus Christi College, Cambridge. Licensed under a Creative Commons Attribution-NonCommercial 4.0 International License.

before 1435 all the way to the photographers and conservators who produced digital images c. 2008. From the book on the shelf to the book on the internet, each mark on and around folio 127r is embedded in larger networks—of paper manufacturers, scribes, books, patrons, readers, editors, catalogers, libraries, platforms, coding standards, and more. The folio 127r marks reproduced here include, more or less in chronological order, a paper watermark, grid lines in faint red pencil, the text, a missing line of text added vertically, the patronage annotation, the summary annotations, a hole chewed by an insect, a modern folio number in pencil, white points holding the page flat for digital photography, and black background from the Mirador viewer on Parker Library on the Web c. 2018 (fig. 7). The web page, moreover, has been rendered by "markup" standards—HTML and TEI. The markup isn't immediately visible but can be exposed with browser tools. It functions like scribal layout marks in a manuscript—structuring how texts and images appear on a page. The long accumulation of marks on and around folio 127r makes it possible to see how makers and users are also networkers—starting on the paper page and continuing on the web page.

The way that medieval and modern marks interact on folio 127r extends throughout MS 80. The very first page features eighteenth-century shelf marks "Sub B.5" and "80" alongside the sixteenth-century title (f. 1r; discussed in chap. 4). By the mid-nineteenth century, folio numbers had been added throughout the manuscript, along with a note about displaced pages—evidence that a modern librarian read the fifteenth-century text: "Two leaves out of place. They belong to the commencement of the MS" (f. 197r; Furnivall 1861, 89). The text's reproduction in printed editions brought more annotations to the manuscript. Chapter numbers from Frederick Furnivall's *History of the Holy Grail* track the end of Nasciens's adventures and the grail's arrival in Britain—also annotated by the scribe and Cok (ff. 53v–59v; *Grail*, XXXIX–XLIII). Around this time, someone noticed that a page had been ripped: next to the repair, a conservator wrote "tear not by F.F." (f. 76r)—that is, I believe, that the editor Frederick Furnivall should not be blamed for the damage. A little farther on, the title of the edition *Merlin* is penciled in the margin where the new "branch" begins—also annotated in Parker's time (f. 88v; Kock 1904–32). In different ways, each of these annotations witnesses the text's passage out of Parker's collection and into modern networks. Through catalogues and editions, Lovelich's translation joined the English literary canon as a romance (see chap. 5). This process has left its marks, inscribing an apparatus that makes the medieval manuscript more like a printed book optimized for scholarly reading. Like earlier annotations, these modern marks make the book more accessible for a particular kind of reader. Librarians and editors are thus also bookmakers who contribute to the meaning of medieval manuscripts.

Just as curators have remade MS 80 as a shelf-book, computer coders have remade MS 80 as a digital book. Parker Library on the Web has created new networks for MS 80—with new annotations. At the same time, coding practices reproduce some of the functions of handwritten annotations from the fifteenth and sixteenth centuries. Parker Library on the Web exists in two major iterations—the custom-built Parker 1.0 (2009–17) and the modular Parker 2.0 (2018–21), both hosted by Stanford University. (Parker 2.1 appeared after this book was completed and is not addressed here.) Both Parker 1.0 and Parker 2.0 derive their manuscript descriptions from the print catalogue by M. R. James (1912), who in turn incorporated parts of the previous catalogue by James Nasmith (1777) (discussed in chap. 4). Parker 1.0 presents a digital edition of James's descriptions, while Parker 2.0 has translated that information into an interoperable cataloguing model that enables search across multiple collections (MODS, Metadata Object Description Schema of the Library of Congress). The metadata schema defines which categories of information are included in the object description and which are not. When a schema changes, some data might be lost while some might need to be created to fill new categories in the schema. On Parker 2.0, some metadata can be traced back to the Nasmith in the eighteenth century. Yet much from the eighteenth century has also been lost: the latest update represents but a fragment of the historical data. The representation of annotations on Parker 1.0 and Parker 2.0 thus exposes how infrastructure remakes books by defining how they can be discovered. Together, Parker 1.0 and Parker 2.0 show how digital platforms can make catalogues more fragmented rather than more complete.

The treatment of MS 80's annotations on Parker 1.0 and 2.0 illustrates their respective relationships with "inherited data" (Fyfe 2016, 569). Parker 1.0 reproduces in full James's description of MS 80's annotations: "Marginal scribbles occur, per totum quod cok, f. 24v and elsewhere: on the later leaves, lists of Latin verbs (alphabetical from A to H) with numbers attached, also notes of a theological character (f. 192r)" (James 1912, 1:164). James ignores Nasmith's transcription of the Lovelich-Barton note on folio 127r; James also says nothing of the sixteenth-century flyleaf comment or title; he lets the vague "elsewhere" stand as a summary of the many folios that bear Cok's "marginal scribbles." James's lack of interest in annotations is no longer a scholarly norm, but it continues to set conditions of access to historical materials. On Parker 1.0, James's brief note appears under the rubric "Additions," with hyperlinks to images of the two folios cited. Initially, "Additions" didn't transfer into Parker 2.0's metadata scheme: there was no indication that MS 80 is a book full of interesting notes on "f. 24v and elsewhere" (as of January 30, 2021, the "Additions" have been restored). The progressive loss of information from Nasmith to James and then (initially) from Parker 1.0 to 2.0 exposes how descriptive standards and metadata schemes set the framework for noticing, maintaining, and distributing historical knowledge.

Parker 1.0 and 2.0 also have distinct relationships with digital annotation. On Parker 1.0, annotation is an editorial principle. The project team used color and text to indicate different sources of information: unmarked text for James, light blue highlighted text marked "Nasmith" for James's predecessor, and beige highlighted text marked "CCCC" for new contributions. Notably, the project team created new titles, much like Parkerian annotators back in the sixteenth century (see chap. 4, fig. 12). Some of the project team's contributions were only accessible to subscribers, including their Summary overview of each manuscript. These short paragraphs function like descriptive annotations appended to the main catalogue entry. For MS 80, most of the 1.0 Summary relates to the Lovelich-Barton annotation on folio 127r: Lovelich was a skinner; John Cok added "notes"; Cok's biography suggests that Parker found the manuscript in London. Although the Summary doesn't identify folio 127r, the content reflects

twentieth-century work in literary history and paleography that does—
cited in Parker 1.0's annotated bibliography (Ackerman 1952a; Doyle 1961;
Meale 1994). Through the 1.0 Summary, folio 127r remains at the center
of MS 80's story, linking together the book's earliest existence as a "request" by Barton and its latest incarnation on a website. Parker 1.0 thus
combines historical annotations with born-digital annotations to present
a new description of MS 80. Like earlier handwritten annotations, these
notes make the book more accessible. The 1.0 Summary, like MS 80's
flyleaf annotation, orients readers who are opening the book for the first
time. The Summary extends some of the functions of manuscript marking
onto a digital platform.

The Parker 1.0 manuscript descriptions are themselves the product of
annotations: "markup" code defines the format, shape, color, and other
functions of text on the web page. And remarkably, the code for each
page includes an annotation about the coder—just like folio 127r in MS
80 includes an annotation about the medieval makers. This text, directed
at human readers, explains how the site was made:

> <div class="msLong_msDescResult">
> The James Catalogue was digitized then marked up following
> the TEI P5 Guidelines. The customized model was provided by
> Giuliano Di Bacco, stored in an ODD file (parkerweb.xml): the
> latter was written by GDB using ROMA vers. 2.x, with manual
> adaptations. The ODD file is used as a source to compile the actual
> schema used to validate the xml: it is advisable to compile it in
> RelaxNG sintax(parkerweb.rnc) through ROMA.</div>

This note preserves information about Giuliano Di Bacco not otherwise
available on the site, much like Cok had information about Lovelich not
otherwise available in the book. Like Lovelich the translator, Di Bacco
the coder "manually customized" the markup model for the digital edition. And just as Cok's note about Barton points to the book's historical
context, this note about Di Bacco contains clues about the coding context
(TEI P5, ODD, XML, ROMA, RelaxNG). Curiously, this annotation contra-
dicts the "About" page on Parker 1.0, which states that the markup model

was the older TEI P4 (the accurate case, according to Whearty 2018, 186; https://tei-c.org/guidelines/p5). The annotation's misdirection is a salient reminder that marginal notes call for just as much interpretation as the main text.

Parker 1.0 is now an archived site on the Stanford Web Archive Portal (SWAP). Although Parker 1.0 is no longer available on the live web, many of its functions can still be accessed in this static form. In this environment, it has acquired more annotations. These notes record the preservation process, akin to some of the curator notes in MS 80 the shelf-book. In the SWAP book, preservation notes are signaled by "<!"—the HTML equivalent of Cok's clef. Each page begins with an annotation that identifies the markup standard:

<!DOCTYPE HTML PUBLIC "-//W3C//DTD HTML 4.01
Transitional//EN" "http://www.w3.org/TR/html4/loose.dtd">

This note, much like the author annotation for Di Bacco, provides clues for digital preservation: the web address "http://www.w3.org" links to the full description of the HTML version used on the page (accessed August 22, 2019). The machine processing instructions that follow are intermittently annotated for human readers:

<!—BEGIN WAYBACK TOOLBAR INSERT—>

<!—
TODO: We should be able to remove js/disclaim-element.js but without it the overlay doesn't show. Probably related to JS code at very bottom of this page.
—>
<!—END WAYBACK TOOLBAR INSERT—>

These notes help human readers distinguish between archiving code (the Wayback Toolbar) and Parker 1.0's own functional code. In the middle, the "TODO" note records an unsolved problem of coding elegance: the page doesn't function properly without an instruction that shouldn't be needed. This coding problem may never be fixed, but the intent "to do" so is now archived, much like a manuscript rubric never meant for posterity.

All in all, the annotations in the code of Parker 1.0 on SWAP document the mechanics of preservation. The annotations interrupt machine processing to address human readers, inserting coders into the long history of bookmakers.

The archived Parker 1.0 preserves not only the Parker website but a trace of the tech medievalism that has shaped concepts of digital preservation since the 1990s. At the end of each archived page, a standard annotation documents each act of access. On SWAP, the note refers again to the web archiving software Wayback:

<!—

FILE ARCHIVED ON 12:28:51 Jan 24, 2017 AND RETRIEVED
FROM THE AN [sic] OPENWAYBACK INSTANCE ON 15:12:16
Aug 22, 2019. JAVASCRIPT APPENDED BY OPENWAYBACK,
COPYRIGHT INTERNET ARCHIVE. ALL OTHER CONTENT
MAY ALSO BE PROTECTED BY COPYRIGHT (17 U.S.C.
SECTION 108(a)(3)).

—>

OpenWayback derives from the software that powers the Wayback Machine at the Internet Archive (https://netpreserve.org; Young 2018). Both versions copy web pages so that they remain at least partly accessible even if the live page disappears for one reason or another. Indeed, many versions of Parker 1.0 have been archived by the Wayback Machine, dating back to the first prototype from 2004. Accessing any archived page produces the same annotation, automatically timestamped. This sample records a recent consultation of one of the earliest public versions of Parker 1.0:

<!—

FILE ARCHIVED ON 23:14:57 Jun 21, 2010 AND RETRIEVED
FROM THE INTERNET ARCHIVE ON 15:48:50 Aug 22, 2019.
JAVASCRIPT APPENDED BY WAYBACK MACHINE,
COPYRIGHT INTERNET ARCHIVE. ALL OTHER CONTENT
MAY ALSO BE PROTECTED BY COPYRIGHT (17 U.S.C.
SECTION 108(a)(3)).

—>

Together, these two samples—one from SWAP and one from the Internet Archive—tell a short story of internet preservation. The Wayback Machine was developed by Brewster Kahle and librarian Peter Lyman to address concerns over the rapid disappearance of digital information as websites aged or their hosts went out of business (Lyman and Kahle 1998). Almost immediately, this encroaching future of cultural loss was dubbed the "digital Dark Ages"—a medieval metaphor used to explain the purpose of the Internet Archive from the time it opened until very recently (Danny Hillis, cited in "About the Archive" 2001–17). The openness of the Internet Archive (anyone can add web pages) is meant to broaden access so that more sites are preserved. Yet both of the Wayback annotations assert copyright with reference to the legal code of the United States. These access notes thus reflect the persistent tension between open and proprietary models of copying: on the internet, the line between sharing and theft dissolves easily (Johns 2010, 474–84). Intellectual property rights have significant ethical and economic value, yet they have been identified since the beginning of the "digital Dark Ages" as barriers to efficient digital preservation of "all other content" (Kuny 1997). The Wayback software performs this barrier even as it promises solutions. The conflict is wonderfully preserved in the persistent error of every OpenWayback retrieval annotation: "the an OpenWayback instance," where the *the* of "the Internet Archive" remains as a fragment. Here, preservation is perfect and wrong at the same time. Similarly, in the framework of tech medievalism, digital civilization can be saved if we avoid medieval error while complying with legal boundaries. Parker 1.0's archive annotations thus encode ongoing social and legal conflicts over the making, using, and networking of digital culture, including digital manuscripts.

Parker 2.0 represents a strategic move toward both openness and sustainability. Rather than using custom coding, it relies on open source components maintained by broad international communities of users and makers. The image viewer, Mirador, is the most obvious example. The International Image Interoperability Framework (IIIF) is another—an open standard that is also a "community of users and developers" committed to the standard (https://iiif.io/community/faq/#what-is-iiif). While these tools do ultimately rely on grants and other institutional investments (Stanford 2020, 208), the results are far more accessible than Parker 1.0's subscription, which was quite expensive and only available to libraries. In the interests of affordable sustainability, Parker 2.0 is part of the larger systems that make up the digital infrastructure of Stanford Libraries (Karampelas 2015). Basic updates to the site are part of regular maintenance across the whole system. Here, "Parker Library" is one collection among many.

These infrastructure changes have altered access to MS 80's annotations. On the one hand, information linked to the Lovelich-Barton annotation on folio 127r becomes the primary framework for understanding the book: the 2.0 Description is the 1.0 Summary, featured directly below the manuscript images as the primary access point for understanding the manuscript. Parker 2.0 thus moves Cok's annotation from the margin to the center of MS 80's description. On the other hand, James's description of MS 80's annotations has disappeared because the 2.0 metadata don't include the 1.0 Additions. James's description is still just a click away—attached as a PDF, as it was on Parker 1.0. But the PDF text is not included in search results: MS 80's annotations are not discoverable through search. Of course, MS 80's annotations are visible to sighted humans who page through the images. But one would have to know to go looking. The translation of Parker 1.0 into 2.0 thus points to the fragility of historical data even when it is carefully migrated. Parker 2.0 is not unique in this regard. All across the internet, digital platforms are getting more uniform—and thus in some cases more distant from the objects they represent, even as they reproduce more images of those objects. Parker 2.0 shows concretely how platforms and coding standards make literary history.

While Parker 2.0 submerged MS 80's annotations, it also produced a new annotation for the digitized manuscript: "Ending imperfectly," linked to the image of folio 200v (see fig. 8). This phrase is not a new contribution from the Parker 2.0 team but rather is inherited from James, who adapted it from Nasmith (Nasmith 1777, 54; James 1912, 1:164). The phrase appears on Parker 2.0 because it was encoded on Parker 1.0 as part of MS 80's table of contents, linked to a specific folio (see chap. 4, fig. 12). All text in this format was translated into "page-level details" on Parker 2.0—called

"Annotations" in the Mirador viewer. Through a succession of transfers, then, a piece of text unrelated to annotations *in* the manuscript became the sole annotation *of* the manuscript in its digital format. Handily enough, the phrase describes well the nature of digital formats: they exist in a perpetual progressive present tense ("ending"). The images and the annotation happen online over and over, never finally or completely ("imperfectly"). On Parker 2.0, this effect is performed in the annotation's own variability: it "pops up" in different places on the screen according to the cursor's placement; there is no end to its variability. The digital annotation of MS 80's folio 200v thus preserves histories of cataloguing back to the eighteenth century even as it reconfigures them as born-digital data.

The Parker 2.0 annotation of folio 200v also performs disparate definitions of the term *annotation*. In this page view, annotations in books, annotations of books, and annotations as books all coexist. In the fifteenth-century book, someone wrote Latin words beginning with *h* in the margin—clearly visible in the digital image. At the same time, "Ending imperfectly" annotates the page image. It describes the book's preservation status, informing readers that the manuscript is incomplete. Finally, in the terminology of IIIF, the page image and the phrase "Ending imperfectly" are themselves "annotations" of the viewing "canvas." In IIIF, "annotations" have "motivations"—comment, description, painting, and so forth (Crane 2017; Sanderson, Ciccarese, and Young 2017). On Parker 2.0, then, a JPEG file representing folio 200v annotates the "canvas" of the Mirador viewer with the "motivation" painting—that is, a coded instruction to cover part of the canvas with the image (metaphorically speaking). In this process, each component is independent but linked. Annotations both produce the page and comment on the page. They produce a new ontology for "the book" as a compilation of relationships.

In the IIIF environment, the relationships between the page images is defined in a file called a "manifest." Here, the image file locations are listed in order so that they can be rendered into a semblance of a book in any IIIF-compliant environment. The manifest functions like a binding, keeping the pages together wherever the book goes (Bolintineanu 2020, 212). In MS 80, however, the page-level detail "Ending imperfectly" isn't (as

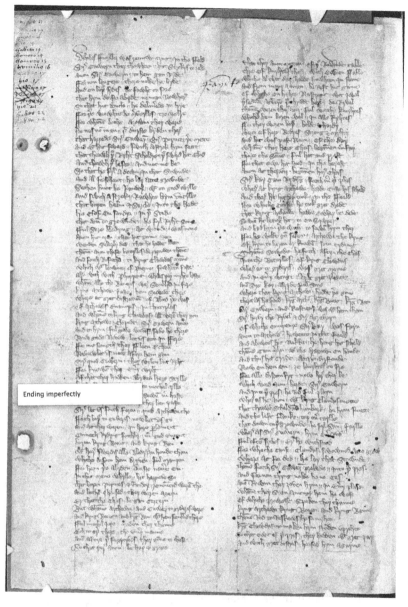

Figure 8 Screen image of MS 80, folio 200v on Parker Library on the Web 2.0, with image viewer Mirador 2.0 (2018–21).

SOURCE: https://parker.stanford.edu/parker/catalog/canvas-7478c6f6063f19d743e91ffe866ae185. Courtesy of Parker Library, Corpus Christi College, Cambridge. Licensed under a Creative Commons Attribution-NonCommercial 4.0 International License.

of this writing) listed in the manifest and thus does not "travel" with the book outside of Parker 2.0. The book's component parts are thus simultaneously linked and separated. In IIIF, then, annotation slips in and out of the book according to the variable arrangements of digital infrastructure. Networked protocols thus turn some of the long-standing functions of manuscript "marking" into new relationships between books and their makers, users, and coders.

The Mirador viewer adds a final form of annotation to MS 80 with its "Information" overlay (see fig. 9). This annotation can be "toggled" from any view of the digital images. It includes the book's title, the legal conditions of access, the colorful Stanford Libraries logo, and links to the catalogue data and the IIIF manifest. The Information annotation thus includes the "whole book"—as a supplement to any part of the book. The relationship between annotations at different scales is thus circular. This circularity is a key characteristic of interoperability: relationships between digital objects can be rendered the same everywhere but they can also be configured differently in different applications. The Information annotation performs the distinct ontology of digital books in IIIF: they exist independently from any given interface, but they don't exist at all without an interface.

The various definitions of *annotation* in digital environments point back to the many ways that annotations in ink and pencil have made, used, and networked the book all along. Parker 2.0 doesn't yet (as of this writing) have user-generated annotations, but they are technically possible. Crowd-sourced transcriptions, for example, might eventually be integrated with Parker Library on the Web (https://fromthepage/theparkerlibrary). Indeed, interactive user contributions are one of the most common associations people have with "annotations" in digital environments. They are integral to the most ambitious goals for digital networking (www.w3.org/TR/annotation-model). In the context of Parker Library, user annotations align with Parker's own reading practices. Yet Parker also expected that future readers would keep their pens and pencils out of his books: his bequest forbade further annotation (Page 1993, 45; CCCC MS 575). Parker thus founded his library with a dual commitment to restriction and openness (the bequest

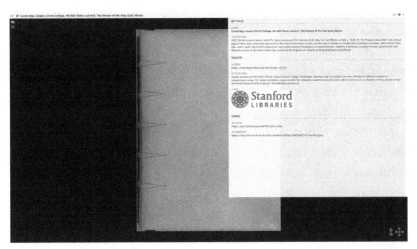

Figure 9   Screen image of MS 80 on Parker Library on the Web 2.0, with Information overlay from Mirador 2.0 (2018–21).

SOURCE: https://parker.stanford.edu/parker/catalog/xd494bt3141. Courtesy of Parker Library, Corpus Christi College, Cambridge. Licensed under a Creative Commons Attribution-NonCommercial 4.0 International License.

specifies that scholars have access to the library and at which hours of the day). This tension remains to some degree even in open digital collections, even when user access can't rip any pages. Networked environments work only when everyone follows the same rules. And the rules are as much a part of the historical record as the content that they deliver.

MS 80 has been collecting all kinds of marks since the fifteenth century. The earliest marks guided the book's production. Later notes witness a variety of interactions with the book: social relationships (Barton and Lovelich), readers' responses (Cok and Parker), self-expression unrelated to the text (signatures and lists), classifications (titles and shelf marks), and conservators' care (repairs and apparatus). With Parker Library on the Web, digital markup echoes all these older handwritten practices while structuring new ways of being for "books." As a function of code— HTML, TEI, IIIF—annotation guides and documents the production of texts and images on digital platforms. Annotations also interpret texts, particularly in TEI. The IIIF standard, meanwhile, adopts the very term *annotation* to classify digital relationships: as an element of infrastructure, annotations are part of the process that renders digital files into a semblance of a manuscript. Annotations are thus integral to format, interface, and platform—beginning with paper and continuing with screens. In books and online, annotations are preservation tools that write the margins into the center of book history. MS 80 is still open to annotation. Even in a vault, marks can still be made. The history of the book is not over.

CHAPTER 4

CATALOGUING LIBRARIES

History, Romance, Website

FINDING A BOOK OFTEN BEGINS with a library catalogue. There, the book's description creates expectations about its text, even before the book is opened. The title alone suggests what might be found inside. Other elements of a catalogue entry add further texture, such as author, date, publisher, subject, language, genre, or format. Even the call number (for printed books) or the shelf mark (for manuscripts) encodes information about the book, such as its subject classification, provenance, or shelf location. Digital books bear similar marks of their production, classification, location, and conditions of access. Even digitized books discovered through general search on Google have been classified and formatted for the algorithms that index them. Outside of libraries, descriptive processes might be less visible than for medieval manuscripts, but they are no less essential in defining books. When we go searching, it's not always obvious how past decisions influence what we might find (Reidsma 2019; Block 2020). Yet every book—on a shelf or online—is marked by the history of its journey into a catalogue or index. These marks shape what can be found and by what pathways. Library catalogues thus prescribe as much as they describe. They project ideas about books even in the absence of the books themselves. Through description and classification, catalogues create, sustain, and sometimes even disrupt literary history.

Library catalogues epitomize the definitions of *book* that I outlined in my introduction: they are devices that store information, formats that structure information, interfaces between users and books, platforms that distribute information, and components of library infrastructure. They can lose their codex format altogether—becoming databases—without losing their basic functions. They, too, have been digitized as part of new library platforms. Whatever the format, catalogues represent books via metadata—information that describes various aspects of the book. Formal metadata schemes define what information can or must be included and in what order. A schema can be as simple as a single field for titles—or as detailed as the hundreds of fields in the US Library of Congress's model for Machine-Readable Cataloguing (MARC), which enables libraries to record and share extensive bibliographic data for many different kinds of objects. Metadata schemes translate what exists (ontology) into what can be known (epistemology): they "must be read as models of knowledge, as discursive instruments that bring the object of their inquiry into being" (Drucker 2009, 11). Conversely, metadata slip back into the objects, framing what users might notice or even what books they might take the time to open: "metadata systems . . . infiltrate the documents themselves and affect the way they are used" (Campbell 2005, 72). In short, metadata make the book.

Parker Library has a particularly rich history of cataloguing. Indeed, the library existed as metadata in a catalogue before it existed as books on shelves. Around 1574, Archbishop Matthew Parker drew up a list of titles that he intended to donate to Corpus Christi College. The list included about four hundred manuscripts and about a thousand printed books (Knight 2013; Echard 2015). At the time, Parker had many more books, which he had collected over decades as a Protestant antiquarian (Crankshaw and Gillespie 2004). The 1574 catalogue thus represents an accumulation of selections over time. It reflects Parker's values and then passes them on to future library users. Parker sought to stabilize the collection by setting management rules, including that two other colleges audit the books annually and impose fines for any losses. To this end, he made three copies of the rules and the booklist (CCCC MS 575; Gonville and Caius College, MS 710/743; Trinity Hall, MS 29). After Parker died in 1575, the books came to Cambridge gradually, perhaps even piecemeal (Dickins 1972). The collection never did exactly match the 1574 list, and the three copies of the list don't quite match each other (Page 1981). These discrepancies underscore how catalogues themselves create collections, even when they don't correspond to any specific set of materials. Given these inconsistencies and the continued growth of the collection after Parker's time, the manuscripts have been catalogued several times since the sixteenth century ("Parker Library" 2019). Each catalogue's "apparatus and architecture" reveal how institutional histories shape metadata (Echard 2015, 98). Together, the Parker manuscript catalogues tell a history of books and texts that begins with Protestant polemics and ends with database debates.

The cataloguing of MS 80 shows in detail how reference tools shape the books they describe and even what books people might imagine reading. MS 80 contains Henry Lovelich's fifteenth-century English translation of a French book about the Holy Grail and King Arthur. Exactly how Lovelich's translation came into Parker's collection is unknown, but he or his associates read it with some care (see chap. 3). In the 1574 Register, the book has a Latin title—*Acta Arthuri Regis*—and is listed with a small group of other books "on the ground under B" (MS 575, 66). These books formed a group in part because they were projected to be too large for the shelves. Shelf placement, as library science has shown, is a "functional system" that carries meaning by revealing classifications by subject, size, and other factors (Bowker and Star 1999, 11). Shelf placement is also a functional system that creates literary history: how many books fit on a shelf before "space management" leads to selections that define a canon (Lerer 2006, 232)? Cataloguers can reflect earlier canonizing decisions, influence later ones, and even make some of their own. Parker brought Lovelich's translation into literary history when he made room for it "on the ground under B" and then surrounded it with other books too big for the shelf.

Later cataloguers gave Lovelich's translation a succession of number classifications that reflect their varied approaches to the library as a knowledge system: 350, 351, 1618, Sub.B.5, LXXX, and 80 (James 1600; Bernard 1697; Stanley 1722; Nasmith 1777; James 1912). The "80" is now canon, written on the book's first folio and stamped in gold on the spine. When the first digital catalogue was published in 2009, the "80" remained, signaling that Parker Library on the Web was a digital edition of its print predecessor and closely tied to the books on the shelves in Cambridge (Parker 1.0, 2009). The result is the kind of "bibliographical ambiguity" (McKitterick 2003, 230) common with photographic copies: a single identifier refers to two quite different objects, one on a library shelf and one elsewhere. The current version of Parker Library on the Web resolves this ambiguity with a new born-digital identifier, xd494bt3141 (Parker 2.0, 2018–21). This identifier points to the digital facsimile of MS 80 but also gathers other digital objects associated with MS 80, such as bibliography and annotations. "MS xd494bt3141" is unique among all digital manuscripts but is also much more than a representation of MS 80. Referential tangles thus persist at the interfaces between machine processing, human reading, and classification. Altogether, the various shelf marks associated with Lovelich's translation track centuries of literary history from the "ground" of 1574 to the "cloud" of 2018.

In this chapter, I investigate how Parker Library catalogues have made and remade the book now called MS 80. Titles, shelf marks, and genre classifications express how Lovelich's translation has been understood in the past and how it might be understood in the future. Across the centuries, cataloguing creates literary value in some stark and surprising ways. In the first phase, Archbishop Parker's selection of Lovelich's translation was motivated by Protestant nationalism. In this context, Joseph of Arimathea and King Arthur had religious and political significance that drew attention to the book's historical value (see also chap. 3). These values persisted throughout the seventeenth century. Toward the end of the eighteenth century, however, the cataloguer James Nasmith reclassified MS 80 as a romance and gave it a new title, setting English literary history on a new course. Nasmith confirmed this disruption with his index entry for "romances." He codified his broader conceptual break with Parker's purposes by establishing a new shelf-marking system, which created "MS 80."

In the twentieth century, M. R. James kept Nasmith's shelf marks but discarded everything else when it came to MS 80, turning it into a relatively unremarkable book. His indexer, Alfred Rogers, even excluded Lovelich's translation from the romance genre. These changes coincide with less enthusiastic assessments of the text by literary historians (discussed in chap. 5). In the digital era, Parker 1.0 largely repeated James's catalogue entry but contextualized it with more recent scholarship and with images of the manuscript that could contradict the catalogue entry. Keyword search, moreover, opened new pathways back into the romance genre via digital indexing. Parker 2.0 has translated all of these features onto a new platform with a new metadata scheme—a process that has again produced new titles, identifiers, and representations of romance. Through new technologies, both websites remobilize Archbishop Parker's founding legacy, framing the collection as an asset worth preserving. The home pages convey "shelving" arrangements just as significant as those that once placed Lovelich's translation "on the ground under B." The websites themselves demonstrate once again how catalogues make books.

History under the Shelf

When Henry VIII began reforming the English church and dissolved the monasteries in 1536, many medieval books were destroyed because of their associations with the Roman papacy. Many reformers continued to view texts from the "Catholic" Middle Ages with suspicion. Discerning antiquarians, however, saw something else: valuable evidence of Britain's ancient Christian history, including connections to apostles that implied that the British church had indeed developed independently from the Roman one. When Matthew Parker became the first Anglican Archbishop of Canterbury in 1559, he brought this spirit to the highest levels of church and state. Under the direction of Queen Elizabeth, he bolstered national arguments for religious independence in part by broadening his efforts to collect medieval books. Queen Elizabeth made the search for antiquities a matter of national policy in 1568 when she instructed any "private persons" holding documents of public interest to share them with Parker so that "the antiquity of the state of these countries may be restored to the knowledge of the world" (CCCC MS 114a, p. 49). Medieval books thus became a matter of imperial sovereignty. Parker obviously didn't keep everything he read, but he did amass a large personal collection that represented a "Protestantized antiquity" (Robinson 1998, 1062). The most valuable books made the Anglican Church look like a return to ancient ways; such books also supported the idea that the English monarchy owed no allegiance to Rome (McKisack 1971, 26–49; Page 1993, 43–61; Summit 2008, 101–35). In this context, Lovelich's translation offered a valuable account of both ancient British Christianity and prestigious Arthurian history (see chap. 3).

The larger purposes of Parker's collection are reflected in the title that he or someone in his circle gave Lovelich's translation. In Parker's 1574 Register, the book is listed as *Acta Arthuri Regis* (CCCC MS 575, 66). This title focuses on Arthur, even though he isn't mentioned until folio 62r and not born until folio 112v. The title thus associates the book with other historical accounts of Arthur in Parker's collection (MSS 21, 45, 50, 174, 182, 281, 292, 311, 354, 363, 374, 414). One of Parker's printed books also intersects with the *Acta*—John Hardyng's chronicle printed in 1543 (CCCC 575, 100; Hardyng 1543). Extracts from Merlin's prophecies, too, are scattered throughout the collection (MSS 6, 175, 313, 405, 476). And near the *Acta* was a book with a full page frontispiece depicting Merlin as he explains the meaning of two quarreling dragons—a scene also recounted in the *Acta Arthuri Regis* (MS 476, f. 2v; MS 80, f. 100r; *Merlin*, lines 2925–3022). The book of "King Arthur's Acts" thus serves as one of many volumes that supported Parker's project to bring British history to bear on Elizabethan and Anglican problems.

The location of the *Acta Arthuri Regis* ratifies the title's gesture toward history. In the 1574 Register, most of the medieval manuscripts are grouped by letters, with many of the largest ones classified as "on the ground" under shelves B, C, and D (Dickins 1972, 28–29; Page 1993, 1–19). The *Acta* book was listed "under B" (see fig. 10). There, it kept company with a number of mostly historical books: John of Tynemouth's *Historia aurea* (MSS 5, 6), chronicles by Thomas Walsingham (MS 7), Vincent of Beauvais's massive *Speculum historiale* (MSS 8, 13, 14), a collection of Old English saints' lives (MS 9), an account of the recovery of Mary Tudor's dowry (MS 132), and a now unidentified copy of the Gospels (James 1912, 1:xliii). In fact, most of the twenty-six books on the ground under B, C, and D were either histories or Bibles. It is worth noting that John of Tynemouth's *Historia aurea* includes both Joseph and Merlin (MS 5, f. 160v–61v; MS 6, f. 145r) and that Vincent of Beauvais's *Speculum historiale* describes a grail book written by a British hermit (MS 14, f. 230r)—described, in turn, by John Bale in his catalogue of British writers (Bale 1557–59, 2:31). The *Acta* book looks very much like an English translation of this *Sanctum Graal* that Vincent says is hard to find ("nec facile") and that Bale claims to have seen. Whether

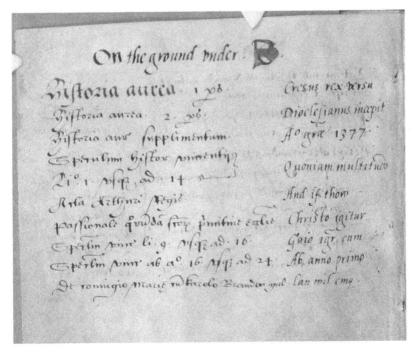

Figure 10 List of books "on the ground under B." Cambridge, Corpus Christi College, MS 575, p. 66.

SOURCE: https://parker.stanford.edu/parker/catalog/ww741yn5061. Courtesy of Parker Library, Corpus Christi College, Cambridge. Licensed under a Creative Commons Attribution-NonCommercial 4.0 International License.

by Bale's influence or some other means, Parker determined that the *Acta* book was worth saving. Once placed "on the ground under B," Lovelich's translation looked like an English source of national history, foregrounding both Arthur and Britain's first apostle, Joseph of Arimathea.

The utility of Parker's collection for Protestant nationalism is confirmed in the printed catalogue by Thomas James (1572–1629). James produced a "union catalogue" of medieval manuscripts in Oxford and Cambridge libraries so that Protestant editors could correct "false" Catholic editions with "true" English sources (Clement 1987, 1991; Summit 2008, 221–33). The catalogue thus opens with accusations of the papacy's "false and fabulous corruption" (James 1600, n.p.). James later declared the catalogue "to the benefit of most *Protestant* writers, and [even] some *Papists*," wondering why it hadn't been more stringently condemned on the papal index of forbidden books (James 1625, 26n; Clement 1987, 18). The title of James's 1611 treatise summarizes his outlook: *A Treatise of the Corruption of Scripture, Councels, and Fathers, by the Prelats, Pastors, and Pillars of the Church of Rome, for Maintenance of Popery and Irreligion*. There, he lays out methods of editing designed to cure the "diseases of books" from "popish corruptions" (James 1611, part V). Although he didn't achieve his grandest editorial ambitions, he spent his life pursuing "purified" patristic texts through English manuscripts.

James's catalogue integrates Lovelich's translation into this Anglican framework by giving it a catalogue number. The catalogue includes twenty-three libraries and 2,823 codices, numbered consecutively for each library rather than according to existing shelf marks (Clement 1987, 12). This uniformity erases the vagaries of local histories in favor of a larger systemic coherence created by the catalogue itself. For Parker's library, the number sequence reflects James's progress through the library, revealing that c. 1600 the manuscripts were roughly grouped in the order of the 1574 Register (James 1912, 1:xliv–xlvii; Clement 1987, 5–11). So the books formerly "on the ground" under B, C, and D form a more or less continuous series from 346 to 370. Lovelich's translation thus becomes MS 350, "*Acta Arthuri Regis*, metro Anglico" (Acts of King Arthur, in English verse) (James 1600, 1:94). The book still keeps company with history books but is now notable for its language and form, making it an unmistakably national source.

The first printed catalogue devoted solely to Parker's manuscripts continued the emphasis on Protestant polemics. It was prepared by William Stanley (1647–1731), then Master of Corpus Christi College (1693–98) (Budny 1997, li). Stanley was a staunch proponent of Anglican rectitude who published (anonymously) several sermons and treatises that combined doctrine with practical guidance. The extended title of his first treatise sums up the tenor of his views: "A discourse concerning the devotions of the Church of Rome, especially, as compared with those of the Church of England in which it is shewn, that whatever the *Romanists* pretend, there is not so true devotion among them, nor such rational provision for it, nor encouragement to it, as in the Church established by law among us" (Stanley 1685). He applied these principles to a guide of practical advice for the "Church of England-man" (Stanley 1688). In his library catalogue, he emphasized an unbroken Reformation pedigree by featuring Parker's name and title in large letters and reusing text from Thomas James (Stanley 1722). Stanley's catalogue thus represents a "printed update" of the 1574 Register.

Stanley revives Parker's own vision for the collection by using the letters in the 1574 Register as shelf marks. To identify each book individually, he adds numbers. Most of the manuscripts have been annotated with these shelf marks on a flyleaf or first folio: these eighteenth-century notes inscribe Parker's sixteenth-century groupings. In Stanley's hands, Lovelich's translation is put back in its place "under B" as "Sub B, V" (Stanley 1722, 64). In the catalogue entry, Stanley also prints the full title now inscribed on folio 1r (rather than the shorter one written in the 1574 Register and reproduced in James): "Acta quædam Arthuri Regis, or the History of King *Arthur* in old *English* Verse." By adding a translation, Stanley underscores the book's national value, with italics for *Arthur* and *English*. And thanks to his index, users can find more books with similar texts: "Arturus Rex" and "Merlinus" each reference several other manuscripts (Stanley 1722, n.p.). These pathways into Arthurian history, combined with Parker's many chronicles, show that the *Acta* remained valuable history into the early eighteenth century.

Understanding the *Acta* as history does take some effort, even for committed Anglican antiquarians. The fact that James and Stanley both specify meter or verse suggests that the book might lean more toward poetry. And by their time, plenty of doubt had been cast on Arthur's historicity. Annotations from Parker's time also point to some of these difficulties, such as a flyleaf comment that warns against the "not very probable things" readers might find in the book (see chap. 3). But this is the very kind of textual challenge for which Reformist antiquarians trained. They leveraged the antiquity of the books themselves to validate any evidence they might find that could support their religious and political goals. In these interpretive practices, ambiguity was friend, not foe. Indeed, even the title *Acta* could encompass fiction as well as fact (as I show in chap. 3). The early cataloguing of Lovelich's translation thus illustrates the complex ways in which the very idea of history emerges from acts of preservation and classification.

Romance in the Index

The passage from history to romance for Lovelich's translation took place suddenly and decisively in the catalogue by James Nasmith, published in 1777. History (as factual events) and romance (as imaginative invention) had been intertwined since the very beginning of Arthurian narrative with Geoffrey of Monmouth's *History of the Kings of Britain*. In the eighteenth century, new approaches to literary history separated romance from history once and for all. Nasmith's catalogue reflects some of this very latest thinking about the role of the romance genre in English national culture (Hurd 1762; Warton 1762; Percy 1765). He would in turn influence literary histories in the 1780s and beyond (discussed in chap. 5). Indeed, Nasmith's classification of Lovelich's translation reverberates all the way through the very latest metadata on Parker Library on the Web. The genre survives as a searchable, indexed category despite the fact that Nasmith's successor, M. R. James, discarded Nasmith's entire entry for MS 80. Through the mechanics of indexing, the word *romance* alone has sufficed to forge meaningful connections from catalogue to catalogue, platform to platform. The genre persists even as its definition fluctuates and remains contested. MS 80's cataloguing thus exposes how classifications write literary history.

Nasmith's catalogue upended the founding logic of Parker's collection. As a fellow at Corpus Christi College (1765–76), he spent five years preparing new manuscript descriptions (McKitterick 1986, 344–48). He departed from the partisan example set by Parker and followed by Thomas James and Stanley. Instead, he presents his catalogue as an antidote to Protestant myopias. He works in the spirit of Edward Bernard—an astronomer who edited Thomas James's catalogue into an even larger catalogue covering libraries throughout England and Ireland (1697). In this massive work, Bernard sought to rationalize idiosyncratic local systems into a single coherent representation of historical knowledge. Tellingly, Nasmith cross-references Bernard's catalogue numbers, not Stanley's or James's. In a similar spirit, Nasmith dedicates his catalogue to the library's knowledge keepers—the Master and Fellows of Corpus Christi College. He presents his catalogue to them as a corrective to Stanley, who omitted more than a hundred manuscripts and lacked "diligence." Nasmith, for his part, promises a detailed and consistent description of every manuscript (1777, n.p.). Most dramatically, Nasmith assigned new shelf marks to every manuscript—a continuous series roughly in order of folio size from I to CCCCLXXXII (482). This system discarded Parker's groupings, leading ultimately to the reshelving of all the books (James 1912, 1:xv). Nasmith's catalogue thus wholly redefined the collection.

Nasmith's renumbering turned Lovelich's translation into "MS 80." This numbering separated the book from the historical volumes that Parker had grouped "on the ground under B." Most of those books were larger and so became a continuous series in the single digits (MSS 5, 6, 7, 8, 9, followed by 13, 14). That is, they are among the largest books in the whole collection. In fact, the ten largest books were all formerly on the ground under B, C, or D: two Bibles (2, 3, 4), four history books (5, 6, 7, 8), and three volumes of church materials (1, 9, 10). The next ten include six from under B, C, or D. By exact measure, Lovelich's translation should have become 25 (according to the "Browse by Size" pages on Parker 1.0, 2017). Obviously Nasmith's system wasn't exact, and some books may now have different dimensions, but the breakup of the "Sub B" group is notable (comparison tables in James 1912, 1:liii). Nasmith's whole undertaking displaces the collection's founding logic, giving material form to Nasmith's divestment from the polemics that were so important for Parker, James, and Stanley. The books on the shelves are still the ones selected by Parker, but new meanings have been projected onto them by the cataloguing system.

Beyond the new shelf mark, Nasmith's entry for MS 80 redirects the genre of Lovelich's translation. He begins with a new title: *The Romance of the St. Grayl*. With this reclassification, Nasmith breaks with history in favor of literature. He recognizes that this is an unusual decision for a cataloguer: "It is with diffidence that I have ventured to affix to this volume a title so different to that which it has borne in former catalogues; especially as I must acknowledge that the excessive length of this poem, which consists of not less than forty thousand lines, deterred me from attempting the perusal of it" (Nasmith 1777, 54). Nasmith, however, was diligent indeed and did read quite a lot of the *Romance of the St. Grayl*. He notes that the book is "imperfect" (incomplete) at beginning and end, he prints lengthy extracts, and he accurately summarizes the plot change at the middle of the book. In commenting on the *Acta* title, he deems it to have been written by Parker's secretary, John Joscelyn: "How little pains this learned man gave himself to discover the true title of this poem, and in what contempt he held these first efforts of the British muse is evident from the following sentence transcribed by him on a blank leaf at the beginning of this volume, 'Oh quantos labores insumpserit hic autor in rebus non ita probabilibus' [Oh such great labors this Author expended on things not very probable]" (Nasmith 1777, 54). Nasmith's criticism of this annotation parallels his criticisms of James and Stanley: he accuses his predecessors of errors and diffidence. He understands the flyleaf comment as a misguided effort to dissuade readers. Nasmith, though, was undeterred. In the process, he discovered a new romance for the English canon.

Nasmith bolsters his argument for the new title with a popular reference work, *The English Historical Library*, by William Nicolson (1655–1727). Nasmith believes that Lovelich's source was probably the "French legend" mentioned by Nicolson (Nasmith 1777, 54; Nicolson 1714, 91).

Notwithstanding Nicolson's status as an Anglican bishop, he shared Nasmith's skepticism of Protestant antiquarians. His "French legend" passage is part of a chapter entitled "Of the Writers of the Affairs of the British Church"—nearly all of whom Nicolson finds untrustworthy. He is particularly skeptical of Bale, who claimed that Joseph of Arimathea wrote epistles to British churches (Bale 1557–59, 1:15–16; Nicolson 1714, 90). Nicolson refers sarcastically to "trusty John Pits" for further information about these epistles: "I can hear of no more ancient Treatise relating to the Ecclesiastical State of Old *Britain*, save only the *Sanctum Graal*" (Nicolson 1714, 91)—which Nicolson hardly considers an ecclesiastical treatise. Pits was an English Catholic who spent most of his career in France (1560–1616). Pits actually sourced his grail comment from Bale, who cited the encyclopedia by Vincent of Beauvais (d. c. 1260), who quoted verbatim from a chronicle by Helinand de Froidmont (d. c. 1230) (Pits 1619, 122; Bale 1557–59, 2:31; Vincent de Beauvais 1591, 327v; Helinand de Froidmont 1855, cols. 814–15). Nicolson summarizes from Vincent of Beauvais and then prints the entry for "Graal" from yet another catalogue, Pierre Borel's *Trésor de recherches* (1655, 242–43). Centuries of cataloguing thus converge in Nasmith's entry for the *Romance of the St. Grayl*—thirteenth-century encyclopedias indexed by Leland and Bale in the sixteenth century, revised by Pits, expanded by Borel, and compared by Nicolson. This thread of references shows precisely how cataloguing defines systems of knowledge. Through Nicolson, Nasmith brought the grail out of history and into romance.

To substantiate MS 80's connection to the "French legend," Nasmith turns to the English text. He prints several lengthy passages that answer key cataloguing questions. The first passage relates to the classification of the grail: is it a vessel touched by Christ or the blood of Christ held in a vessel? MS 80 "proves" that it can be either or both, "holy vessel" and "royal blood" (MS 80, f. 42r; *Grail*, XXXIV:1–3). The other passages that Nasmith prints are also concerned with a classification question: who is responsible for this text? Possibilities include God, a hermit, a translator named Robert, a scribe named Blaise, the unclassifiable Merlin, and Lovelich (see chap. 1). The extracts in Nasmith's catalogue help answer this question by describing the translation process (MS 80, ff. 88r–v, 95r;

Grail, LVI:509–40; *Merlin*, 1643–76). These same passages were previously annotated in Parker's time, when identifying sources was also a primary concern (see chap. 3). Nasmith thus singles out the same passages as Parker but for different purposes: where Parker sought reliable historical sources, Nasmith finds the origins of romance. Nasmith's final proof of the "French legend" source is provided by the annotation that says that Lovelich translated at the request of Henry Barton—duly transcribed at the end of the catalogue entry (MS 80, f. 127r). Here, "Henry Lonelich, Skynner" appears in print for the first time—the romance writer who channeled the "British muse." With this extended entry (the longest for a single item in the whole catalogue), Nasmith set English literary history on a new path.

Nasmith uses the catalogue's index to establish romance as a genre classification. Alongside MS 80, Nasmith lists seven other texts, all in French. First, he brings in the French prose *Lancelot* (MS 45). Next, he lists five of the six texts from MS 50: Wace's *Romanz de Brute*; a "romanz" of a knight, a lady, and a clerk; *Amis et Amilun*; "lestorie" of four sisters; and the *Romanz de Gui de Warwyc* (Nasmith 1777, 32–33). Finally, he adds MS 91, another case where his "diligent" reading overturns Stanley and leads to a new title, *La Romance de Louis de Gaures* [Gavre] (Nasmith 1777, 61). Nasmith's approach to these texts shows his particular interest in literature, also evident in his unpublished catalogue for Cambridge University Library (McKitterick 1986, 347). Through the index, Nasmith defines a corpus of romances within Parker's collection. His catalogue had immediate impact on the modern reception of medieval romance. It inspired one of the first editions of the "French legend" tied to MS 80 (Michel 1841, v–vi, n25). And the new title, *Romance of the St. Grayl*, led to the edition of MS 80 itself (Furnivall 1861; see chap. 5). Indeed, the title alone gave MS 80 a reputation as one of the "most remarkable" manuscripts held by Corpus Christi College (Stokes 1898, 192–93). Nasmith's catalogue thus influenced literary history and the nationalist English canon throughout the eighteenth and nineteenth centuries.

Nasmith's catalogue remained in place for more than a hundred years. It still seemed perfectly adequate to the Fellows of Corpus Christi College in the early 1900s. The visionary cataloguer M. R. James, however, had other ideas. As fellow and provost of King's College, Cambridge, James set out to modernize as many manuscript catalogues as he could, implementing new descriptive standards drawn from print bibliography (Hanna 2017). His influence can still be felt across nearly every manuscript library in Cambridge and beyond. Nonetheless, when he proposed a new catalogue for Parker Library, the Fellows hesitated to consign Nasmith to the "dim abode of dead catalogues" and so agreed on condition that James incorporate as much of Nasmith as he deemed "worthy of preservation" (James 1912, 1:xxxi). In this stipulation, the Fellows, perhaps surprisingly, recognized the risks of innovation when it comes to what is now called metadata curation. They understood that new reference tools tend to replace their predecessors—with the potential loss of valuable historical data. They thus imposed a compromise meant to safeguard Nasmith's most significant contributions and to make James's catalogue a complete repository of accumulated knowledge. In the end, however, James's catalogue fragmented manuscript data in ways that have had long-term repercussions on the digital representation of Parker Library.

For MS 80, James determined that Nasmith's entry contained nothing "worthy of preservation." Overall, the entry obscures the literary status that Nasmith promoted. Even though on the whole James kept about half of Nasmith's material and reprinted his preface (James 1912, 1:xxxi, lxix–lxxi), James's goal was to be "the fashioner of a fresh key to one of the richest storehouses of ancient learning in the country" (1912, 1:xxxii). And so, like his predecessors, he imprinted his own values on the manuscript descriptions. He highlighted decorations, for example, but deleted almost everything Nasmith had to say about annotations. While the catalogue can surely "guide [specialists] to some discoveries [and] stimulate curiosity in some beginners" (James 1912, 1:vi), it also guides them in particular directions. For MS 80, the results might well guide both specialists and beginners away from the book (see fig. 11). James removes all mention of "romance," for example, using instead the titles of printed editions (Furnivall 1861, 1863, 1874–78; Kock 1904). He obscures Lovelich's identity as author by printing his name as "Louelich"—a form never previously used in catalogues, editions, or scholarship (James 1912, 1:164). This choice is particularly pointed since "Lovelich" had recently been in the philological news (Bradley 1902a; Skeat 1902a, 1902b; Furnivall 1903; Kock 1904). In lieu of Nasmith's "one continuous narrative" (1777, 54), James presents MS 80 as a book containing two separate narratives, "The Graal" and "Merlin," which prioritizes printed editions over the manuscript and obscures the design of the book. Indeed, James says nothing of the layout for illustrations even though he describes in detail an equally incomplete manuscript of Geoffrey Chaucer's *Troilus and Criseyde*, to which Nasmith gave only a sentence (MS 61; Nasmith 1777, 40; James 1912, 1:126–27). Finally, in place of the two quite intriguing annotations transcribed by Nasmith, James characterizes all the notes as "marginal scribbles," with just a few comments about the ones least related to the text ("lists of Latin verbs," "notes of a theological character"). In discarding the annotations that Nasmith used to make Lovelich the author of a worthy romance, James reflects new standards for poetry that had turned MS 80 into a "bad romance" (as shown in chap. 5) In the end, James turned a book that Nasmith found quite interesting into one that is difficult to notice.

The catalogue's index enshrines an even more pointed dismissal of MS 80 from the romance genre. The index was compiled from James's text by Alfred Rogers of Cambridge University Library (James 1912, 1:v). Rogers indexed twenty-three topical categories, including several literary genres: chronicles, poems, stories, verses . . . and romances (Rogers 1912, 497). The entry for Romances, however, wasn't copied from Nasmith and does not include MS 80 (Rogers 1912, 541). Rogers's romances overlap with Nasmith's for the prose *Lancelot* (MS 45) and the collection of French verse texts (MS 50). Meanwhile, the *Romance de Louis de Gaures* (MS 91) has also been declassified, perhaps because James didn't include the word *romance* in his title or description. Instead, MS 91 and MS 80 are both indexed only by their authors, titles, and editors (Rogers 1912, 519, 527, 528, 530, 532, 548). As a result, MS 80 is represented in such a way as to be hardly recognizable: Lovelich is the author of the *Grail* only; the *Merlin* is associated only with Merlin's prophecies (MS 405); there is no heading "Arthur, King." MS 80 thus has many entries but no genre. It can only be discovered by those who already know how to look. Rogers's indexing strategies erase

80. Louelich. The Graal.   { Sub. B. 5
          Merlin.   { T. James 350

Paper, 15⅜ × 11, ff. 200, double columns of 65, 69, 74 etc. lines. Cent. xv, in a current hand.
Vellum guards from a MS. of cent. xii with Lessons from 1 Reg.
Collation : A gone B¹⁶ (wants 1–9 : 10, 11 are now ff. 197, 198 : 12–16 in situ) C¹⁶ D¹⁶ (wants 4) E¹⁶–O¹⁶ [B 10, 11] P (1 and 2 left).

Contents :

1. The History of the Saint Graal by Henry Louelich, beginning
   imperfectly (what is now f. 197 contains the beginning of
   what is left : it was originally f. 10) ending f. 88 *b.*
   Ed. Furnivall, Roxburghe Club 1861–3, and E. E. T. S. Extra
   series (1874 etc.)
2. Merlin .   .   .   .   f. 88 *b*
   Ending imperfectly 200 *b.*
   Ed. E. A. Kock. E. E. T. S. Extra series (1904).

Marginal scribbles occur, per totum quod cok, 24 *b* and elsewhere : on the later leaves, lists of Latin verbs (alphabetical from A to H) with numbers attached, also notes of theological character (192 *a*).

Figure 11 Description of MS 80 in M. R. James, *A Descriptive Catalogue of the Manuscripts in the Library of Corpus Christi College, Cambridge* (Cambridge: Cambridge University Press, 1912), 1:164.

the literary history that Nasmith wrote into his own index. Rogers's index reveals, already in a print format, the powers and perils of keyword search.

Meanwhile, Rogers classified some new texts as romances, illustrating further how catalogues shape literary history. In addition to the prose *Lancelot* and the French verse texts (MSS 45, 50), Rogers lists four other texts under "Romances": the "Story of Alexander" (MS 450, item 13), "Barlaam et Josaphat" (MS 66, item 15), "Story of Charlemagne and a Fairy" (MS 181, item 6), and "Fragment, *cover*" (MS 494). This last presents the clearest case for romance, based on James's description: "The covers are lined with portions of 2 leaves of a xivth cent. MS. in double columns in French prose, perhaps from a romance. The name Galelzout occurs several times" (James 1912, 2:446). This fragment is part of the same French prose corpus as the prose *Lancelot* (MS 45), although it now lines the cover of a book given to the library after Parker's time. The other items are all in Latin prose, none described as romances by James or Nasmith. "Barlaam et Josaphat" is a substantial work of nearly fifty folios (MS 66A, ff. 139r–208r), but the

Alexander and Charlemagne "romances" are no more than paragraphs (MS 181, pp. 276–77; MS 450, f. 50r). By giving them titles, James brought them to light; Rogers in turn classified them as romances. For whatever reason, Rogers found fantastical Latin fragments more obviously "romance" than either the *Grail* or *Merlin*. And a barely readable fragment became a more visible romance than Lovelich's translation. As a result, experienced re-searchers and "curious beginners" alike would find no English romances in Rogers's index. This guidance might then define what texts could be imagined as part of English literary history.

A hundred years later, notions of literary value had changed substan-tially, along with cataloguing methods and technology. In the late 1990s, curators at Parker Library began exploring the idea of photographing the manuscripts and publishing images on the internet. The public proposal for Parker Library on the Web c. 2000 included a plan for new manuscript descriptions to accompany a comprehensive online resource. This plan, however, proved too ambitious. In the end, the descriptions published in 2009 can best be described as digital editions of James's entries. The encoding process, though, was hardly a straightforward task (Paul 2018; Nigel Morgan, CCCA, Box 5). To make some of their editorial decisions evident, the project team annotated text that James had reused with a light blue "Nasmith" and their own contributions with a beige "CCCC." Text deleted from Nasmith by James, or from James by the Parker project team, however, can only be identified through detailed comparisons across all three catalogues (Echard 2015, 104–5). Parker 1.0 was thus a new catalogue that mixed inherited data with new information. Access to some of the most valuable information, moreover, required a hefty fee: the project team's bibliography, notes, summaries, and high-resolution images were restricted to subscribing libraries. Search functions, too, were limited to subscribers. Parker 1.0 thus created two different literary histories: free access represented scholarship c. 1900 while subscription access repre-sented scholarship c. 2000. In this time lag, MS 80 was either an obscure book with unreadable scribbles or a well-connected book with an intrigu-ing backstory. These infrastructure arrangements told two very different histories of literature in general and of romance in particular.

On the subscription version of Parker 1.0, MS 80 became a very different book from the one that James projected (see fig. 12). The project team's integration of twentieth-century scholarship revived some of Nasmith's enthusiasm, as well as some of his catalogue data. As a result, MS 80 became once again an interesting romance and, even more, an integral part of fifteenth-century literary activity around London (see chap. 2). For example, Lovelich appeared as a recognizable author—with a full name and full edition titles. The formatting on Parker 1.0 also elevated MS 80's annotations in the ordering of information. Meanwhile, red hyperlinks connected directly to images of the folios, where users could see the annotations for themselves and begin paging through the book. Finally, the Summary of scholarship since James highlighted information related to the author annotation transcribed by Nasmith: Lovelich was a skinner; many marginal notes were written by John Cok, "a priest at the Augustinian hospital of St. Bartholomew at Smithfield"; therefore, Parker probably found the book in London. These "new" facts are documented in the annotated bibliography (Ackerman 1952a; Doyle 1961; Meale 1994). Through this combination of framing and formatting, Parker 1.0 made Lovelich an author worth reading and MS 80 a book worth opening.

More broadly, digital indexing on the subscription version of Parker 1.0 dramatically changed the picture of the romance genre. Results were not limited to James's judgments or word choices but extended to the bibliography titles and to the Comments and Summaries written by the project team. The Summaries distill a manuscript's context and significance, as understood by their authors (Suzanne Paul, Nigel Morgan, Neil Coates, Rebecca Rushforth, and Elizabeth Boyle). They were, however, somewhat of an "afterthought" and written without a controlled vocabulary (Paul 2018); at least one of their authors has judged at least one of her Summaries "flawed" (Boyle 2020, 154). Nonetheless, the 1.0 Summaries include much valuable information and are now a substantial corpus of searchable text. Idiosyncratic word choices still determine the search results, but the context for romance expands in meaningful ways. Machine indexing can only return items that contain the same character string, unless additional tagging or text encoding has taken place. For the most part, Parker 1.0

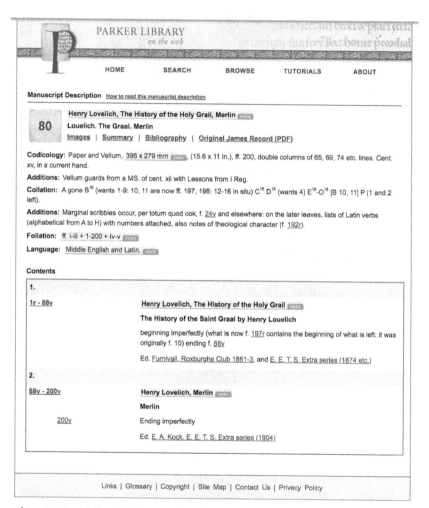

Figure 12 Description of MS 80 on Parker Library on the Web 1.0 (subscription version, 2009–17).

SOURCE: https://swap.stanford.edu/*/http://parker.stanford.edu. Courtesy of Parker Library, Corpus Christi College, Cambridge.

relied on character-string search, with some structured tagging ("About the Project" 2010). In this context, keyword search becomes the equivalent of a catalogue index—even if the two are not equivalent at all.

Search results for *romance* on Parker 1.0 reveal how machine indexing coauthors literary history. These results also bring out the enduring influence of nineteenth-century publications on digital platforms. The archived Parker 1.0 doesn't preserve the site's search technologies, but probable results can be reconstructed by cross-referencing individual 1.0 pages with their source (a searchable PDF of James's catalogue) and with search results on Parker 2.0 that can be traced back to 1.0 data. By this means, it becomes apparent that a major source of *romance* search results on Parker 1.0 was a nineteenth-century catalogue that James used frequently in his descriptions: *Catalogue of Romances in the Department of Manuscripts in the British Museum* (Ward and Herbert 1883–1910). This three-volume work, decades in the making, represents the high point of the romance genre's nineteenth-century reputation. Through keyword search, this catalogue title associates seventeen Parker manuscripts with romance: chivalric adventures in French (MS 50), Merlin's prophecies (MS 405, ff. 3v–5v), Alexander the Great (MSS 129, 219, 370, 414), animal fables (MSS 177, 481), saints' lives and miracles (MSS 42, 43, 275, 292, 318, 462), and Latin exempla (MSS 385, 406, 441). Together, these items represent a capacious definition of the genre, many of them relevant to understanding MS 80. Yet James did not connect MS 80 to the *Catalogue of Romances*, even though its authors cite Furnivall's Lovelich edition (Ward and Herbert 1883–1910, 1:341, 342). In James's descriptions, the only romance in Parker's collection is the French prose *Lancelot* (MSS 45, 494). Nonetheless, James's use of the British Museum catalogue of romances made nineteenth-century literary history a vector of discovery on a twenty-first-century digital platform. In this way, romantic medievalism from the nineteenth century has sedimented into digital data, regardless of how differently "romance" is now understood.

Search results from the Parker 1.0 Bibliography expanded the romance genre further, bringing MS 80 back into the fold. In this way, Parker 1.0 reversed James, just as James had reversed Nasmith. In addition to results related to the British Museum *Catalogue of Romances*, twentieth-century scholarship using the word *romance* would have associated a number of new items with the genre: the Bury Bible (MS 2 via Gerould 1935); several copies of Ranulf Higden's *Polychronicon* (MSS 21, 117, 164, 259, and 367 via Loomis 1952); the chronicle of William of Newburgh (MS 262 via Rollo 1998); the Latin history of King "Waldeus" by John Bramis (MS 329 via Smyly 1919). Finally, relatively recent publications would have brought Nasmith's two favored romances back into the genre: *La Romance de Louis de Gaures* (MS 91 via Visser-Fuchs 1998) and Lovelich's translation (MS 80 via Kock 1904, 1913; and Meale 1994). All in all, the eclectic results of keyword search on Parker 1.0 provide a surprisingly meaningful framework for understanding Lovelich's translation: chronicles point to the narrative's relations with history; saints' lives illuminate Joseph of Arimathea; the Bible conditions the Holy Grail's Christological symbolism; Alexander the Great was one of the "Nine Worthies," along with King Arthur; Merlin's prophecies are embedded in the narration of Arthur's reign.

The Parker 1.0 Bibliography also included Comments—annotations by the bibliographers that explained each item's connection to a manuscript (authored by Rebecca Rushforth, Neil Coates, Elizabeth Boyle, Keith Waters, and Denis Casey). Since the Comments were also searchable, they were another source of "romance"—dependent less on published titles than on the bibliographers' judgment. The bibliographers didn't use a controlled vocabulary any more than James did; each wrote narrative descriptions in their own idiom. Nonetheless, the Comments confirm the romance classification of MS 80 and the other items in Nasmith's original index entry (MSS 45, 50, 91). Thus, despite all that has changed in literary history since the eighteenth century, and all the different ways of defining *romance*, the digital platform conveyed a relatively stable sense of genre.

The Parker 1.0 Comments locate the very origin of English romance in Parker's collection. The search results bring forward one new text never previously catalogued as a romance—the Old English *Apollonius of Tyre* (MS 201). The 1.0 Comments describe this text as "the first English romance" (via Archibald 1991, 145), translated from a "Latin romance" (via Lapidge 1985, 72). *Apollonius of Tyre* gives Lovelich's translation an English, rather than French, lineage. Through the Comments, Parker 1.0 pointed toward a literary history that would make MS 80 the culmination of an ancient English practice of making romance out of translation. This reframing restored MS 80 to its various roles within Parker's founding purposes, which included the recovery of knowledge about the origins of the national language. Parker 1.0 thus brought the collection closer to the sixteenth century than it had been for quite some time, even as the digital platform incorporated Nasmith's eighteenth-century vision as well as the latest twentieth-century scholarship. Through innumerable intentions and accidents, Parker Library on the Web fulfilled the Fellows' vision of c. 1900 that a new catalogue not consign the old ones to the "dim abode" of obsolescence.

New platforms, however, do not necessarily maintain older data. One of the primary challenges in digital preservation is precisely how to sustain inherited data when formats, protocols, and basic infrastructure change over time. Parker Library on the Web is certainly no exception to these challenges. It was launched with the best intentions for sustainability—a subscription fee to pay for maintenance and a commitment to migrate to new technologies within ten years (Harrassowitz 2009). Right on schedule, Stanford Libraries archived Parker 1.0 and launched Parker 2.0 in January 2018. The new site is driven by open-source technologies and integrated within larger infrastructure systems across Stanford Libraries. These changes make maintenance efficient, but they also make new literary histories.

The protocols and networking standards that drive Parker 2.0 affect the manuscript descriptions as well as the results of keyword searches. Some new information has been created, and some old information has been lost. Parker 2.0 might be best described as an abstract of Parker 1.0. Understanding what has happened to the cataloguing and indexing is essential to understanding how to use Parker 2.0—which will, inevitably, change again. Indeed, Parker 2.0 became Parker 2.1 in March 2021 (changes not addressed here, as they took place as this book went to press). Parker Library on the Web is very much a dynamic site, with energetic and thoughtful managers, most notably Benjamin Albritton of Stanford Libraries. As Albritton has noted, Parker 2.0 challenges managers and users alike to "confront the differences between a web delivery platform and a published manuscript catalogue" (Albritton 2020, 10). The break with cataloguing is thus a matter of infrastructure. Even if Parker 2.0 no longer functions quite like I describe here by the time readers come to this book, this analysis might help future researchers understand how the history of digital platforms has shaped their own conditions of access to manuscripts, catalogues, libraries, and perhaps many other things.

The representation of MS 80 on Parker 2.0 provides a succinct view of how cataloguing combines with platforming to project literary history onto manuscripts (see fig. 13). The page layout, for example, places the manuscript images above the description. This priority derives from one of the most significant technological changes—the development of the International Image Interoperability Framework (https://iiif.io) and the Mirador image viewer (https://projectmirador.org). The IIIF standard foregrounds the value of using images outside their host institution: they can be integrated into other applications in any IIIF-compliant environment (Albritton 2020, 11). As with previous innovations at Parker Library, this new conception of the collection has generated new titles and shelf marks. The title that "travels" with MS 80's images to other viewing environments includes the complete name of the home repository, as well as a digitally enhanced shelf mark, "080," to ensure sequential order in machine sorting: "Cambridge, Corpus Christi College, MS 080: Henry Lovelich, The History of the Holy Grail, Merlin." In various settings, this title serves as a complete description of location, author, and text. On Parker 2.0, versions of this title appear four times on MS 80's main page—a persistent reminder of the book's context. A second identifier is analogous to a shelf mark in that it is unique to digital objects associated with MS 80: "xd494bt3141" is part of MS 80's web address on Parker 2.0 and of the "manifest" file used in IIIF to assemble the digital manuscript in image viewers (Mirador or others). This unique identifier enables interoperability across platforms and applications: many shelf marks include "80" but there is only one "xd494bt3141." Just like Nasmith in the eighteenth century, Parker 2.0 signals a new conception of the collection with new identifiers akin to new shelf marks. With Parker 2.0, the "Parker Manuscripts" become one collection among many, part of much larger systems of data, protocols, and libraries.

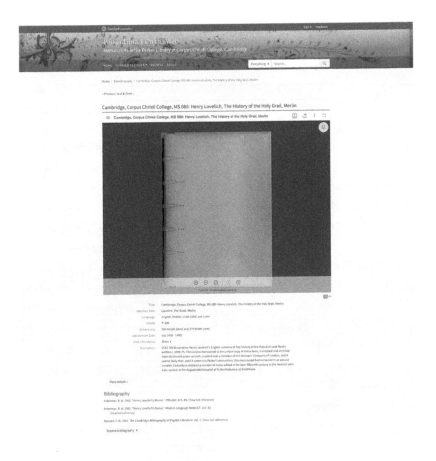

Figure 13   Description of MS 80 on Parker Library on the Web 2.0 (2018–21).

SOURCE: https://parker.stanford.edu/parker/catalog/xd494bt3141. Courtesy of Parker Library, Corpus Christi College, Cambridge. Licensed under a Creative Commons Attribution-NonCommercial 4.0 International License.

The main page for MS xd494bt3141 shows just a snippet of the manuscript description. The most prominent and informative text on the page is the Description—imported wholesale from the 1.0 Summary. Users coming to MS 80 for the first time are thus presented with a book clearly contextualized by both the literary practices of fifteenth-century London and Parker's own collecting practices. The framing by the Parker 1.0

project team (previously restricted to subscribers) is now the most accessible entry point for learning about a manuscript. The rest of the description "pops up" when users click on "More Details." Here, the Parker 1.0 edition of James has been translated into a metadata scheme. In the early years of Parker 2.0, the scheme didn't include the "Additions" category and so lost James's note about MS 80's annotations. Currently, the record has been modified to include "Additions," as well as a link to an "Augmented James Record," which is a representation of the Parker 1.0 entry (accessed January 30, 2021). These changes preserve more of the record's data lineage. Parsing the record, however, still requires some in-depth comparative cataloguing. Unless one is already familiar with MS 80, for example, one can't exactly tell which information about the manuscript's "material" to believe—vellum or vellum and paper. Similarly, it's hard to know what to make of the "language" data—Middle English and Latin. For some users, these kinds of inconsistencies might undermine trust (Paul 2018). Yet they are also useful in publicizing the fact that the information isn't entirely reliable; some of it was wrong in 1912 and is still wrong today. It was never curated to support data-driven research like "quantitative codicology" (Da Rold 2020a, 61) or collation visualizations (Porter 2018c). In this environment, responsibility for historical knowledge shifts away from the library as a "reliable or omniscient guide" (Albritton 2020, 12). Inconsistency turns into an accurate representation of the uncertainty that attends every catalogue—starting with Parker's own 1574 Register, which exists in three slightly different copies (Page 1993, 3-15). Yet each catalogue also presents itself as authoritative. All in all, as a catalogue Parker 2.0 is both more accessible than ever to "curious beginners" and more demanding than ever of specialist expertise—not only in manuscript studies but in comparative cataloguing. Parker 2.0 serves as a salutary reminder that digital platforms carry histories that need to be analyzed and integrated in our understanding of how they are guiding users to and through their materials.

The fate of romance on Parker 2.0 further exposes the impact of platform technologies on literary history. Keyword searches can be initiated from any page through an open search box that defaults to "Search

Everything." The results largely confirm the expanded genre corpus encoded in Parker 1.0, with some revealing exceptions that remind us that platforms don't always become more complete with each update. Sometimes they lose things. The specific data sets that produce the romance corpus, moreover, are somewhat different from Parker 1.0 in ways that might have meaningful impacts on other kinds of search. MS 80, for example, is a romance on Parker 2.0 because of reference titles—the same ones as on Parker 1.0 (Kock 1904, 1913; Meale 1994), plus a few more recent additions (Eddy 2012; Warren 2018a). However, one of the publications that most pointedly reevaluated the status of Lovelich's translation as a romance, by Roger Dalrymple (2000), isn't included in search results for "romance." The reason is a quirk of metadata scope: the word *romance* is not used in the article title, although it is part of the title for the book that includes the article. Another platforming process has attached erroneous "notes" to these post-1.0 references (Dalrymple 2000; Eddy 2012; Warren 2018a): each is annotated, erroneously but appropriately, with a note from MS 16II about Henry III processing with a relic of Holy Blood (as of July 7, 2020). Notes aren't included in search results, and new notes aren't generally created for post-1.0 references. Nonetheless, somehow Parker 2.0 has produced a "comment" on MS 80 as a grail romance. These results show that even errors and accidents can contribute good information.

In addition to bibliography, "Search everything" includes item titles and Page Details (called Annotations in the Mirador viewer). The results from both sources depend on a combination of James's choices, Parker 1.0 titles, and Parker 1.0 formatting decisions. MS 405, for example, remains in the 2.0 romance corpus because James happened to transcribe the beginning of a French text in which the author extols the difficulties of writing in "romance" (f. 196v). Elsewhere, the 1.0 decision to give the title "Saints Lives and Romances" to MS 318 ensures that everything related to this manuscript is swept up in romance search. Finally, MS 385, with a Latin exemplum (p. 243), is associated with romance because it has the only one of James's seventeen references to the *Catalogue of Romances* that was encoded on the same line as an image link. On Parker 1.0 Contents, all the other references were formatted after a line break—and none of the text after line breaks transferred into Parker 2.0 (at least not in the early years). On Parker 1.0, the *Catalogue of Romances* was a major source for romance search results. This case shows the influence that even formatting can have on the migration of data from platform to platform—with potentially significant impact on search and discovery and, thus, on how users can perceive historical materials.

All in all, Parker 2.0 has lost two romances from 1.0, each for a different reason that illustrates platform authoring. MS 370, with Latin texts about Alexander the Great, had been connected by James to the *Catalogue of Romances*: this reference was accidentally overlooked in the 1.0 Bibliography (and so not linked to MS 370 on 2.0); none of James's four references to the *Catalogue* was in the first line of 1.0 Contents (and so none became 2.0 Page Details). The corpus of Alexander romances on Parker 2.0 has thus shrunk by one (MSS 129, 219, and 414 remain). Most dramatically, the prose *Lancelot* (MS 45)—associated with Lovelich's translation since Parker's time—cannot be found as a romance on Parker 2.0. Instead, the barely legible binding fragment pasted into MS 494 is more visible. How has MS 45 disappeared from romance search? For almost every possible platform reason: the 1.0 title is "The Pseudo-Map Prose Lancelot"; the French character string "roman" isn't indexed with "romance"; 1.0 Comments aren't part of 2.0 search; James's note "Romance of Lancelot" was encoded after a line break on 1.0 Contents; the 1.0 Summary doesn't use the word *romance*. These results show the powers and perils of keyword search. The scope of full-text search can greatly expand results, but results will always depend on the idiosyncrasies of inherited data and platform processing. These procedures also author literary history.

The "romance" results on Parker 2.0 actually illuminate MS 80 in many meaningful ways. The manuscripts associated with the character string represent many topics relevant to Lovelich's text: British history in chronicles, Christian themes, chivalric conduct, linguistic translation. The usefulness of this corpus for literary history shows that even "bad data" can produce good results. When the indexes that used genre classification (Nasmith; Rogers) were replaced by machine-generated indexes that match character strings (Parker 1.0; Parker 2.0), genre remained part of search and discovery even though it wasn't a metadata category. In the future, even if genre is written into the metadata, the results will still project a historically and technologically specific corpus—not a "truer" one. Each catalogue—or web delivery platform—reclassifies the collection. The accidents of search on Parker Library on the Web show that classification and computation prescribe as much as they describe.

The wide impact of platforming decisions on literary history surfaces at the heart of the technological transformation that defines Parker 2.0—the adoption of IIIF. The shared protocol facilitates collection aggregation, bringing together manuscript images from otherwise isolated repositories. The Biblissima project, for example, is designed to unify access to digital manuscripts and digital data about manuscripts (https:// biblissima.fr). On Biblissima, the Parker data available for keyword search are the descriptions—that is, the 1.0 Summaries (as of January 30, 2021). The Parker romances are thus associated with a host of items from other libraries—but there are only five of them: the "French romance" *Histoire des Seigneurs de Gavres* (MS 91), "fragments of a French romance, the prose *Lancelot*" (MS 494), the "Old English romance *Apollonius of Tyre*" (MS 201), some "romance material" in a hagiography collection (MS 318), and a copy of the Latin *Thebaid* adapted from a Greek source by Statius (MS 230). The *Thebaid* joins the corpus solely because the 1.0 Summary author wrote a brief literary history of medieval romance: "The text was of interest in the Middle Ages, used as a source for the twelfth-century French romance, *Le Roman de Thèbes*, and by Boccaccio and Chaucer." This Summary/Description alludes to centuries of translation that stretch from Greek epic to the height of the English canon, passing through French and Italian. The *Thebaid*'s association with the romance corpus on Biblissima thus derives directly from the platforming of medieval English literature on Parker 1.0.

On Biblissima, MS 80 has lost its genre again. In this interoperable environment, however, new pathways have also been formed. Their potential to contribute to new literary histories will require yet more histories of cataloguing, indexing, and platforming. With shared protocols, images and descriptions can circulate in more flexible ways, but they can also become harder to find once unmoored from their home collections. When items from disparate sources are aggregated, they retain only the metadata elements that they share. Large-scale interoperability generally means small-scale metadata, at least so far. In this environment, how do you find a manuscript that you aren't already looking for? Discoverability thus remains a challenge within IIIF (Benjamin Albritton, email communication, January 7, 2019). These are the conditions of all kinds of research now, not just manuscripts and not just romance. Analysis of the underlying infrastructures is integral to understanding the histories that have been carried forward and those that might have been processed into oblivion. Platforms will never be complete representations, no matter how universal their protocols or how successful their institutional collaborations. Rather than waiting for the better data that will never come, literary history can also study the platforms as they are. Platforms work profoundly yet fleetingly on our understanding of books and texts. We won't know what they've done unless we keep looking.

Library on the Internet

The changes that Parker 1.0 and 2.0 have brought to the history of cataloguing at Parker Library extend beyond the manuscript descriptions. As websites, they represent the library's own history as an institution created and sustained within very specific historical conditions. Those conditions now extend beyond Cambridge to the infrastructure of the internet itself. In the process of integrating new technologies, Parker Library on the Web has redefined the nature of the manuscript collection and even the concept of "the book" (see chaps. 3 and 6). The websites also publicize and reconfigure Parker's founding legacy. In the design of the home pages, new technologies are counterbalanced by the prestige of the most ancient materials in the collection and Parker's own reputation as a significant figure in English national history. Each home page uses the latest networked standards to convey its connections to the library's most distant origins. This message minimizes the difference that digital makes, leveraging historical value to enhance digital value. In this frame, MS 80 is part of a long history of English bookmaking.

As digital access points, the home pages of Parker Library on the Web "house" the collection in ways that echo Parker's 1574 Register, which defined the contractual conditions of his bequest to Corpus Christi College. Parker envisioned a careful coordination of access and preservation: the library was to be open daily but only to fellows (with a few special exceptions); writing in the books was forbidden; the collection was to be audited annually; fines were imposed for missing leaves, quires, or books; if too many books were lost, the collection would be entrusted to another college (MS 575; Graham 2006, 338-40). The library's first catalogue was thus a preservation tool that supported the annual audit. Parker 1.0 was envisioned as the culmination of this curatorial spirit—expanding access but also using fees to safeguard the new digital materials (Harrassowitz 2009). Parker 2.0 has made the collection even more accessible with the removal of fees and a maintenance plan integrated with core library functions at Stanford. In both cases, the digital books need curatorial care, or they, too, could be lost, just like books on a shelf.

Even on the open internet, access includes some restrictions, or at least conditions. Parker Library on the Web is quite transparent in spelling out conditions of use. The changes from Parker 1.0 to 2.0 reflect broader changes in the management of digital assets that have taken place between 2008 and 2018. Parker 1.0, for example, treats the website like a published book protected by copyright law: a navigation link for "Copyright" leads to a page that outlines the legal codes of both the United Kingdom and the United States. A separate navigation link delineates the "Privacy Policy," addressing how users' data will be handled in accordance with the UK Data Protection Act of 1988. Both pages are written in a gentle, informative tone even as they expose the fact that accessing a website is anything but private or free. By contrast, Parker 2.0 presents itself as part of the open web, where users engage digital content in many different ways, not all of them related to copyright. Parker 2.0 draws a distinction between publishing and sharing. Copyright remains in force for publishing while a generous "Creative Commons" license allows flexibility for noncommercial uses (More Details, Mirador Information). Equally significant, the rights notices are linked to the images rather than the home page: in accordance with the purposes of IIIF, the notices travel with the images when they are integrated elsewhere. Similarly, privacy notices are part of Stanford Libraries rather than specific to Parker 2.0. With some effort, users can reach a page where they can "opt out of analytics" (https://library. stanford.edu/opt-out). Powered by Google, the "opt out" model registers the seismic shift in digital-identity tracking that has taken place since the UK Data Protection Act of 1988. Users now have more control, but their participation is the default. Internet users thus "pay" for "free" information by providing their access data. On an internet powered by IIIF and Google, the Parker 2.0 home page is in fact no longer the "home" for the manuscript images: users can reach the images without ever passing through the home page. At the technical level, the home page is no longer a portal to the collection but one page among others. The passage from Parker 1.0 to 2.0 thus illustrates the recent history of the internet, in which websites are now less like books and more like loose-leaf pages.

In their respective moments of creation, Parker 1.0 and 2.0 were each new experiences for their first users. Both sites convey an understanding of their novelty and take responsibility to teach users about their functions. On both sites, "About" links bring up extensive documentation explaining the history of the library, the catalogues, the production of the website, the institutional partners, and the role of conservation in digital reproduction. Every contributor is named, every technology identified, every funding source credited. This transparency demystifies the material production of digital infrastructure. Both sites further their openness by inviting interaction with the people who maintain the sites—"Contact Us" (1.0) or "Feedback" (2.0). And both sites include instructions for newcomers. Parker 1.0 was in fact a comprehensive portal for manuscript studies—a catalogue, a handbook, an institutional history, and an internet tutorial all in one. Even without a subscription, "curious beginners" could learn a lot about medieval books with video tutorials (complete with transcriptions), a compendium of other digital resources for manuscript studies, an extensive listing of "Tools and Resources," and a glossary of technical terminology (a revised digital edition of Michelle Brown's *Understanding Illuminated Manuscripts* [1994]). Parker 2.0 is less comprehensive but equally attentive to users' need for orientation, with a series of "Hints and Tips" for understanding the site's structure. The focus is more on the technology and less on manuscript study in general, in accordance with the shift away from the centralized structure of a "portal." Indeed, so many digital resources for manuscript studies populate the internet that it has become unreasonable to curate them in any comprehensive way. Here again, Parker 2.0 takes its place in a larger ecosystem where expectations have shifted from centralized guidance to user-defined search. Users themselves need to take responsibility for identifying the quality and utility of digital resources. In this way, "Parker Manuscripts" is no longer (only) a collection but also just one Google search result among millions of others.

These distinctions between a centralized portal and decentralized interoperability are expressed in the descriptive language of each home page. Both Parker 1.0 and 2.0 emphasize a spirit of "welcome." On Parker 1.0, the word repeats twice: "WELCOME. Corpus Christi College and the Stanford University Libraries welcome you to Parker on the Web—an interactive, web-based workspace designed to support use and study of the manuscripts in the historic Parker Library at Corpus Christi College, Cambridge." With the promise of an interactive "workspace," the website is presented as an extension of the reading room in Cambridge. Parker 2.0 adapts this text by replacing "web-based workspace" with "digital exhibit"—a phrase that conveys less permanence but also alludes to users' ability to make their own exhibits out of the site's digital materials. The paragraph then continues with a more expansive description of both the library in Cambridge and the digital exhibit: "The Parker Library is a treasure trove of rare medieval and Renaissance manuscripts, as well as early printed books. Almost all manuscripts in the Parker Library collection have been fully digitised and are available in this exhibit, along with associated bibliographic references and annotations made by scholars from around the world" (Parker 2.0). This summary reflects 2.0's departure from cataloguing by mentioning bibliography and annotations (Page Details) but not descriptions. Instead, the exhibit focuses on images. Indeed, Parker 2.0 has a second web address that locates the site among other digital exhibits hosted by Stanford Libraries (https://exhibits.stanford.edu/parker). Here,

Parker 2.0 is one collection among many. In this sense, it harkens back to the earliest printed catalogues: Thomas James (1600) and Edward Bernard (1697) both sought to facilitate research across collections more than they sought to describe the Parker collection as such. All in all, the home page texts call attention to the social implications of their technical formats.

To mitigate the disruptive effects of networked technologies, both iterations of Parker Library on the Web use web-design strategies to reinforce the sites' connections to Corpus Christi College and to Parker himself. Thus, even as internet distribution unmoors "Parker Library" from Cambridge, the websites preserve a strong sense of historical location (see fig. 14). Parker 1.0 features Parker's name in the largest letters on the page—even though James had broken with precedent and not

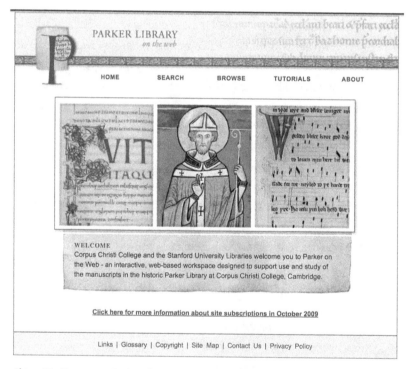

Figure 14   Home page, Parker Library on the Web 1.0 (nonsubscription version, 2009).

SOURCE: https://web.archive.org/web/20100211002937/http://parkerweb.stanford.edu/parker/actions/page.do?forward=home. Courtesy of Parker Library, Corpus Christi College, Cambridge.

used the name in his catalogue title. On the internet, Parker's name anchors the web address, "parkerweb.stanford.edu," counterbalancing the new technology (web) and the geographical displacement (stanford.edu). Parker is also evoked in the *P* that structures the home page like a manuscript page: the *P* encloses a snippet of handwriting and is set against an image of vellum, all positioned across a blue border decoration and some faded lines of Latin. The patch of vellum is repeated on each Description page as a frame for the shelf marks, also in red. Even the font (named in the source code) comments on the history of writing technologies: "MS Trebuchet Sans Serif" is a "humanist" typeface named after a medieval siege engine and designed specifically for the internet (https://en.wikipedia.org/wiki/Trebuchet_MS). The whole page is bound by a thin lined frame, leaving a wide margin of white space to fill a computer screen. This framing device, used throughout the site's pages, echoes the table formats found in print catalogues. The page thus fuses the aesthetics of manuscript, print, and digital formats. It keeps a visual sense of book history even as it produces new digital ontologies.

The home page for Parker 2.0 conveys even stronger connections to Cambridge—even as the site's technologies multiply where the collection images might be used (see fig. 15). A thin red banner along the top anchors the site in "Stanford Libraries." In the next layer, a wider border portrays a close-up of a medieval manuscript decoration—overlain with the site name in large crisp white letters, "Parker Library on the Web," followed by the subtitle "Manuscripts in the Parker Library at Corpus Christi College, Cambridge." The Cambridge location is in fact named four times on the page. The image below the border illustrates these words with a photo of the historic Wilkins Reading Room (1827). At the center of the photo's sight lines—and of the web page—is a portrait of Parker himself, hung high at the end of the room. A semitransparent banner stretches across the photo, just below Parker's image, naming Corpus Christi College and the University of Cambridge; it includes the college's logo, a pelican representing Christ's sacrifice. This photo portrays the physical space where James would have started his catalogue, where editors would have transcribed MS 80, and where I myself first saw the manuscript. The room's architecture

Corpus Christi College and the Stanford University Libraries welcome you to Parker Library on the Web, a digital exhibit designed to support use and study of the manuscripts in the historic Parker Library at Corpus Christi College, Cambridge. The Parker Library is a treasure trove of rare medieval and Renaissance manuscripts, as well as early printed books. Almost all manuscripts in the Parker Library collection have been fully digitised and are available in this exhibit, along with associated bibliographic references and annotations made by scholars from around the world.

Explore the collection

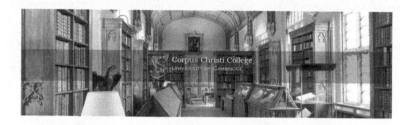

Figure 15   Home page, Parker Library on the Web 2.0 (2018–21)

SOURCE: https://parker.stanford.edu. Courtesy of Parker Library, Corpus Christi College, Cambridge.

is neogothic—a romanticized revival of medieval forms. The Parker 2.0 home page thus depicts the library as a nineteenth-century museum. In this way, it connects with the cultural influences that have shaped both manuscript cataloguing and MS 80's literary history.

Finally, the home pages use manuscript images to create an even deeper sense of history. These images convey continuity from the most ancient items in the collection to the most recent technologies. Parker 1.0 features three images. In the middle sits Saint Dunstan, Archbishop of Canterbury in the tenth century—Parker's most prestigious predecessor (MS 181, f. 1r). Dunstan is flanked by a decorated initial from the life of the even more ancient St. Guthlac (MS 389, f. 22v) and by a snippet of a Middle English motet (MS 8, f. Ar). Collectively, these images reference Parker's animating vision of English vernacular Christianity. They evoke the library's origins in Reformation politics. The snippet from the life of St. Guthlac, moreover, includes an example of Parker's characteristic red underlining—one of the ways in which he marked the manuscripts to call attention to valuable information (see chap. 3). Parker's annotation practice is echoed in the website's use of red lettering and hyperlinks, which also reflect the color brand of both Stanford and Corpus Christi College. Red is thus a visual symbol of the site's simultaneous origins in the sixteenth century and the twenty-first, in Cambridge and in California. Moving a digital pointer across the images causes new images to "pop up," modified to include a semitransparent layer that describes the images and identifies their sources (see fig. 16). For brief moments, the uniquely historical and the uniquely digital coincide.

The images on Parker 2.0 also showcase the collection's history along with the site's technical accomplishments. Scrolling down below the Wilkins Reading Room photo, users encounter six navigation options,

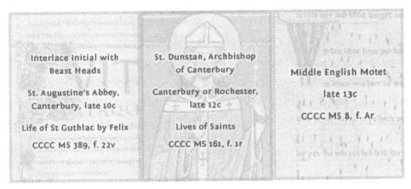

Figure 16   Home page manuscript identifications, Parker Library on the Web 1.0 (nonsubscription version, 2009–17). Composite image from three screen images.

SOURCE: https://web.archive.org/web/20100211002937/http://parkerweb.stanford.edu/parker/actions/page.do?forward=home. Courtesy of Parker Library, Corpus Christi College, Cambridge.

each defined by both text and image. On the first row to "Explore the Collection," a figure reads a book for the Manuscripts, the Wheel of Fortune humorously (?) illustrates "Page-level Details" (which may or may not be helpful, depending on what users seek), and a figure holds a scroll for the "Bibliography." On the second row to "Explore Special Topics," a figure writes in a book for Bibliography, two friendly (?) beasts beckon viewers into the tutorial for "The Basics for Parker 2.0," and a figure pointing to his eye guides users toward "The Manuscript Viewing Window." These navigation boxes exemplify the practice of redundant messaging that makes web design more accessible for more users (https://webaim. org/intro). Unlike the images featured on Parker 1.0, these images function referentially even if one knows nothing more about their source or content. Clicking on them doesn't reveal their identity but rather opens a page with the advertised function.

Identifying the images, though, enhances their messaging and further illustrates how Parker 2.0 has processed data from Parker 1.0. On the 2.0 home page, the image sources don't "pop up" but they can be found relatively easily with a modest understanding of IIIF, HTML, and advanced browser tools. The process of identifying these images exposes again the separation between images and cataloguing on Parker 2.0. The home page's source code includes links in IIIF syntax that define what part of a JPEG file to display. The links include the shelf mark along with the folio, so the full images can be found in the Parker 2.0 exhibit. The folios' Page Details, however, rarely include image descriptions. For someone unfamiliar with a particular manuscript, More Details are necessary. There, the PDF of James's description usually does describe the images. However, in 2020, the image details were easier to find on the archived 1.0 Contents lists (now included in 2.1 More Details as "Augmented James Record"). These arrangements mean that search cannot reliably identify specific images or even which manuscripts are illustrated. Like the re-indexing of "romance," the loss of both data and metadata for "decoration" affects what kinds of research questions the site can answer. At the level of cataloguing, there are no illustrated manuscripts; at the level of platform technology, "Image" is the site's very definition (the second *I* of IIIF). Digital platforming thus creates not only new "ways of being" (ontologies) for books but also new ways of classifying (also ontologies, in the parlance of metadata curation). In the move from catalogue (1.0) to web delivery platform (2.0), the target of classification has shifted from content (texts and images in books) to form (file formats that represent books).

The images on the 2.0 home page ultimately combine iconographic messaging with historical significance, much like 1.0. The "Manuscripts" are presented by Luke, from the Gospels of St. Augustine (MS 286, f. 129v)—the collection's oldest book. Parker held it in high esteem as evidence of the ancient origins of Christianity in Britain and at Canterbury in particular. The image for "Page-level Details" derives from a copy of the *Historia Anglorum* (MS 66, p. 66), an English history that signals Parker's nationalist interests. Isaiah from the Bury Bible guides us to "Bibliography"—a small snippet from a very large book, also among the library's most famous (MS 2II, f. 220v). The "Hints and Tips" for Bibliography come from a famous writer—St. Jerome, depicted composing the *Life of St. Paul* (MS 389, f. 1v). This book also came from Canterbury and provided the image from St. Guthlac's life on Parker 1.0. The friendly beasts for "The Basics of Parker 2.0" come from the beginning of the Bury Bible (MS 2I, f. 1v). King David points to the "Viewing Window" from within a gilded *D* in the lavishly illustrated Peterborough Psalter (MS 53, f. 38v). Finally, the floral border at the top of the page is symbolically in the "English" style and from the "first" book in the catalogue (MS 1, f. 31r). Collectively, these images represent some of the library's most famous manuscripts. They are associated with the issues of greatest concern to Parker. Thus on Parker 2.0, the latest syntax of interoperability mobilizes the library's oldest materials. The home page ultimately conveys a succinct summary of centuries of writing, reading, and collecting that has culminated in new methods for doing all those things on the internet.

Lovelich's translation has made a long journey from the ground to the cloud. As presented in Parker's 1574 Register, the book had multiple roles: chronicle (shelved with a world encyclopedia), linguistic evidence (alongside texts in Old English), Christian example (next to English saints' lives), and literature (not far from Chaucer's *Troilus and Criseyde* and the French prose *Lancelot*). Each successive catalogue shifted the book's company and even its place on the shelf. Early cataloguers hewed closely to Parker's investments in Protestant historiography (James 1600; Stanley 1722). Nasmith, though, valued the text's connection with French romance (1777). By contrast, M. R. James obscured many elements of interest for literary history, such as annotations, sources, and authorship (1912). Parker Library on the Web has made those elements more discoverable even though it remains based on James and has inherited eighteenth-century notions of "romance" (2009, 2018–21). Along the way, MS 80 made its way into various thematic catalogues. Its link to a French source brought it into the catalogue of Parker's French manuscripts (Wilkins 1993). Its doodles and index fingers drawn in pen attracted attention for the *Index of Images in English Manuscripts* (Nichols 2008, 42). If M. R. James had been more thorough, MS 80 might have made it into the *Index of Middle English Prose*—which includes Chaucer's *Troilus and Criseyde* because of several marginal notes (Rand 2009, 6–7). Collectively, these catalogues have made many books out of Lovelich's translation: a history of King Arthur, a romance of the Holy Grail, a tedious book of "scribbles," and an illustrated English manuscript.

Each catalogue has something different to say about MS 80. To understand the manuscript, or any Parker manuscript, one needs all the catalogues, not just the first or the last. Parker stored his metadata on vellum; Stanford uses networked digital standards. Today, no single catalogue has all the information. Each, though, contributes something significant. Parker constructed a library of titles before the library of books (1574). Thomas James produced a tool for comparing texts in different repositories (1600). Bernard brought that idea to a national scale (1697). Stanley printed a guide to some of the shelving outcomes of Parker's metadata (1722). Nasmith upended these calculations with a new shelf-mark system that led to the books' reshelving (1777). M. R. James followed the same order but with newly standardized descriptions (1912). Parker 1.0 used digital technologies to publish a catalogue that was also a handbook, facsimile, bibliography, and database (2009–17). Finally, Parker 2.0 has disaggregated those functions so that data can be repurposed elsewhere (Albritton

2020, 10). Yet Parker 1.0 remains the best tool for understanding complex manuscripts—including Parker's metadata, MS 575 (formerly classed with the printed books; Vaughn and Fines 1960). Fortunately, Parker 1.0 has archived well because it was encoded in static text-based markup. Meanwhile, Parker 2.0 isn't intended to function like a catalogue (Albritton 2020). Yet where else would one go to start learning about the manuscripts? Under these circumstances—which aren't unique to Parker Library— historiographies of metadata are an essential part of manuscript studies.

The history of cataloguing at Parker Library is also the history of the elusive goal of a "union catalogue" of all surviving medieval manuscripts. Such a catalogue would reveal relationships among books that have been scattered across the world for a number of geopolitical reasons. Back when Parker was collecting books, he had in hand some of the earliest British efforts toward such a catalogue—printed lists by John Leland (1549) and John Bale (1557–59). In the 1590s, Thomas James looked across libraries in Cambridge and Oxford to encourage editors to collate texts (1600). Bernard expanded this idea by collating catalogues themselves from across England and Ireland (1697). In the twentieth century, microfilm and other duplication technologies spurred new efforts to aggregate manuscript catalogues (Richardson 1937; Wilson 1956; Born 1964). Since the 1990s, such efforts have continued in electronic formats, such as Digital Scriptorium in the United States, E-Codices in Switzerland, and Biblissima in France. Yet to this day a multitude of standards are in use, and fragmentation remains the norm, even within a single repository like the British Library (Prescott 2013). The scope of cataloguing remains largely national at best, just as in Parker's day. For many reasons, then, a vast gap remains between what is desirable, what is technically possible, and what is feasible within and across institutions.

Literary history is written in this gap. Medieval studies does have a lot of "bad data." In some sense, digital cataloguing is doing what MS 80's editor, Frederick Furnivall, was doing in the nineteenth century: "Prints of MSS. are all good, though those without mistakes are better than others" (Furnivall 1864b, xxv). We might say interoperable data are all good, though those created as structured data are better than others. Furnivall may have given English literary history a lot of bad data—including the text of MS

80—but those editions can be put to good use by contextualizing their production (as I show in chap. 5). And even bad data can produce good romance, as my investigation of genre indexing shows. While it is true that Parker Library on the Web is made of relatively little structured data—in the sense of "information on which a formalized language of analysis has been imposed" (Drucker 2009, 11)—it can yield many meaningful results through search. Even if better data are curated, users' habits and expectations are enormously variable and difficult to predict. More "paradata" that contextualizes digital images and their metadata might help users better understand the scope and limits of digital materials (Paul 2018; Stanford 2019; Whearty forthcoming). In the meantime—or really, all the time—comparative histories of cataloguing help explain what might be found, or not, when a word is listed in an index or typed into a search box.

The passage of Parker Library on the Web itself into catalogues and archives provides a glimpse of the near future of book history. At Stanford, Parker 1.0 has been partially preserved on the Stanford Web Archive Portal and duly recorded in the library catalogue with metadata (https:// searchworks.stanford.edu/view/wd621jt4618). The original entry for the site also remains in the catalogue, with defunct links. In both cases, Parker 1.0 is classified with three genres, reflecting its varied functions: database, facsimile, and catalogue. Some might even encounter the site by looking for the romance genre since one of the languages listed in the metadata is "romance (other)." Meanwhile, Parker 2.0, has not been catalogued: it is an open platform discoverable through search engines rather than library catalogues. Parker 2.0 is, however, entangled with Parker 1.0 on the Internet Archive: entries for "parker.stanford.edu" stretch back to 2010 (parkerweb.stanford.edu goes back to 2004). The newest archived copies are barely legible, however, because Parker 2.0 is a dynamic site with very few static pages of the sort easily captured by web archiving software. Parker Library on the Web is thus bibliographically ambiguous, like a book with more than one shelf mark. It has even been classified as both an ebook and a print book (Worldcat.org, reviewed July 21, 2020). Preserved in multiple fragments, it embodies the fragmented future of books on the internet.

CHAPTER 5

EDITING ROMANCE

Poetry, Print, Platform

THE FIRST MEDIEVAL BOOK most people read is a modern edition. It might be a cheap paperback assigned for a class. Or it might be a hefty hardback checked out from a library, dense with notes. Or it might be a website, plainly formatted for durable access. Whatever the format, edited texts play key roles in reflecting and creating literary value. Editions become authoritative often for no other reason than that they are more accessible than manuscripts; they are also easier to read, easier to handle. Publishing decisions directly influence the canon of medieval literature by shaping what can be widely read, taught, and studied. Conversely, the established canon motivates publishing decisions: famous authors have steady markets. The history of publishing thus turns into the history of the canon. Editions, though, tend to have long shelf lives. Indeed, some nineteenth-century editions remain the only editions of certain texts. As a result, editions informed by outdated practices remain authoritative amid even the most recent scholarship. Even when newer editions exist, the mass digitization of public domain books over the past fifteen years has made nineteenth-century editions readily available—more or less for "free" and more or less "new" from the perspective of many readers, including new generations of students. Through mass digitization, the nationalist values that shaped many nineteenth-century editorial decisions remain very much part of how we access medieval literature.

Editions are themselves a significant part of book history. They exemplify the definitions of *book* that I outlined in my introduction. Editions are devices that store texts, formats that structure texts, interfaces between manuscripts and readers, platforms that distribute texts, and components of educational infrastructure. Editions, like catalogues, can lose their codex format altogether—becoming databases—without losing their core functions of preserving, interpreting, and distributing texts. Each format, though, fulfills these core functions in distinct ways. Whether in print or online, editions contribute to literary history through both their texts (philology) and their formats (codicology). As publications, editions are produced by what I call "platform philology"—practices of textual production that obscure the individuals who bring texts out of manuscripts and into wider circulation. Editions also embody "platform codicology"— practices in publishing that influence how edited texts circulate as part of larger collections. To the extent that editions make "embodied arguments" about texts (Nowviskie 2000), they also make embodied arguments about the platforms that distribute them. In the case of digitized editions produced from printed editions, platform authoring is compounded by multiple layers of selection and technology—from the literal platform of a library shelf to internet protocols. A digitized print book is effectively a "family of new editions and impressions comprising at least six parts": TIFFs, JPEGs, PDFs, OCR-derived text, XML file (for web display), and a web interface (Cordell 2017, 214). At the juncture of all these formats, platforms edit texts, publish books, and write literary history.

The editions of MS 80 arise from these entanglements of philology, codicology, and literary value. The story of how the text first came into print tracks the rise of the romance genre as a crucible for the value of literature to the English nation. Literary historians started repositioning the significance of romance in the eighteenth century (Johnston 1964; Matthews 1999; Santini 2010). The first person to recommend printing MS 80's Arthurian romance was Thomas Percy in his influential *Reliques of English Poetry* (1765). The genre classification was soon confirmed in a new catalogue of the Parker Library manuscripts by James Nasmith (1777) (discussed in chap. 4). From there, rumor of an intriguing "Romance of the Holy Grail" at Corpus Christi College in Cambridge passed through the literary histories of Thomas Warton (1778) and George Ellis ([1805] 1848) to land in the hands of Frederick J. Furnivall in the late 1850s. At that time, Furnivall was a charismatic teacher at the Working Men's College in London—a Christian Socialist enterprise that offered adult education courses meant to "assimilate" the working class to middle-class values (Pearsall 1998, 126). To this end, Furnivall taught medieval literature. He attributed "the flame of his enthusiasm for the older literature" to the Arthurian poetry of Alfred Tennyson, which he first read as a teenager in 1842 (Alois Brandl in Munro 1911, 11). When Furnivall decided to edit MS 80, the idea was romantic in every sense.

MS 80 came into print through Furnivall's purposeful efforts to create publishing platforms. He worked with three organizations dedicated to publicizing the national and imperial value of medieval English—the Philological Society, the Roxburghe Club, and the Early English Text Society (EETS). As a member of the Philological Society, Furnivall met a member of the exclusive Roxburghe Club, which agreed to sponsor his edition from MS 80, *Seynt Graal, or The Sank Ryal: The History of the Holy Graal* by "Henry Lonelich, Skynner" (Furnivall 1861, 1863). At the time, the Philological Society had just begun preparing a historical dictionary of English, which eventually became the *Oxford English Dictionary* (*OED*). Furnivall thus used MS 80 to compile words worth citing. To complete the dictionary, though, Furnivall needed far more text than the Roxburghe Club would ever publish. So he founded EETS as a subscription service open to all, with the goal of expanding both the corpus of the English language and the audience for Arthurian romance. To keep the EETS presses rolling, he started an "Extra Series" to reprint rare editions as affordable paperbacks—like his own Roxburghe *Grail* (Furnivall 1874–78). Within a few decades, EETS had redefined medieval literature as a nationalist heritage available even to those of modest means (Matthews 1999, 138–61). EETS also helped bring medieval literature—especially romances—into university teaching (Ganim 1996; Singleton 2005; Spencer 2015). As EETS director for forty years and dictionary editor for ten, Furnivall provided the philological foundation for much of what we now know of medieval English literature and language—and he established his methods with MS 80.

Through these layers of authenticating platforms, Furnivall's rather unscholarly methods fade from view. He once claimed that he could teach prospective editors everything they needed to know in about half an hour (Alois Brandl in Munro 1911, 13). He thought nothing of sending his inexperienced students to the British Museum to copy texts that he then published as authoritative editions. His carefree amateurism was both brilliant and scandalous (Dinshaw 2012, 24–29). He understood printing as a distribution platform in which quantity was more valuable than quality: "Prints of MSS. are all good, though those without mistakes are better than others" (Furnivall 1864b, xxv). Mistakes and all, Furnivall's editions are still very much part of English literature and language. As one volume appeared after another, the EETS series legitimized each editor, regardless of the reliability of any individual text. EETS itself came to be seen "as a kind of national monument" (Spencer 2013, 28–29). One of Furnivall's biographers could thus declare him "hardly a scholar at all" yet also the de facto author of Middle English literature (Pearsall 1998, 133, 136). His influence is far-reaching indeed: paper slips written by Furnivall are still in use at the OED (Gilliver 2016, 582); EETS editions provide many of the OED's historical citations; the dates given by EETS editors became the dates cited in the OED; for many texts, EETS editions remain the only editions. In this way, each platform reinforced the others, deflecting attention from some of the shakier foundations of philological practice.

Despite Furnivall's enthusiasm, the romance genre had lost its luster by the end of the nineteenth century. New assessments of poetry gradually marginalized medieval romance as a lesser art, lacking rhetorical refinement (Ganim 1996, 156). As a result, throughout the twentieth century, guides for literature students classified Lovelich's translation as a "bad romance" and overtly discouraged readers. By the time the second half of MS 80 was finally published as *Merlin*, the edition prompted an excoriating assessment of both Lovelich as an author and the Holy Grail as a subject (Kock 1904; Kempe 1905). Thirty years later, though, when the last *Merlin* volume appeared, the reviewer in the *Times Literary Supplement* did find Lovelich's identity intriguing: *Merlin* may be "one of the dullest of Middle English romances," yet "one cannot help but be interested in a skinner who wrote romance" (Review of *Merlin* 1932). Indeed, as I've shown in earlier chapters, Lovelich's social context would ultimately revive scholarly appreciation of his work. And as methods of literary criticism have diversified, the romance genre has also attracted new kinds of interest (Furrow 2009; Ingham 2014; Little and McDonald 2018). Today, the terms of value are quite different from those of the eighteenth-century literary historians who first brought MS 80 to wider attention, but the result is similar: romance is again a foundational genre for English literary history.

In the twenty-first century, digital platforms have made nineteenth-century editions more accessible than ever. Digitized copies of Roxburghe and EETS editions can be found in various places on the internet—ProQuest, Google Books, HathiTrust, and the Internet Archive. Thus despite all the changes in the scholarly appreciation of romance in general and Lovelich in particular, older literary histories are still influential. Furnivall's own relatively indiscriminate editorial selections have directly influenced today's digital libraries. He practiced a "romance of the copy" in which an editor's handwritten transcription was treated as equivalent to both the medieval manuscript and the printed edition. Similarly, digital platforms treat disparate formats as interchangeable. Indeed, mass printing and mass digitizing have many similarities. The Roxburghe Club approach to reprinting, for example, has been compared to Google's approach to scanning: reproductions increase access and can influence reading patterns (Husbands 2013, 130). Similarly, the kind of "mass collaboration" that Furnivall organized for the Philological Society's Dictionary Committee has been compared to digital crowdsourcing (Gilliver 2016, 44n13). Digital platforms also reflect the same mix of financial models as the nineteenth-century print publishers: patronage (now including grants from foundations), subscriptions, and consumer marketing. Furnivall himself published with all three models simultaneously (1864a, 1864b, 1864c). From the perspective of editorial practice, then, digital libraries remain fundamentally tied to print models even as they have increased the range of source materials and the rate of copying. These parallels pinpoint what today's knowledge economy has inherited from the nineteenth century—which is the first step toward making good use of "bad data" like a Furnivall edition.

One of the latest formats for circulating old texts is the "print-on-demand" (POD) codex—a book printed from a digitized print book. POD editions of public domain texts illustrate the workings of platform codicology in concert with platform philology and literary history. As nineteenth-century books in libraries, Roxburghe Club and EETS editions have been swept up in the mass digitization of printed books begun in 2004 by Google and now sustained by various for-profit and nonprofit organizations. On platforms such as Google, HathiTrust, and the Internet Archive, printed books have become machine-readable and human-searchable through image processing, metadata curation, and OCR (Optical Character Recognition). Digitized editions in PDF include digital watermarks and library stamps that show for-profit and nonprofit organizations collaborating to fund the labor of digitization in a complex amalgam of convergent and divergent interests (Thylstrup 2018). Meanwhile, POD marketers sell the aura of literary tradition to make free content (public domain text) worth paying for when transferred from one Portable Document Format to another—the codex. The price of a POD codex represents the value of the format itself in the digital economy. For rare editions of medieval texts, a POD codex culminates two centuries of editorial platforming.

A great variety of platforms have kept Lovelich's translation in continuous circulation since 1861. In this chapter, I analyze the shifting relations among text, codex, and genre that have coedited MS 80. First, I follow the vagaries of MS 80's reputation as a romance—from the eighteenth century to now. From this angle, MS 80 cuts a new path through the history of Middle English literature told by David Matthews from "the text in the manuscript, the text in its editions, the circulation of the text, the transmission of editions, the social and scholarly placement of editors" (Matthews 1999, xv). To this list of editorial components must now be added the digital platforms that are reediting the print inheritance. I connect these most recent publications with MS 80's longer editorial history, beginning with the Roxburghe Club, EETS, and the *OED*, then continuing with ProQuest, Google, HathiTrust, and the Internet Archive. The passage of Lovelich's text from manuscript to the internet shows that financial models for publishing have as much impact as genre on the idea of medieval literature. Finally, I look again at this history from the perspective of formats: deluxe hardback codex, cheap paperback codex, PDF, web interface, and POD codex. Today, platform philology and platform codicology combine to bring old ideas about romance back into the marketplace. POD editions that are both new and old recall the somewhat haphazard conditions that extracted text from MS 80 in the first place. In the repackaging of a Roxburghe edition as a cheap paperback, format itself generates new ways of reading romance.

Romance in Literary History

MS 80 became a romance in the 1760s when literary historians began recasting the genre's place in the development of English poetry. The manuscript was first mentioned by Thomas Percy in his *Reliques of English Poetry* (1765). Percy prefaced the ballads of King Arthur with an essay, "On the Ancient Metrical Romances." In promoting the value of romances as context for ballads, Percy criticized previous antiquarians as "men void of taste and genius" who rejected romance in favor of "dull and insipid" rhymes (ix). To replace these bad judgments with a proper understanding of the "rise and progress of English poetry," he recommended publishing a collection of romances. He posits that even though most romances are not as good as works by "genius" Geoffrey Chaucer, many are much better than the poetry of "tedious" John Gower or "dull and prolix" John Lydgate (Percy 1765, ix). Percy concludes with a numbered list of prospects for the romance canon—including Lovelich. Under item 7, the stanzaic *Le Morte Arthure* (BL Harley MS 2252), Percy adds: "In the Library of [Corpus Christi] Coll. Cambridge, No. 351 is a MS. entitled in the Cat. *Acta Arthuris Metrico*

Anglicano, but I know not whether it has any thing in common with [*Le Morte Arthure*]" (xix). This summary refers (imprecisely) to the catalogue edited by Edward Bernard (1697), based on Thomas James (1600). James's bare description of English meter (*metro Anglico*) thus became the basis for Lovelich's entry into English literary history.

Percy's sense of the national significance of medieval romance echoes his contemporaries Richard Hurd and Thomas Warton. In *Letters on Chivalry and Romance* (1762), Hurd positioned romance as central to the aesthetic history of poetry, as well as to the social history of chivalry (Johnston 1964, 60–74; Matthews 1999, 14–16). Like Percy, he put "genius" and "romance" into the same sentence: "may there not be something in the Gothic Romance peculiarly suited to the views of a genius, and to the ends of poetry?" (Hurd 1762, 4). Around the same time, Warton made the case for appreciating romance in *Observations on the Fairy Queen of Spenser* (1754, 1762). He broadened his claims with the first volume of the three-volume *History of English Poetry* (1774–81), which begins with the essay "The Origin of Romantic Fiction in Europe." Here, Warton consolidated all the previous gestures toward romance into a full-scale narrative argument that made romance the foundation of national literary traditions.

More or less simultaneously, Percy's intuition about the *Acta Arthuris Metrico Anglicano* was ratified by a new cataloguer, James Nasmith. Around 1770, Nasmith was preparing new descriptions of the Parker Library manuscripts. For MS 80, he took the unusual step of creating a new title: *The Romance of the St. Grayl* (Nasmith 1777, 54). Nasmith believed that Archbishop Matthew Parker's secretary, John Joscelyn, had given the wrong title, having made little effort to discover the "true title" and therefore judging the poem with "contempt" (54). Contrary to Joscelyn, Nasmith proclaimed Lovelich an admirable conduit of the "British Muse" (54). He then printed a two-page edition of the passages where Lovelich describes his authorship; Nasmith also edited the annotation that identifies Lovelich and his patron, Henry Barton (see chap. 3). In printing extracts from MS 80, Nasmith sought to prove that Lovelich translated a French text and that the content involved the lofty subject of the "monarchs and champions of the British line" (57). With this lengthy entry, Nasmith elevated the romance genre and set MS 80 on a new course through literary history.

Even before Nasmith's catalogue was published, it had a direct impact on Warton's *History of English Poetry*. As Warton was completing volume 2, he learned of Nasmith's new account of the *Acta Arthuris* manuscript. After reading the entry, he wrote a footnote meant to be appended to the mention of the French translator "Robert Borron" in volume 1 (1:115). The nine-page note begins by referring to "an English poem on the SANG-REAL, and its appendages, containing forty thousand verses." Warton proceeds to print almost the entirety of Nasmith's catalogue entry (including the extracts), followed by a summary of Arthur's "romantic history" starting with Geoffrey of Monmouth (c. 1135). This lengthy excursus supports Warton's assessment of MS 80: "The book is a translation made from Robert Borron's French romance called LANCELOT, abovementioned, which includes the adventure of the San-Greal, by Henry Lonelich Skynner [sic], a name which I never remember to have seen among those of the English poets" (Warton 1778, 2:n.p.). Warton had not heard of Lovelich because Nasmith had only just turned him into a poet of "romantic fiction."

A few decades later, George Ellis integrated the romance theories of Warton and Percy into an anthology, *Specimens of Early English Metrical Romances* (1805). Ellis made romance popular by highlighting "good stories" rather than debates over origins, summarizing the plots in his own words with brief "specimens" of Middle English interspersed (Matthews 1999, 70–77). In the words of the antiquarian James Halliwell, Ellis did "for ancient romance what Percy had previously accomplished for early poetry. . . . Our country almost ceases to be merry England without its ballads and its romances" (preface to Ellis [1805] 1848, iv). In this nationalist and popularizing frame, Ellis nonetheless dismisses Lovelich rather efficiently in the introduction to "Romances Relating to Arthur": "Warton . . . has given us an extract from the St. Graal, a metrical fragment, said to consist of 40,000 lines, composed in the reign of Henry VI by Thomas Lonelich [sic]. . . . It is difficult to feel much interest, after perusing the deplorably dull extract given by Warton" (Ellis [1805] 1848, 75). The extract, selected by Nasmith to show the use of sources, could only disappoint someone looking for narrative action. Ellis can't even be bothered to remember the poet's name.

Aided by Ellis's *Specimens*, romances became central to the popular perception of the Middle Ages in nineteenth-century England. Arthurian subjects in particular acquired a mystical aura fed by the poetry of Tennyson and Walter Scott (Merriman 1973; Mancoff 1990). In fact, Scott provided Ellis with various materials printed in the *Specimens*, including details about the metrical *Morte Arthur* that follow Ellis's Lovelich comment (Ellis [1805] 1848, 76). Tennyson, for his part, published Arthurian poetry to great acclaim across several decades, echoing broader popularity in visual arts (Staines 1982; Mancoff 1990, 2000; Bryden 2005). Tennyson's reputation was such that even the most basic allusion to the Holy Grail could summon his poetic authority. Not even a clergyman writing church history could resist: when Walter Hook came across MS 80 in Nasmith's catalogue, he took note of "the very curious account of 'The Romance of the Holy Grayl,' which may be compared with Tennyson's magnificent poem" (Hook 1872, 510). Hook's topic was ecclesiastical affairs, and he mentioned only a handful of Archbishop Parker's books. Nonetheless, when Hook read the same catalogue entry that Ellis disdained, he drew the opposite conclusion. Hook exemplifies how romantic medievalism could produce literary value out of the barest suggestion.

Furnivall was so in thrall to romantic medievalism that he found even Ellis's dismissal of Lovelich an exciting discovery. Like Hook, Furnivall saw medieval literature through the filter of Tennyson's poetry. In fact, he opens his Lovelich edition with an epigraph from Tennyson's "Sir Galahad":

> A gentle sound, an awful light!
> Three angels bear the Holy Grail.
> With folded feet, in stoles of white,
> On sleeping wings they sail.
> Ah, blessed vision! Blood of God!
> My spirit beats her mortal bars.
> As down dark tides the glory slides,
> And, star-like, mingles with the stars.
> (Tennyson 1842, lines 41–48; Furnivall 1861, i)

The voice here is Galahad's, encountering the grail for the first time. With this epigraph, Furnivall associates his edition with a poem so well known that he doesn't print the title or name the author. He then links Galahad's view of the grail to another popular text, *The Most Ancient and Famous History of the Renowned Prince Arthur King of Britaine*—the title of a recent edition of Thomas Malory's *Morte Darthur* (1816). Quoting from this Malory, Furnivall exclaims over the grail and turns to the moment he discovered Lovelich in Ellis's *Specimens*:

> The very name of the vesture [samite] even stirred one's imagination. What could the wondrous texture be? And the Body and Spirit it covered,—what was not that to Galahad? What might it not be to us if we could but know more about it? When, therefore, while reading one day for my class at the Working Men's College, I came on the passage in Ellis's *Specimens of Early English Romances* (p. 75; Bohn, 1848), which states that a metrical Romance of the St. Graal, said to consist of forty thousand lines, composed in the reign of Henry VI, by Henry Lonelich, was preserved in MS in the library of Corpus Christi College, Cambridge, and had not been printed, I could not help exclaiming, "Unprinted! What a shame! Please God, I'll get it printed. Why, it's almost as bad as leaving Wycliffe's Bible unprinted so long."—Forty thousand lines about the San Graal with possibly, nay certainly, untold glories and wonders without end, lying hid in Corpus Library! The thing was hardly credible; while all our English world too was delighting in "The Idylls of the King" [Tennyson 1859]. (Furnivall 1861, ii)

Furnivall describes here the entirety of his approach to medieval literature—a potent combination of romantic identification (anyone can think like Galahad) and energetic publicity (if Tennyson's Arthurian poems are popular, so will be any Arthurian poem). His imagination carries him instantly from possibility to certainty. He has total faith in his ability to access the text. He considers all old materials equally valuable (a Bible, a romance); all should be printed so that more people can read them.

The first obstacle on Furnivall's editorial quest was financial: how to pay for the printing? Despite his conviction that Tennyson made all

Arthurian subjects marketable, commercial publishers were skeptical. One after another turned down the "probable treasures of the Lonelich romance" because they couldn't make a profit on "an unknown poet"; they suggested that publishing with a private society or club would be more viable (Furnivall 1861, ii). Luckily enough, Furnivall was well acquainted with the treasurer of the Roxburghe Club, Beriah Botfield, who had joined the Philological Society around the same time as Furnivall (Philological Society 1847). When Botfield donated several Roxburghe editions to the Society's Dictionary Committee, Furnivall offered his editorial services for free if the Club would pay the costs of printing the "Romance of the St. Graal" (Furnivall 1861, ii). With Botfield's agreement, Furnivall had secured a patron for his treasured romance.

Before Furnivall could travel to Cambridge, he encountered a second obstacle, born of his own imagination. While editing Robert Mannyng's *Handlyng Synne* (Furnivall 1862), he happened "by chance" upon the etymology for *dimity*: he was distraught to learn that this course fabric had the same etymology as the grail's velvety *samite*:

> What! My samite allied to dimity,—bed-ticking and dusters! Here was a roll in the mud for all my rose-pink notions! And a terrible suspicion followed: What if the Lonelich Romance should be dimity too? Had not Ellis spoken of the dulness [sic] of an extract from it? Was it sure that he did so because the grapes were sour? Yes, it *was* sure, and should be. How *could* a history of the Graal be dull? So I was reassured, and went up soon after to Corpus, eager to examine my treasure, hoping to gloat over it and handle it for three days. (Furnivall 1861, iii)

Furnivall imagines that Ellis judged Lovelich harshly to cover the fact that he hadn't actually read the text. Furnivall's imagination, however, rescues him as quickly as it got him in trouble and carries him to Cambridge, where "the long-wished-for 'Romance of the San Graal' was put into my hands" (1861, iii). The volume is "stout," the writing "pale from damp and age, and awkward at first to read" (1861, iii). Like a suitor to a blind date, Furnivall tries to love his treasure but must admit a further obstacle: he finds the verse "dimity unmistakeable" after all. Yet, once again, romantic ideals to the rescue: "the subject of the Grail would ennoble any covering of words" (1861, iv). Like his eighteenth-century predecessors, albeit for different reasons, Furnivall separates content and form. Style concerns him so little that he prints eighty-nine pages of French prose to "complete" the text missing from the beginning of MS 80—and then an entire volume of the French prose *Queste del Saint Graal* to create a complete grail narrative for the Roxburghe Club (1864c). By abstracting story from style, Furnivall negotiates the simultaneity of "good" and "bad" romance.

Furnivall concludes his own romance of the grail with Tennyson— again so famous that he isn't named: "Anyone who does not find the 'thing' 'ful swete' can pass it by; enough for me to know that our great Victorian poet has glanced over these pages with interest; I trust he will accept them as a slight acknowledgement of the debt of gratitude all English-reading men now owe him, for the perfect words, and noble and beautiful thoughts, that are the delight of many a working-man in his workshop, as I well know, as well as of the Queen in her palace" (1861, xii). Furnivall drafts Tennyson's reputation as both a royal favorite and a people's poet to dismiss any potential critics of Lovelich. He casts Arthurian poetry as the great healer of social stratification—a romance of national unity that culminates when Furnivall's editions reach Tennyson's own library (Furnivall 1861, 1863, 1864c; Staines 1982, 66n9). Furnivall thus made MS 80 integral to a medieval English canon founded on nineteenth-century romantic medievalism.

Since the Roxburghe *Grail* couldn't satisfy Furnivall's desire to bring Arthurian romance to popular audiences, he reached agreement with the commercial publisher Macmillan to publish a shorter text, the stanzaic *Morte Arthur* (1864b). This very text was associated with MS 80 by Percy (1765), popularized by Ellis ([1805] 1848, 143–47), and previously edited for the Roxburghe Club (Ponton 1819). Macmillan's edition signals its popular orientation by opening with a drawing of an injured Arthur surrounded by fawning women in the delicate style of romantic chivalry. Furnivall dedicates the edition to Tennyson "with affectionate admiration" and begins the preface by invoking Tennyson's poems: he hopes their popularity will inspire enough sales to cover the costs of printing (Furnivall 1864b, vii).

More ambitiously, he hopes Arthurian enthusiasm will launch EETS: he asks for "the support of any readers this book may have, for that Society (the Early English Text Society) whose chief object is the printing in an accessible form of all the English Romances relating to Arthur and his Knights" (Furnivall 1864b, xxv). In this plea, Furnivall ties EETS to Arthurian romance, making the Roxburghe *Grail* and the Macmillan *Morte* founding documents for the then-emerging canon of medieval English literature.

The first EETS volumes, as promised, focused on Arthurian materials (Furnivall 1864a; Skeat 1865; Wheatley 1865–69; Brock 1871; Skeat 1871). The first Extra Series reprints brought more romances into circulation (Skeat 1867, 1868). On EETS's tenth anniversary, Furnivall started reprinting the Roxburghe *Grail*. The announcement, likely written by Furnivall, reiterates the spirit of his Roxburghe preface by separating Lovelich's style from the grail content:

> The glory of the Holy Grail renders radiant Arthur's court, spite of all its crimes. May its rays give brilliance to Lonelich's lines, and make them shine with an effulgence not their own! But, though poor, Lonelich's poem is the only full English History of the coming of the Grail to White Britain, which is England. It is part of that series of Arthur-Romances which the Committee from the first promist [sic] to print entire; and its curious mixture of monkish superstitions, legends, and fights, will interest the student of the Middle-Age romance and belief. (Early English Text Society 1874, 19)

Even though this announcement introduces Lovelich with the derogatory phrase "prosy poetaster," his text is redeemed here by its "radiant" content. The English language, moreover, gives the text national significance. And in a mistake perhaps revelatory of imperial racism, Britain is called "White" instead of "Blue" (as in the text; see chap. 1). Indeed, elsewhere the report extols EETS's patriotic contributions and global reach (Early English Text Society 1874, 10). The EETS *Grail* thus put Lovelich onto the shelves of individual and institutional subscribers throughout the British Empire, Europe, and the United States. The edition made the text canon for both literary and cultural history.

While EETS was printing medieval texts as quickly as financing allowed, the educational establishment turned away from romance toward poetry. By the end of the nineteenth century, romance started to engender "disenchantment" because it didn't fulfill expectations for the "irreducible aura" that came to define "literariness" (Ganim 1996, 163). While intrinsic literary qualities had never been part of the arguments in favor of romance, neither did style disqualify the genre from historical significance: Lovelich could write in "bad verse" and still be well worth reading ("Romance" 1861). A punctual measure of how romance lost out to new definitions of poetry can be taken from Matthew Arnold's introduction to an 1880 anthology for students. Arnold presents his influential view that historical significance should be excluded in determining the "best" poetry: "A poet or a poem may count to us historically, they may count to us on grounds personal to ourselves, and they may count to us really" (Arnold 1880, xx). The anthology begins with Chaucer—deemed the first poet to exceed mere historical value and achieve "real poetry" (Arnold 1880, xxxvi). Romances, meanwhile, are "rym doggerel" that no one needs to read (Arnold 1880, 1). Arnold's view of poetry shaped many guides to literature in the twentieth century—to the detriment of romance in general and Lovelich in particular. In the 1890s, W. P. Ker sealed the fate of romance when he judged it lacking in "freedom" and "dramatic imagination" compared to epic (Ker 1897, 37–39). In his influential telling, a "good" romance is one that is no longer medieval but instead a modern novel that is really an epic (1897, 415–21). These aesthetic values mark the end of the romantic medievalism that brought MS 80 into print.

And so, having become a romance, Lovelich's text entered the twentieth century as a bad romance. If the combination of Arnold's poetry and Ker's epic devalued all romances, Lovelich's fell the hardest. The irascible George Saintsbury (1845–1933) launched the new era with *A Short History of English Literature* (1898). Although not particularly short, at eight hundred pages, Saintsbury's history has had a long shelf life in reprints. Thanks to EETS, Saintsbury wrote with more information about medieval literature than any of his predecessors—and set a high bar for negativity directed at Lovelich: "[one of the] most curious books in existence, the wonderful interest and charm of the matter, which might have been thought likely either to stir a translator into genius or compel him to silent despair, being approached with a cheerful doggedness of incompetency difficult, if not impossible, to parallel elsewhere. Hardly any other story could possibly survive such a translator; no other translator, one would hope, could have failed to catch fire from such a story" (Saintsbury 1898, 195). In the Arnoldian frame, the "charm of the matter" no longer redeemed perceived failures of poetic style. Saintsbury thus finds Lovelich "dull," "ineffective," and "intolerable"—with "no spark of illumination" (1898, 194–95). A few years later, in *The English Novel*, he characterizes Lovelich as "execrable" and "abominable" (Saintsbury 1913, 11, 16). Readers seeking guidance through English literary history were thus warned away from Lovelich's romance in the strongest possible terms. Such judgments in reference books acquire the authority of established knowledge among specialists and nonspecialists alike, narrowing the canon from the printed corpus to the sanctioned corpus.

The most damning assessment of Lovelich came from EETS itself. In 1904, the long-awaited *Merlin* was finally published, edited by the Swedish scholar Ernst Kock (instead of by Mary Bateson, as previously planned [Kölbing 1890, xix]). To mark the occasion, EETS republicized the *Grail*. The report at the front of Kock's volume promises that the *Grail* will be reprinted along with "a capital summary of the rise and development of the Legend of the Graal" by Dorothy Kempe (Early English Text Society 1904, 3). Kempe was a recent Oxford graduate who went on to write a number of books, including a classic of girls' education, *English Girlhood at School* (1929) (Haigh 2004). Her introduction to Lovelich presents the latest orthodoxies of literary history: medieval literature is worthy for either sublime poetry (Arnold 1880) or epic heroism (Ker 1897)—neither of which she finds in Lovelich. While she admires Arthurian literature as a mirror of "the intellectual growth of a people," she deems Lovelich's version "the least attractive stage of its growth, for as a literary monument, or as a work of art, his History of the Holy Grail is valueless" (Kempe 1905, v). The only possible interest is the "strange and anomalous . . . introduction of the Christian Legendary element," a derivative echo of the French tradition (Kempe 1905, v). Kempe goes on to compare Lovelich unfavorably to Malory: Lovelich "proves himself no story teller, and his version of the famous episodes may be commended with the rest of his voluminous and incoherent ramblings, to a merciful oblivion" (Kempe 1905, vi). She judges the entire grail tradition flatly "ridiculous" (Kempe 1905, xxxvii). And so, between the covers of the reprint, Lovelich appears unworthy of printing. In this position, Kempe's essay carries the authority of canon, repeated even now at the front of every EETS reprint of Furnivall's edition.

Kempe's disparagements reverberate through twentieth-century criticism. John Wells largely repeats her opinions as (uncredited) facts in the *Manual of the Writings in Middle English*: the *Grail* is of "little or no artistic or literary value. Its theme exhibits one of the least interesting phases of the growth of the [Arthurian] legend, due largely to the infusion of Christian legendary elements"; the *Merlin* is "distressingly tedious" (Wells 1916, 77, 45). Here, the Christian elements that made the book attractive centuries earlier now ensure its status as an unattractive romance. The updated *Manual* of 1967 did little for Lovelich's reputation: he had "no talent for writing and no ear for verse," although as "a man of substance who respected poetry," he deserved some attention (Newstead 1967, 49). In this case, upper-middle-class social values provide some margin of redemption. In the same era, George Kane seems morally committed to discouraging future readers: "The personality that [Lovelich] reveals in these monuments of dullness is oppressive by its excessively unhumorous application and diligence; there is not one relieving feature in the thousands upon thousands of lines that he wrote, not one moment of brightness, or any change of any kind from level mediocrity.... Lovelich was an unimaginative and insensitive clod, capable only of further inflating his already huge originals" (Kane 1951, 16–17; cited in Dalrymple 2000, 157). Even Robert Ackerman, who studied Lovelich extensively in the 1950s, reached harsh conclusions: "the most clumsy and tedious poet of the fifteenth century" (1952a, 153; cited in Dalrymple 2000, 157), with "scarcely a trace of talent" (Ackerman 1952b, 484); Lovelich had "no ear whatever," wrote with "utmost awkwardness" and "plodding dullness," and "lacked nearly every qualification for his task" (Ackerman 1959, 488, 507, 519). All these comments—from Wells to Ackerman—occur in reference books meant to guide students of medieval literature. They are the kinds of texts oft consulted but rarely cited. Their influence is undoubtedly broad but hard to document as it may take place in the flash of a page quickly turned, a note not taken, a question not asked, an edition not read.

Guides to romance and Arthurian literature maintained Lovelich's bad reputation throughout the twentieth century. Derek Pearsall put the poem's very existence in quotation marks, discarding every distinctive feature as "odd" and insignificant (1976, 71). Derek Brewer classed the text among the "flood" of fifteenth-century translations, which have "human importance" even though they also deserve "literary contempt"; Lovelich's work is merely "immensely long" in a century marked by "modest achievement" (1983, 88). W. R. J. Barron saw only the "limping verse" of an "immensely long" poem (1987, 152n12; cited in Dalrymple 2000, 157). Even specialists in Arthurian literature have been mostly discouraging: "derivative" and "uncomplicated" for "historically and aesthetically uncritical" audiences (Hodder 1999b, 82); a "vast and unwieldy" work "of somewhat indeterminate metrical form" (Cooper 2003, 151). These relatively recent judgments witness the slow pace of change in literary history. Reference books, by their nature, often rely on previous reference books to navigate vast quantities of material. Ideas become sedimented as common knowledge rather than situated within specific aesthetic histories. Authors and publishers endeavor to represent "consensus" but end up canonizing idiosyncratic opinions. In this way, the "dullest" poet of the "dullest" century remains the latest news, just as he was in 1805.

Fortunately, not all readers are swayed by the authority of handbooks. Anyone who consulted Kock's *Merlin*, despite the warnings, could find subtle clues that the manuscript might be a little interesting: Kock's footnotes point to scribal corrections, some "blank spaces" in the text columns, marginal annotations, and the occasional doodle (e.g., Kock 1904–32, 206, 238, 245, 260). Manuscript studies became one of the first ways in which scholars found Lovelich worthwhile (Meale 1994; Warren 2008; Eddy 2012). The romance genre also elicited new interest as scholars developed social approaches to literature (e.g., Knight 1986). Understanding Lovelich, then, as a member of a particular London community shaped another set of approaches that refreshed Lovelich's reputation (Dalrymple 2000; Radulescu 2013; Warren 2016; see chap. 2). Finally, translation studies developed into a sophisticated field in which Lovelich's text no longer looked derivative (Warren 2007; Finotello 2014; see chap. 1). Carole Meale combined all these perspectives to contextualize MS 80 in a mercantile environment, declaring Lovelich's poems "two of the most interesting" in late medieval London (Meale 1994, 217). Since the 1990s, then, a new course has been set.

In the last decade, reference works have started to reflect these changes. In the article "Romance" for the *Oxford History of Literary Translation in English*, Rosalind Field calls Lovelich's work "lengthy and often clumsy" yet notes that Lovelich has "a recognizable voice and a civic context for an ambitious" translation (2008, 308). In *Later Medieval English Literature*, Douglas Gray calls the translations "rather good" and the poetry "competent, if not inspired" (2008, 386–87). And in the latest *Handbook of Arthurian Romance*, Gareth Griffith dispenses almost entirely with the defensive posture to offer a thematic analysis of shame, just as one might for any text (2017). Likewise, the digital library Literature Online (LION) by Chadwyck-Healey (now ProQuest) includes a biography for Lovelich that engages recent scholarship and wholly breaks the cycle of negativity in a reference work ("Lovelich" 2017). LION effectively circles back to Nasmith, classifying Lovelich's text as a romance by association with its French source. LION also picks up "romance" from titles in another ProQuest product, the *Annual Bibliography of English Language and Literature* (*ABELL*). In the latest digital handbook, then, Lovelich is the author of a romance in both eighteenth-century and twenty-first-century terms, having passed through the romantic hyperbole of the nineteenth century and the poetic strictures of the twentieth. The vagaries of Lovelich's reputation testify to the powerful yet unstable work of literary canons.

Text on Platforms

The literary history of romance brought MS 80's text into print, and the platform history of publishing has now brought it onto LION in the form of digitized editions. Platforms build on each other, the products of one becoming components of another. With editions, this process of textual transmission amounts to philology by platform. The story of LION's Lovelich editions thus unravels in reverse but progresses sequentially from the Roxburghe Club to EETS to ProQuest. At each stage, MS 80 was partly incidental to editorial selections based on collections: Furnivall sought any and all Arthurian romances; EETS Extra Series reprinted what others had already printed; LION reproduced EETS to represent medieval English literature. This history of editions is entangled, from start to finish, with the *Oxford English Dictionary*. Here, too, selections for linguistic data proceeded through collections. Furnivall was working on the Dictionary Committee when he edited MS 80 for the Roxburghe Club; Roxburghe, EETS, and LION have all contributed citations to the *OED*; *OED* citations have made Lovelich an author of the English language. Since the 1850s, then, the social and financial organization of publishing platforms has had as much influence on the English canon as the literary historians of romance. Today, these dynamics continue on digital platforms. The very latest editors of MS 80 are the machine processes that display text on LION and other digital platforms such as Google, HathiTrust, and the Internet Archive. These digitized editions consolidate inherited canons even as their metadata reconfigure literary history. They are the products of platform philology.

Furnivall's Roxburghe *Grail* illustrates the formative work of platforms in producing medieval literature. The edition came about because of Furnivall's role as cochair of the Philological Society's Dictionary Committee, founded in 1857 (Benzie 1983, 81–116). The dictionary needed editions of medieval texts to document the history of English. In the early days, the project relied on publications by private clubs and societies—such as the Roxburghe Club. This group of forty bibliophiles published deluxe editions for their own private libraries, using rare books to shore up English cultural imperialism (Matthews 1999, 85–89; Husbands 2017; White 2020). One of the club members, Beriah Botfield, had joined the Philological Society around the same time as Furnivall in 1847 (Philological Society 1847). Botfield regularly donated Roxburghe editions to the Dictionary Committee. So when commercial publishers refused to print the grail romance, Furnivall pitched it to Botfield (Furnivall 1861, ii). The Roxburghe *Grail* then became an outlet for dictionary work. Several members of the Philological Society contributed signed notes to Furnivall's edition (Hensleigh Wedgwood, Benjamin Davies) while the dictionary editor Herbert Coleridge (1830-61) provided a prefatory essay on "Arthur" (Furnivall 1863, xxi–xxxii, reprinted in Furnivall 1864b, xxviii–lvi). Coleridge and Furnivall also produced dictionary materials from MS 80, printed at the end of the Roxburghe volumes: "List of a Few Words casually extracted for use in the Philological Society's proposed English Dictionary, by the late Herbert Coleridge and F. J. Furnivall" (Furnivall 1861, 493); "List of Some of the Noteworthy Words, Meanings, and Constructions" (Furnivall 1863, 397). The dictionary project thus made the edition possible while the edition contributed to the dictionary. Linguistic data from the Roxburghe *Grail*, however "casually extracted," ultimately furnished the *OED* with some authoritative documentation of the history of English.

Furnivall treated the edition itself as a platform with various interchangeable components. Not only did Philological Society members write linguistic notes; the text was mostly transcribed by someone else—Harry Seeley, who also contributed to Furnivall's other Roxburghe editions around the same time (Furnivall 1861, iv, xiii; 1862, xxii). The Roxburghe *Grail* also includes a parallel edition of a French prose text, representing Lovelich's source, transcribed by Eleanor Dalziel, who married Furnivall soon after (Furnivall 1861, iv; Benzie 1983, 24). In each of these early editions, Furnivall describes his own role as minimal: "only putting together disjointed words" (1861, xii), "helping occasionally" (1862, xxii), and reluctantly giving up his vacation to complete Seeley's work (1863, x–xi). He functions mainly as a proofreader—and not a very good one, by his own admission (1862, xxiii–xxv). When he offers excuses for his "freshman's first performance" as editor, he neglects to mention Seeley's qualifications, which are far more pertinent (1862, xxv). Seeley would have been around twenty years old and hardly trained for the task: at the time, he was a student of Furnivall's at the Working Men's College with interests in geology (he eventually became a rather important paleontologist [Lydekker 1909]). He contributed just one note to the edition—a detailed geological explanation of the phrase "chalk in the clay" (Furnivall 1861, 324; *Grail*, XXV: 242). Furnivall's approach to using amanuenses amounts to a platform theory of editing: at the base is a hand (*a manu*)—anyone's hand.

After publishing the Roxburghe *Grail*, Furnivall founded EETS in 1864 to scale up his values: Arthurian enthusiasm, patriotic lexicography, and platform philology. EETS had a popularizing spirit. Just as the Dictionary Committee welcomed "Englishmen to come forward and write their own Dictionary for themselves" (*Proposal* 1859, 8), EETS welcomed English men and women to come forward and edit their literature for themselves. EETS's first governance board included, not surprisingly, many members of the Philological Society (Singleton 2005, 91n2). They sought a broad subscriber base to pay for the printing, with Tennyson among the first to join (Benzie 1983, 120). Throughout the 1850s and 1860s, then, Furnivall was leveraging the prestige of romantic poetry to elevate medieval romance— and ultimately the English language itself. The editions and the dictionary both aimed to consolidate English heritage as an elite, racialized culture that could nonetheless be acquired by anyone.

The editions of MS 80 tell a representative history of EETS's first fifty years. The original printings include reports that detail the Society's operations and aspirations. The first *Grail* volume coincided with EETS's tenth anniversary, prompting a lengthy report. By this time, the Society's ambition had grown to encompass "the printing of the whole of the unprinted MSS. of Early English" (Early English Text Society 1874, 13). The report, likely written by Furnivall, claimed that EETS had already reinvented the history of English literature: with so many new texts printed, it was no longer possible to describe Chaucer as the "Father of English Poetry" (11). The expanded canon enhanced not only the history of the English language but the status of the English nation and the global reach of the British empire: EETS was bringing "the teaching of English culture within the reach of every student and boy in the British Empire, the United States, Germany, and Austria" (10). Nonetheless, to achieve the Society's printing goals, more subscribers were needed; current subscribers were urged to sign up their friends (12, 27). In this report and others, acquiring new subscribers is a form of patriotism (Matthews 1999, 147–48; Singleton 2005, 99–100). The more subscribers, the more texts, the more honor to the nation.

These principles were repeated in 1904 in the first *Merlin* volume. The preface reprints the description of EETS used in many volumes over many years, likely written by Furnivall. EETS is given a profound national purpose: its publications provide essential knowledge of English character, illustrating "the thoughts, the life, the manners and customs of our forefathers and foremothers" (Early English Text Society 1904, 2). The editions make this historical information accessible to "the ordinary student" (2), binding the nation together through shared knowledge. The editions also provide "the beginnings (at least) of proper Histories and Dictionaries of that Language and Literature," which themselves will instruct the general public in their own culture (2). All these functions combine to improve England's reputation in the eyes of other nations, "wiping away the reproach under which England had long rested, of having felt little interest in the monuments of her early language and life" (2). This ambitious goal requires many more editions: "Until all Early English MSS are printed, no proper History of our Language or Social Life is possible" (2). Since printed editions have such lofty purpose, the report accuses nonsubscribers of bad citizenship: "very small numbers of those inheritors of the speech of Cynewulf, Chaucer and Shakespeare . . . care two guineas a year for the records of that speech. 'Let the dead past bury its dead' is still the cry of Great Britain and her Colonies, and of America, in the matter of language" (2). The report pleads repeatedly for help in increasing subscriptions so that completed editions can go to press (2, 4, 5). Despite the perpetual shortage of funds, EETS published a steady stream of editions that increased the corpus of English language and literature. On this basis, EETS claimed also to increase England's national and imperial reputation.

Meanwhile, the Philological Society's dictionary project was pursuing the same goals using editions for evidence of etymologies and historical usage. In the early days, the Dictionary Committee used a lot of Roxburghe editions, including Furnivall's *Grail* (Philological Society 1861). Over time, EETS editions provided citations, while the need for citations motivated editing (Willinsky 1994, 33; Matthews 1999, 147). The dictionary project was heralded from the beginning in nationalist terms and became a symbol of imperial supremacy (Willinsky 1994). Furnivall himself did not mince words in an 1862 report to the Philological Society, composed in the midst of his work on Lovelich: "We have set ourselves to form a National Portrait Gallery, not only of the worthies, but of all of the members, of the race of English words which is to form the dominant speech of the world" (cited in Gilliver 2016, 46). This exhortation, true to Furnivall's romantic spirit, included a line from Tennyson's *The Princess* (1847): "Fling our doors wide! All, all, not one, but all." Furnivall's philosophy of lexicography thus echoes his editorial and social ideals: egalitarian in the service of national prestige. The actual work proceeded rather chaotically—largely because of Furnivall (Gilliver 2016, 41–90). But these shaky foundations recede from view in the aura of authority that has accrued to the *OED*. Just as EETS's reputation lends legitimacy to each individual volume, the *OED*'s reputation lends legitimacy to each individual citation. And those citations would collectively provide imperial English with solid historical foundations.

The mutual relationship between dictionary work and editorial work plays out clearly in Lovelich's case. On the one hand, a query from the dictionary editor Henry Bradley about the dating of the word *lonely* created doubts about the spelling of Lovelich's name—leading to documentation that his name was not in fact "Lonelich" as previously printed (Bradley 1902a; Furnivall 1903). On the other hand, EETS editions of Lovelich's text provided nearly eight hundred citations for the *OED* (OED.com). These citations show how the happenstance of attention has shaped the history of English. The *Grail*, for example, has many more citations (590) than the *Merlin* (199), likely because the *Grail* was printed during the period of most active collection for medieval sources, whereas the last volume of *Merlin* was printed in 1932, after the first edition of the *OED* had been completed. A disproportionate number of words are cited from Lovelich as either the first evidence of a word's existence (71 words) or the first evidence of a particular meaning (209 words). A portion of these words are attested only in Lovelich's text, with no other citations for the word's existence or meaning—for example, *apressly, ascomfit, inlance, presumptuosity*. These words are duly classified as "obsolete, rare." Some arise from untranslated French; they may or may not have been in broader use in the fifteenth century. Conversely, some relatively common words are listed with Lovelich as the oldest attestation of particular meanings, when it is highly likely that others also used the word in similar fashion—for example, *bloodshed, endlessly, eyebrow, shatter.* Citations from Lovelich for thoroughly common words further demonstrate how printed editions shaped citation patterns across the dictionary—for example, *about, again, day, lady, of, well.* The history of English is thus also the history of editorial publishing in the nineteenth century.

Today, the *OED* is a digital platform available by subscription—just like LION, which includes the EETS backlist up to 1991. Both platforms exemplify how digital databases process texts inherited from nineteenth-century print. On OED.com, each entry shows the date of its revision: many entries that cite Lovelich are unrevised, representing original nineteenth-century research. But even the most recently updated entries include material originally prepared in the nineteenth century: as a matter of policy, the *OED* doesn't delete (Gilliver 2016, 557). Meanwhile, since the 1990s, the *OED* has used full-text digital databases to generate new citations—including LION and the journal archive JSTOR (Gilliver 2016, 566). Editorial publishing is thus still defining the history of English. The full-text databases construct canons as they seek to appeal to the broadest possible subscriber base (LION) or save the most shelf space (JSTOR). Even though these large-scale projects can disrupt canons through keyword search, editorial decisions still shape the corpus. JSTOR, for example, began with "stable" disciplines and excluded "turbulent" fields like literature (Gitelman 2014b, 78). Metadata decisions introduced further biases (Block 2020). OED.com inherits these kinds of editorial intentions and accidents from every platform used for citations. Layers and layers of editorial canonizing, stretching back to the 1850s and beyond, filter into each digital platform.

By design, digital platforms minimize their editorial contributions to bolster the authenticity of their texts. This, too, they inherit from nineteenth-century print platforms. ProQuest, for example, markets LION's value based on the fact that texts have been "re-keyed to 99.99% textual accuracy" (Literature Online Brochure, accessed April 30, 2020). For the MS 80 texts, this promise echoes the murky circumstances of the

Grail transcription in the 1850s: rekeyed by whom? LION texts, moreover, may be accurate in relation to print editions, but the editions' relationships with their sources aren't recoverable from the platform: the scrolling page of text has been stripped of original prefaces, apparatus, and most notes. Nonetheless, a rekey editor selected five notes for the *Grail* (from the hundreds in the printed volumes), and another editor (or the same) added fourteen chapter divisions to the *Merlin* (vols. 1 and 2; 3 is not included). The resulting digital edition is optimized for cross-database keyword search. On ProQuest, this textual universe includes dissertations, journal articles, bibliographies, and other collections of literature. Across these databases, discovery by keyword search and metadata rests on the redefinition of editing as "rekeying." Digital platforms thus rely on a new generation of amanuenses. Like Furnivall, ProQuest obscures its editorial interventions as the condition for profiting from them.

The metadata for Lovelich on LION show how platforms rewrite literary history as they reedit texts (surveyed March 22, 2020). First, Lovelich is unequivocally a poet because his texts are part of the "English Poetry Full-Text Database." The automated process of metadata aggregation, however, has given the *Grail* a new nonpoetry title: "The Legend of the Holy Grail"—the title of Kempe's 1905 essay. In this twist, the text is no longer the "romance" that Nasmith made it but a "legend" outside of literature and history, ever tied to its rejection by Kempe. Meanwhile, Lovelich's "other poem" is titled "Merlin, BY LOUELICH THE SKINNER"—a spelling that looks like a misprint for "Lovelich" but is actually a transcription from the manuscript that had been printed in an earlier catalogue and reprinted in Kock's edition. Scrolling down, readers would think that the text is only about fifteen thousand lines, as nothing indicates the absence of text from volume 3 of the printed edition. More confusing, MS 80's approximate date given by Furnivall (c. 1450) has been translated into a specific lifespan for Lovelich—born 1425, died 1475. This false information emerges from the data template: "c. 1450" becomes the exact middle years of the 1400s. In fact, Lovelich's birth and death dates are unknown, although he appears active in various records from 1401 to 1411 (see chap. 3). "Louelich, 1425–75" and the "legend" in the poetry database show how machine processing can turn errors into facts. Platforms can actively re-write literary history. LION's Lovelich biography, however, corrects the misleading judgments that have accumulated in reference works since El-lis's *Specimens*. And platform searches for *romance* produce a wide range of results that fully contextualize the history of the genre, including Lovelich's French source and all the texts classified as romances by EETS (see chap. 4). LION is thus simultaneously one of the best places to learn about Lovelich and one of the worst.

The metadata for Lovelich's editions across other platforms further document how platform philology produces both more connections and more errors. In the Dartmouth Library catalogue, for example, "Henry Lovelich" is the Author/Creator of three "book chapters": LION *Grail*, LION *Merlin*, and EETS *Merlin* (vol. 3). This is a complete corpus of MS 80's edited text, in a combination of digital and print formats. These are not, however, all the editions. Four more items are listed by "Herry Lovelich," which are digitized editions on the HathiTrust platform: Roxburghe *Grail* (vol. 2), EETS *Grail* (vol. 5, by Kempe), and EETS *Merlin* (vols. 1 and 2). This corpus is incomplete even though HathiTrust hosts multiple copies of all the Roxburghe and EETS volumes: the metadata register five more variations on Lovelich's name, disparities that block the merger of records representing the "same" volume. Meanwhile, no search on the Dartmouth catalogue by author or title returns the EETS Extra Series editions that are actually on the local shelf—that is, all of the *Grail* and the first two volumes of *Merlin*. Long ago, the Extra Series was classified as a "journal" with no separate entries by title, author, editor, or even volume number (Dewey Decimal 820.6.E12pe). *Merlin* volume 3, meanwhile, is classified as a "book chapter," as if the Original Series were one book (Library of Con-gress PR1119.A2). This volume's absence from LION may thus result from something like a shelf-reading error, since many libraries likely catalogued volume 3 separately from the Extra Series volumes. All these variations (and more I haven't detailed) reveal that even as digital platforms aggregate more and more metadata, they remain fragmented by local histories that include nineteenth-century cataloguing decisions. In the absence of meta-data reconciliation, updating can become backdating—and even erasure.

Platforms like HathiTrust host digitized editions produced by scanning rather than by "rekeying" like LION. The newest editions of MS 80 are thus text files generated by OCR processing from scanned images. These editions combine machine authoring with the human craft of software design (Cordell 2017, 196, 199). The corpus of Lovelich's OCR editions exposes the editorial work of machine processing because the files have been processed on three different platforms, producing variants when the "same" print volume is processed by different OCR software. Across Google, HathiTrust, and the Internet Archive, Lovelich is identified variously as "Herry Loneuch," "Kerry Lovelich," and "Lo118lich." Even the born-digital watermark "Google" can be processed into "L^ooQle." Meanwhile, the Middle English character yogh (ȝ) can come across fairly consistently as either "je" (Internet Archive) or "3e" (HathiTrust). These digital variants harken back to the idiosyncrasies of manuscripts and serve as reminders of the variable and even unreliable conditions of full-text search.

The passage of text from MS 80 into print and ultimately onto the internet has been structured by platform philology. These practices have a host of contradictory effects. Furnivall's treatment of his collaborators as interchangeable "hands" erased the intellectual contributions of women (Eleanor Dalziel is only one example). At the same time, he brought relatively unskilled, unprivileged women and men into scholarship. He was well known for his "undiscriminating mode" of recruiting editors (Singleton 2005, 115). Similarly, Google's "ScanOps"—the unit that processed book scans into PDFs—taught specific skills to low-wage workers but also created gendered and racialized hierarchies by segregating ScanOps from higher-paid units staffed predominantly by white male engineers (Zeffiro 2019, 142–46). In print and online, these platform practices increase the pace of editing at the cost of equitable labor practices. Efficiencies are also created by selecting collections rather than individual texts: edit the manuscripts from the closest library; scan the whole library shelf of printed books. Yet collection-based reproduction also recycles the values that shaped the collections, giving them new platforms where their historical context becomes harder to perceive with each iteration. Already in the passage of Lovelich's text from Roxburghe to EETS, Furnivall's romanticism fades from view: Tennyson's poetry disappears when the preface is removed. By the time the LION editions reach my local library catalogue, Furnivall himself has disappeared. Even so, metadata and full-text search across platforms can redirect these sedimented canons in provocative and illuminating ways. Alongside the erasures and errors, new connections emerge. The future of literary history is thus indebted to the generative and enduring effects of platforms on the accessibility of medieval texts.

Codex on Demand

The corollary of platform philology is platform codicology—publishing arrangements that distribute editions in collections. When published in a series, an edition is not only an individual book but also part of a larger corpus of similar books. The characteristics of the series influence the meaning of each individual volume. Here, too, nineteenth-century print practices and twenty-first-century digital systems operate in mutually informing ways. The publishing platforms that distributed medieval texts—Roxburghe and EETS—developed material consistencies that made each individual volume recognizable as part of a larger collection. As the series accumulated on shelves, they became coherent canons. And when they accumulated on library shelves, their classification in cataloguing systems contributed to selection patterns for mass scanning projects, with far-reaching consequences for the digital libraries that have become so integral to the knowledge economy. Digitized books produced from scans extend questions of format to new technologies. Platform components such as file specifications, interfaces, hardware, and software structure access to networked libraries and can reframe literary genres along the way.

Digital platforms maintain different relationships with offline books and libraries, depending in part on their financial models. While online books can make offline books seem obsolete, offline books can authenticate and legitimize digital facsimiles. In some cases, authenticity justifies access fees; in others, it maintains users' trust amid the many free resources that are also notoriously unreliable. To position themselves in this broader information economy, where trust itself is an unstable commodity, digital platforms deploy what I call a "rhetorical codex"—an idea of the book as a unique offline object. These relationships are thrown into stark relief by the print-on-demand market—books printed one at a time from PDFs that represent out-of-copyright texts. This corpus has become quite large as a result of the mass scanning of library books over the past fifteen years. PDFs hosted in open repositories can be remarketed en masse as reprints by anyone with access to an industrial printing machine. Each book is printed "on demand"; it is custom-made (for a customer) but also the product of vast technological infrastructures—from scanning to mail-delivery systems. POD turns online texts back into offline books. With common covers and other shared features, POD books form collections that accumulate on screens and shelves as coherent canons. Amid digital platforms offering text for free, POD marketers sell the value of the codex format as an expression of canonical value. Since a POD book is an actual codex, marketers trade the rhetorical codex of digital platforms for the rhetoric of literary history.

The print editions of Furnivall's *Grail* illustrate succinctly how platform codicology contributes to literary canons. As a Roxburghe Club volume, the *Grail* was part of an exclusive series intended for the private libraries of club members. By the time of Furnivall's edition, the club had established a consistent design: deluxe folio-size paper, distinctive bindings, uniform typography, a neogothic frontispiece listing the members (limited to forty), and woodcut images in the style of early modern printed books. The Roxburghe *Grail* features all these elements, including woodcuts. The images fill space at the beginning and end of each volume, meeting a standard expectation for decoration. They are somewhat tangentially related to the Christian and chivalric themes of Lovelich's translation. Volume 1 has one image from an early modern edition of Dante's *Divine Comedy* (probably Dante 1491; Wikimedia) and another depicting Adam and Eve's expulsion from the Garden of Eden (Furnivall 1861, xxii, 497). Volume 2 has another image of Christian temptation, two images of men on horseback, and a reader at a lectern (Furnivall 1863, xx, xlviii, 404, 412). These images combine early modern and neogothic medievalism to align the *Grail* with every other volume on club members' shelves.

When Furnivall reprinted the text of his Roxburghe edition in EETS, the change of format conveyed a change of meaning. Whereas the Roxburghe *Grail* comprises two large volumes with two columns of text on each page, the EETS *Grail* comprises four small volumes with a single text column per page. Whereas Roxburghe books were destined for private distribution and not intended for libraries (Matthews 1999, 87), EETS books reached hundreds of subscribers and are still available in reprints even now. In reformatting the edited text, the EETS volume also shifted its meaning: in a Roxburghe binding, the *Grail* is a rare text worthy of an expensive format; in an EETS binding, it is a popular text worthy of a broad audience. EETS, too, developed a consistent format that conveyed this message: plain covers with titles and series numbers on the spine (see fig. 17). Over time, the typography and design have varied but at any given moment, the format is the same for every volume. Both publication series accumulate on shelves as coherent collections that lend their authority as series to each individual volume.

The Roxburghe and EETS editions have now all been reproduced on digital platforms. Their path from print codex to digitized book passed through library platforms—shelves and institutions that classified and sustained them into the twenty-first century. The Lovelich editions thus bear witness to the social, financial, and technical arrangements of the digital libraries that have transformed the knowledge economy in recent years. Mass scanning began in libraries in 2004, sponsored by Google. Google itself began as part of a digital library project at Stanford in the late 1990s: founder Larry Page pivoted away from mass digitization to launch a company focused on search technologies, only to return to library books as sources of revenue-generating information (Thylstrup 2018, 38–40). Today, PDFs produced by Google are also hosted on other platforms, notably HathiTrust and the Internet Archive. Each digital platform hosts a unique corpus of Lovelich editions, represented by many variations in metadata. Some editions are represented only once and on only one platform. No two PDFs, however, are exactly alike. Even PDFs of the "same" book from the "same" library can represent distinct scanning events years apart, as evidenced by both metadata and unique image characteristics. And despite

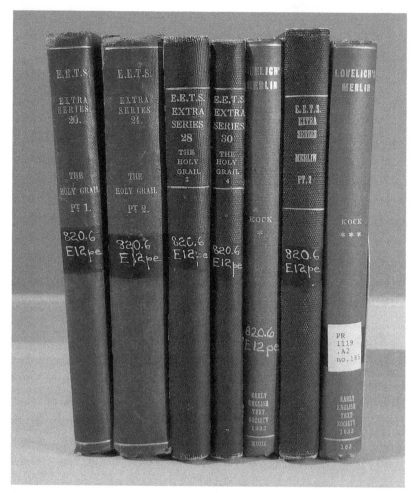

Figure 17 Edition of MS 80 in seven volumes. Early English Text Society, Dartmouth College Library. Photo by Michelle Warren (January 6, 2019).

scanning projects' reputation for reproducing whole shelves for the sake of efficiency, no platform has a complete set of EETS editions from one library. Similarly, the Roxburghe *Grail* is represented by more copies of volume 2 than volume 1. These patterns show that even Google-sponsored digitization from library shelves involves many kinds of selection and exclusion (Chalmers and Edwards 2017). As a result, each platform represents a specific partial collection even as they all make claims on "universality."

Their gaps and inconsistencies expose how selections have shaped even the largest digital libraries. These selections intersect with those that have shaped the printed canon of medieval literature. Digital libraries are thus perhaps more likely to consolidate old canons than they are to disrupt and open new perspectives.

The Lovelich PDFs illustrate these intersections between platform codicology and literary value. The codicology of a PDF produced from a printed codex includes the entire computational apparatus that creates and sustains digital objects. At the level of format, a digitized edition of an EETS volume actually has more in common with the digitized edition of MS 80 on Parker Library on the Web than with the printed EETS source. All the digitized books are made of TIFFs and JPEGs and can become PDFs; all have the same, variable dimensions (the size of the viewing window on a screen of a certain size); all open with interfaces that provide similar viewing options (single page, two-page opening, gallery view, etc.). And all show evidence of handcrafted production. Google's industrial production model preserves evidence of the digital bookmaking process. These "glitches" can even be considered a defining feature of the model (Conway 2013). Common errors include reversed pages, differences in scale between odd and even pages, and color images combined with images processed to black/white contrast (see fig. 18). These results document how the digital-capture process produces data that look like facsimile images only after extensive processing (Chalmers and Edwards 2017; Thylstrup 2018, 41–42). The most well-documented glitches involve the hands of people who scanned the books. These images portray the labor of handcrafting that is a basic component of digital platforms. People's hands are scanned more often with small volumes—like EETS editions—because they require more handholding to produce useable images. These digital fingerprints mark a point where manuscript, print, and digital meet again and again—echoes of the faint fingerprint that marks MS 80 itself (f. 1v). In some cases, processing software detects these handprints and generates color changes to "erase" them. Even when the process is algorithmically successful, however, it can usually be detected by a human eye. When the process fails, the results depict infrastructure in the act of bookmaking.

Digital images of printed books are ultimately somewhat incidental to the functions of digital platforms: one of the most powerful advantages of digital libraries is text search, which doesn't require page images. Nonetheless, digital platforms remain invested in images and in the rhetorical codex—the idea of the book as a format that authenticates information. The rhetorical codex distracts users from the fact that "full-text search" is often anything but (Pope and Holley 2011). The nature of this rhetorical codex depends on the platform's financial model. Google's paradigm has drifted away from the codex over time to promote information, while the nonprofit platforms have maintained and even strengthened their rhetorical commitments to shelves and "paper libraries" (Internet Archive). The nonprofit HathiTrust, for example, is defined as a consortium of offline libraries; only member institutions can access its full library of digitized editions; sometimes access is even specifically tied to a member institution's ownership of the printed codex source. The Internet Archive, meanwhile, has defended the codex-like properties of digital files in court. Countering a lawsuit from publishers about Controlled Digital Lending, Brewster Kahle has underscored the symmetry of online and offline libraries: both exist to "buy, preserve, and lend books" (Kahle 2020). This defense, ironically, relies on the logic of commodity transactions: if you buy something, you can do what you want with it. For profit-oriented platforms, by contrast, books are "information" that they own: customers acquire the storage format, not the content. In this model, books are licensed, not owned. At different times, Google has deployed both sides of this argument against authors, publishers, and libraries themselves (Thylstrup 2018, 45–55). Google is now a bookstore that profits from libraries, monetizing the codex by turning it into pure rhetoric. All these platform maneuvers determine access to the history of printed books and their texts in ways that directly impinge on how texts (including editions of medieval texts) reach both popular and specialist audiences.

These tensions between codex (form) and information (content) play out in platform interfaces. In its early phases, Google deployed the codex rhetorically to negotiate the ontological shift from shelf to screen. The very

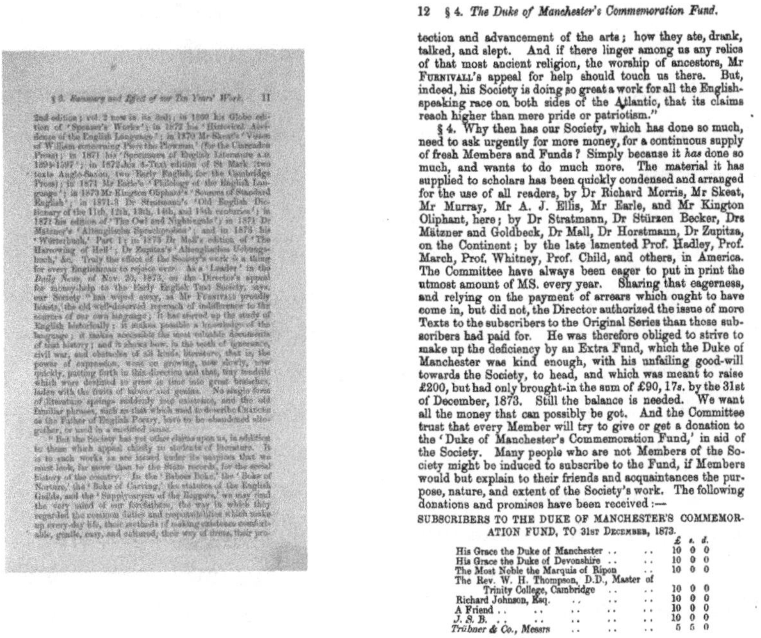

12 § 4. *The Duke of Manchester's Commemoration Fund.*

tection and advancement of the arts; how they ate, drank, talked, and slept. And if there linger among us any relics of that most ancient religion, the worship of ancestors, Mr FURNIVALL's appeal for help should touch us there. But, indeed, his Society is doing so great a work for all the English-speaking race on both sides of the Atlantic, that its claims reach higher than mere pride or patriotism."

§ 4. Why then has our Society, which has done so much, need to ask urgently for more money, for a continuous supply of fresh Members and Funds? Simply because it *has* done so much, and wants to do much more. The material it has supplied to scholars has been quickly condensed and arranged for the use of all readers, by Dr Richard Morris, Mr Skeat, Mr Murray, Mr A. J. Ellis, Mr Earle, and Mr Kington Oliphant, here; by Dr Stratmann, Dr Stürzen Becker, Drs Mätzner and Goldbeck, Dr Mall, Dr Horstmann, Dr Zupitza, on the Continent; by the late lamented Prof. Hadley, Prof. March, Prof. Whitney, Prof. Child, and others, in America. The Committee have always been eager to put in print the utmost amount of MS. every year. Sharing that eagerness, and relying on the payment of arrears which ought to have come in, but did not, the Director authorized the issue of more Texts to the subscribers to the Original Series than those subscribers had paid for. He was therefore obliged to strive to make up the deficiency by an Extra Fund, which the Duke of Manchester was kind enough, with his unfailing good-will towards the Society, to head, and which was meant to raise £200, but had only brought-in the sum of £90, 17*s*. by the 31st of December, 1873. Still the balance is needed. We want all the money that can possibly be got. And the Committee trust that every Member will try to give or get a donation to the 'Duke of Manchester's Commemoration Fund,' in aid of the Society. Many people who are not Members of the Society might be induced to subscribe to the Fund, if Members would but explain to their friends and acquaintances the purpose, nature, and extent of the Society's work. The following donations and promises have been received:—

SUBSCRIBERS TO THE DUKE OF MANCHESTER'S COMMEMORATION FUND, TO 31ST DECEMBER, 1873.

	£	s.	d.
His Grace the Duke of Manchester	10	0	0
His Grace the Duke of Devonshire	10	0	0
The Most Noble the Marquis of Ripon ..	10	0	0
The Rev. W. H. Thompson, D.D., Master of Trinity College, Cambridge	10	0	0
Richard Johnson, Esq.	10	0	0
A Friend	10	0	0
J. S. B.	10	0	0
Trübner & Co., Messrs	5	5	0

Figure 18 Scanned pages, left reversed to right and mismatched sizes. In *History of the Holy Grail*, edited by Frederick J. Furnivall. Early English Text Society, Extra Series 20 (1874), 11–12. Digitized from Stanford University Library; uploaded to Archive.org on August 9, 2008.

SOURCE: https://archive.org/details/historyholygrai01lovegoog/page/n19/mode/2up.

title "Google Books" elevates the idea of the codex; it replaced "Google Print," which implied closer ties to paper. The branding notice that prefaces older PDFs also centers the codex. The first sentence emphasizes library shelves, their books, and the careful craft of preservation: "This is a digital copy of a book that was preserved for generations on library shelves before it was carefully scanned by Google as part of a project to make the world's books discoverable online" (e.g., Furnivall 1862). The notice also emphasizes the value of books as sources of historical knowledge: "Public domain books are our gateways to the past, representing a wealth of history, culture, and knowledge that's often difficult to discover." And the unique properties of specific print copies further enhance the historical value of digital copies: "Marks, annotations and other marginalia present in the original volume will appear in this file—a reminder of this book's long journey from the publisher to a library and finally to you." These rhetorical moves make a digitized print book sound very much like a digitized manuscript. The platforming of editions thus offers important lessons for book history, including digitized medieval manuscripts, where interfaces and rhetoric are also influencing access and interpretation.

Over time, Google has pivoted away from the rhetorical codex. Indeed, all along, codex properties have been treated as "bugs rather than features" by the technologies of industrial text extraction (Chalmers and Edwards 2017). Even the original branding notice carefully distinguished between the public ownership of the books ("we are merely their custodians") and the private control of the digital files: "make non-commercial use of the files; refrain from automated querying; maintain attribution; keep it legal." Currently, Google has repositioned the value of the codex format in the information economy by reducing "Books" to a small appendage to the large colorful "Google" on the main search page. A single line defines the site as an information index: "Search the world's most comprehensive index of full-text books" (accessed July 25, 2020). Similarly, the preface for newer PDFs foregrounds the commercial value of information rather than the preservation value of books. It no longer promises to organize or "care" but rather to extract information: "This is a reproduction of a library book that was digitized by Google as part of an ongoing effort to preserve the information in books and make it universally accessible" (2017). This pithy statement is accompanied by a "QR code" that opens the book on Google (if processed on a networked device). Links below the digitized book lead eventually to more details about "terms of service." These terms apply to the "Google Books Digital Content Store"—a title that foregrounds the sales motive. Here, it becomes clear that accessing Google Books is just one component of one's relationship with Google, privacy, copyright, and content ownership. "Universally accessible" applies not only to information that users seek but to users themselves, whose information Google seeks: "you give Google a perpetual, irrevocable, worldwide, royalty-free, and non-exclusive license to reproduce, adapt, modify, translate, publish, publicly perform, publicly display, create derivative works of, and distribute any User Content that you submit, post, or display on or through, the Service, without any compensation or obligation to you" (Google Books Terms of Service, copyright 2011, accessed May 4, 2020). These statements show Google conflating "the economic logics typical of platforms with the public interests and quasi-universal services formerly characteristic of many infrastructures" (Plantin et al. 2018, 306). The results leave library books behind. They suggest some of ways in which infrastructure arrangements, including capital financing, construct cultural heritage as private property.

The Google Books interface doesn't leave behind the codex altogether: the printed paper book still has commercial value as a portable, nonelectric storage device for PDFs. People still like to hold books, read outside, and handwrite notes in margins. By maintaining page-images that are otherwise unnecessary for digital information retrieval, PDF facsimiles of public domain books can convert back into paper books. Google Books access pages thus offer "print-on-demand" purchase options alongside free digital formats. Through POD, Google has spun off the codex format to third-party marketers. Lovelich editions are thus available from a range of publishers who have harvested digital files to generate vast print-on-demand collections. Most of these marketers, like Google, offer free access to digital formats while selling print formats. Many POD books also appear directly on Google Books—with the preview and "search inside" functions unavailable. In these cases, the metadata for a POD codex—which doesn't exist until it is purchased—has been reimported as an unsearchable printed book by the platform that produced the searchable PDF. In this circular repetition, the paper codex manifests the separation between free text and profitable formats: the only reason to list an unsearchable POD book on Google Books is sales. The listing, moreover, is a material fiction that exemplifies the hybrid temporalities of all digitized editions: it will be printed in the future but can be purchased now. This temporal reversal crystallizes how digital reproduction acts on historical books, including medieval manuscripts: reproduction creates feedback loops that also ensnare the original shelf-books.

The corpus of POD editions based on MS 80 represents a microcosm of the broader POD market and its place in book history. As Whitney

Trettien has shown in a case study of John Milton's *Areopagitica*, POD editions are integral to the knowledge economy, "reconfiguring our material relationship with literary history" and exposing how "network capitalism" operates (Trettien 2013, pars. 28, 2). A POD codex has a hybrid temporality—centuries old, hot off the press—that foregrounds "the mediated nature of *all* historical texts—indeed, of the notion of 'textuality' itself" (Trettien 2013, par. 28). In the case of POD editions of printed editions of a medieval manuscript, the implications for literary history are even more stark than for early modern printed books: "The evident artificiality of POD reprints invites a productive skepticism of textual editing, offering a tool with which to probe the histories, assumptions and even moralism implicit in how scholars mediate literary history" (Trettien 2013, par. 26). For Lovelich, these editorial histories stretch through Reformation medievalism, Enlightenment medievalism, and Romantic medievalism, each entangled with various forms of nationalism and imperialism. Literary history has also been mediated by the practices of platform philology that turned MS 80's handwriting into printed text and that printed text into digital text. At each step, technology infrastructures have been essential components of accessing and distributing romance. And at each step—including the production of MS 80 itself—copying technologies make it possible for more people to hold their own piece of valuable cultural heritage.

Literary history is an explicit part of POD marketing that seeks to profit from free text. Lovelich editions offered for sale between September 2018 and April 2020 represent the gamut of marketers' strategies. The texts are consistently described as "culturally important" works that contain knowledge worth "protecting, preserving, and promoting" (e.g., Alpha Editions, Kessinger Publishing, BiblioBazaar). This romance of cultural rescue rests on the scarcity of old books: POD editions preserve "a vanishing wealth of human knowledge" (BiblioLife). The sales pitch also defers to established scholarly authority, claiming that the works have been specifically selected for their "great significance and value to literature" (Alpha Editions) or as part of the "knowledge base of civilization as we know it" (Scholar Select brand, printed by multiple presses, including the advertising company Creative Media Partners).

Scholars' authority is reinforced by libraries': their stamps show that the originals "have been housed in our most important libraries around the world" (Scholar Select). These claims to canonical value derive from very specific date calculations: the expiration of copyright in the United States. The aura of cultural prestige thus obscures the prosaic pathways of preservation: publication date; purchase by a library that participated in mass scanning; a binding compatible with mass scanning; presence in a digital repository that allows file harvesting. In the POD world, texts that would otherwise be deemed outdated or obsolete—such as literary histories by the likes of Ellis or Saintsbury—become historical "treasures." Similarly, nothing Dorothy Kempe has to say about Lovelich or the Holy Grail can undermine the value of the reprint.

The POD editions also embody platform codicology. They are produced from a combination of unique features and shared technologies. In the first instance, the page images reproduce the annotations and other "imperfections" from a specific library book: marketing materials point to these anomalies as signs of authenticity that "intentionally preserve" history and guarantee that the reprint faithfully reproduces a valuable original (e.g., Forgotten Books, Scholar Select, Alpha Editions). The PDF itself preserves the unique conditions of its own production, such as reversed pages and scanned hands (see figs. 18 and 19). These born-digital imperfections make the book less reliable as a facsimile of its source but more reliable as a record of digitization (see fig. 20, a print of fig. 19). Digital flaws are not addressed in marketing, as they undermine the value of POD itself as a technology. The digital correction of flaws in the source book, however, can make reprints superior. Forgotten Books, for example, touts the use of "state-of-the-art technology to digitally reconstruct the work . . . repairing imperfections in the aged copy." Nobel Press credits humans with the quality of its restorations: "This book . . . has been restored by human beings, page by page, so that you may enjoy it in a form as close to the original as possible." BiblioLife also highlights its investment in readers' experience: "we undertake the difficult task of re-creating these works as attractive, readable, and affordable books . . . [for] a global audience" (flyleaf, 2018). The company is particularly proud of its proprietary font, EasyScriptTM,

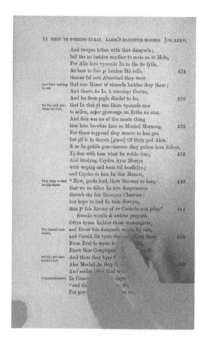

Figure 19   Pixelated handprint. In *History of the Holy Grail*, edited by Frederick J. Furnivall. Early English Text Society, Extra Series 28 (1877), 14–15. Digitized from Stanford University Library copy; uploaded to Archive.org on October 23, 2008.

SOURCE: https://archive.org/details/historyholygrai00lovegoog/page/n24/mode/2up.

which "provides readers with larger than average typeface, for a reading experience that's easier on the eyes" (flyleaf, 2018). These narratives of improvement follow the conventions of progress that have long shaped both technology and literary history as a practice always "on the improve" (Matthews 1999, xvi). These publishers seek to profit from the authenticity of originals while displacing them with better books.

The covers of POD editions reproduce platform formatting in the tradition of the Roxburghe Club and EETS. From a bibliographic standpoint, the POD editions are retitled and reauthored by the PDF metadata. Kempe's *Legend of the Holy Grail*, for example, is the title of three volumes with different content and different dimensions. The covers, moreover, illustrate two ways to signify the value of a POD codex—make it new with

14   THEY 'VE NOTHING TO EAT. LABEL'S DAUGHTER MOURNS.   [CH. XXXV.

And tweyne leften with that damysele ;
but the ne hadden neyther to mete ne to Mele,
For Alle here vyaunde In to the Se fylle,
As here to fore ȝe herden Me telle.   424
thanne ful sore Abaached they were
and have nothing to eat.   that non Maner of viaunde hadden they there ;
And therto fer In A straunge Contre,
And fer from peple disolat to be,   428
for the work produces no food.   that In that yl was there vyaunde non
to sellen, neþer growenge on Erthe ne ston.
And this was on of the moste thing
that hem browhte Into so Mochel Morneng,   432
For thens supposid they neure to han gon
but ȝif it be thoruh [grace] Of Only god Alon.
& so In goddis gouernaunce they putten hem Echon,
To don with hem what he wolde don ;   436
And knelyng, Cryden hym Mercye
wiþ weping and teris ful tendirlye ;
and Cryden to him In this Manere,
They pray to God to help them.   " Now, goode lord, thow Socoure vs here,
that we ne fallen In non desperaunce
thorwh the fals Enemyes Chawnce ;
but kepe vs lord In thin Servyse,
that þi fals Enemy of vs Cachcho non prise."   444
Swoche wordis & swiche preyeris
Oftyn tymes hadden these messengeris ;
The damsel complains.   and Euere this damysele wepto ful sore,
and Cursid the tyme the ... Cam thore,
From Evel to werse to ... ,
Euere thus Complayne ...
and the two men comfort her.   And there they hyre ...
Also Mochel As they ...
And seiden that God w...
(: proclaimment)   Er Come ...
"and th... ..., we,
For ȝow... vs m...

CH. XXXV.]   KING LABEL'S DAUGHTER WILL TURN CHRISTIAN.   15

Thanne Axode sche ham of here Creaunce,
And they hire tolde with-owten variaunce
how that be Iosephe of Barthamye
they it Resceyveden ful trewelye,   460
And be Al holy Chirche lawe,
Of whoche Creawnce they weren ful fawn.
thanne tolden they hyre In Eche degre
What powere [Crist hadde,] & what dignete,   464
and how that socouren he wolde his frend,
And from perylen to-bringen him to good End.
" For who that In hym hath Affyaunce,
he wele hym kepen with-owten variaunce ;   468
and from Alle perylles, I the Enawre,
hym delyveren, as Seith the holy scripture."
"In feith," quod this damysele tho,
" ȝif ȝowre lord sweche Merveilles May do   472
as ȝe me now tellen here,
on hym wil I trosten In Alle Manere.
ȝif he owt of this peryl vs now brynge,
and to vs wil owht sende In Socourynge,   476
And therto A-sckapen from Al this fere,
I hym promyse In Alle Manere
From this day forward his Servaunt to be,
And hym to Serven In Alle Manere degre."   480
" Iia, damysele," quod they Anon,
"Now weten we wel Everychon
that with-owten dowto fal Sekerly
we scholen haven Socour Ryht hastely   484
Al oth... we thanne he wolde han do
... promys ȝe han mad so."
And there they hyre Alle thre   488
...wht ful Sekerlo ;
... Neuere be woxe ferto,
Angwisch As they hadden tho.
...yht Gan Comen faste,
loked Atte laste,   492

Figure 20   Erased pixelated handprint. In *History of the Holy Grail*, edited by Frederick J. Furnivall. Early English Text Society, Extra Series 28 (1877), 14–15. Printed by Forgotten Books (2018) from a file derived from the same scanning event as Figure 19.

brightly colored stock photos and clean fonts, or make it old with neoclassical or neogothic patterns (see figs. 21 and 22). The latter strategy harks back to both the Roxburghe Club and EETS—which used similar italic fonts to lend a sense of historical value to nineteenth-century prints. And like their predecessors, POD publishers use the same cover style for every title. These practices, combined with metadata quirks, have produced four copies of *The History of the Holy Grail* that look identical even though each has different content from different sources. The myriad of consistencies and discrepancies across the corpus of Lovelich POD editions points back to those of the editorial processes that produced the print volumes in the first place—from Furnivall crowdsourcing transcription from manuscripts to EETS reformatting and reprinting text from Roxburghe editions. Platform codicology reveals the long-term repercussions of platform philology,

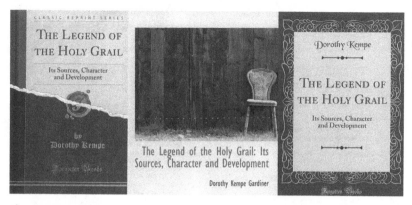

Figure 21   Covers from three print-on-demand editions of Dorothy Kempe's *Legend of the Holy Grail*. Early English Text Society, Extra Series 95 (1905). Left to right: Forgotten Books (paperback, 2017), BiblioLife (paperback, 2009), and Forgotten Books (hardback, 2018).

Figure 22   Covers from three print-on-demand editions of *The History of the Holy Graal*, edited by Frederick J. Furnivall (Roxburghe Club, 1861). Left to right: HardPress (2013), Nabu Press (2012), and Palala Press (2015).

inviting new queries into textual transmission from manuscript to print to digital. Prompted by the dissonant temporalities of a POD codex, we can see more clearly yet another way in which nineteenth-century medievalism continues to find steady markets. Publishers' confidence in the market value of neomedieval and neoclassical nostalgia points once again to how the social construction of popularity—and Arthurian popularity in particular—is woven into the history of technology.

Finally, the cost of POD editions suggests how platform algorithms configure book history. Since the texts are in the public domain and the page-image PDFs are freely available online, the price of a reprint is literally the price of the codex device. Between 2018 and 2020, the typical price range for Lovelich editions was $17–$37. Another set of prices, however, aligned these cheap reprints with rare books—in the $600–$800 range. Indeed, on Amazon, search results for reprints are mixed in with offerings from sellers of rare books. For example, a Roxburghe *Grail* from 1861 could be purchased for $738.83, while a POD reprint of the same title listed for $659 (October 26, 2018, https://perma.cc/HAR7-6J79). Similarly, a *Merlin* reprint listed for $851.90, while a first-run edition from 1913 could be had for $36.95 (March 31, 2020). All these prices stem from the market value of single copies calculated either historically or algorithmically. The prices should represent differences in rarity but instead represent the failure of algorithms to distinguish between an original and a reprint. The automated calculation of scarcity produces a market reversal: a POD codex becomes a high-priced rare commodity because it looks like a single unique copy. This breakdown of network capitalism, like handprints in a PDF, exposes the inner workings of the information economy. Somewhere deep in proprietary code, an algorithm turned affordable books into rarified commodities. The unreliability of these calculations serves as a salutary reminder that "value" is assigned to books and texts for all kinds of reasons—including some that have more to do with platforms and infrastructure than with the books and texts themselves.

More stable POD pricing is available from EETS itself, via Oxford University Press (OUP). But even here, network glitches create a mix of greater access and greater obscurity. POD has realized Furnivall's founding vision of keeping the EETS backlist in print. In fact, he built "POD" into the EETS business model from the beginning: the number of subscribers determined the print runs; back issues were reprinted when enough new subscribers prepaid. The new POD editions from OUP preserve evidence of EETS's long-standing commitment to reprinting: some reproduce notices from the German-American company Kraus Reprints (1970s to 1990s) or the British company Boydell and Brewer (1990s to 2000s). Some POD editions also mark their place in the digital economy with an OUP copyright notice that asserts "database rights." The POD covers translate this dual inheritance with a cost-effective inversion of EETS's visual branding: white paper covers with brown lettering instead of brown cloth covers with gold lettering. Digital transfers, though, have also produced some metadata errors that disrupt the coherence of the EETS platform. The complete backlist, for example, is not available in every country: Lovelich's *Grail* did not appear on "global.oup.com.us" (United States), only on "global.oup.com.gb" (Great Britain) (October 26, 2018). And even there, it has no author and is listed under "T" for "The History of the Holy Grail IâV." In other words, searching for Lovelich on OUP might lead one to conclude that the *Grail* is out of print. I was eventually able to purchase a copy through "oup.com.gb" and have it mailed to the United States. Intriguingly, it arrived with contradictory printing notices—one stating that it was printed in the United States and the other that it was printed by CPI Group in Croydon, UK (cpi-print.co.uk). However it was actually produced, this codex presents itself as a geopolitical assemblage that fuses times, places, and technologies. It maintains national boundaries while transcending them. In this way, it replicates the romantic tradition that brought the *Grail* into print in the first place.

EETS is still producing the medieval English canon—well past the year 2000, just as Furnivall imagined (Early English Text Society 1904, 4). New volumes use clean, modern fonts and arrive in the mail with vivid color dustjackets—bright brown with orange undertones, each adorned with a color image related to the edited text. In most libraries, these covers will be discarded and, with them, the volumes' only information about the EETS publishing platform: "The Early English Text Society was founded in 1864 by Frederick James Furnivall, with the help of Richard Morris, Walter Skeat, and others. The Society's device is a representation of the Alfred Jewel, which was found near Athelney in Somerset in 1693 and is now preserved in the Ashmolean Museum, Oxford." This compressed story of medieval English studies is anchored in specific times and places that span more than a millennium—King Alfred (849–99) to 1693 to 1864 to "now." The ephemeral format—the disposable dustjacket—nonetheless casts the volume into a more limited story line. The Alfred "device" is pressed into the cloth cover under the dustjacket; a rendition with thicker lines is printed on POD volumes. To recover the history of EETS from a library shelf, however, future readers will need to look online. The future of medieval literary history is thus also the history of these arrangements between format and infrastructure.

MS 80's path through English literary history has all the twists and turns of a good romance. It represents a microcosm of how literary history interacts with politics, culture, and pedagogy. Since the eighteenth century, Lovelich's text has been cast variously as a "good" example of English romance, a "bad" example of poetry, a "good" source of grail lore, an essential Arthurian narrative, and a worthless Arthurian narrative. In the 1850s, a particularly harsh literary judgment sparked Furnivall's editorial fervor. Through the idealized lens of romanticism, he set up models for philology and codicology that continue to reverberate through digital platforms: crowdsourcing, subscription financing, patronage, mass copying, reprinting. As editions based on MS 80 pass from one technology to another—print, PDF, database—they show how formats and interfaces make literary meaning. Collectively, editions have made many books out of MS 80: a rare and prestigious tome, an affordable paperback, authoritative linguistic data, treasured cultural heritage. One way or another, the so-called dullest English romance ever written has never been out of print. Bad romances and bad editions can still make for good literary history.

CHAPTER 6

REPRODUCING BOOKS

Binding, Microfilm, Digital

THE FIRST MEDIEVAL MANUSCRIPT most people open is likely a web page. The wide accessibility of digital images of manuscript pages over the last few decades is one of the most remarkable developments in book history. Even though only a fraction of all surviving manuscripts has been photographed, digital repositories have grown large enough to generate new styles of engagement with medieval books. They are also defining new canons of material culture by exposing patterns of selection: famous books and famous libraries attract the most investment. In this way, digitization projects replicate some of the same factors that drive medieval manuscript collecting in the first place. Like acquisition, reproduction has the capacity to concentrate both capital and literary canons. Even before digital images, other forms of photography drew medieval manuscripts into these circuits: relatively expensive print facsimiles offered collectors ownership of rare books; relatively cheap microfilms promised large-scale preservation. Whatever the format, photography exposes the longer legacies of capital accumulation that have been instrumental in the preservation and distribution of medieval manuscripts since they were first made.

Photographs of manuscripts expand the repertoire of "the book" that I outlined in my introduction. They are devices that store visual information, formats that structure visual information, interfaces between source documents and users, platforms that distribute visual information, and components of infrastructure. Images are, like textual editions, only partial representations of their sources: "The camera edits" (Galey 2014, 154; also Flüeler 2015). And like textual editions, they sometimes substitute for their sources. Otherwise, what would be the point of photographing books? The challenge for bringing photographs into book history is thus to define exactly how their "forms effect meaning" (McKenzie 1986, 4). Digital photographs raise unique issues since their form is variable according to interface and other factors (Tarte 2011a; Green 2016; Endres 2019; Stanford 2020). The energy that scholars have applied to thinking about these issues with digital images was once applied to microfilm. Indeed, the two technologies have a number of material, economic, legal, and social parallels (Cady 1990). They have generated similar dreams of vast, efficient scholarly infrastructure, as well as similar problems in achieving those dreams: copyright, cataloguing, and preservation, to name a few. Looking back to microfilm from the vantage point of digital photography clarifies the role of technology infrastructure in book history.

MS 80 has been reproduced several times as part of Parker Library. In the mid-twentieth century, when the text's reputation as an English romance translated by Henry Lovelich was at its lowest point, the manuscript was selected for a new material investment—a new binding. As one of Parker's books, it wouldn't be left to disintegrate. The new binding reproduced the core function of a codex—a book that opens and closes without damage to the pages—in the style of a valuable printed book. Around the same time, MS 80 was microfilmed, along with most of the other manuscripts, as part of a collection-wide preservation project. In the 2000s, MS 80 was digitized, along with all the other Parker manuscripts that could be safely photographed, for Parker Library on the Web (Parker

1.0, 2009). In 2018, the images were reconfigured on a new digital platform (Parker 2.0) (see also chaps. 3 and 4). Each reproduction has multiplied the referents for "MS 80." As an individual book, MS 80 might not stand out for special attention. As part of Parker Library, it benefits from the collection's reputation as a national treasure, preserved largely intact for centuries, containing some of the oldest books in the English language.

MS 80's reproduction history shows the interdependence of copying technologies. Rather than a succession from handcraft to industrial machinery, each reproduction depends on the others; today, they all function simultaneously. The structure of the binding affected how the book could be photographed, and the process of taking photographs affected the binding. Meanwhile, the legacies of microfilm formats have influenced the architecture of digital interfaces (Porter 2018c). And microfilms are themselves now sometimes read on computers or even digitized as part of networked digital libraries. All these formats—the manuscript on the shelf in its modern binding, microfilm copies, and digital image files—are sustained by substantial infrastructures. Just as a book can be left to rot, so can its digital derivatives. They both require electricity, climate control, and a host of other material conditions. As a result, manuscripts and their reproductions are embedded in circuits of global capital, where private companies supply digital storage via cables and satellites manufactured from nonrenewable resources. Profit considerations shape the corporate energy policies that keep the "cloud" running, hastening environmental degradation in the process. From the perspective of infrastructure, these are all components of medieval manuscripts. Accessing medieval manuscripts, online or off, means accessing the complex legacies that copy and preserve them.

The expense of preserving valuable, but unprofitable, cultural heritage makes patronage a further component of reproduction infrastructure. Even the production of MS 80 in the fifteenth century was financed by mercantile patronage (see chap. 3). Today, wealthy merchants and organizations continue to provide the capital to maintain and reproduce historic books. Cultural heritage investment campaigns commonly mobilize public value as a shared responsibility to preserve precious objects and increase access to them: "Helping to embody a story that has already been deemed important, digitizations may be taken to represent a particular people's literature or national identity" (Mak 2014, 1517). Digitization is understood as a global medium that enhances the value of "treasures" precisely by making them available to more people through the internet. One result of this framing is a kind of protection from critical analysis, in the name of the common good (Mak 2014, 1517). Yet these investments are inseparable from the longer histories of capital accumulation that sustain wealthy foundations. If it can feel uncomfortable to recognize the histories of violence that underlie philanthropy, it is even more uncomfortable to overlook them. Analysis and gratitude can go hand in hand. Indeed, every dimension of this book is a product of foundation philanthropy and its violent histories. Empire, too, is a curatorial infrastructure for medieval manuscripts. Ignoring these histories as unseemly or embarrassing undermines the integrity of scholarship, abstracting it from its own material conditions. History deserves a longer shelf life.

In this chapter, I tell the material and geopolitical history of MS 80 since the mid-twentieth century. I begin in 1956—when MS 80 was rebound at a Cambridge bookshop. This work was paid for by a grant from the Pilgrim Trust, an American foundation based in Britain. The grant provided for the replacement of about one-third of the most fragile bindings across the collection. Around the same time, if not before, MS 80 was microfilmed. The infrastructure that supported the mass microfilming of medieval manuscripts was also supported by American organizations—the Library of Congress, the Modern Language Association, the American Council of Learned Societies, and the Rockefeller Foundation, among others. Microphotography and computing evolved side by side throughout the twentieth century, converging in the development of digital photography. So once again, starting in 2005, MS 80 was reproduced as part of the collection-wide project to digitize the medieval manuscripts and publish Parker Library on the Web. This project, too, ultimately rested on private American resources—from Stanford University, the Andrew W. Mellon Foundation, and the Gladys Krieble Delmas Foundation. The launch of Parker 2.0 in 2018 reformatted MS 80 into a new kind of digital object, under new institutional arrangements. All these reproductions bear the stamp of colonial capitalism even as they expand and reorient the knowledge economy.

Rebinding British Heritage

On the shelf, MS 80 and its neighbors all look alike: light brown leather, shelf marks stamped in gold-colored ink, five evenly spaced cords along each spine (see fig. 23). Other than MS 80, this group represents different kinds of Latin reference works: a psalter (MS 75), an ecclesiastical history (MS 76), an ecclesiastical handbook (MS 77), an encyclopedia (MS 78), and a pontifical (MS 79). Although MS 80 is in English verse, it, too, contributes to Christian history with its account of Joseph of Arimathea's evangelization of Britain. The uniformity of the bindings thus inadvertently ratifies Archbishop Parker's understanding Lovelich's translation as national religious history (see chap. 3). The binding's form, meanwhile, calls up another time frame for MS 80—its nineteenth-century editions. The bindings' style echoes the printed collections by the Roxburghe Club and the Early English Text Society (EETS) (see chap. 5). The Parker bindings were in fact designed to mimic printed books that mimicked medieval books: the raised cords on the spines are decorative replicas of the kind of sewing that holds together manuscript quires, used to lend an aura of tradition to printed books held together by glue (Jefferson 2007). On the shelf, the rebound manuscripts give the impression of a coherent modern library even though they were made by two different bookshops. MS 80 is thus one of many manuscripts that has become a copy of a medieval book while remaining a medieval book.

Inside, each rebound manuscript is annotated with the name of the foundation that paid for the work: the Pilgrim Trust (see figs. 24 and 25). Transmitted February 25, 1952, this grant of £2,500 supported the rebinding of about a third of the collection (CCCA; Budny 1997, liii–lvii). The history of the Pilgrim Trust makes the bindings more than pragmatic conservation tools. They are also products of American nostalgia for British colonialism. The trust was founded in 1930 by Edward S. Harkness (1874–1940), a wealthy philanthropist from the United States. Harkness sought to commemorate

Figure 23 MS 80 on the shelf in the vault at Parker Library next to five other manuscripts with 1950s bindings: MSS 75, 76, and 80 made by John P. Gray; MSS 77, 78, and 79 made by Wilson and Sons.

SOURCE: Photo by Michelle Warren (March 13, 2018). Reproduced courtesy of Parker Library, Corpus Christi College, Cambridge.

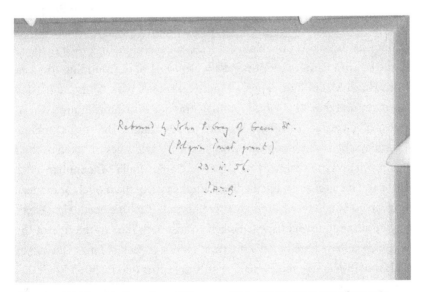

Figure 24 MS 80's rebinding note on 1950s paper: "Rebound by John P. Gray of Green St. (Pilgrim Trust grant). 23.ii.56. J.P.T.B" [February 23, 1956; John Patrick Tuer Bury, Parker Librarian, 1937–56].

SOURCE: https://parker.stanford.edu/parker/catalog/xd494bt3141. Courtesy of Parker Library, Corpus Christi College, Cambridge. Licensed under a Creative Commons Attribution-NonCommercial 4.0 International License.

Figure 25   Letterhead of the Pilgrim Trust, from the cover letter for the rebinding grant (CCCA).

SOURCE: Photo by Michelle Warren (March 13, 2018). Reproduced by kind permission of the Master and Fellows of Corpus Christi College, Cambridge.

his English ancestry by helping Great Britain recover from the Great War of 1914–18. The title "Pilgrim" commemorates an idealized vision of the English settlers who colonized the lands of the Wampanoag People in what is now called Massachusetts: "it was called Pilgrim Trust, to signify at once its dedication to an adventurous ideal and its link with the land of the Pilgrim Fathers" (Wooster 1949, 129). One of the founding trustees, Lord Hugh Macmillan, reported that Harkness's wife, Mary, suggested the name and that all involved found it "fraught with appropriate associations." The trustees deepened the idea by adopting as the trust's emblem "a scallop shell which pilgrims wore in the Middle Ages in token of their having visited the shrine of St. James of Compostella" (Macmillan 1952, 283–84). This gesture made medieval English piety the model for modern English colonialism. Macmillan wrote himself into this nostalgic genealogy by alluding to Geoffrey Chaucer's *Canterbury Tales* in the title of the autobiography where he tells the trust's story, *A Man of Law's Tale* (1952). This romanticizing medievalism recalls the spirit that inspired Frederick Furnivall to edit MS 80—first under the patronage of the exclusive Roxburghe Club (1861–63) and then for the more accessible but still nationalist EETS (1874–78) (see chap. 5). All told, the Pilgrim Trust laces nostalgic medievalism with an equally nostalgic colonialism—directing both toward the patriotic rescue of British culture.

Harkness gave the trust an open-ended mandate to make grants in any area "promoting [Great Britain's] future well-being," which it continues to do to this day (Macauley 1931, 72; Wooster 1949, 128–30; LMA/4450). The trustees interpreted their task as supporting cultural heritage, the arts, and social welfare—"the material side and social side" (Macmillan 1952, 287). From 1930 to 1950, material grants ranged from the restoration of Durham Castle to the archives of Westminster Abbey. The trust also purchased and then gifted to libraries and museums Sir Isaac Newton's library, Charles Darwin's manuscripts, and part of the Codex Sinaiticus (now called "one of the most important books in the world" and the subject of a major digital research project [www.codexsinaiticus.org; Prescott and Hughes 2018]) (Macmillan 1952, 294–304). The English trustees prioritized historic preservation, particularly of medieval materials, because they believed that Americans found restoration projects particularly "delightful," presumably because they combined nostalgia with modernization (Macauley 1931, 73; Curti 1998, 309–13). Macmillan, as chairman in 1952, made the grant to Parker Library as an expression of this philanthropic principle. The trustees thus translated a value that they considered distinctly American into British heritage projects. The gesture solidified the ascendency of the new American empire over its own colonial origins.

The Pilgrim Trust is part of a broader practice of early twentieth-century American philanthropy that continues to shape the course of libraries, universities, museums, and cultural institutions throughout the world. Harkness controlled an immense inherited fortune that made him among the wealthiest Americans of his day, right behind John D. Rockefeller Sr. (1839–1937) and Andrew Carnegie (1835–1919). Edward Harkness's father, Stephen (1818–88), gave Rockefeller his first substantial loan in Cleveland, Ohio, and became a silent partner in Standard Oil (Goulder 1972, 90–98). Stephen's widow, Anna, set a model of philanthropy, founding the Commonwealth Fund, which continues to operate with a focus on healthcare. Edward became its president but conducted most of his own philanthropy by spending nearly all his capital—unlike Rockefeller and Carnegie. His gifts, however, mirror theirs in ranging from ancient art to contemporary social issues, with a prominent place for universities and a marked Anglophilia. He initiated the "Harkness Table" method of seminar-style teaching associated with Exeter Academy, the residential house system at Yale and Harvard, the drama school at Yale, the medical school at Columbia, the humanities division at Cal Tech, and the division of Egyptian Antiquities at the Metropolitan Museum of Art, just to name a few (Wooster 1949; Perry 1951; Towler 2006). His name endures on many buildings, including the central administrative building at Clark Atlanta University, a historically Black institution that Harkness (anonymously at the time) and Rockefeller (also anonymously) pushed to reorganize in 1930: they sought to stabilize Black colleges in Atlanta but also to deradicalize Black leadership (Avery 2013, 165–66; Francis 2019; Morey 2019). In providing the funds to build a new central campus at Clark Atlanta, Harkness stepped into one of the defining features of American philanthropy: using profits derived from racist discrimination to support institutions that counter the effects of racist discrimination.

The wealth that underlies the Pilgrim Trust derives ultimately from the theft of lands from Indigenous Peoples. Stephen Harkness and John D. Rockefeller Sr. made fortunes starting from Cleveland because they profited from US government policies that promoted industrial development at the direct expense of Indigenous sovereignty. The brutal process of dispossession included the 1811 defeat of the Shawnee chief Tecumseh, the 1830 Indian Removal Act, the 1862 Homestead Act, the 1862 Morrill Act (which allocated lands specifically to fund universities), and the 1887 Dawes General Allotment Act (which broke up large tribal reservations, resulting in extensive new land acquisitions by white settlers) (Dunbar-Ortiz 2015; Estes 2019; Lee and Ahtone 2019). Some of the industrialists and bankers who extracted capital from these stolen lands invested their concentrated wealth in cultural foundations—like the Pilgrim Trust, the Commonwealth Fund, and the Rockefeller Foundation. Some of this capital underwrote the purchase of medieval manuscripts and other artifacts of European cultural heritage. On a small scale, Edward and Mary Harkness gave twenty medieval manuscripts to the New York Public Library (including the "Harkness Gospels," MS 115). On a larger scale, J. P. Morgan (1837–1913) and Henry E. Huntington (1850–1927) amassed collections that became new centers of scholarship for medieval and early modern studies (Echard 2000). Universities where book and text technologies have flourished also profited from Indigenous lands, such as Stanford University and the University of Michigan (e.g., Steeh 2002). Histories of US slavery are also bound up with the accumulated wealth that sustains philanthropies, universities, and book collections (Wilder 2013). The rebinding note in MS 80 surfaces these debts to colonial capital carried to some degree by every modern repository. These are the conditions that keep the books open. Ultimately, MS 80 is in good shape in part because Edward Harkness directed the profits of Standard Oil toward the preservation of British heritage.

Microfilming National Documents

A decade or so before the Parker Library grant, the Pilgrim Trust made a different kind of preservation grant—to the British Records Association for microfilming. Macmillan explained that microphotography could "at a surprisingly low cost . . . provide facsimile film copies of important series of documents, thus ensuring against loss by enemy action or otherwise the historical material which they contain" (Macmillan 1952, 303). This brief description alludes to the constellation of interconnected factors that led to the rapid expansion of medieval manuscript photography in the 1930s and 1940s: heightened fears among scholars and government officials that unique documents of national interest could be destroyed by war; increased affordability of photographic technologies; American philanthropists' investments in European cultural heritage. The relatively small grant by the Pilgrim Trust mirrors the projects of larger foundations, scholarly organizations, government offices, and private businesses. The microfilm of MS 80 is part of this history of microphotography, which was developed as a nationalist expression of document rescue. The politics of reproduction extend to the format itself, which turns a codex into a roll that requires a machine interface.

Photographic reproduction at Parker Library in the 1920s and 1930s shows the early entanglement of American and British interests. In 1920, in the wake of the Great War of 1914–18, the Modern Language Association of America (MLA) formed a "Committee on the Reproduction of

MSS and Rare Books" ("Fourth Session" 1920). The project extended the vision of the MLA president, medievalist John Manly, who had started a "Committee on the Reproduction of Early Texts" back in 1907 as a kind of photographic EETS ("Proceedings" 1907, xi). Manly's motivations in 1920 were severalfold: improve scholarship by attracting private patronage; coordinate collaborative research through the MLA; preserve vulnerable documents of cultural significance; maintain access to rare materials as American collectors drove up prices beyond the means of libraries (Manly 1920; Carpenter 1921, 35). At the time, curators at the British Museum told the MLA that they hoped to create "collotypes [facsimiles] of all unique books in existence" (Carpenter 1921, 45). At Parker Library, the MLA ultimately photographed five manuscripts and one printed book between 1925 and 1950 (MSS 145, 292, 358, 402, 470; EP.H.6; "Reproductions" 1950). In the 1930s, the deputy keeper of manuscripts at the British Museum, Robin Flower, carried out experiments in forensic microphotography with Parker's MS 173 and published a collotype facsimile for EETS (Flower and Smith 1941). These early investments in copying technologies at Parker Library respond to broader concerns that wartime violence could destroy precious national documents.

American interests in British manuscripts spiked again with the new war that began in 1939, with the same fears of document destruction. When Britain declared war on Germany, the American microfilm entrepreneur Eugene Power had already been filming early modern books at the British Museum with a grant from the Carnegie Foundation, with the goal of "restoring" endangered documents (Power 1938, 45)—an idea born with microphotography itself almost a century earlier ("Photographic Copies" 1854). In 1940, the American Council of Learned Societies (ACLS), the Library of Congress, and the Rockefeller Foundation organized an emergency effort that became the British Manuscript Project (BMP, 1941–45). With filming organized by Power, the project focused on materials of interest to American scholars; simultaneously, Power was filming for the US Office of Strategic Services (Born 1960, 353–54; Power 1990, 122–42, 385–90). For a time, it seemed possible that the corpus of medieval English manuscripts could be reduced to Power's microfilms at the Library of Congress. The

BMP ultimately produced 2,652 reels, later catalogued at the University of Michigan with another Rockefeller grant (Power 1990, 147). In the midst of the project, librarians at the US Library of Congress envisioned returning to London after the war to produce a complete photographic facsimile of British Museum manuscripts (Wilson 1943a, 307)—and even a fully imperial scheme of worldwide copying (Power 1944). With the support of the Carnegie and Rockefeller foundations, manuscript microfilms sparked grandiose visions of concentrated cultural capital in the United States.

The BMP collection includes a number of highly prized manuscripts of medieval English literature by canonical authors such as Geoffrey Chaucer, John Lydgate, and Thomas Hoccleve (Born 1955; https://quod.lib.umich.edu/cgi/b/bib/bib-idx?c=bmp). The infrastructure that produced these copies combined scholarly interests, military intelligence, private profit, and philanthropy: since Power was filming in Britain before the war, he was able to meet the needs of the wartime military; because he was involved with intelligence work, he was allowed to have expensive equipment that otherwise would have been prohibited; after the war, cameras used for intelligence gathering were reassigned for scholarly projects (Mak 2014, 1518–19; Fyfe 2016, 554–59; Power 1990, 133–149). As a result of these arrangements, the quantity of medieval manuscripts on microfilm by the 1960s was deemed "incalculable" (Born 1964, 83). The microfilm reproduction of medieval manuscripts across these decades is one piece of a much larger investment in creating a self-sufficient knowledge economy in the United States. In this light, manuscript microfilms are the material remains of a nationalist definition of European heritage constructed by a convergence of academic, government, and private interests.

Somewhere along the way, most of the Parker manuscripts were reproduced as a microfilm collection. I haven't been able to reconstruct very many details, but Parker Library was selling films in the 1990s, and as recently as 2015, a collection of some four hundred books on 155 reels could be purchased for £10,700 from World Microfilms. At least some films were made before the 1950s bindings, as they show features that differ from current books (Budny 1997, 104). MS 80, for example, lies open without restraints, whereas the 1950s bindings were deemed too tight for photography during the digitization project (Jefferson 2007). Whatever the exact circumstances, microfilm copies have been readily available and regularly used as substitutes for the manuscripts. The idea that films could replace books was built into the practice of microfilm as a preservation technology, first deployed on a mass scale amid fears that wartime bombings could destroy whole libraries. By definition, then, microfilm defined the codex—even a very valuable one—as a potentially replaceable storage device. The unique book with a fixed geolocation would become a film roll that could be copied many times over and used simultaneously in many locations. In this process, every kind of document becomes the same kind of document: the first book printed in English, Caxton's *Recuyell of the Histories of Troy*, could be reproduced as easily as a 1914 copy of the *Saturday Evening Post* (Power 1990, 232). In the United States, microfilming was seen as democratizing and even antifascist in releasing control of information from foreign governments (Carpenter 2007).

For book history, microfilms introduce a new scale of infrastructure into the repertoire of "the book." Today, that infrastructure often includes a computer. The interface of a microfilm book has always been an industrial apparatus that uses electricity. In the same period that digital reproduction has made microfilm seem obsolete, microfilm interfaces have become computers that turn the roll into a specific kind of digital book. When I set out to access MS 80's microfilm in October 2018 at the Dartmouth Library, I encountered a desktop computer processing unit, a keyboard, a mouse, a rectangular monitor, and a microform reader designed for both film (16 mm or 35 mm width) and fiche (flat sheets, positive or negative images). The reader functions as a digital scanner, operated by the software ScanPro 2000: to advance the film, you use the mouse to click on screen images of buttons. The graphics and the machine itself look to be of c. 2000 vintage. Images can be viewed on the screen or captured in JPEG (the computer was not connected to the internet or to a printer). This setup turns microfilm into a moving digital image. Scrolling through the film, the image pixelates as the processor catches up. The reproduction is thus unforgettably mediated by a fragile combination of mechanical magnification and electronic transmission. At the same time, the film transmits the heft of the material book quite effectively: since the book was photographed lying open, the thickness of the whole book is visible in each image, shifting from left to right leaf by leaf as the film advances. On high speed, the pixelated images reveal the infrastructure that produces the movie—a computer processor of limited capacity.

The microfilm computer is not designed for reading books, however. This lesson unspooled when I tried to save a digital image of a complete book opening. Since the rectangular screen isn't wide enough to show the whole image, I tried to zoom in but the image didn't shrink enough. I then used the mouse to click the rotate button, expecting to take advantage of the vertical screen—only to find half of the screen blocked out, still showing the same partial view (see fig. 26). Of course. The image size is a function of the lens on the scanner, not the screen or the software. I had been seduced by "screen essentialism" (Montfort 2004)—the idea that a digital image is an object that exists independently from its rendering on the screen. The microfilm computer makes the mechanics of digital representation starkly clear: the amount of film transmitted to the screen is determined by the distance between the film and the lens. This distance has been optimized for pages, not books. Similarly, the monitor, which seemed impressively large at first, is hardware for digital page views of proportionally rectangular scale. Despite the potentially flexible capacity of the software, the microfilm computer is tethered to a fixed image dimension—one not designed for books. The images of MS 80 have also not been designed for reading: the gutter of each opening is a stark black line, obliterating the beginning of every line of the right-hand page. The text could not be edited from these images. Together, this film and this machine point to the misalignment of efficient copying with efficient reading. They show how preservation technologies make selections, silently redirecting the future archive toward some purposes and not others.

The location of this Dartmouth microfilm computer in 2018 loops back to the 1930s, when manuscript microfilming was getting started and Harkness was founding the Pilgrim Trust. This part of MS 80's story is quite accidental but also quite revelatory of the nationalist and racial histories of technology and patronage. The computer was installed in the library's

Figure 26 Microfilm of MS 80 in a computer monitor. Project Room, Dartmouth College Library.

SOURCE: Photo by Michelle Warren (October 3, 2018).

Project Room—adjacent to the Orozco Room, named for the famous mural by José Clemente Orozco, *The Epic of American Civilization* (1932–34). The mural is a searing depiction of colonial brutality, industrial corrosion, and the perversions of elite culture. The commission was initiated by two Dartmouth art history professors, aided by their recently graduated student Nelson D. Rockefeller (Class of 1930), who convinced his mother to allocate Rockefeller family funds to the project (Coffey 2020, 28). The mural is now maintained with funds provided by another family foundation, the Mantons (also patrons of restoration at Westminster Abbey). Dartmouth also hosts a digital Orozco exhibit, funded partly by the Mellon Foundation (Nadeau 2017; www.dartmouth.edu/digitalorozco). Orozco's mural—painted around the same time that Harkness founded the Pilgrim Trust, funded by the Rockefeller fortune, sustained by yet other family philanthropies—lays bare the debts that patronage owes to colonial brutality.

The door to the Project Room is framed by a pointed comment on technology and civilizational violence. Orozco set the door at the beginning of the conquest of the Americas, with a menacing crusader figure on the right and a stack of machine parts on the left (see fig. 27). According to the interpretive brochure, the panels are titled *Cortez and the Cross* and *Machine Totem*; the depiction of Hernán Cortés (1485–1547) is "machine-like"; the machines themselves are sinewy and lifelike (Nadeau 2017). These panels exemplify the mural's overall concern with "the broader plight of humanity under the conditions of private ownership, exploitation, and social inequality that capitalism entails" (Mary Coffey, in Nadeau 2017, 15). The driver of destruction here is the menacing Christian cross that looms directly above the door. Walking through the door means walking into this history. Going about one's work on the other side means working within the framework of all that has been destroyed in the name of "civilization." As an access point for MS 80, the Project Room draws the grail history into a fuller time line of colonial Christianity. The grail, too, is an instrument that destroys the "unworthy": most who seek it die; it reveals itself to only a few pure knights. The twentieth-century microfilm of a fifteenth-century book set in the early Christian era tangles temporalities in ways that parallel the machine totem of the Spanish conquest.

Figure 27   Entrance to the Project Room, Dartmouth College Library, framed by two sections of José Clemente Orozco's mural: *The Epic of American Civilization: Machine Images* and *Cortez and the Cross* (panels 10 and 11), 1932–34, fresco. Hood Museum of Art, Dartmouth College: Commissioned by the Trustees of Dartmouth College; P.934.13.12–.13.

SOURCE: Photo by Michelle Warren (October 3, 2018).

The microfilm and the mural also share debts to nationalist patronage. In the years that Orozco was painting the mural, the Library of Congress undertook its first major microfilming project with a $490,000 grant from John D. Rockefeller Jr.; another Rockefeller gift paid for the library's first photoduplication lab in 1938 (Meckler 1982, 30–31). These arrangements made it possible for the Library of Congress to support expanded copying for all sorts of materials, including the manuscript microfilms made for the BMP (1941–45) and the MLA (1939–50)—projects that focused specifically on materials "of particular interest to American scholars" (Power 1990, 385). Those interests benefited from a targeted shift in philanthropic priorities at the Rockefeller Foundation—which replaced racial equity projects with scholarly infrastructure projects. In 1929, the Social Science Research Council laid out comprehensive goals for microfilm reproduction at a Rockefeller-funded conference in Hanover, New Hampshire (Binkley 1936, iii). At the time, the SSRC had four active committees focused on race, particularly in relation to African Americans. During 1930, however, all four committees were dissolved as they lost their Rockefeller funding (Morey 2019). By 1938, the Library of Congress had its Rockefeller photoduplication lab. Soon, Power would be sending microfilms of British manuscripts to the Library of Congress. The collaborations among the SSRC, ACLS, and MLA in support of scholarly microfilm came at the direct expense of earlier initiatives for racial justice. These connections show that technologies of cultural preservation are inseparable from social and political definitions of who and what is worth saving.

Power, too, connected scholarly copying to racial politics. Already in 1939, Power's microfilm product list represented a spectrum of rare materials in need of rescue through photography—old books and "old cultures." With encouragement from the Carnegie Foundation, he hosted an exhibit for the 1939 World's Fair in San Francisco, featuring microfilms of both "English Books before 1550" and "Indian Art" (Power 1990, 119). He reprised the showing at the MLA meeting in 1941 (Power 1990, 119). Power's "Indian Art Exhibit" exemplifies the trope of the "vanishing Indian," in which white settlers both regret and celebrate the idea that Indigenous Peoples are disappearing. Power later styled himself a patron of Inuit art—with some help from the industrialist, book collector, and patron of the Houghton Library at Harvard University, Arthur Houghton Jr. (Power 1990, 172–85). Power's practices align the rescue of old books via microfilm with a settler colonialist ideology that cast Indigenous Peoples as equally old and fragile. This same ethos came into other media just a few decades later with Stewart Brand's "America Needs Indians," a multimedia exhibit in which he sought to bring attention to "forgotten people"—at the same time that he was developing new visions of "cyberculture" (Turner 2006, 66–69; Smith 2012, 43–56; Nakamura 2014, 931). Brand and Power both granted new technologies more agency than Indigenous Peoples themselves in the maintenance of authentic memories.

The intersections of microfilm, race, and libraries are succinctly expressed by William Jerome Wilson (1884–1963)—fellow in medieval history at the Library of Congress and author of a report to the ACLS on the progress of the BMP in 1943. The challenges of cataloguing microfilms of manuscripts sparked Wilson's technological imagination. First, he delineates the problems that arise when films are treated as surrogates rather than as new bibliographic objects: without their own call numbers, the films could not be incorporated into the card catalogue; thus, their content could not be discovered (Wilson 1943b, 302–3). Instead, films needed to be treated like books so that scholars could "browse" them like other materials (Wilson 1943a, 216). At the same time, the unique affordances of microfilm invited new technologies—such as "some simple device which would throw the image on any blank wall, something about the shape of a large flashlight that could be screwed into any electric light socket" (Wilson 1943a, 215). Wilson also imagined libraries sharing their materials and catalogues via television: "the principles are known by which any library could be equipped to show a rare book or a section of its card catalog to a distant scholar, sitting in his own study before his television screen and turning the pages or flipping the cards by remote control!" (Wilson 1942, 7). The seemingly mundane tasks of cataloguing would thus generate new scholarly technologies. Wilson represents one of the earliest examples of tech medievalism (see introduction).

All this cataloguing and connectivity, however, had a pernicious racial component. Some scholars and librarians in the United States thought that "the deteriorating state of affairs" in Europe meant that the center of learning would be shifting from Europe to the United States: scholars would therefore need a full collection of manuscript copies in order to carry on what Europeans could no longer sustain: "Someone, observing sadly the racial and cultural divisions of Europe, has remarked that only in America has it been possible to develop anything that can properly be termed a European race and a European civilization. Perhaps the compilation of a complete bibliographical catalog of the priceless manuscript records of Europe also awaits American execution, with the microfilm copy as the medium" (Wilson 1943b, 309). This "someone" was suggesting that the war that began in 1939 resulted partly from Europe's lack of racial coherence—whereas white Europeans in the United States, despite their different national origins, saw themselves as a unified race. From within this framework of white supremacy, Wilson posited that good American microfilm cataloguing could give Europe what Europe lacked—a unified cultural record. A consolidated bibliography would lead to a consolidated identity. This racialization of European heritage—tied to manuscript microfilms—reflects the totalizing views of culture, and race, implicit in the very idea of mass reproduction.

Digitizing Global Assets

By the 1990s, digital technologies were writing a new chapter in cultural heritage reproduction. Computing, digital photography, and the internet were converging to make networked images of manuscripts a new component of the knowledge economy. The new technologies, like microfilm before, developed through disparate and complex interactions among military, commercial, and educational interests. Many elements were supported by national interests but also crossed into increasingly global networks. As objects of both national and world heritage, medieval manuscripts in libraries were swept up in many new initiatives for networked representation. The internet appealed for its broad reach and increasingly global audience, while individual projects often traded on local or national values. The first website at the British Library, in 1993, for example, featured an image of the Magna Carta—considered the founding document of Britain's constitutional monarchy but also "one of the most famous documents in the world" (https://bl.uk/magna-carta). The British Library soon added images from the *Beowulf* manuscript— representing the origin of British literature (Prescott 1998). These digital strategies reframed medieval English documents as global assets.

The project to digitize the medieval manuscripts of Parker Library exemplifies these trends. The first feasibility study was carried out in 1996 and updated in 1997, along with a study for a revenue-generating visitor center (CCCA, Box 5). The Parker digitization project was announced publicly in 2000 as part of the capital campaign to celebrate the 650th anniversary of Cambridge University. "The Parker Library Appeal" makes clear that the Parker Library is both a major asset and a major liability. The expense of renovating both the books and the building would require a proposed investment of £20 million ("Parker Library Appeal" 2000, 34). At the time, digitization seemed to offer a way to sell a book while keeping the book, converting cultural riches into monetary ones. Indeed, the Parker librarian Christopher De Hamel aimed to make the library self-sustaining, with digitization just one of several revenue streams (De Hamel 2005–8; 2010, 10; CCCA, Box 2). The project was expected to last four years, with four researchers producing a new electronic catalogue and others photographing the manuscripts ("Parker Library Appeal" 2000, 32). The project would use the latest technology, much as Parker had done with printing in his own time (De Hamel 2005–8, no. 3, p. 4). Digital reproduction would broaden access to the library's treasures for everyone while maintaining exclusive forms of access for major donors.

"The Parker Library Appeal"—a glossy brochure full of colorful photos—made investment in the library seem worthwhile and even patriotic by emphasizing both the ancientness and Englishness of the collection. The library was said to represent a complete "time capsule of English learning" ("Parker Library Appeal" 2000, 22). The cover made the point succinctly with an image of Elizabeth I, reproduced from Matthew Parker's copy of the Corpus Christi College Statutes (MS 582). Digital reproduction was presented as both a continuation of these ancient, national documents and an innovation that would turn the collection into a global asset: "The Parker Library has been described as 'a major surviving fragment of the medieval information super-highway.' For centuries, the great courts and abbeys of Europe could only communicate by writing on animal skin (vellum) with vegetable dye inks, using the common language of Latin. At Corpus Christi, we believe that the new information communication technologies will enable Matthew Parker's treasures to become accessible to people around the world, so that his extraordinary bequest will become part of the international heritage" ("Parker Library Appeal" 2000, 32). The analogy between the library and the internet is presented without attribution yet as a quotation. It appears with the authority of a source and the ubiquity of common knowledge. This conception of internet distribution makes global access a new source of prestige for the library: its national treasures will acquire an even more impressive international reputation. However rhetorically savvy, the appeal was more successful for the building than for digitization: by 2010, the manuscripts had a new home in a state-of-the-art vault, complete with sensitive alarms, temperature and humidity controls, and fire protections ("Parker Library" 2010). Adjacent to the vault, a large and well-appointed reading room houses librarians and readers in equal comfort.

The digitization project developed instead through foundation grants and collaboration with Stanford University—a private institution founded in 1885 at the latter end of American westward expansion, now one of the wealthiest institutions in the world. Andrew M. Thompson, an alumnus of both Stanford and Corpus Christi College, is credited with "catalyzing" the project ("About Earlier Phases" 2018–21). De Hamel described meeting Thompson in January 2002 at the San Francisco Airport in California. An investment banker, Thompson "conjured images of huge wealth for the College from trading metaphorically in the Parker Library, our most valuable asset" (De Hamel memo, November 13, 2006; CCCA, Box 2). Within the year, discussions were under way with Michael Keller, head of Stanford Libraries, and Don Waters, program officer at the Mellon Foundation. A pilot project was carried out in 2004–5 ("About the Project" 2010). The project, though, remained mired in uncertainty and mismatched expectations on all sides. At one point, administrators at Corpus Christi College envisioned that Stanford would become a comprehensive fundraising partner (CCCA, Box 2); at another, Thompson and De Hamel proposed a licensing fee in the millions for Stanford to gain full rights to the images (Keller 2018). This was obviously not a feasible arrangement for a university library. The archived emails and memos suggest that the project nearly collapsed more than once.

Throughout its development, the digitization project reflected De Hamel's vision that the library should be open to all—including children, to inspire care for historical archives in the next generation (De Hamel 2010). The digital project extended what he saw as the library's founding identity: "In theory, it has been open to readers since 1574, but for several centuries it was almost impossible to gain admission. These days we are glad to welcome scholars of all nationalities to see and study the treasures of the Parker Library. Corpus Christi College is delighted that the new Parker Library on the Web facility now allows even more people access to these breathtaking manuscripts, which are truly the heritage of the world" (Harrassowitz 2009; press release, November 2008). By casting the collection as "world heritage," the sales pitch for Parker Library on the Web turned a national asset into a global responsibility. Although buoyed by the most "breathtaking" books, the project treated the collection itself as a treasure, such that even "unloved" manuscripts were included (Paul 2018). This approach enabled a manuscript like MS 80—disparaged even by its editors (see chap. 5)—to become a new kind of object.

The production phase of Parker Library on the Web was made possible by foundation grants in the tradition of Harkness, Carnegie, and Rockefeller. Like them, the Mellon Foundation links cultural heritage philanthropy with social equality values: archival projects are treated as the natural allies of initiatives that address racial injustice. In this framework, preservation serves the common good, and broadening access serves democratic ideals. Andrew W. Mellon (1855–1937) was active in the same years as Harkness, Carnegie, and John D. Rockefeller Sr. Andrew's father, Thomas, initiated the family wealth in banking in Western Pennsylvania; his holdings eventually included Rockefeller's Standard Oil, where Stephen Harkness also invested. Andrew Mellon became Secretary of the Treasury in 1921 and was ambassador to Britain from 1932 to 1933. His philanthropy mostly supported educational and social causes in Pittsburgh, including what is now Carnegie Mellon University. The foundation was established posthumously in 1969 by Andrew's two children, Alisa (1901–69) and Paul (1907–99), with a focus on the arts, humanities, and education (Mellon 1992; Cannadine 2006). Paul attended Cambridge University and mirrored

Edward Harkness in Anglophilia as well as patronage, including two additional residential colleges at Yale. These histories are echoed in the smaller grant for the Parker project from the Delmas Foundation: Gladys Krieble Delmas (1913–91) inherited an industrial fortune, which she used to support the arts and academia, including the American Philosophical Society and the Institute for Advanced Study in Princeton (Sutton 1992). These grants for Parker Library on the Web, like the Pilgrim Trust grant for rebinding and Rockefeller investments in microfilm technology, connect the reproduction of British cultural heritage to deep legacies of capital accumulation in the United States.

The Mellon and Delmas grants supported the direct labor of producing Parker Library on the Web. Photography took place from 2005 to 2009, with nine different camera operators from Cambridge University Library on the project for varying lengths of time ("About the Project" 2010). Here, a different set of political factors weave into digital books. These "modern copyists" were mostly Polish citizens, whose migration was facilitated by the open labor policies of the European Union (Whearty 2018, 197). With the 2016 passage of the Brexit referendum, Britain left the European Union and moved toward polices that would bar such migrations. The rise of anti-immigration legislation is affecting every sector of society, including cultural heritage projects—themselves integral to European Union economic strategy (Niggemann, Decker, and Lévy 2011). As Bridget Whearty concludes: "we are implicated in the infrastructures and politics that shape the lives of these modern makers of medieval books" (Whearty 2018, 197). To the extent that Parker Library on the Web is a "global" asset of deep national significance that was produced in part through policies designed to support the union of "European" identities, it is the product of a very specific history of internationalization. As a post–World War II organization, the European Union was meant to counter the extreme nationalism blamed for the war: it originated at the same time that William Jerome Wilson was imagining that American microfilm collections could help unify the "European race" by creating a unified record of manuscripts (Wilson 1943b, 309). Once again, via Polish photographers working in Cambridge, racism cuts a complex path through the history of British manuscript copying.

The media files eventually published with Parker 1.0, and now used on Parker 2.0, bear only partial witness to the many improvisations that produced them. Like the manuscripts themselves, they have come through occasionally inhospitable environments in which the photographers and the larger team enabling their work solved problems large and small. Conservator Melvin Jefferson has described in detail how cradles were adapted to enable the photography of various types of materials, from stiff bindings to disbound leaves, as well as the protocols for continuity of temperature and humidity (Jefferson 2007). In the early phases, though, the team faced many obstacles—from unsteady floorboards to poor air quality to discolored lighting. Many details have not been recorded. Others are proprietary and confidential as they involve financing, intellectual property, and internal college administration. The available archive offers glimpses (CCCA, Boxes 2 and 5), as do the living memories of participants (although I have not undertaken a project ethnography). The gaps in this record of recent history are salutary reminders that all archives and manuscript collections preserve irretrievable combinations of intentions and accident—all of which shift meaning over time.

The digitization of books like MS 80 was directly facilitated by the 1950s rebindings. These bindings were generally too tight to allow the books to open sufficiently, but their historical significance was also deemed minimal; therefore, they could be modified. The "disastrous" 1950s hide glue was replaced with purified wheat-starch paste; the spines were modified to include a paper hollow to support the leaves when the book opens (Jefferson 2007). All of this work was facilitated by a new state-of-the-art conservation studio, built in 2005 to serve historic collections in various Cambridge institutions (Jefferson 2007). High-tech conservation was thus the prerequisite for high-tech photography. Each manuscript was first checked for its ability to open on a photography cradle without being damaged; adjustments and repairs were made to enable the photography; after photography, the physical state of each manuscript was again checked. The project's digital outputs include a database on the conservation status of every manuscript, including those that were too fragile to be photographed (Jefferson 2007). MS 80 on the shelf is thus now a codex reproduced in both 1956 and c. 2006. Even in the vault, it is at once a medieval paper manuscript, a modern printed book, and a digital book.

Once a book can be safely opened in a photography cradle, many further steps intervene before it appears on anyone's networked device. Many different people with specialized skills contribute to the process in tandem with multiple software and hardware components. At Parker Library, each image capture was processed into several files: an archival master in TIFF format, one uncropped submaster in compressed TIFF format showing the color bar used to verify image fidelity, one cropped submaster in compressed TIFF format without a color bar, and a compressed derivative of each submaster in the JPEG2000 format ("About the Project" 2010). While many of these processes are automated, the algorithms and software have been designed by people—many but not all now anonymous (the TIFF compression algorithm, for example, is called "LVW" after Abraham Lempel, Jacob Ziv, and Terry Welch [Wikipedia]). A digital image displayed on Parker Library on the Web is thus a copy of copies, encoded to optimize access via a web browser. Parker 2.0 shows traces of this processing history: thumbnail images in search results show uncropped pages with a color bar and the full shape of the magnetic page holders made of bone (as of October 27, 2020; Jefferson 2007; see fig. 28). Though small, these images allude to the immensity of the physical labor, storage arrangements, and technical machinery required to enable colored pixels to appear in proper order on a screen.

From a user's perspective, the digital reproduction of a manuscript includes the interface that structures access to the images. On a purely visual level, the image viewers on Parker 1.0 and 2.0 present similar editions of the manuscripts. Their similarities are also typical of other digital manuscript platforms, suggesting that there is currently a visual canon for digital books, much as there was for the 1950s bindings at Parker Library. In both cases, the visual interface in one medium mimics the format of other technologies. Whereas the bindings draw their design vocabulary from printed books, image viewers draw theirs from microfilm: "scroll view" like a roll and "gallery view" like a fiche (Porter 2018c). Zoom features are the digital equivalent of analog magnification. Image viewers

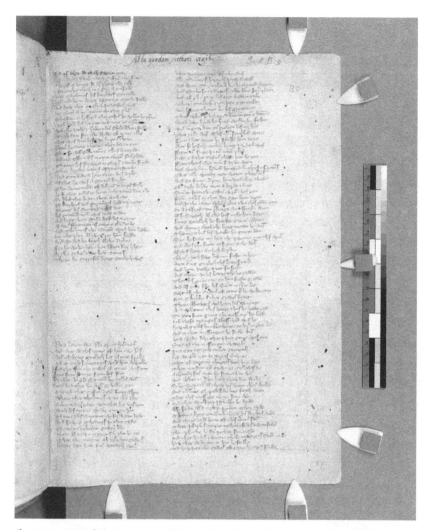

Figure 28 MS 80, folio 1r, uncropped thumbnail on Parker Library on the Web 2.0 (2018–21).

SOURCE: https://purl.stanford.edu/xd494bt3141. Courtesy of Parker Library, Corpus Christi College, Cambridge. Licensed under a Creative Commons Attribution-NonCommercial 4.0 International License.

for manuscripts also adapt models developed for digitized print books (Prescott and Hughes 2018). Image viewers thus reproduce the modern history of reproduction. The consistency of these forms across platforms has structured digitized manuscripts as facsimile books, optimized for reading styles closely analogous to both the codex and the microfilm. From this view, MS 80 is more or less "the same" on Parker 1.0 and 2.0.

In other ways, though, MS 80 is a different form of book on 1.0 than it is on 2.0. These differences expose the work of infrastructure in book-making. On Parker 1.0, the interface is made of customized code, making it a unique artifact. The digital images are "fixed" inside the viewer, just as they are on the shelf. With the option for page animations and the default view to an open book, the interface emphasizes the codex-like properties of digital reproductions. The zoom function also maintains the semblance of analog magnification, with plus and minus icons similar to microfilm readers. With these strategies, the interface minimizes the difference that the digital makes, treating the digital book primarily in its guise as a storage device for the manuscript's visual properties. The viewer itself is integrated in a custom platform that provided a comprehensive portal for manuscript studies (see chap. 4). Parker 1.0 thus presented MS 80—and the other manuscripts—within the epistemological frames of print cataloguing and editing.

Parker 2.0, by contrast, makes the digital book more like a platform—reprogrammable for uses beyond the collection itself. The image viewer, Mirador, is open-source software that can display any files encoded with the standards of the International Image Interoperability Framework (IIIF) (http://projectmirador.org). To reproduce a semblance of a codex, a collection of images is "bound" together by a "manifest" that lists the file locations in order—analogous to a book binding (Bolintineanu 2020, 212). The manifest has its own web address and can be ported to other IIIF image viewers, meaning that the Parker manuscript images can be viewed outside of Parker Library on the Web. A digital book might bear the marks of Mirador functions (like color contrast adjustments), or it might have entirely different features in another application. A book can also be disaggregated page by page, like a collection of loose leaves. In this configuration, "MS

80" and Mirador are both interchangeable components of other systems; they are not tied to Parker 2.0 or even to each other. The model is distributed rather than integrated (van Zundert 2018). With these strategies, the interface opens toward new born-digital ontologies for medieval books.

The interface of MS 80 includes the complete websites of Parker 1.0 and 2.0, from their home pages to their navigation structures (see chaps. 3 and 4). Parker 1.0 presented a number of welcoming features but drew a bright red line (literally) between free features and those that could be accessed by subscribers only. Above the image viewer, a red banner declares: "The zoom view option is available to subscribed users only." And on the home page, a red hyperlink directs users to subscription information. Redirected to the site of the German publisher Harrassowitz, users would learn that access to the site's full features—high resolution images, bibliography, summaries, advanced browse options, and search—came with a hefty price tag: $9,500 purchase with annual maintenance fee of $480 or annual subscription of $3,500, with discounts for consortia of libraries (Harrassowitz 2009). The marketing materials described in detail the maintenance expenses covered by the fees—and specified that a sustainable business model was a condition of the grants that paid for the four-year project to build the site. All through the planning phases, the website was described as a free resource ("Parker Library Appeal" 2000; De Hamel 2005–8). In the end, though, the subscription model addressed the fact that the digital images were—like the manuscripts—a major asset as well as a major liability. The high price was widely criticized for creating a new barrier to scholarship ("monstrously expensive," Prescott 2012). And indeed, it divided the scholarly community—and thus scholarship—according to institutional wealth. These divisions were not entirely new: travel was already a barrier, and libraries limit access to rare materials for many reasons. Even though other manuscript projects were publishing free websites, costs must be born somewhere: ideology aside, the internet is not free. The Parker 1.0 subscription thus registered the material challenges of digital stewardship.

The final archive version of Parker 1.0 includes a red banner linking to the 2015 press release for Parker 2.0. The announcement reveals how much had changed in digital reproduction over a ten-year span. The primary concern for access is not cataloguing or metadata but image sharing via IIIF. A second major concern is affordable sustainability: the subscription business model would be replaced with free access, facilitated by replacing custom components with templates so that updating is integrated with the standard systems of Stanford University Libraries (Karampelas 2015). Together, these two strategies maximize access and longevity—the core commitments of the Parker digitization project from the beginning. These strategies make Parker Library on the Web an exemplary model of resource stewardship—migrating within the ten-year time frame originally promised and doing so in a way that minimizes the cost of future migrations. Indeed, free access has been one of the most touted—and welcome—features of Parker 2.0. Free, however, doesn't mean without constraint. Every resource—digital or otherwise—has structures that make some things highly visible and other things difficult or impossible to see. For Parker 1.0, subscription made the manuscripts difficult to see for those without institutional access. This barrier, though, was a condition of making the digital images visible at all. Now, on Parker 2.0, access is free but some components have disappeared (see chap. 4). Each arrangement brings its advantages and disadvantages, depending on users' circumstances. From the perspective of book history, the arrangements themselves are part of the manuscripts.

The infrastructure contrast between Parker 1.0 and 2.0 mirrors ongoing tensions across digital platforms between different funding models: subscription, advertising, and nonprofit. Parker 1.0 followed the subscription model set by EETS in print and by Power in microfilm. The digitized editions of EETS (Literature Online: LION) and Power's microfilms (EEBO) also became subscription platforms, first by Chadwyck-Healey and now by ProQuest. In this model, subscribers purchase access licenses, not objects. This model turns books into information. Parker 2.0, by contrast, shifts the model of digital stewardship to free access, most common for libraries and nonprofits like the Internet Archive and HathiTrust. Meanwhile, Google offers free access in exchange for users' data, which can then be sold to advertisers. Each model produces a distinct style of "book" (as I discuss in chap. 5). From this perspective on infrastructure, digitized manuscripts and digitized print have more or less similar formats according to the arrangements that pay for their storage. Subscription models make the costs of infrastructure visible and distributed (however unevenly), while the library-service model makes the accounting less visible and also less distributed. Each model constructs "the book" and its communities of care differently; each relies on different theories and practices of infrastructure security.

Almost as soon as Parker 1.0 was completed, Mellon made additional grants to Stanford, Johns Hopkins University, and the University of Toronto for a number of born-digital research projects under the umbrella title "Manuscript Studies in an Interoperable Digital Environment" (2011–15). Among these projects, "Parker's Scribes" was designed to make use of Parker 1.0 as the foundation for new manuscript research focused on annotations (Gillespie and Horobin 2015). As a project adviser, I visited Parker Library in 2012—encountering MS 80 yet again, in the newly renovated reading room. In the end, though, "Parker's Scribes" encountered numerous technical barriers, in part because interoperability was not yet, so to speak, operable (Alexandra Gillespie, personal communication, January 23, 2020). Research into interoperability standards continued at Stanford throughout this period, supported in part by additional Mellon grants (https://mellon.org/grants/grants-database). The grants contributed to the development of both Mirador and IIIF. Parker 2.0 puts these research results into practice. The site, then, is "free" in part because it has been paid for by other means.

The price of digital access includes the carbon footprint of hosting networked images. From the beginning, curators at Parker Library recognized the digital files as new physical assets that would require conservation measures akin to the manuscripts themselves ("About the Project" 2010). Digital reproduction increased costs by increasing the amount and type of materials that needed preservation. Every cultural heritage institution faces this dilemma. The physical conservation of the books and the data requires control of both temperature and humidity. In the context of climate change, rising global temperatures endanger the longevity of both books and bits. These factors combine in a circular fashion: climate change puts archives and library collections at risk; preserving collections contributes to climate change (Pendergrass et al. 2019). Parker Library provides one example of this global issue: when the new vault introduced air conditioning for the first time, the bursar became concerned about costs and had to be convinced that, even with no one in the library on weekends, the books still needed to stay cool (Paul 2018). The books are safer in the vault, but they are also permanently more expensive—as are the data files derived from them. The package of master TIFFs of the Parker manuscripts takes 75 terabytes of digital storage. They are archived in several ways: spinning disk servers at Stanford, spinning disk servers at Corpus Christi College, offsite "cloud" storage with Amazon Web Storage (likely on tape), and offsite "cloud" storage with IBM (likely on tape) (email from Ben Albritton, August 1, 2019). Preservation of these files requires periodic updating, some of which is outsourced to the for-profit storage vendors. The prospects for sustainability rely on continued institutional investments, which depend partly on perceptions of the ongoing value of the files. The business practices of Amazon and IBM are also part of the story.

Finally, the technology that powers Parker Library on the Web includes software components fraught with the ethnoracial and discriminatory histories of the internet. These components illustrate how meaningful histories drift into infrastructure only to be subsumed by habits that render them meaningless. These components are not at all unique to the Parker platform—which only broadens their significance as bookmakers. The indexing functions for search on both Parker 1.0 and 2.0, for example, have been created by the Apache Group. Currently, the name story for the Apache Software Foundation, whose logo is a feather, acknowledges its ties to "cultural appropriation" (Keene 2010–19). While the Apache website originally stated that the name derived from a "really good" pun on "a patchy Web server," founder Brian Behlendorf later described instead an "out of the blue" connotation of "Take no prisoners. Be kind of aggressive and kick some ass" (McMillan 2000, 2). Since 2013, this settler colonialist stereotype has been displaced by a narrative that shows some awareness of Indigenous history, although it is still in the mode of appropriation: "The name 'Apache' was chosen from respect for the various Native American nations collectively referred to as Apache, well-known for their superior skills in warfare strategy and their inexhaustible endurance" ("Why" 2019). Meanwhile, the naming story for the JavaScript applications that built the custom image viewer on Parker 1.0 seems to have no cultural awareness beyond "coffee" (Murphy 1996), which itself shows how thoroughly Dutch colonial practices in Indonesia have been naturalized in global markets. The creator of the Saxon XLST Processor used to transform documents in XML (Extensible Markup Language) into HTML is silent on the name of his company, but clearly it leans into Anglo-Germanic associations forged amid nineteenth-century nationalism (Saxonica.com; Rambaran-Olm 2019). Finally, the JPEG2000 image standard by "Aware SDK" alludes to the racially fraught field of biometrics, now the main business of Aware. com (Resnikoff 2018). This detail illustrates the debt that all imaging technologies have to surveillance. The JPEG2000, moreover, is built on the JPEG—a standard with its own discriminatory legacy: it was originally developed with a test image selected in 1973 of "Lena," a Swedish model who had posed for a Playboy centerfold. "Lena" is still the most used test image in the world and widely criticized for contributing to discriminatory environments in computing (Bartley 2019). Collectively, these names and practices are a meaningful part of tech infrastructure. They tend to naturalize into a semblance of meaninglessness, but nonetheless they carry forward histories of oppression. Correctives to these toxic legacies include critical infrastructure practices—such as "losing Lena" and Indigenous data sovereignty projects (Duarte 2017; Srinivasan 2017; Christen 2019). The bounds of ethical tech include, minimally, remembering these wider histories and integrating them into book history.

MS 80 is many books in one. On the shelf "next to 79," MS 80 is a twentieth-century book produced by American Anglophilia and bookbinders' equally nostalgic vision of medieval book technologies. On the microfilm computer, MS 80 is a twentieth-century roll produced by the nationalist development of document preservation, particularly American visions of the transfer (*translatio*) of learning and empire westward from Europe to the United States. On Parker Library on the Web, MS 80 is a twenty-first-century digital interface, sustained again by American commitments to English heritage as a global asset. All along the way, librarians at Parker Library leveraged these interests to serve their own responsibilities to conserve a collection of great significance to British history. These arrangements are but a sampling of the complex networks that keep old books open around the world.

As a fifteenth-century book made of paper, MS 80 itself provides a model for durable preservation media. In the 1930s, the same institutional arrangements that supported microfilm also devised new standards for paper. At the time, modern wood-pulp paper was rapidly deteriorating, taking culture and scholarship with it. As one of the early proponents of microfilming, Robert Binkley, wrote: "the records of our time are written in dust" (Binkley 1929, 171). As secretary and then chair of the ACLS/SSRC Joint Committee on Materials for Research, formed in 1930, Binkley set medieval paper as the standard for durability, "taking as a standard the fine old papers of the fifteenth and sixteenth centuries" (Binkley 1929, 175). The ultimate result is the "acid-free, archival-quality" paper used in book publishing today. Funding for paper research came from the same sources as microfilm—Carnegie, Rockefeller, ACLS, SSRC, and the US government (Carpenter 2007; Gitelman 2014a, 53–82). The very material of MS 80 thus cycled into the reimagining of technological innovation in the early decades of the twentieth century. In this way, medieval paper itself became a source of tech medievalism. Today, digital materials are written in electrical pulses that dissipate even more quickly than dust. Are the "digital Dark Ages" inevitable, or will "digital vellum" come to the rescue? Will copying continue to get cheaper, or will climate change reconfigure the calculations? It remains to be seen which book will last longest—MS 80 on the shelf, MS 80 on a film roll, or MS 80 on the internet.

CONCLUSION

INDEXING THE GRAIL, ROMANCING THE INTERNET

ONE BOOK, SIX STORIES, HUNDREDS OF YEARS. The longer I've looked at MS 80, the more I've seen. Modern paper, slightly pinkish. A leaf of vellum, stiff and covered with writing on one side. Finally, creamy brownish paper, slightly wavy, brownish ink. Small, mostly unobtrusive holes, round and oblong. Faint reddish rulings marking out two columns, small pricking holes to guide the straight lines. Blank spaces in the midst of text columns, a patch, indented scratches, watermarks, chain marks from paper molds, round discolorations here and there. Annotations in the margins, flourishes ascending from some top lines of text, verses written vertically, faces, fingers, folio numbers in pencil, quire signatures in ink, stray pen marks, paragraph marks, a woman's name, erasures. A black ink stain on the outer edge, about forty page-edges wide. Next to the book, on the table in the Wilkins Room at Corpus Christi College, my laptop and so much more to see (fig. 29). The title "Henry Lovelich, The History of the Holy Grail, Merlin." The Stanford Libraries logo. "Search everything" on Parker Library on the Web, a blue and red "IIIF" icon, white triangles holding the pages flat, bibliography, and much more. The book is multiplying, but it can still get lost. Each time it's found, it's different from the time before.

The short story of MS 80 goes something like this. In the twelfth century, Geoffrey of Monmouth launched King Arthur into the mainstream of British history with *The History of the Kings of Britain*. Geoffrey's account became widely influential, intermingling with many other Arthurian stories in many languages. In the early thirteenth century, French writers incorporated some of Geoffrey's historical structure into an expansive narrative of the Holy Grail and King Arthur, full of new characters and convoluted plots. Numerous manuscripts in varied configurations preserve this French prose cycle, some with illustrations. One of them sparked the imagination of two members of the London Skinners' Guild in the early fifteenth century, Henry Lovelich and Henry Barton. Lovelich translated a portion of the French cycle into English couplets, preserved in a single manuscript made of paper c. 1425, with an incomplete design for illustrations. The book was then annotated extensively in the mid to late fifteenth century and again in the mid to late sixteenth century, when it was selected for the collection of England's first Anglican Archbishop, Matthew Parker. Thus preserved, it received new cataloguing attention in the seventeenth and eighteenth centuries before being edited in the nineteenth century and then rebound and microfilmed in the twentieth. In the twenty-first century, it has joined the digital world, where translation, annotation, cataloguing, editing, and reproduction all happened again by and for new communities.

In the preceding chapters, I have offered an "exploded view" of this story. Each chapter has constructed a network from the book's movements through various hands, formats, and institutions. Together, the chapters echo the interlaced structure of Lovelich's narrative, itself an echo of the cyclic strategies of French prose narrative. Arthur's story came to function like a programmable platform with ready-made components adaptable to different uses. In exposing the components, I have highlighted the technologies and patronage arrangements that produce the value of texts and books. I have tried to make visible some of the hidden processes that

Figure 29   MS 80 on a table next to a laptop. Wilkins Room, Parker Library, Corpus Christi College.

SOURCE: Photo by Michelle Warren (March 13, 2018). Reproduced courtesy of Parker Library, Corpus Christi College, Cambridge.

create aesthetic hierarchies, which shape decisions about preservation and access, which in turn structure access in ways that further delimit literary history. This model of book history integrates finding aids into the analysis of what is found—and what is found into an analysis of finding aids. The tools for engaging digital images say as much about digital infrastructure as they do about medieval books (Warren, ByrneSim, and Braunstein 2018). The book "before digital" is now entangled with the book "in digital" as well as with the book "after digital"—that time just beyond the horizon when today's digital objects may have faded. I've used a particularly poignant episode in the history of Arthurian literature to articulate the epistemological stakes of search. The ever-shifting nature of search is remaking literary history even as I mark the end of this story.

Each shift creates "the text." They are collectively "the book." The book "itself" is not a single object but rather a repertoire of forms, each with a story to tell. Each form reconfigures what it inherits from its predecessors—an English translation of a French book, a printed edition of a manuscript text, a digital edition of a printed catalogue. Even confused or erroneous metadata become vital sources of information for certain questions, as are failed page loads and paywall notices. Each form—manuscript, print, microfilm, media file, among others—enables distinctive types of inquiry, with zones of interchangeability. Comparative studies of media, platforms, and interfaces help define the shapes of those zones and thus also each form's unique affordances. Through the infrastructures that create and sustain these forms, the knowledge economy is saturated with colonial, imperial, and racist formations.

Across these centuries and formats, MS 80 owes its existence and persistence to many communities—from the fifteenth-century Skinners' Guild to sixteenth-century antiquarians to twentieth-century philanthropists to twenty-first-century photographers. Communities of care have been posited as the most significant factor in digital preservation. Care, however, is uneven and unpredictable. Value at one point in time can be discounted at a later one, and vice versa. These changes are not always rational or predictable. And how large does a community have to be to count as significant? Is two enough? Perhaps, if they are willing and able to put in the time. Institutions such as archives, libraries, and museums make care for books less contingent on individuals, yet they, too, have to set priorities for labor, space, and other resources. One archivist's care can still make the difference between a useful catalogue and a mess in a box. Digital reproduction only amplifies the tension between preservation and access that has always been at the core of document management. It represents a new tool in the long-standing question of who gets to touch what and why.

Now what? How do I end a network of stories? About a book still in motion? A few years ago, I worried—and some publishers confirmed—that a book about one book wouldn't get very far. Now, it seems that it can go anywhere and has no natural end point. Once "search" itself became the topic, the questions and the stories just kept multiplying beyond the wildest dreams I might have had in 1996. I've had to leave out so many, including deeper forays into scholarship from the various relevant disciplines.

Sometimes tracking MS 80 across platforms has felt like unraveling a vast conspiracy theory. Was everything really connected to everything? Or were the connections themselves an artifact of my enclosure within systems that built on each other and thus produced connections among themselves out of their own production process? New stories are still emerging, like new episodes in a medieval romance cycle. In this spirit, I'll conclude here by picking up some threads from earlier events in the story.

One catalyst for this book was the dissonance I experienced between the book I saw in Cambridge in 1996 and the "Lovelich" I found in literary histories. The issue of value judgments runs through many of the chapters. Was Lovelich a bad poet? Was Furnivall a bad editor? Is a microfilm a bad copy? Is Google a bad library? Is a JPEG a bad substitute for a manuscript? The answers to these and other questions of judgment depend on point of view and definitions of purpose. I have mostly avoided making judgments in favor of explanations of judgments: aesthetic pluralism calls for fewer definitive conclusions. I started my career defending editions amid some acrimonious debates in the 1990s in which some scholars promoted manuscripts as the only valid materials for studying medieval literature (detailed in Warren 2003). I formed a belief, which has never wavered, that all sources are good so long as they are matched with questions they can answer (Warren 2015). Digital reproductions are yet another kind of source—good for some things and not for others.

Another starting point for this book was reading about "digital vellum" in 2015 (Lepore 2015). The metaphor sparked my imagination, as well as my curiosity, leading me eventually to the "digital Dark Ages" and a host of "digital grails." Uncovering the work of tech medievalism also uncovered how ideals both inspire and constrain the imagination, stimulate justice and obscure violence. Tech medievalism isn't going away any time soon. Artificial Intelligence is the latest scientific area to promote solutions via the Holy Grail (e.g., Boden 2016, 21); digital preservation is still responding to "warnings of an impending 'digital dark age'" (Owens 2018, 1). But these metaphors also lead the way back through the infrastructures that produce and sustain them. They uncover, eventually, the histories of computing and infrastructure that are also part of the survival of medieval manuscripts.

The entry for *grail* in the *Oxford English Dictionary* is a case in point. The dictionary was conceived amid the same currents of romanticism and imperialism that brought Lovelich into print in 1861—with Frederick Furnivall as editor of both. The *OED*'s "grail" documentation includes Alfred Tennyson's poem "Sir Galahad" (1842, epigraph to Furnivall's Lovelich edition) and an EETS edition of an Arthurian romance (Wheatley 1865–69). The citations also include one metaphor—an English critique of American capitalism: "The quest for the almighty dollar is their Holy Grail" (Stead 1894, 123). This offhand comment witnesses the near-beginning of the modern metaphoric grail that refers to any desirable and elusive goal. Today, digital indexes turn up thousands of such citations in many genres, from journalism to science to literature. At the same time, the word frequency algorithm on OED.com counts *grail* as a low-usage word "unknown to most people." Even if the *OED* editors eventually update the entry with a sampling of post-1894 citations, the low-frequency classification might not change. Algorithms can't count the cultural weight of a word. The dissonance between the grail's popularity and the algorithm's frequency tally casts broader doubt on the algorithmic representations that shape everything from library catalogue searches to online shopping. Are the first results really the most relevant? As a relatively infrequent yet highly recognizable word, *grail* defies computational assessment. In this guise, it gives the lie to its own use as a metaphor for solutions and teaches us to search for what isn't being shown.

This book took a decisive new turn with the change of interface on Parker Library on the Web in January 2018, when Parker 1.0 closed and Parker 2.0 opened. The migration illustrates an important lesson that digital project creators have learned since the 1990s: interfaces and data need to be treated separately. Projects that designed custom interfaces with integrated data typically operate for five to ten years and then degrade or break suddenly when an operating system updates. In this environment of perpetual obsolescence, data need to be stored in simplified forms that can be processed by many different interfaces over time. Yet both literary history and book history teach that form (interface) and content (data) are inseparable. Meaning—in the broadest sense—derives from their interplay. In the study of literature and books in digital environments, then, interfaces are integral and meaningful even if they are variable and ephemeral. Indeed, as this book went to press, Parker 2.0 became Parker 2.1 (Albritton 2021). That story will have to wait for another day.

In the interests of sustainability and forward migration, interfaces are becoming more standardized. They are forming design canons that will gradually have more and more impact on the data that can be imagined or seem worth producing. Manuscript scholars have been asking how interfaces for digital images can answer questions besides "what does a page look like" (e.g., Stokes 2015; Porter 2018b, 2018d; Endres 2019). Can such interfaces become infrastructure? Or will they be temporary research tools? Will digital images themselves engender "new historical devices" (Trettien 2015, 187–88)? Comparative interface studies, as part of the habitual practice of literary history and book history, can document and interpret how these "forms effect meaning" (McKenzie 1986, 4). Every interface reveals and also hides. In this way, the organization of information conditions the very possibilities of thought.

The environment in which I wrote this book is already fading. Toward the end of my work, during October 2019, I encountered new interfaces on several of my habitual digital platforms—Bodleian Library, Early English Books Online, Google Books. Around the same time, the office building where I work was being closed for new interfaces—climate control systems and an elevator. In packing up my books and papers, I found again the 1996 letter confirming my first appointment to see MS 80. In the same drawer, a folder labeled "Electronic Networking" was full of printouts and handwritten notes about how to find medieval documents on the internet—including a 1998 announcement of a new digital manuscript platform called Digital Scriptorium and a grainy photocopy entitled "Websites for Using the Internet." However quaint that may sound now, in the 1990s such lists were essential research tools. As I was unpacking these memories, the internet turned fifty years old on October 29, 2019. I realized that my search for MS 80 had grown up with the scholarly internet. In this time span, the nature of search has changed substantially. All along, though, the internet has been making medieval books.

The origin of the internet is often told as a romance plot, with heroic protagonists surmounting unimaginable obstacles. Indeed, the protagonists themselves have contributed to this romance (Streeter 2011). The heroic plotline obscures the extensive collaborations that led to the first internet message in 1969, as well as "the command economy of military procurement" that paid for the research (Abbate 1999, 145). The romance also obscures the histories of violence that underwrote the infrastructure. In this parallel story, excavated by Ingrid Burrington, the cables and wires that carried the first network signal from Los Angeles to Menlo Park crossed a landscape rent by racism and environmental destruction: the genocide of Indigenous Peoples up and down the California coast since the days of Spanish conquest, the polluted waters of industrial manufacturing, and anti-Black violence of the 1960s (Burrington 2019). I grew up in some of these same places and went to some of these same universities in the 1980s and 1990s. I first "found" MS 80 just a few miles from the destination of the first internet message—in a book on a shelf in the Stanford University library. The histories carried, and buried, by internet infrastructure are also carried and buried by medieval books, wherever they may lie.

ACKNOWLEDGMENTS

This book has been decades in the making, though written only very recently with a tremendous amount of support through trying times. The scale of acknowledgments that I might make is rather daunting. And I know that I have forgotten the details of many kindnesses and encouragements that made all the difference at one moment or another. May these few words represent much more than what they actually say.

This is a book of stories about the institutions and materials that sustain books. My broadest acknowledgment is rooted in the institution where this work has come to completion—Dartmouth College in Hanover, New Hampshire. Every word of that description points to the homeland of medieval English literature—Britain. The systems of wealth accumulation that produced the fifteenth-century manuscript that I study here are continuous with those that produced Dartmouth College in the eighteenth century—namely, settler colonialism and the theft of Abenaki lands by the British monarchy. As fate would have it, those continuities include the very merchant organization that produced the manuscript I study here—the Skinners' Guild (fur traders). The college's namesake, the second Earl of Dartmouth, William Legge (1731–1801), descended from Thomas Legge, who in 1347 became the first skinner to serve as mayor of London (Lambert 1934, 37; Brydges 1812, 105–24). The Earl of Dartmouth still makes ceremonial visits to New Hampshire—a remnant of aristocratic privilege that has nothing and everything to do with this book. Acknowledging how the profits of settler colonialism and slavery sustain the college and all of its employees and students is the very minimum responsibility of settlers like me, who benefit from those profits. Informed acknowledgment is only one step in seeking respectful relations with Indigenous Peoples, but it is an essential one (Calloway 2010; Vowel 2016; Zuroski 2020). Acknowledgment helps make visible the settler protocols that make it hard for settlers to see who has paid what price for the preservation and destruction of cultural heritage. Incorporating these protocols into research narratives is another aspect of the critical infrastructure practices that animate this book.

The pathways of this research have been inspired—and often defined—by the librarians who operate the libraries that safeguard the books and host the people who study them. At Stanford University, Mary Jean Parrine initiated my training in bibliography back in the 1990s; most recently, Benjamin Albritton has been a generous fount of insights into digital infrastructure. At the University of Miami, Cecilia Leathem advocated for all kinds of resources for medieval studies; the Interlibrary Loan department often surprised me by procuring shipments of rare nineteenth-century books. At Dartmouth College, Laura Braunstein has been a joyful friend, coauthor, and colleague; Jay Satterfield supported lots of ideas for research and teaching adjacent to this project that have influenced my work. Most significant of all, of course, has been the warm welcome and collaboration of librarians at Parker Library at Corpus Christi College, Cambridge: Gillian Cannell in the first instance back in 1996 and again in 2012, along with Christopher De Hamel; Alexander Divine, Anne McLaughlin, and archivist Lucy Hughes in person in 2018 and via email ever since. I met Suzanne Paul after her time at Parker Library, but our immediate "meeting of minds" broadened my understanding of what my research might mean. Similarly, Emma Stanford, then of the Bodleian Library, introduced me to new dimensions of digital preservation.

The earliest champion of this project was Paul Strohm. More than once, a bracing email from Paul rekindled my own enthusiasm. Paul introduced me to Caroline Barron and Andrew Prescott, whose expertise and warm welcome into new areas of research have been invaluable. Alexandra Gillespie, too, invited me into discussions that completely transformed my concept of book history. Peggy McCracken and Patty Ingham were there at the beginning and still in 2020, confirming my ideals as well as my riskier experiments. Many other medievalist colleagues have shared curiosity and expertise at conferences and other venues. I have particularly fond memories of events at the Medieval Academy of America (2002), the Medieval London Seminar (2003, 2006), the International Congress on Medieval Studies (2004, 2005, 2012), Theory and Practice of Translation in Paris (2004), the French of England at Fordham University (2007), New Chaucer Society (2010, 2012), and the launch conferences for Parker Library on the Web 2.0 (2018). I am grateful to Keith Busby for recent discussions of French manuscripts. Members of the Dartmouth Medieval Seminar were convivial conversationalists over many years. I'll never forget Cecilia Gaposchkin's skepticism that format could really matter to a text: I've been trying to explain it better ever since. At the University of New Hampshire, Cord Whitaker let me talk about library catalogues with undergraduates. Graduate students at the Medieval Studies Institute at the University of Indiana-Bloomington, especially Kayla Lunt and Denise Weisz, made me feel like a star.

My education in the digital humanities has been belated and erratic but, somehow, inevitable. With support from a 2015 Innovative Research Award from the Dean of Faculty for Arts and Sciences at Dartmouth, I was able to a launch an experimental project called *Remix the Manuscript* and travel to a number of workshops and institutes: Institute for Liberal Arts Digital Scholarship (Hamilton College), the Rare Book School (University of Pennsylvania), the Digital Humanities Summer Institute (University of Victoria), the Medieval Academy of America (Yale University), and a THATCamp at the University of Maryland.

Colleagues of more recent acquaintance have been an inspiration to ambition, ethical research, and honest confrontations with the complex privileges of academic work. I appreciate so much the discussions shared with former postdoctoral fellows of Dartmouth's Society of Fellows, especially Tatiana Rainoza, Yesenia Baragán, Kate Hall, Yvonne Kwan, and Nathalie Batraville. The people I've met through Dartmouth's Mellon Mays Undergraduate Fellowship have impacted me profoundly, shaping everything I've done since 2010. I cherish especially the long-lasting friendships of Amanda Hall, Aimée Lê, and Mukhtara Yusuf, whose timely text messages mean the world.

Over the years, several undergraduate research assistants have contributed to this research. Most notably, Emily Ulrich brought her infectious enthusiasm for manuscript studies to a meticulous mapping of annotation patterns (supported by a grant from the Leslie Humanities Center, Dartmouth College). Some rather tedious work reconciling bibliographic styles was completed by Brooke Hadley (Choctaw), Lexington Foote, and Teresa Alvarado-Patlán.

Throughout the chapters herein, I've drawn from several previously published articles, with kind permission from the publishers. Chapters 1 and 2 adapt ideas originally published in "Translation" (Warren 2007). Chapter 2 incorporates research from "On the Line of the Law: The London Skinners and the Biopolitics of Fur" (Warren 2016). Chapters 2 and 3 draw snippets from "Lydgate, Lovelich, and London Letters" (Warren 2008). Chapter 4 incorporates "Making a Home for Medieval Manuscripts on the Internet" (Warren 2020). Finally, Chapters 4 and 5 both include material from "Good History, Bad Romance, and the Making of Literature" (Warren 2018a).

This book would not exist without the life-changing fellowships awarded by the American Council of Learned Societies (2018–19) and the John Simon Guggenheim Foundation (2019–20). I truly intended to abandon this project and turn my energies elsewhere. Instead, I received gifts of time and confidence that have brought inspiration well beyond what I imagined. For these gifts, I owe further debts of gratitude to all those who helped me. Charlotte Bacon taught me the difference between a good proposal and a great one. Paul Strohm, Carolyn Dinshaw, Alexandra Gillespie, and Jeffrey Cohen generously wrote recommendations, trusting in my visions to venture into new research areas. Administrators at Dartmouth College made creative and generous financial arrangements to support a full two years of leave, notably Interim Provost David Kotz, Dean Elizabeth Smith, and Associate Dean Chris Strenta. Finally, Dartmouth colleagues Sara Chaney and Dean Lacy took up leadership roles that I had been fulfilling, ensuring that critical work around diversity and inclusion carried forward with unwavering energy and commitment.

In some sense, this book also saved my life. Fidgeting while thinking of the next word to type, I discovered a lump. Yes, that kind of lump. Through treatments and recovery, two years turned into three. So many nurses, therapists, and doctors became my coauthors. I am particularly grateful to Jennifer Chickering, who brought my hands back to strength so that I could write again. Through the lingering effects of fatigue and anxiety, I leaned on the generosity of readers as never before. I couldn't have been more fortunate than to work with Elaine Treharne, Ruth Ahnert, and Erica Wetter at Stanford University Press. They provided the perfect combination of cheerleading and critique through more months and more drafts than they bargained for. In January 2020, a marvelous group of colleagues gathered to discuss a partial draft, supported by a grant from the Leslie Humanities Center at Dartmouth College: Dot Porter, Alexandra Gillespie, Lisa Gitelman, Laura Braunstein, Daniel Chamberlain, Jacqueline Wernimont, Bridget Whearty, and Georgia Henley. Later, I received truly superlative editorial feedback from Summer McDonald and astute indexing from Cathy Hannabach through the agency Ideas on Fire. Joe Abbott provided expert copyediting.

The end of this journey coincides with the COVID-19 pandemic. The scale of loss and traumas is just beginning to sink in. For those able, or required, to continue with academic work during this time, the wonders and limitations of digital infrastructure have been thrust to the center of attention in new ways. Limited to digital resources in the final stages of this book about digital resources, I've thought more than ever about the meaning of touch—of people, of manuscripts, of library tables, and of all the other furnishings of scholarship. There was a time when I traveled regularly to London, Oxford, and Cambridge for research related to this book, supported by a series of travel grants from the University of Miami and Dartmouth College. I haven't yet been back to a library, but I hope my book shows how much they matter. Digital resources are their own kind of resource—not a substitute for any other kind.

The heaviest burden of the years writing this book has been carried by my wife Rebecca Biron—for the caretaking but also for reading all the least coherent drafts, more than once. Among my highest achievements are the smiley faces she scribbled into the margins next to the really good sentences. I can't possibly say all that I would like to say—especially since these are the last words to type. The best expression of gratitude right now will be to click "send." Meanwhile, our son, Quinn, keeps everything in perspective. As I'm agonizing over truly finishing a project I've carried for so long, he points out that, in the end, a book is just someone's afternoon reading.

REFERENCES

Abbate, Janet. 1999. *Inventing the Internet.* Cambridge, MA: MIT Press.

"About the Archive." 2001-17. *Internet Archive.* April 13, 2001–February 6, 2017. https://web.archive.org/web/*/https://archive.org/about.

"About Earlier Phases of Parker on the Web." 2018-21. Parker Library on the Web 2.0. https://parker.stanford.edu/parker/about/about-earlier-phases-of-parker-on-the-web.

"About the Project." 2010. Parker Library on the Web 1.0. https://web.archive.org/web/20100623003724/http://parkerweb.stanford.edu/parker/actions/page?forward=about_project.

Ackerman, Robert W. 1952a. "Henry Lovelich's Name." *Modern Language Notes* 67 (8): 531-33. JSTOR.

———. 1952b. "Herry Lovelich's *Merlin*." *PMLA: Publications of the Modern Language Association of America* 67 (4): 473-84. JSTOR.

———. 1952c. *An Index of the Arthurian Names in Middle English.* Stanford: Stanford University Press.

———. 1959. "English Rimed and Prose Romances." In *Arthurian Literature in the Middle Ages*, edited by Roger Sherman Loomis, 480-519. Oxford: Clarendon Press.

Albritton, Benjamin. 2020. "Parker on the Web." In Albritton, Henley, and Treharne 2020, 9–13.

———. 2021. "Parker on the Web 2.1 Launches." *Special Collections Unbound*
(blog). March 3, 2021. https://library.stanford.edu/blogs/special-collections
-unbound/2021/03/parker-web-21-launches.

Albritton, Benjamin, Georgia Henley, and Elaine Treharne, eds. 2020. *Medieval
Manuscripts in the Digital Age*. London: Routledge.

Allison, Arthur, James Currall, Michael Moss, and Susan Stuart. 2005. "Digital
Identity Matters." *Journal of the American Society for Information Science and
Technology* 56 (4): 364–72. Wiley Online Library.

Anderson, Sheila. 2013. "What Are Research Infrastructures?" *International Journal of Humanities and Arts Computing* 7 (1–2): 4–23. EBSCO.

Appleford, Amy. 2015. *Learning to Die in London, 1380–1540*. Philadelphia: University of Pennsylvania Press.

Archibald, Elizabeth. 1991. *Apollonius of Tyre: Medieval and Renaissance Themes
and Variations*. Cambridge: D. S. Brewer.

Archimedes Palimpsest. 2008–11. http://openn.library.upenn.edu/Data/0014/Archi
medesPalimpsest.

"Archimedes Palimpsest." 2018. *Wikipedia*. Revision History, December 18, 2018.
https://en.wikipedia.org/wiki/Archimedes_Palimpsest.

Archimedes Palimpsest. 2019. Google Books. Accessed November 9, 2019. https://
books.google.com/books?id=_zX8OG3QoF4C. Reviews archived at https://
perma.cc/F97E-TMVQ and https://perma.cc/56NW-XZTC.

ArchimedesPalimpsest.org. 2018. Accessed December 18, 2018. http://archime
despalimpsest.org.

Arnold, Matthew. 1880. "General Introduction." In *The English Poets*, edited by
Thomas Humphry Ward. Vol 1. London: Macmillan. HathiTrust.

Aron, Jacob. 2015. "Glassed-In DNA Makes the Ultimate Time Capsule." *New
Scientist*, February 11, 2015. www.newscientist.com/article/mg22530084
-300-glassed-in-dna-makes-the-ultimate-time-capsule.

Avery, Vida L. 2013. *Philanthropy in Black Higher Education: A Fateful Hour Creating
the Atlanta University System*. New York: Palgrave Macmillan.

Bale, John. 1546. *The Actes of Englysh Votaryes*. Antwerp. EEBO, Text Creation
Partnership. http://name.umdl.umich.edu/A02573.0001.001.

———. 1549. Preface to *The Laboriouse Journey and Serche of Iohan Leylande, for
Englandes Antiquitees*, by John Leland. London. EEBO.

———. 1557–59. *Scriptorum illustriu[m] maioris Brytannie*. 2 vols. Basel. EEBO.

Barron, Caroline. 1969. "Richard Whittington: The Man behind the Myth." In
Studies in London History Presented to Philip Edmund Jones, edited by Albert E. J.
Hollaender and William Kellaway, 197–248. London: Hodder and Stoughton.

———. 1974. *The Medieval Guildhall of London*. London: Corporation of London.

———. 2004. *London in the Later Middle Ages: Government and the People, 1200–1500*. Oxford: Oxford University Press.

———. 2016. "What Did Medieval Merchants Read?" In *Medieval Merchants and Money: Essays in Honor of James L. Borton*, edited by Martin Allen and Matthew Davies, 43–70. London: Institute of Historical Research.

Barron, W. R. J. 1987. *English Medieval Romance*. London: Longman.

Bartley, Kyra, director. 2019. *Losing Lena*. www.losinglena.com.

Bayers, Chip. 2013. "Tech's Holy Grail: Finding the Next Steve Jobs." *USA Today*, October 17. www.usatoday.com/story/tech/columnist/2013/10/17/where-is-the -next-steve-jobs-apple-cook-mayer-zuckerberg-ellison-gates/2990343.

"BBC Domesday Project." 2018. *Wikipedia*. Accessed August 14, 2018. https:// en.wikipedia.org/wiki/BBC_Domesday_Project.

Benson, Larry D., ed., and Edward E. Foster, rev. 1994. *King Arthur's Death: The Middle English Stanzaic Morte Arthur and Alliterative Morte Arthure*. Kalamazoo, MI: Medieval Institute.

Benzie, William. 1983. *Dr. F. J. Furnivall: Victorian Scholar Adventurer*. Norman, OK: Pilgrim.

Bergeron, David M. 1993. "Pageants, Politics, and Patrons." *Medieval & Renaissance Drama in England* 6:139–52. JSTOR.

Bernard, Edward, ed. 1697. *Catalogi librorum manuscriptorum Angliae et Hiberniae in unum collecti cum indice alphabetico*. 2 vols. Oxford. EEBO. Archive.org. Google.com.

Bernstein Consortium. 2019. *The Memory of Paper*. Updated October 30, 2019. www.memoryofpaper.eu/BernsteinPortal.

Binkley, Robert C. 1929. "The Problem of Perishable Paper." In *Atti del 10 congresso mondiale delle biblioteche e di bibliografia* 4:77–85, Rome. Reprinted in *Selected Papers of Robert C. Binkley*, edited by Max Fisch, 169–78. Cambridge: Harvard University Press, 1948. Archive.org.

———. 1934. "New Tools, New Recruits for the Republic of Letters." Edited by Peter Binkley. Typescript. www.wallandbinkley.com/rcb/works/new-tools-new -recruits-for-the-republic-of-letters.html.

———. 1936. *Manual on Methods of Reproducing Research Materials*. Ann Arbor, MI: Edwards Brothers. HathiTrust.

Blaess, Madeleine. 1957. "L'Abbaye de Bordesley et les livres de Guy de Beauchamp." *Romania* 78:511–18.

Blanchette, Jean-François. 2011. "A Material History of Bits." *Journal of the Association for Information Science and Technology* 62 (6): 1042–57. EBSCO.

Blaney, Jonathan, and Judith Siefring. 2017. "A Culture of Non-citation: Assessing the Digital Impact of British History Online and the Early English Books

Online Text Creation Partnership." *Digital Humanities Quarterly* 11 (1): www
.digitalhumanities.org/dhq/vol/11/1/000282/000282.html.

Block, Sharon. 2020. "Erasure, Misrepresentation, and Confusion: Investigating
JSTOR Topics on Women's and Race Histories." *Digital Humanities Quarterly*
14 (1): www.digitalhumanities.org/dhq/vol/14/1/000448/000448.html.

Boboc, Andrea. 2006. "Justice on Trial: Judicial Abuse and Acculturation in Late
Medieval English Literature, 1381-1481." PhD diss., University of Michigan.
ProQuest (AAT 3224823).

Boden, Margaret. 2016. *AI: Its Nature and Future*. Oxford: Oxford University Press.

Boffey, Julia. 2010. "London Books and London Readers, c. 1475-1550." In *Cultural Reformations: Medieval and Renaissance in Literary History*, edited by
Brian Cummings and James Simpson, 420-37. Oxford: Oxford University
Press.

Bolintineanu, Alexandra. 2020. "Books Consumed, Books Multiplied: Martianus Capella, Ælfric's *Homilies*, and the International Image Interoperability
Framework." In Albritton, Henley, and Treharne 2020, 205-15.

Bolton, Maggie. 2019. "Fellowship and Furs: The Skinners' Company of London
and Its Two Fraternities, with Special Reference to the Fraternity of the Assumption of Our Lady, 1350-1450." MA diss., University of London.

Borel, Pierre. 1655. *Trésor de Recherches et Antiquitiz Gauloises et Francoises*. Paris.
Archive.org.

Born, Lester. 1955. *British Manuscripts Project: A Checklist of the Microfilms Prepared
in England and Wales for the American Council of Learned Societies, 1941-1945*.
Washington, D.C.: Library of Congress. https://quod.lib.umich.edu/cgi/b/bib/
bib-idx?c=bmp.

———. 1960. "History of Microform Activity." *Library Trends* 8 (3): 348-58. http://
hdl.handle.net/2142/5884.

———. 1964. "Planning for Scholarly Photocopying." *PMLA: Publications of the
Modern Language Association of America* 79 (4): 77-90. JSTOR.

Bower, Peter. 2001. "The White Art: The Importance of Interpretation in the
Analysis of Paper." In *Looking at Paper: Evidence and Interpretation*, edited
by John Slavin, Linda Sutherland, John O'Neill, Margaret Haupt, and Janet
Cowan, 5-16. Ottawa: Canadian Conservation Institute.

Bowers, John M. 2001. *The Politics of Pearl: Court Poetry in the Age of Richard II*.
Cambridge: D. S. Brewer.

Bowker, Geoffrey C., and Susan Leigh Star. 1999. *Sorting Things Out: Classification
and Its Consequences*. Cambridge: MIT Press.

Boyle, Elizabeth. 2020. "*Philologia* and Philology: Allegory, Multilingualism, and
the Corpus Martianus Capella." In Albritton, Henley, and Treharne 2020,
154-62.

Bradley, Henry. 1902a. "Henry Lonelich the Skinner." *The Athenaeum*, no. 3914 (November 1): 587. HathiTrust.

———. 1902b. "The Translator of 'The Graal.'" *The Athenaeum*, no. 3918 (November 29): 722. HathiTrust.

Brand, Stewart. 1987. *The Media Lab: Inventing the Future at MIT*. New York: Viking.

———. 1999a. *The Clock of the Long Now: Time and Responsibility*. New York: Basic Books.

———. 1999b. "Escaping the Digital Dark Age." *Library Journal* 124 (2): 46–49. ProQuest.

Brandsma, Frank. 2010. *The Interlace Structure of the Third Part of the Prose Lancelot*. Cambridge: D. S. Brewer.

Brantley, Jessica. 2009. "The Prehistory of the Book." *PMLA: Publications of the Modern Language Association of America* 124 (2): 632–39. JSTOR.

Brewer, Derek. 1983. *English Gothic Literature*. London: Macmillan.

Brock, Edmund, ed. 1871. *Morte Arthure, or, the Death of Arthur*. EETS OS 8. London: Trübner.

Brown, Michelle P. 1994. *Understanding Illuminated Manuscripts: A Guide to Technical Terms*. Malibu: J. Paul Getty Museum. Digital version: www.bl.uk/catalogues/illuminatedmanuscripts/glossary.asp.

Bryan, Elizabeth. 1999. *Collaborative Meaning in Medieval Scribal Culture: The Otho Laȝamon*. Ann Arbor: University of Michigan Press.

———. 2016. "Matthew Parker and the Middle English Prose Brut." In *The Prose Brut and Other Late Medieval Chronicles: Books Have Their Histories, Essays in Honour of Lister M. Matheson*, edited by Jaclyn Rajsic, Erik Kooper, and Dominique Hoche, 165–80. Woodbridge, Suffolk: Boydell and Brewer.

Bryden, Inga. 2005. *Reinventing King Arthur: The Arthurian Legends in Victorian Culture*. Aldershot: Ashgate.

Brydges, Egerton. 1812. *Collin's Peerage of England*. Volume 4. London. Google Books.

Buckland, Michael. 2017. *Information and Society*. Cambridge, MA: MIT Press.

Budny, Mildred. 1997. *Insular, Anglo-Saxon, and Early Anglo-Norman Manuscript Art at Corpus Christi College, Cambridge: An Illustrated Catalogue*. Vol. 1. Kalamazoo, MI: Medieval Institute.

Bulteel, John. 1656. *Londons Triumph*. London. EEBO.

Burrington, Ingrid. 2016. *Networks of New York: An Illustrated Field Guide to Urban Internet Infrastructure*. Brooklyn, NY: Melville House.

———. 2019. "How We Misremember the Internet's Origins." *New Republic*, October 29, 2019. https://newrepublic.com/article/155532/misremember-internets-origins.

Busby, Keith. 2002. *Codex and Context: Reading Old French Verse Narrative in Manuscript*. 2 vols. Amsterdam: Rodopi.

Bush, Vannevar. 1945. "As We May Think." *The Atlantic*, July. www.theatlantic.com/magazine/archive/1945/07/as-we-may-think/303881.

Butterfield, Ardis. 2009. *The Familiar Enemy: Chaucer, Language, and Nation in the Hundred Years War*. Oxford: Oxford University Press.

———. 2012. "Rough Translation: Charles d'Orléans, Hoccleve, and Lydgate." In *Rethinking Translation: Ethics, Politics, Theory*, edited by Emma Campbell and Robert Mills, 204–25. Cambridge: D. S. Brewer.

Cady, Susan A. 1990. "The Electronic Revolution in Libraries: Microfilm Déjà Vu?" *College and Research Libraries* 51 (4): 374–86. https://doi.org/10.5860/crl_51_04_374.

Calendar of Records of the Skinners' Company. 1965. Typescript. Guildhall Library, MS SL 37: S 628.

Calendar of the Patent Rolls. 1891. Edward III, Vol. 1. London: Her Majesty's Stationery Office.

———. 1905. Richard II. Vol. 5. London. His Majesty's Stationery Office.

———. 1907. Henry VI. Vol. 3. London: His Majesty's Stationery Office.

Calhoun, Joshua. 2020. *The Nature of the Page: Poetry, Papermaking, and the Ecology of Texts in Renaissance England*. Philadelphia: University of Pennsylvania Press.

Calloway, Colin. 2010. *The Indian History of an American Institution: Native Americans and Dartmouth*. Hanover, NH: Dartmouth College Press. https://doi.org/10.1349/ddlp.699.

Campbell, D. Grant. 2005. "Metadata, Metaphor, and Metonymy." *Cataloging and Classification Quarterly* 40 (3–4): 57–73.

Campbell, Emma, and Robert Mills, eds. 2012. *Rethinking Medieval Translation: Ethics, Politics, Theory*. Woodbridge, Suffolk: D. S. Brewer.

Cannadine, Davie. 2006. *Mellon: An American Life*. New York: A. A. Knopf.

Carley, James P. 1994. "A Grave Event: Henry V, Glastonbury Abbey, and Joseph of Arimathea's Bones." *Culture and the King: The Social Implications of the Arthurian Legend. Essays in Honor of Valerie M. Lagorio*, edited by Martin B. Shichtman and James P. Carley, 129–48. Albany: State University of New York Press.

———. 1996. "Polydore Vergil and John Leland on King Arthur: The Battle of the Books." In *King Arthur: A Casebook*, edited by Edward Donald Kennedy, 185–204. New York: Garland.

———. 2008. "Glastonbury, the Grail-Bearer and the Sixteenth-Century Antiquaries." In *The Grail, the Quest and the World of Arthur*, edited by Norris J. Lacy, 156–72. Cambridge: D. S. Brewer.

———. 2011. "Arthur and the Antiquaries." In *The Arthur of Medieval Latin Literature*, edited by Siân Echard, 149–78. Cardiff: University of Wales Press.

Carlson, David R., ed. 2003. *Concordia (The Reconciliation of Richard II with London)*, by Richard Maidstone and translated by A. G. Rigg. Kalamazoo, MI: Medieval Institute.

Carlton, David, and Richard J. Moll. 2018. "The Arundel *Coronacio Arthuri*: A Middle English Sword in the Stone Story from London, College of Arms MS Arundel 58." *Arthurian Literature* 34:130–57.

Carpenter, Frederic Ives. 1921. "The Photographic Reproduction of Rare Books." *Papers of the Bibliographical Society of America* 15 (1): 35–46. JSTOR.

Carpenter, Kenneth. 2007. "Toward a New Cultural Design: The American Council of Learned Societies, the Social Science Research Council, and Libraries in the 1930s." In *Institutions of Reading: The Social Life of Libraries in the United States*, edited by Thomas Augst and Kenneth Carpenter. Amherst: University of Massachusetts Press. JSTOR.

Carter, John, and Graham Pollard. 1934. *An Enquiry into the Nature of Certain Nineteenth Century Pamphlets*. London: Constable.

Catto, Jeremy. 1985. "John Wyclif and the Cult of the Eucharist." *Studies in Church History: Subsidia* 4:269–86. https://doi.org/10.1017/S0143045900003677.

Caxton, William, trans. 1485. *Ryal Book*. Westminster: William Caxton. EEBO.

Cerf, Vint. 2015. "Digital Vellum." Lecture presented at the Chautauqua Institution, August 7, 2015. https://beta.prx.org/stories/156917.

———. 2016. "Digital Vellum and Archives." Lecture presented at *The Networking and Information Technology Research and Development Program (NITRD)*, August 12, 2016. https://web.archive.org/web/20190701115037/https://www.nitrd.gov/nitrdgroups/index.php?title=DigitalVellumAndArchives.

Chalmers, Melissa, and Paul Edwards. 2017. "Producing 'One Vast Index': Google Book Search as an Algorithmic System." *Big Data & Society* 4 (2): https://doi.org/10.1177/2053951717716950.

Chambers, R. W., and Marjorie Daunt. 1931. *A Book of London English, 1385–1425*. Oxford: Clarendon Press.

Chase, Carol. 2003. "The Gateway to the *Lancelot-Grail Cycle: L'Estoire del Saint Graal*." In Dover 2003, 65–74.

Christen, Kim. 2019. "In Transition." www.kimchristen.com/about.

Chun, Wendy Hui Kyong. 2008. "The Enduring Ephemeral, or the Future Is a Memory." *Critical Inquiry* 35 (1): 148–71. JSTOR.

———. 2011. *Programmed Visions: Software and Memory*. Cambridge, MA: MIT Press.

Clement, Richard W. 1987. "Thomas James's *Ecloga Oxonio-Cantabrigiensis*: An Early Printed Union Catalog." *Journal of Library History* 22 (1): 1–22. JSTOR.

———. 1991. "Librarianship and Polemics: The Career of Thomas James (1572–1629)." *Libraries and Culture* 26 (2): 269–82. JSTOR.

Cloonan, Michèle. 1993. "The Preservation of Knowledge." *Library Trends* 41 (4): 594–605.

Coffey, Mary K. 2020. *Orozco's American Epic: Myth, History, and the Melancholy of Race*. Durham, NC: Duke University Press.

Coleman, Janet. 1981. *Medieval Readers and Writers, 1350–1400*. New York: Columbia University Press.

Combes, Annie. 2003. "The *Merlin* and Its *Suite*." Translated by Carol Dover. In Dover 2003, 75–85.

Connolly, Margaret. 1998. *John Shirley: Book Production and the Noble Household in Fifteenth-Century England*. Aldershot: Ashgate.

Conway, Paul. 1996. *Preservation in the Digital World*. Council on Library and Information Resources. www.clir.org/pubs/reports/conway2/index.

———. 2013. "Preserving Imperfection: Assessing the Incidence of Digital Imaging Error in HathiTrust Preservation." *Digital Technology and Culture* 42 (1): 17–13. http://hdl.handle.net/2027.42/99522.

Cook, Megan. 2019. *The Poet and the Antiquaries: Chaucerian Scholarship and the Rise of Literary History, 1532–1635*. Philadelphia: University of Pennsylvania Press.

Cooper, Helen. 2003. "The *Lancelot-Grail Cycle* in England: Malory and His Predecessors." In Dover 2003, 147–62.

Cooper, Lisa, and Andrea Denny-Brown, eds. 2008. *Lydgate Matters: Poetry and Material Culture in the Fifteenth Century*. New York: Palgrave Macmillan.

Cordell, Ryan. 2017. "'Q i-jtb the Raven': Taking Dirty OCR Seriously." *Book History* 20:188–225. Project MUSE.

Cottingham, Katie. 2015. "How to Preserve Fleeting Digital Information with DNA for Future Generations." American Chemical Society, August 17, 2015. www.acs.org/content/acs/en/pressroom/newsreleases/2015/august/dna-storage.html.

Crane, Tom. 2017. "Annotations: How IIIF Resources Get Their Content." Accessed November 24, 2019. https://resources.digirati.com/iiif/an-introduction-to-iiif/annotations.html.

Crankshaw, David J., and Alexandra Gillespie. 2004. "Parker, Matthew (1504–1575)." In *Oxford Dictionary of National Biography*. https://doi.org/10.1093/ref:odnb/21327.

Crowder, C. M. D. 1977. *Unity, Heresy, and Reform, 1378–1460: The Conciliar Response to the Great Schism*. New York: St. Martin's.

Curti, Merle. 1998. *American Philanthropy Abroad*. London: Routledge.

Da Rold, Orietta. 2020a. "A Note on Cambridge, Corpus Christi College, 210." In Albritton, Henley, and Treharne 2020, 57–63.

———. 2020b. *Paper in England: From Pulp to Fictions.* Cambridge: Cambridge University Press.

Dalrymple, Roger. 2000. "'Evele knowen ʒe Merlyne, jn certeyn': Henry Lovelich's *Merlin.*" In *Medieval Insular Romance: Translation and Innovation*, edited by Judith Weiss, Jennifer Fellows, and Morgan Dickson, 155–67. Cambridge: D. S. Brewer.

"Danny Hillis." 2019. *The Long Now Foundation.* http://longnow.org/people/board/dannyo/full.

Dante Alighieri. 1491. *La Commedia.* Edited by Piero da Figino. Venice: Petrus de Plasiis.

Davies, Matthew. 2011. "'Monuments of Honor': Clerks, Histories and Heroes in the London Livery Companies." In *Parliament, Personalities and Power: Papers Presented to Linda S. Clark*, edited by Hannes Kleineke, 145–65. Woodbridge, Suffolk: Boydell.

———. 2012. "Crown, City and Guild in Late Medieval London." In *London and Beyond: Essays in Honour of Derek Keene*, edited by Matthew Davies and James Galloway, 248–68. London: Institute of Historical Research.

———. 2016. "'Writying, making and engrocyng': Clerks, Guilds and Identity in Late Medieval London." In *Medieval Merchants and Money: Essays in Honor of James L. Borton*, edited by Martin Allen and Matthew Davies, 21–42. London: Institute of Historical Research.

Dee, John. 1577. *General and Rare Memorials Pertayning to the Perfect Arte of Navigation.* London. Huntington Library. EEBO.

———. 2004. *The Limits of the British Empire.* Edited by Kan MacMillan. Westport, CT: Praeger.

De Hamel, Christopher. 2005–8. *The Parker Chronicle: A Newsletter for the Friends of Parker Library.* Vols. 1–4. Cambridge, UK: Corpus Christi College.

———. 2010. Interview. *The Pelican* (19): 8–11.

———. 2016. *Meetings with Remarkable Manuscripts.* London: Allen Lane.

Dekker, Thomas. 1628. *Brittannia's Honor.* London. EEBO.

De Kosnik, Abigail. 2016. *Rogue Archives: Digital Cultural Memory and Media Fandom.* Cambridge, MA: MIT Press.

Dickins, Bruce. 1972. "The Making of the Parker Library." *Transactions of the Cambridge Bibliographical Society* 6 (1): 19–34. JSTOR.

"Digital Dark Age." 2006. *Wikipedia.* Created November 29, 2006. https://en.wikipedia.org/wiki/Digital_dark_age, archived at https://perma.cc/5W47-WRVJ.

"Digital Dark Ages." 2004–21. Google Trends. https://trends.google.com/trends/explore?date=2004-01-01%202021-09-25&geo=US&q=%22digital%20dark%20ages%22.

"Digital Dark Ages." 2005. *Library and Information Science Wiki.* Created October 10, 2005. https://liswiki.org/wiki/Digital_Dark_Ages, archived at https://perma.cc/5CM2-R4UP.

Dinshaw, Carolyn. 2012. *How Soon is Now? Medieval Texts, Amateur Readers, and the Queerness of Time.* Durham, NC: Duke University Press.

Dover, Carol, ed. *A Companion to the Lancelot-Grail Cycle.* Cambridge: D. S. Brewer.

Doyle, A. I. 1961. "More Light on John Shirley." *Medium Aevum* 30 (2): 93–101. JSTOR.

———. 1983. "English Books in and out of Court from Edward III to Henry VII." In *English Court Culture in the Later Middle Ages,* edited by V. J. Scattergood and J. W. Sherborne, 163–81. New York: St. Martin's.

———. 1997. "The Study of Nicholas Love's Mirror, Retrospect and Prospect." In *Nicholas Love at Waseda: Proceedings of the International Conference, 20–22 July 1995,* edited by Shoichi Oguro, Richard Beadle, and Michael G. Sargent, 163–74. Cambridge: D. S. Brewer.

Drimmer, Sonja. 2018. *The Art of Allusion: Illuminators and the Making of English Literature, 1403–1476.* Philadelphia: University of Pennsylvania Press.

Driver, Martha W. 2014. "Pageants Reconsidered." In *Makers and Users of Medieval Books: Essays in Honor of A. S. G. Edwards,* edited by Carol M. Meale and Derek Pearsall, 34–47. Cambridge: D. S. Brewer.

Drucker, Johanna. 2008. "The Virtual Codex from Page Space to E-space." *A Companion to Digital Literary Studies,* edited by Ray Siemens and Susan Schreibman. Oxford: Blackwell, 2008. www.digitalhumanities.org/companionDLS.

———. 2009. *SpecLab: Digital Aesthetics and Projects in Speculative Computing.* Chicago: University of Chicago Press.

———. 2013. "Performative Materiality and Theoretical Approaches to Interface." *Digital Humanities Quarterly* 7 (1): www.digitalhumanities.org/dhq/vol/7/1/000143/000143.html.

Duarte, Marisa Elena. 2017. *Network Sovereignty: Building the Internet across Indian Country.* Seattle: University of Washington Press.

Duffy, Eamon. 2005. *The Stripping of the Altars: Traditional Religion in England, c.1400–c.1580.* 2nd ed. New Haven, CT: Yale University Press.

Dunbar-Ortiz, Roxanne. 2015. *An Indigenous Peoples' History of the United States.* Boston: Beacon.

"Early English Books Online (EEBO) on the ProQuest Platform." 2020. *ProQuest*

LibGuides. Accessed April 9, 2020. https://proquest.libguides.com/eebopqp/about.

Early English Text Society. 1874. "Tenth Report of the Committee." In *History of the Holy Grail*, edited by Frederick J. Furnivall, 1–44. EETS ES 20. London: Trübner. Archive.org.

———. 1904. "Report." In *Merlin*, edited by Ernst Kock, 1–10. EETS ES 93. London: Kegan Paul, Trench, and Trübner. HathiTrust.

Ebin, Lois E. 1988. *Illuminator, Makar, Vates: Visions of Poetry in the Fifteenth Century*. Lincoln: University of Nebraska Press.

Echard, Siân. 2000. "House Arrest: Modern Archives, Medieval Manuscripts." *Journal of Medieval and Early Modern Studies* 30 (2): 185–210. Project MUSE.

———. 2008. *Printing the Middle Ages*. Philadelphia: University of Pennsylvania Press.

———. 2015. "Containing the Book: The Institutional Afterlives of Medieval Manuscripts." In *The Medieval Manuscript Book: Cultural Approaches*, edited by Michael Johnston and Michael Van Dussen, 96–118. Cambridge: Cambridge University Press.

Eddy, Nicole. 2012. "Marginal Annotation in Medieval Romance Manuscripts: Understanding the Contemporary Reception of Genre." PhD diss., University of Notre Dame. ProQuest (AAT 3534385).

Ellis, George. (1805) 1848. *Specimens of Early English Metrical Romances: To Which Is Prefixed an Historical Introduction on the Rise and Progress of Romantic Composition in France and England*. Revised by James O. Halliwell. London: Henry Bohn. HathiTrust.

Ellis, Thomas O., John F. Heafner, and William L. Sibley. 1969. *The Grail Project: An Experiment in Man-Machine Communications*. Santa Monica, CA: RAND Corporation. www.rand.org/pubs/research_memoranda/RM5999.html.

Emerson, Lori. 2014. *Reading Writing Interfaces: From the Digital to the Bookbound*. Minneapolis: University of Minnesota Press. Project MUSE.

Endres, William. 2019. *Digitizing Medieval Manuscripts: The St. Chad Gospels, Materiality, Recoveries, and Representation in 2D and 3D*. Amsterdam: Amsterdam University Press.

Erickson, Thomas. 1990. "Working with Interface Metaphors." In *The Art of Human-Computer Interface Design*, edited by Brenda Laurel, 65–75. Reading, MA: Addison Wesley.

Erler, Mary C. 2016. "The Guildhall Library, Robert Bale and the Writing of London History." *Historical Research* 89 (243): 176–86. EBSCO.

Estes, Nick. 2019. *Our History Is the Future: Standing Rock versus the Dakota Access Pipeline, and the Long Tradition of Indigenous Resistance*. Brooklyn, NY: Verso.

Etherton, Judith. 2004 "Cok [Coke], John (c.1393–c.1468)." In *Oxford Dictionary of National Biography*. https://doi.org/10.1093/ref:odnb/5818.

Fabry-Tehranchi, Irène. 2014. *Texte et images des manuscrits du "Merlin" et de la Suite Vulgate (XIIIe–XVe siècle)*. Turnhout: Brepols.

Field, Rosalind. 2008. "Romance." In *Oxford History of Literary Translation in English*, edited by Roger Ellis, 296–331. London: Oxford University Press.

Fildes, Nic, Alan Smith, David Blood, Ændrew Rininsland, Max Harlow, and Caroline Nevitt. 2018. "Broadband Speed Map Reveals Britain's New Digital Divide." *Financial Times*, July 18, 2018. LexisNexis.

Finney, Andy. 1986–2006. "The Domesday Project." www.atsf.co.uk/dottext/domesday.html.

Finotello, Ambra. 2014. "Transformations of the Merlin Legend in Late-Medieval England: Contextualizing Translation in *Of Arthour and of Merlin*, Henry Lovelich's *Merlin*, and the Prose *Merlin*." PhD diss., Bangor University. http://e.bangor.ac.uk/5006/1/AFinotello%20Thesis.pdf.

Flower, Robin, and Hugh Smith, eds. 1941. *The Parker Chronicle and Laws (Corpus Christi College, Cambridge, MS 173): A Facsimile*. EETS. London: Humphrey Milford.

Flüeler, Christoph. 2015. "Digital Manuscripts as Critical Edition." *Schoenberg Institute for Manuscript Studies* (blog). June 30, 2015. https://schoenberginstitute.org/2015/06/30/digital-manuscripts-as-critical-edition.

"Fourth Session, Thursday, December 30." 1920. *PMLA: Publications of the Modern Language Association* 35 (Appendix): xvii–xviii. JSTOR.

Foys, Martin. 2007. *Virtually Anglo-Saxon: Old Media, New Media, and Early Medieval Studies in the Late Age of Print*. Gainesville: University Press of Florida.

———. 2018. "The Remanence of Medieval Media." In *The Routledge Research Companion to Digital Medieval Literature*, edited by Jennifer E. Boyle and Helen J. Burgess, 9–30. London: Routledge.

Francis, Megan Ming. 2019. "The Price of Civil Rights: Black Lives, White Funding, and Movement Capture." *Law & Society Review*, 53:275–309. Wiley Online Library.

Furnivall, Frederick J., ed. 1861. *The History of the Holy Graal*, by Henry Lovelich. Vol. 1. London: Roxburghe Club. HathiTrust.

———, ed. 1862. *Roberd of Brunne's Handlyng Synne*. London: Roxburghe Club. Archive.org.

———, ed. 1863. *The History of the Holy Graal*, by Henry Lovelich. Vol. 2. London: Roxburghe Club. HathiTrust.

———, ed. 1864a. *Arthur*. EETS OS 2. London: Trübner. HathiTrust.

———, ed. 1864b. *Le Morte Arthur*. London: Macmillan. HathiTrust.

———, ed. 1864c. *La Queste del Saint Graal*. London: Roxburghe Club. HathiTrust.

———. 1873. "Mr. Hutton and Tennyson's 'King Arthur.'" *Notes and Queries*, ser. 4, vol. 11 (January 4): 3–4. https://books.google.com/books?id=jJJb4ZPLWsAC.

———, ed. 1874–78. *The History of the Holy Grail*, by Henry Lovelich. 4 vols. EETS ES 20, 24, 28, 30. London: Trübner.

———. 1903. "Henry Lovelich, Skinner." *The Athenaeum*, no. 3924 (January 10): 50–51. HathiTrust.

Furrow, Melissa. 2009. *Expectations of Romance: The Reception of a Genre in Medieval England*. Cambridge: D. S. Brewer.

Fyfe, Paul. 2016. "An Archaeology of Victorian Newspapers." *Victorian Periodicals Review* 49 (4): 546–77. Project MUSE.

Gadd, Ian. 2009. "The Use and Misuse of *Early English Books Online*." *Literature Compass* 6 (3): 680–92. http://doi.org/10.1111/j.1741-4113.2009.00632.x.

Gairdner, James, ed. 1876. "Chronicle of London." In *The Historical Collections of a Citizen of London*, 55–239. London: Camden Society.

Galey, Alan. 2014. *The Shakespearean Archive: Experiments in New Media from the Renaissance to Postmodernity*. Cambridge: Cambridge University Press.

Ganim, John. 1996. "The Myth of Medieval Romance." In *Medievalism and the Modernist Temper*, edited by R. Howard Bloch and Stephen G. Nichols, 148–66. Baltimore: Johns Hopkins University Press.

Genet, J.-P. 1984. "English Nationalism: Thomas Polton at the Council of Constance." *Nottingham Medieval Studies* 28:60–78.

Geoffrey of Monmouth. 2007. *The History of the Kings of Britain*, edited by Michael D. Reeve and translated by Neil Wright. Woodbridge, Suffolk: Boydell.

Gerald of Wales. 2018. *De principis instructione (Instruction for a Ruler)*, edited and translated by Robert Bartlett. Oxford: Clarendon Press.

Gerould, Gordon Hall. 1935. "Arthurian Romance and the Date of the Relief at Modena." *Speculum* 10:355–76.

Gillespie, Alexandra. 2006. *Print Culture and the Medieval Author: Chaucer, Lydgate, and Their Books*. Oxford: Oxford University Press.

———. 2007. "The History of the Book." *New Medieval Literatures* 9:245–86.

Gillespie, Alexandra, and Simon Horobin. 2015. "Parker's Scribes." https://web.archive.org/web/20150406092334/http://web.stanford.edu/group/dmstech/cgi-bin/drupal/node/41.

Gillespie, Alexandra, and Deirdre Lynch, eds. 2021. *The Unfinished Book*. Oxford: Oxford University Press.

Gillespie, Vincent. 2011. "Chichele's Church: Vernacular Theology in England after Thomas Arundel." In *After Arundel: Religious Writing in Fifteenth-Century England*, edited by Vincent Gillespie and Kantik Ghosh, 3–42. Turnhout: Brepols.

Gilliver, Peter. 2016. *The Making of the "Oxford English Dictionary."* Oxford: Oxford University Press. Oxford Scholarship Online.

Gitelman, Lisa. 2014a. *Paper Knowledge: Toward a Media History of Documents.* Durham, NC: Duke University Press.

———. 2014b. "Searching and Thinking about Searching JSTOR." *Representations* 127 (1): 73–82. JSTOR.

Given-Wilson, Christopher, ed. 2005. *The Parliament Rolls of Medieval England, 1275–1504.* Leicester: Scholarly Digital Editions. www.sd-editions.com/PROME/home.html.

Gordon, George, and William Noel. 2017. "The Needham Calculator (1.0) and the Flavors of Fifteenth-Century Paper." *Schoenberg Institute for Manuscript Studies* (blog). January 30, 2017. https://schoenberginstitute.org/2017/01/30/the-needham-calculator-1-0-and-the-flavors-of-fifteenth-century-paper.

Goulder, Grace. 1972. *John D. Rockefeller: The Cleveland Years.* Cleveland: Western Reserve University.

Grafton, Anthony. 2017. "Matthew Parker: The Book as Archive." *History of the Humanities* 2 (1): 15–50. https://doi.org/10.1086/690571.

Graham, Timothy. 2006. "Matthew Parker's Manuscripts: An Elizabethan Library and Its Uses." In *The Cambridge History of Libraries in Britain and Ireland,* edited by Elisabeth Leedham-Green and Teresa Webber. Vol. 1, 322–41. Cambridge: Cambridge University Press.

Graham, Timothy, and Andrew G. Watson, eds. 1998. *The Recovery of the Past in Early Elizabethan England: Documents by John Bale and John Joscelyn from the Circle of Matthew Parker.* Cambridge: Cambridge Bibliographical Society.

Gray, Douglas. 2008. *Later Medieval English Literature.* Oxford: Oxford University Press.

Green, Johanna. 2016. "Textuality in Transition: Digital Manuscripts as Cultural Artefacts." In *Occupying Space in Medieval and Early Modern Britain and Ireland,* edited by Gregory Hulsman and Caoimhe Whelan, 65–86. Bern: Peter Lang.

Griffith, Gareth. 2017. "*Merlin*: Christian Ethics and the Question of Shame." In *Handbook of Arthurian Romance,* edited by Leah Tether and Johnny McFadyen, 477–92. Berlin: De Gruyter.

[Griffiths, Jeremy]. 1985. "A New 'Myrrour', by the Scribe of the Petworth Chaucer." In *English Books, 1450–1900,* no. 112. Bernard Quaritch Limited, Catalogue 1054. London: Stockwell.

———. 1995. "Thomas Hingham, Monk of Bury and the Macro Plays Manuscript." *English Manuscript Studies* 5:214–19.

Haigh, John. 2004. "Gardiner [née Kempe], Dorothy (1873–1957). In *Oxford Dictionary of National Biography.* https://doi.org/10.1093/ref:odnb/51780.

Hanawalt, Barbara. 1998. *"Of Good and Ill Repute": Gender and Social Control in Medieval England.* Oxford: Oxford University Press.

———.2017. *Ceremony and Civility: Civic Culture in Late Medieval London.* Oxford: Oxford University Press.

Hanna, Ralph. 2017. "Manuscript Catalogues and Book History." *The Library: The Transactions of the Bibliographical Society* 18 (1): 45–61. Project MUSE.

Hardman, Phillipa. 1994. "Reading the Spaces: Pictorial Intentions in the Thornton MSS, Lincoln Cathedral MS 91, and BL MS Add. 31042." *Medium Aevum* 63 (2): 250–74. JSTOR.

———.2006. "Lydgate's Uneasy Syntax." In *John Lydgate: Poetry, Culture, and Lancastrian England,* edited by Larry Scanlon and James Simpson, 12–35. Notre Dame: University of Notre Dame Press.

Hardyng, John. 1543. *The Chronicle of Iohn Hardyng.* Edited by Richard Grafton. London. EEBO.

Harrassowitz, Otto. 2009. "Parker Library on the Web." https://web.archive.org/web/20090414101321/http:/www.harrassowitz.de/Parker_on_the_Web.html.

Harvey, Ross, and Jaye Weatherburn. 2018. *Preserving Digital Materials.* 3rd ed. London: Rowman and Littlefield.

Hayles, N. Katherine. 1999. *How We Became Posthuman: Virtual Bodies in Cybernetics, Literature, and Informatics.* Chicago: University of Chicago Press.

———.2003. "Translating Media: Why We Should Rethink Textuality." *Yale Journal of Criticism* 16 (2): 263–90. Project MUSE.

Hedstrom, Margaret. 1999. "Digital Preservation: Matching Problems, Requirements, and Solutions." National Science Foundation Workshop on Data Archiving and Information Preservation, March 26–27, 1999. https://web.archive.org/web/20010725045334/http://cecssrv1.cecs.missouri.edu/NSFWorkshop/hedpp.html.

Helinand de Froidmont. 1855. *Chronicon.* In *Patrologia Latina,* edited by Jacques-Paul Migne, vol. 212, col. 771–1082. https://books.google.com/books?id=BZ9BAAAAcAAJ.

Hendriks, Cor. 2015. "De Geheimen van de Graal (3): Jozef in de gevangenis." *Rob Scholte Museum* (blog). November 24, 2015. http://robscholtemuseum.nl/cor-hendriks-de-geheimen-van-de-graal-3-jozef-in-de-gevangenis, archived at https://perma.cc/S8WD-QSJP and https://perma.cc/NST2-SRZ9.

———.2017. "De Geheimen van de Graal (12): De dood van Merlijn." *Rob Scholte Museum* (blog). November 25, 2017. http://robscholtemuseum.nl/cor-hendriks-de-geheimen-van-de-graal-12-de-dood-van-merlijn, archived at https://perma.cc/MR3E-HDH2 and https://perma.cc/T5CN-5SBP.

Henry, Avril. 1983. "The Illuminations in the Two Illustrated Middle English

Manuscripts of the Prose *Pilgrimage of the Lyfe of the Manhode*." *Scriptorium* 37:264–73.

Hill, Tracey. 2011. *Pageantry and Power: A Cultural History of the Early Modern Lord Mayor's Show, 1585–1639*. Manchester: Manchester University Press. JSTOR.

Hodder, Karen. 1999a. "Henry Lovelich's *History of the Holy Grail*." In *The Arthur of the English: The Arthurian Legend in Medieval English Life and Literature*, edited by W. R. J. Barron, 78–80. Cardiff: University of Wales Press.

———. 1999b. "Henry Lovelich's *Merlin* and the Prose *Merlin*." In *The Arthur of the English: The Arthurian Legend in Medieval English Life and Literature*, edited by W. R. J. Barron, 80–83. Cardiff: University of Wales Press.

Hook, Walter Farquhar. 1872. *Lives of the Archbishops of Canterbury*. Vol 9. London: Richard Bentley and Son. HathiTrust.

"Hooking Up." 2019. *Twelfth Annual Schoenberg Symposium on Manuscript Studies in the Digital Age*. November 21–23, 2019. www.library.upenn.edu/about/exhibits -events/ljs-symposium12.

Horobin, Simon. 2010. "Manuscripts and Scribes." In *Chaucer: Contemporary Approaches*, edited by Susanna Fein and David Raybin, 67–82. University Park: Penn State University Press.

———. 2013. "John Cok and His Copy of *Piers Plowman*." *Yearbook of Langland Studies* 27:45–58.

Horobin, Simon, and Aditi Nafde. 2015. "Stephan Batman and the Making of Parker Library." *Transactions of the Cambridge Bibliographical Society* 15 (4): 561– 81. JSTOR.

Horrox, Rosemary. 1988. "The Urban Gentry in the Fifteenth Century." In *Towns and Townspeople in the Fifteenth Century*, edited by John Thompson, 22–44. Gloucester: Alan Sutton.

Hu, Tung-Hui. 2015. *A Prehistory of the Cloud*. Cambridge, MA: MIT Press.

Hudson, Anne. 1988. *The Premature Reformation: Wycliffite Texts and Lollard History*. Oxford: Clarendon Press.

Hurd, Richard. 1762. *Letters on Chivalry and Romance*. London. *Eighteenth Century Collections Online*. Gale.com: Document no. CW3313766938. Microfilm Range 6603.

Husbands, Shayne. 2013. "The Roxburghe Club: Consumption, Obsession and the Passion for Print." In *Manuscripts and Printed Books in Europe, 1350–1550: Packaging, Presentation and Consumption*, edited by Emma Cayley and Susan Powell, 120–32. Liverpool: Liverpool University Press.

———. 2017. *The Early Roxburghe Club, 1812–1835: Book Club Pioneers and the Advancement of English Literature*. London: Anthem.

Ingham, Patricia Clare. 2014. "Discipline and Romance." In *Critical Contexts: Mid-*

dle English Literature, edited by Holly Crocker and Vance Smith, 276–82. New York: Routledge.

Ja, Rashiq. 2015. "Digital Dark Age: Information Explosion and Data Risks." *Infosec Institute*. Posted March 23, 2015. Accessed August 15, 2018. https://resources.infosecinstitute.com/digital-dark-age-information-explosion-and-data-risks/#gref.

Jacob, E. F., ed. 1947. *Register of Henry Chichele, Archbishop of Canterbury 1414–43*. Vol. 4. Oxford: Clarendon Press.

James, M. R. 1912. *A Descriptive Catalogue of the Manuscripts in the Library of Corpus Christi College, Cambridge*. 2 vols. Cambridge: Cambridge University Press. HathiTrust. Archive.org. Google.com. https://parker.stanford.edu./parker/about/corpus-christi-college-manuscript-catalogues.

James, Thomas. 1600. *Ecloga Oxonio-Cantabrigiensis*. 2 vols. London. EEBO. Archive.org. Google.com

———.1611. *A Treatise of the Corruption of Scripture, Councels, and Fathers, by the Prelats, Pastors, and Pillars of the Church of Rome, for Maintenance of Popery and Irreligion*. London. EEBO.

———.1625. *An Explanation or Enlarging of the Ten Articles in the Supplication of Doctor Iames*. Oxford. EEBO.

Jefferson, Lisa. 2000. "The Language and Vocabulary of the Fourteenth- and Early Fifteenth-Century Records of the Goldsmiths' Company." *Multilingualism in Later Medieval Britain*, edited by D. A. Trotter, 175–211. Cambridge: D. S. Brewer.

Jefferson, Melvin. 2007. "Parker Library Conservation Now." Parker Symposium, Corpus Christi College, September 2007. Text and slides on Parker Library on the Web 1.0. https://swap.stanford.edu/20170127003235/https://parker.stanford.edu/parker/actions/page.do?forward=conservation.

Johns, Adrian. 1998. *The Nature of the Book: Print and Knowledge in the Making*. Chicago: University of Chicago Press.

———.2010. *Piracy: The Intellectual Property Wars from Gutenberg to Gates*. Chicago: University of Chicago Press.

Johnston, Arthur. 1964. *Enchanted Ground: The Study of Medieval Romance in the Eighteenth Century*. London: Athlone Press.

Jordan, Thomas. 1671. *London's Resurrection to Joy and Triumph*. London. EEBO.

Kahle, Brewster. 1997. "Preserving the Internet." *Scientific American* 276 (3): 82–83. JSTOR.

———.2020. "Libraries Have Been Bringing Older Books to Digital Learners: Four Publishers Sue to Stop It." *Internet Archive Blogs* (blog). July 22, 2020. https://blog.archive.org/2020/07/22/libraries-have-been-bringing-older-books-to-digital-learners-four-publishers-sue-to-stop-it.

Kane, George. 1951. *Middle English Literature*. London: Methuen.

Karampelas, Gabrielle. 2015. "Parker Library on the Web Celebrates 10th Anniversary with a New Service." Stanford University Libraries, press release, July 14, 2015. https://swap.stanford.edu/20161206075618/http://library.stanford.edu/news/2015/07/parker-library-web-celebrates-10th-anniversary-new-service.

Karras, Ruth Mazo. 2003. *From Boys to Men: Formations of Masculinity in Late Medieval Europe*. Philadelphia: University of Pennsylvania Press.

Keene, Adrienne. 2010–19. *Native Appropriations* (blog). http://nativeappropriations.com.

Keller, Michael. 2018. Welcoming Remarks for *Celebrating Parker 2.0 at Stanford University: Stanford Text Technologies Fourth Annual Collegium*. Palo Alto, CA, March 25–28, 2018.

Kempe, Dorothy. 1905. *The Legend of the Holy Grail: Its Sources, Character, and Development*. EETS ES 95. London: Kegan Paul, Trench, and Trübner.

Ker, W. P. 1897. *Epic and Romance*. London: Macmillan. Archive.org.

Kerling, Nellie. 1973. *Cartulary of St. Bartholomew's Hospital*. London: St Bartholomew's Hospital.

Kiernan, Kevin S. 1991. "Digital Image Processing and the *Beowulf* Manuscript." *Literary and Linguistic Computing* 6 (1): 20–27. Oxford Academic.

Kilbride, William. 2016. "Saving the Bits: Digital Humanities Forever?" In *A New Companion to Digital Humanities*, edited by Susan Schreibman, Ray Siemens, and John Unsworth, 408–19. Chichester: Wiley Blackwell.

Kingsford, Charles L., ed. 1905. *Chronicles of London*. London: Oxford University Press.

Kirschenbaum, Matthew. 2008. *Mechanisms*. Cambridge, MA: MIT Press.

Kirschenbaum, Matthew, and Sarah Werner. 2014. "Digital Scholarship and Digital Studies: The State of the Discipline." *Book History* 17:406–58. Project MUSE.

Kline, David. 1996. "Is Government Obsolete?" *Wired*, January 1, 1996. www.wired.com/1996/01/government.

Knies, Rob. 2008. "Translating the Web for the Entire World." *Microsoft Research Blog*. March 5, 2008. www.microsoft.com/en-us/research/blog/translating-web-entire-world.

Knight, Jeffrey Todd. 2013. *Bound to Read: Compilations, Collections, and the Making of Renaissance Literature*. Philadelphia: University of Pennsylvania Press. Project MUSE.

Knight, Stephen. 1986. "The Social Function of the Middle English Romances." In *Medieval Literature: Criticism, Ideology, and History*, edited by David Aers, 99–122. New York: St. Martin's.

Kock, Ernst, ed. 1904–32. *Merlin,* by Henry Lovelich. 3 vols. EETS ES 93, 112; EETS OS 185. London: Kegan Paul, Trench, and Trübner.

Kölbing, Eugen. 1890. *Arthour and Merlin.* Altenglische Bibliothek IV. Leipzig: Reisland.

Kosciejew, Marc. 2015. "Digital Vellum and Other Cures for Bit Rot." *Information Management* 49 (3): 20–25. ProQuest.

Kuny, Terry. 1997. "A Digital Dark Ages? Challenges in the Preservation of Electronic Information." Paper presented at the Sixty-Third Annual Meeting of IFLA: International Federation of Library Associations and Institutions, Copenhagen, Denmark, September 4, 1997. https://archive.ifla.org/IV/ifla63/63kuny1.pdf.

Lagorio, Valerie. 1971. "The Evolving Legend of St. Joseph of Glastonbury." *Speculum* 46 (2): 209–31. JSTOR.

Lambert, John James. 1934. *Records of the Skinners of London, Edward I to James I.* London: George Allen and Unwin.

Lambert, Laura. 2005. *The Internet: A Historical Encyclopedia.* Vol. 2. Santa Barbara: ABC-CLIO.

Lancashire, Anne. 2002. *London Civic Theatre: City Drama and Pageantry from Roman Times to 1558.* Cambridge: Cambridge University Press.

Lapidge, Michael. 1985. "Surviving Booklists from Anglo-Saxon England." In *Learning and Literature in Anglo-Saxon England,* edited by Helmut Gneuss and Michael Lapidge, 33–89. Cambridge: Cambridge University Press.

Lawton, Lesley. 1983. "The Illustration of Late Medieval Secular Texts, with Special Reference to Lydgate's *Troy Book.*" In *Manuscripts and Readers in Fifteenth-Century England: The Literary Implications of Manuscript Study,* edited by Derek Pearsall, 41–69. Cambridge: D. S. Brewer.

Laynesmith, Joanna. 2004. *The Last Medieval Queens: English Queenship, 1445–1503.* Oxford: Oxford University Press.

Lee, Robert, and Tristan Ahtone. 2020. "Land-Grab Universities." *High Country News,* March 30, 2020. www.hcn.org/issues/52.4/indigenous-affairs-education-land-grab-universities.

Leland, John. 1544. *Assertio inclytissimi Arturii regis Britanniae.* London. EEBO.

———. 1549. *The Laboriouse Journey and Serche of Iohan Leylande, for Englandes Antiquitees.* London. EEBO.

Lennon, Brian. 2018. *Passwords: Philology, Security, Authentication.* Cambridge, MA: Harvard University Press.

Lepore, Jill. 2015. "The Cobweb." *New Yorker,* January 26, 2015, 34–41.

Lerer, Seth. 1993. *Chaucer and His Readers: Imagining the Author in Late-Medieval England.* Princeton, NJ: Princeton University Press.

———. 2006. "Falling Asleep over the History of the Book." *PMLA: Publications of the Modern Language Association of America* 121 (1): 229–34.

———. 2015. "Bibliographical Theory and the Textuality of the Codex: Toward a History of the Premodern Book." In *The Medieval Manuscript Book: Cultural Approaches*, edited by Michael Johnson and Michael Van Dussen, 17–33. Cambridge: Cambridge University Press.

Lesk, Michael. 1997. "Going Digital." *Scientific American* 276 (3): 58–60. JSTOR.

Lesser, Zachary. 2019. "Xeroxing the Renaissance: The Material Text of Early Modern Studies." *Shakespeare Quarterly* 70 (1): 3–31. https://doi.org/10.1093/sq/quz001.

Lindenbaum, Sheila. 1999. "London Texts and Literate Practice." In *The Cambridge History of Medieval English Literature*, edited by David Wallace, 283–309. Cambridge: Cambridge University Press.

Little, Katherine C., and Nicola McDonald, eds. 2018. *Thinking Medieval Romance*. Oxford: Oxford University Press.

Liu, Alan. 2018. *Friending the Past: The Sense of History in the Digital Age*. Chicago: University of Chicago Press.

Loomis, Laura Hibbard. 1952. "The Athelstan Gift Story: Its Influence on English Chronicles and Carolingian Romances." *PMLA: Publications of the Modern Language Association* 67:521–37.

Lovelich, Henry. 1874–78. *The History of the Holy Grail*. 4 vols. Edited by Frederick J. Furnivall. EETS ES 20, 24, 28, 30. Various prints, reprints, microfilms, photocopies, and digitized copies.

Lovelich, Henry. 1904–32. *Merlin*. 3 vols. Edited by Ernst A. Kock. EETS ES 93, 112; EETS OS 185. Various prints, reprints, microfilms, photocopies, and digitized copies.

"Lovelich, Henry, fl. 1450." 2017. *ProQuest Biographies*. Document ID 2137899144. Ann Arbor, MI: ProQuest.

Lowden, John. 2011. "The Strange and Eventful History of the Archimedes Palimpsest." In Netz et al. 2011, 1:97–118.

Lydekker, Richard. 1909. "Prof. H. G. Seeley, F. R. S." *Nature* 79 (2046): 314–15. www.nature.com/articles/079314b0.pdf.

Lydgate, John. 1906–35. *Troy Book*. Edited by Henry Bergen. 4 vols. EETS ES 97, 103, 106, 126. London: Kegan Paul, Trench, Trübner.

———. 1911–34. *The Minor Poems of John Lydgate*. Edited by Henry Noble MacCracken. 2 vols. EETS ES 107, EETS OS 192. Oxford: Oxford University Press.

———. 1923–27. *Fall of Princes*. Edited by Henry Bergen. 4 vols. Washington, DC: Carnegie Institution.

Lyman, Peter, and Brewster Kahle. 1998. "Archiving Digital Cultural Artifacts." *D-Lib Magazine*, July/August. www.dlib.org:80/dlib/july98/07lyman.html.

Macauley, Thurston. 1931. "The Pilgrim Trust." *North American Review* 231 (1): 72–74. JSTOR.

MacLean, Margaret, and Ben H. Davis. 1998. *Time & Bits: Managing Digital Continuity.* Los Angeles: J. Paul Getty Trust.

Macmillan, Hugh. 1952. *A Man of Law's Tale: The Reminiscences of the Rt. Hon. Lord Macmillan.* London: Macmillan.

Magennis, Hugh. 2015. "Not Angles but Anglicans? Reformation and Post-Reformation Perspectives on the Anglo-Saxon Church, Part 1: Bede, Ælfric and the Anglo-Saxon Church in Early Modern England." *English Studies* 96 (3): 243–63.

Mak, Bonnie. 2011. *How the Page Matters.* Toronto: University of Toronto Press.

———. 2014. "Archaeology of a Digitization." *Journal of the Association for Information Science and Technology* 65 (8): 1515–26. EBSCO.

Malik, Om. 2003. *Broadbandits: Inside the $750 Billion Telecom Heist.* Hoboken: Wiley and Sons. https://books.google.com/books?id=h432909LpTsC.

Malo, Robyn. 2013. *Relics and Writing in Late Medieval England.* Toronto: University of Toronto Press.

Malory, Thomas. 1816. *The Most Ancient and Famous History of the Renowned Prince Arthur, King of Britaine.* Edited by William Stansby (1634). Vol. 1. London: Wilks. HathiTrust.

Mancoff, Debra. 1990. *The Arthurian Revival in Victorian Art.* New York: Garland.

———. 2000. "'Pure Heart and Clean Hands': The Victorian and the Grail." In *The Grail: A Casebook,* edited by Dhira Mahoney, 447–64. New York: Garland.

Manley, Lawrence. 1995. *Literature and Culture in Early Modern London.* Cambridge: Cambridge University Press.

Manly, John. 1920. "The President's Address: New Bottles." *Publications of the Modern Language Association of America* 35 (Appendix): xlvi–lx. JSTOR.

"Manuscript Studies in an Interoperable Digital Environment." 2011–15. Stanford University. https://web.archive.org/web/20160307061351/http://web.stanford.edu/group/dmstech/cgi-bin/drupal.

Matheson, Lister M. 1985. "The Arthurian Stories of Lambeth Palace Library MS 84." *Arthurian Literature* 5:70–91.

———. 1998. *The Prose Brut: The Development of a Middle English Chronicle.* Tempe, AZ: Medieval & Renaissance Texts & Studies.

Mattern, Shannon. 2017. *Code and Clay, Data and Dirt: Five Thousand Years of Urban Media.* Minneapolis: University of Minnesota Press.

Matthews, David. 1999. *The Making of Middle English, 1765–1910.* Minneapolis: University of Minnesota Press.

McGill, Meredith. 2018. "Format." *Early American Studies* 16 (4): 671–77. Project MUSE.

McIlwain, Charlton. 2020. *Black Software: The Internet and Racial Justice, from the AfroNet to Black Lives Matter*. Oxford: Oxford University Press.

McKenzie, Donald F. 1986. *Bibliography and the Sociology of Texts*. London: British Library.

McKisack, May. 1971. *Medieval History in the Tudor Age*. Oxford: Clarendon Press.

McKitterick, David. 1986. *Cambridge University Library, a History: The Eighteenth and Nineteenth Centuries*. Cambridge: Cambridge University Press.

———. 2003. *Print, Manuscript and the Search for Order, 1450–1830*. Cambridge: Cambridge University Press.

———. 2013. *Old Books, New Technologies: The Representation, Conservation and Transformation of Books since 1700*. Cambridge: Cambridge University Press.

McLaren, Mary-Rose. 2002. *The London Chronicles of the Fifteenth Century: A Revolution in English Writing*. Woodbridge, Suffolk: D. S. Brewer.

McMillan, Robert. 2000. "Apache Power." *Linux Magazine*, April 20, 2000. https://web.archive.org/web/20190128065900/http://www.linux-mag.com/id/472/.

Meale, Carol M. 1985. "Manuscripts, Readers, and Patrons in Fifteenth-Century England: Sir Thomas Malory and Arthurian Romance." *Arthurian Literature* 4:93–126.

———. 1986. "The Manuscripts and Early Audience of the Middle English *Prose Merlin*." In *The Changing Face of Arthurian Romance*, edited by Alison Adams, Armel Diverres, Karen Stern, and Kenneth Varty, 92–111. Woodbridge, Suffolk: Boydell.

———. 1989. "Patrons, Buyers and Owners: Book Production and Social Status." In *Book Production and Publishing in Britain, 1375–1475*, edited by Jeremy Griffiths and Derek Pearsall, 201–38. Cambridge: Cambridge University Press.

———. 1993. "'. . . alle the bokes that I haue of latyn, englisch, and frensch': Laywomen and Their Books in Late Medieval England." In *Women and Literature in Britain, 1150- 1500*, edited by Carol M. Meale, 128–58. Cambridge: Cambridge University Press.

———. 1994. "'gode men / Wiues maydnes and all men': Romance and Its Audiences." In *Readings in Medieval English Romance*, edited by Carol M. Meale, 209–25. Cambridge: D. S. Brewer.

———. 2013. "The Patronage of Poetry." In *A Companion to Fifteenth-Century English Poetry*, edited by Julia Boffey and A. S. G. Edwards, 7–18. Cambridge: D. S. Brewer.

Meckler, Alan Marshall. 1982. *Micropublishing: A History of Scholarly Micropublishing in America, 1938–1980*. Westport, CT: Greenwood Press.

Meder, Theo, and Cor Hendriks. 2005. *Vertelcultuur in Nederland: Volksverhalen uit de collective Boekenoogen (ca. 1900)*. Amsterdam: Aksant.

Mellon, Paul. 1992. *Reflections in a Silver Spoon: A Memoir*, with John Baskett. New York: William Morrow.

Merriman, James. 1973. *The Flower of Kings: A Study of the Arthurian Legend in England between 1485 and 1835*. Lawrence: University Press of Kansas.

Meuwese, Martine. 2007. "Crossing Borders: Text and Image in Arthurian Manuscripts." *Arthurian Literature* 24:157–77.

———. 2008. "The Shape of the Grail in Medieval Art." In *The Grail, the Quest and the World of Arthur*, edited by Norris J. Lacy, 13–27. Cambridge: D. S. Brewer.

Micha, Alexandre, ed. 1979. *Merlin: Roman du XIIIe siècle*. Geneva: Droz.

———. 1980. *Etude sur le "Merlin" de Robert de Boron, roman du XIIIe siècle*. Geneva: Droz.

Michel, Francisque. 1841. *Le Roman du saint-graal*. Bordeaux: Prosper Faye.

Middleton, Roger. 2003. "Manuscripts of the *Lancelot-Grail Cycle* in England and Wales: Some Books and Their Owners." In Dover 2003, 219–35.

———. 2006. "The Manuscripts." In *The Arthur of the French*, edited by Glyn S. Burgess and Karen Pratt, 8–92. Cardiff: University of Wales Press.

Middleton, Thomas. 1619. *The Triumphs of Love and Antiquity*. London. EEBO.

Minnis, Alistair. 2012. "Creating English Literature, ca. 1385–ca. 1425: Inks, Pigments, and the Textual Canon." http://ydc2.yale.edu/node/573/attachment; https://desmm.yale.edu.

Mod, Craig. 2018. "The 'Future Book' Is Here, But It's Not What We Expected." *Wired*, December 28, 2018. www.wired.com/story/future-book-is-here-but -not-what-we-expected.

Moll, Richard. 2003. *Before Malory: Reading Arthur in Later Medieval England*. Toronto: University of Toronto Press.

Montfort, Nick. 2004. "Continuous Paper: The Early Materiality and Workings of Electronic Literature." Paper presented at the Modern Language Association Convention, December 28, 2004. http://nickm.com/writing/essays/continuous_paper_mla.html.

Montfort, Nick, and Ian Bogost. "Platform." 2014. In *The Johns Hopkins Guide to Digital Media*, edited by Marie Laure-Ryan, Lori Emerson, and Benjamin Robertson, 393–95. Baltimore: Johns Hopkins University Press. Project MUSE.

Mooney, Linne R., Simon Horobin, and Estelle Stubbs. 2011. *Late Medieval English Scribes*. https://www.medievalscribes.com.

Mooney, Linne R., and Estelle Stubbs. 2013. *Scribes and the City: London Guildhall Clerks and the Dissemination of Middle English Literature, 1375–1425*. York: York Medieval Press.

Moran, Patrick. 2014. *Lectures cycliques: Le Réseau inter-romanesque dans les cycles du Graal du XIIIe siècle*. Paris: Champion.

Morey, Maribel. 2019. "Rockefeller, Carnegie, and the SSRC's Focus on Race in the 1920s and 1930s." *Items: Insights from the Social Sciences* (blog). January 8, 2019. https://items.ssrc.org/insights/rockefeller-carnegie-and-the-ssrcs-focus-on-race-in-the-1920s-and-1930s.

Munro, John James, ed. 1911. *Frederick James Furnivall: A Volume of Personal Record.* London: Henry Frowde, Oxford University Press. HathiTrust.

Murphy, Kieron. 1996. "So Why Did They Decide to Call It Java?" *InfoWorld*, October 4, 1996. www.infoworld.com/article/2077265/so-why-did-they-decide-to-call-it-java-.html.

Murphy, Peter. 2019. *The Long Public Life of a Private Poem: Reading and Remembering Thomas Wyatt.* Stanford: Stanford University Press.

Mynors, R. A. B. 1963. *Catalogue of the Manuscripts of Balliol College, Oxford.* Oxford: Clarendon Press.

Nadeau, Nils, ed. 2017. *Orozco at Dartmouth: The Epic of American Civilization.* Hanover, NH: Hood Museum of Art and Dartmouth College Libraries. Exhibition Brochure. https://hoodmuseum.dartmouth.edu/sites/hoodmuseum.prod/files/hoodmuseum/publications/270152_orozco_eng_2017.pdf.

Nakamura, Lisa. 2014. "Indigenous Circuits: Navajo Women and the Racialization of Early Electronic Manufacture." *American Quarterly* 66 (4): 919–41. Project MUSE.

Nasmith, James. 1777. *Catalogus Librorum Manuscriptorum quos Collegio Corporis Christi et B. Mariae Virginis in Academia Cantabrigiensis legauit Reverendissimus in Christo Pater Matthaeus Parker, Archiepiscopus Cantuariensis.* Cambridge. HathiTrust. Archive.org. Google.com. https://parker.stanford.edu./parker/about/corpus-christi-college-manuscript-catalogues.

Netz, Reviel, and William Noel. 2007. *The Archimedes Codex: Revealing the Secrets of the World's Greatest Palimpsest.* London: Weidenfeld and Nicolson.

Netz, Reviel, William Noel, Natalie Tchernetska, and Nigel Wilson, eds. 2011. *The Archimedes Palimpsest.* 2 vols. Cambridge: Cambridge University Press.

Newstead, Helaine. 1967. "Arthurian Legends." In *A Manual of the Writings in Middle English*, edited by J. Burke Severs, 1:38–79. New Haven: Connecticut Academy of Arts and Sciences.

Nichols, Ann E. 2008. *An Index of Images in English Manuscripts: From the Time of Chaucer to Henry VIII.* London: Harvey Miller.

Nicolson, William. 1714. *The English Historical Library.* 2nd ed. London. Archive.org.

Niggemann, Elisabeth, Jacques De Decker, and Maurice Lévy. 2011. *The New Renaissance: Report from the Comité des Sages Reflection Group on Bringing Europe's Cultural Heritage Online.* www.eurosfaire.prd.fr/7pc/doc/1302102400_kk7911109enc_002.pdf.

Nightingale, Pamela. 1995. *A Medieval Mercantile Community: The Grocers' Com-*

pany and the Politics and Trade of London, 1000–1485. New Haven, CT: Yale University Press.

Noble, Safiya. 2018. *Algorithms of Oppression: How Search Engines Reinforce Racism*. New York: New York University Press.

Noel, William. 2011. "Introduction: The Archimedes Palimpsest Project." In Netz et al. 2011, 1:1–20.

———. 2012. "Revealing the Lost Codex of Archimedes." Filmed April 2012 in Doha, Qatar. TEDxSummit video, 14:47. www.ted.com/talks/william_noel _revealing_the_lost_codex_of_archimedes.html.

Nowviskie, Bethany. 2000. "Interfacing the Edition." Lecture presented at *Literary Truth and Scientific Method*, Charlottesville, VA, April 10, 2000. www2.iath .virginia.edu/bpn2f/1866/interface.html.

O'Callaghan, Michelle. 2009. *Thomas Middleton, Renaissance Dramatist*. Edinburgh: Edinburgh University Press.

O'Donnell, Daniel. 2004. "The Doomsday Machine, or, 'If You Build It, Will They Still Come Ten Years From Now?': What Medievalists Working in Digital Media Can Do to Ensure the Longevity of Their Research." *Heroic Age*, no. 7: www.heroicage.org/issues/7/ecolumn.html.

Owens, Trevor. 2018. *The Theory and Craft of Digital Preservation*. Baltimore: Johns Hopkins University Press, 2018.

Page, Raymond I. 1981. "The Parker Register and Matthew Parker's Anglo-Saxon Manuscripts." *Transactions of the Cambridge Bibliographical Society* 8:1–17.

———. 1993. *Matthew Parker and His Books*. Kalamazoo, MI: Medieval Institute.

Palmer, Tamara. 2015. "Steve Jobs' Unmarked Grave Becomes Holy Grail." *NBC Bay Area* (October 20): www.nbcbayarea.com/news/local/Steve-Jobs-Un marked-Grave-Becomes-Holy-Grail-334782051.html.

"Parker Library." 2010. Archive.org. www.corpus.cam.ac.uk/parker-library.

"Parker Library." 2018. Archive.org. www.corpus.cam.ac.uk/about-corpus/parker -library.

"Parker Library." 2019. Archive.org. www.corpus.cam.ac.uk/about-corpus/parker -library.

"Parker Library Appeal: An Appeal for Funds for the New Parker Library." 2000. Corpus Christi College. Cambridge: Cambridge University Press.

Parker Library on the Web 1.0. 2009. Nonsubscriber site, archived February 11, 2010. https://web.archive.org/web/20100211002937/http://parkerweb.stanford .edu/parker/actions/page.do?forward=home.

Parker Library on the Web 1.0. 2017. Subscriber site, archived January 24, 2017. https://swap.stanford.edu/*/http://parker.stanford.edu.

Parker Library on the Web 2.0. 2018–21. https://parker.stanford.edu. Partial archive of static pages on https://archive.org.

Parker, Matthew. 1572. *De antiquitate Britannicae ecclesiae & priuilegiis ecclesiae Cantuariensis*. London. EEBO.

Parkes, Malcolm. 1991. "The Literacy of the Laity." In *Scribes, Scripts and Readers: Studies in the Communication, Presentation and Dissemination of Medieval Texts*, 275–98. London: Hambledon Press.

Parks, Lisa, and Nicole Starosielski, eds. 2015. *Signal Traffic: Critical Studies of Media Infrastructures*. Urbana: University of Illinois Press.

Paul, Suzanne. 2018. "Function." Typescript. Keynote lecture presented at *Celebrating Parker 2.0 at Stanford University: Stanford Text Technologies Fourth Annual Collegium*. Palo Alto, CA, March 25–28, 2018.

Pearsall, Derek. 1976. "The English Romance in the Fifteenth Century." *Notes and Queries*, n.s., 29:56–83.

———.1998. "Frederick James Furnivall (1825–1910)." In *Medieval Scholarship: Biographical Studies in the Formation of a Discipline*. Vol. 2, *Literature and Philology*, edited by Helen Damico, 125–38. New York: Garland.

Peele, George. 1585. *The Device of the Pageant Borne before Woolstone Dixi*. London. EEBO.

Pendergrass, Keith L., Walker Sampson, Tim Walsh, and Laura Alagna. 2019. "Toward Environmentally Sustainable Digital Preservation." *American Archivist* 82 (1): 165–206. http://nrs.harvard.edu/urn-3:HUL.InstRepos:40741399.

Percy, Thomas. 1765. "On the Ancient Metrical Romances." In *Reliques of Ancient English Poetry*. Vol. 3, i–xxiv. London. HathiTrust.

Perry, Lewis. 1951. "Edward and Mary Harkness." *Metropolitan Museum of Art Bulletin* 10 (2): 57–59. JSTOR.

Peterson, Erik. 2011. "*Itinera Archimedea*: On Heiberg in Constantinople and Archimedes in Copenhagen." In Netz et al. 2011, 1:119–27.

Phillips, Kim M. 2007. "Masculinities and the Medieval English Sumptuary Laws." *Gender and History* 19 (1): 22–42. Wiley Online Library.

Philological Society. 1847. *Transactions* 3 (58). Google Books.

———.1861. *List of Books*. London: Trübner. *Nineteenth Century Collections Online*. Gale.com: Document no. GHNBTN040644608.

"Photographic Copies of Ancient Manuscripts." 1854. *Notes and Queries* 222 (January 28): 83. Oxford Academic Journals Online.

Pits, John. 1619. *Relationes historicae de rebus Anglicis*. Paris. https://books.google.com/books?id=lLNhAAAAcAAJ.

Plantin, Jean-Christophe, Carl Lagoze, Paul N. Edwards, and Christian Sandvig. 2018. "Infrastructure Studies Meet Platform Studies in the Age of Google and Facebook." *New Media & Society* 20 (1): 293–310. SAGE.

Plotnikoff, David. 1997. "Purple Moon's Sly Rockett Wisks Girls to Computers." *San Jose Mercury News*, October 19, 1997. LexisNexis.com.

Pollard, Alfred W., and G. R. Redgrave. 1926. *A Short-Title Catalogue of Books Printed in England, Scotland, and Ireland and of English Books Printed Abroad, 1475–1640*. London: Bibliographical Society.

Ponceau, Jean-Paul. 1983. "Étude de la tradition manuscrite de *l'Estoire del Saint Graal*, récit du XIIIème siècle." Thèse de 3e cycle. Université de Paris IV-Sorbonne.

———. 1997. *L'estoire del saint graal*. 2 vols. Paris: Champion.

Ponton, Thomas, ed. 1819. *Le Morte Arthur: The Adventures of Sir Launcelot du Lake*. London: William Bulmer for the Roxburghe Club.

Pope, Julia, and Robert Holley. 2011. "Google Book Search and Metadata." *Cataloging and Classification Quarterly* 49 (1): 1–13. Taylor and Francis Online.

Porter, Dot. 2018a. "Is This Your Book? What We Call Digitized Manuscripts and Why It Matters." *Dot Porter Digital* (blog). July 16, 2018. www.dotporterdigital.org/is-this-your-book-what-digitization-does-to-manuscripts-and-what-we-can-do-about-it.

———. 2018b. "The Uncanny Valley and the Ghost in the Machine: A Discussion of Analogies for Thinking about Digitized Medieval Manuscripts." *Dot Porter Digital* (blog). October 31, 2018. www.dotporterdigital.org/the-uncanny-valley-and-the-ghost-in-the-machine-a-discussion-of-analogies-for-thinking-about-digitized-medieval-manuscripts.

———. 2018c. "Using VisColl to Visualize Parker on the Web: Reports on an Experiment." *Dot Porter Digital* (blog). March 18, 2018. www.dotporterdigital.org/using-viscoll-to-visualize-parker-on-the-web-reports-on-an-experiment.

———. 2018d. "Zombie Manuscripts: Digital Facsimiles in the Uncanny Valley." *Dot Porter Digital* (blog). May 12, 2018. www.dotporterdigital.org/zombie-manuscripts-digital-facsimiles-in-the-uncanny-valley.

Power, Eugene B. 1938. "A Report of Progress on Filming English Books before 1550." *Journal of Documentary Reproduction* 1 (1): 45–49.

———. 1944. "The Manuscript Copying Program in England." *American Archivist* 7 (1): 28–32. JSTOR.

———. 1990. *Edition of One: The Autobiography of Eugene B. Power, Founder of University Microfilms*. Ann Arbor, MI: University Microfilms International.

Prescott, Andrew. 1998. "Constructing the Electronic *Beowulf*." In *Towards the Digital Library: The British Library's 'Initiatives for Access' Programme*, edited by Leona Carpenter, Simon Shaw, and Andrew Prescott, 30–49. London: British Library Publications. Archived at https://perma.cc/EBK8-3MFK.

———. 2012. "An Electric Current of the Imagination: What the Digital Humanities Are and What They Might Become." *Journal of Digital Humanities* 1 (2): http://journalofdigitalhumanities.org/1-2/an-electric-current-of-the-imagination-by-andrew-prescott.

———.2013. "The Function, Structure, and Future of Catalogues." *Digital Riffs* (blog). January 11, 2013. http://digitalriffs.blogspot.com/2013/01/the-function -structure-and-future-of.html.

Prescott, Andrew, and Lorna Hughes. 2018. "Why Do We Digitize? The Case for Slow Digitization." *Archive Journal* (September): www.archivejournal.net/ essays/why-do-we-digitize-the-case-for-slow-digitization.

Prise, John. 1573. *Historiae Brytannicae defensio*. London. EEBO.

"Proceedings of the Twenty-Fifth Annual Meeting." 1907. *Publications of the Modern Language Association* 22 (Appendix): iii–xix. JSTOR.

Proposal for the Publication of a New English Dictionary by the Philological Society. 1859. London: Trübner. Google Books.

Putnam, Lara. 2016. "The Transnational and the Text-Searchable: Digitized Sources and the Shadows They Cast." *American Historical Review* 121 (2): 377– 402.

Quandt, Abigail. 2011. "Conserving the Archimedes Palimpsest." In Netz et al. 2011, 1:128–71.

Radulescu, Raluca. 2013. *Romance and Its Contexts in Fifteenth-Century England*. Woodbridge, Suffolk: Boydell and Brewer.

Rambaran-Olm, Mary. 2019. "Misnaming the Medieval: Rejecting 'Anglo-Saxon' Studies." *History Workshop Online*, November 4, 2019. www.historyworkshop .org.uk/misnaming-the-medieval-rejecting-anglo-saxon-studies.

Rand, Kari. 2009. *The Index of Middle English Prose, Handlist XX: Manuscripts of the Library of Corpus Christi College*. Woodbridge, Suffolk: D. S. Brewer.

Rankin, Joy Lisi. 2018. *A People's History of Computing in the United States*. Cambridge, MA: Harvard University Press.

Rawcliffe, Carole. 1993. "Barton, Henry." In *The History of Parliament: The House of Commons, 1386–1421*, edited by J. S. Roskell, Linda Clark, and Carole Rawcliffe. Accessed November 1, 2018. www.historyofparliamentonline.org/vol ume/1386-1421/member/barton-henry-1435.

Reidsma, Matthew. 2019. *Masked by Trust: Bias in Library Discovery*. Sacramento, CA: Library Juice Press.

"Reproductions of Manuscripts and Rare Printed Books." 1950. *PMLA: Publications of the Modern Language Association of America* 6 (3): 289–338. JSTOR.

Resnikoff, Howard. 2018. "Howard L. Resnikoff, 1937–2018." *Boston Globe*, May 13, 2018. www.legacy.com/obituaries/bostonglobe/obituary.aspx?pid=188984732.

Review of *Merlin*, by Ernst Kock. 1932. *Times Literary Supplement*, September 15, 1932 (1598): 646. *The Times Literary Supplement Historical Archive, 1902–2014*. Gale.com: Document no. EX1200043192.

Richardson, Ernest. 1937. *A Union World Catalogue of Manuscript Books*. Vol 6. New York: H. W. Wilson. HathiTrust.

Riddy, Felicity. 2000. "Middle English Romance: Family, Marriage, Intimacy." In *The Cambridge Companion to Medieval Romance*, edited by Roberta L. Krueger, 235–52. Cambridge: Cambridge University Press.

Rikhardsdottir, Sif. 2012. *Medieval Translations and Cultural Discourse: The Movement of Texts in England, France, and Scandinavia*. Cambridge: D. S. Brewer.

Riley, Henry Thomas, ed. and trans. 1859–61. *Liber Albus*, by John Carpenter. London: Longman, Brown, Green, Longmans, and Roberts. Archive.org.

———.1868. *Memorials of London and London Life*. London: Longmans, Green.

Roberts, Jane. 2011. "On Giving Scribe B a Name and a Clutch of London Manuscripts from c. 1400." *Medium Aevum* 80:247–70.

Robinson, Benedict. 1998. "'Darke Speech': Matthew Parker and the Reforming of History." *Sixteenth Century Journal* 29 (4): 1061–83.

Robinson, Pamela R. 2003. *Catalogue of Dated and Datable Manuscripts, c. 888–1600, in London Libraries*. 2 vols. London: British Library.

Robinson, Richard, trans. 1582. *A Learned and True Assertion of the Original, Life, Actes, and Death of the Most Noble, Valiant, and Renoumed Prince Arthure, King of Great Brittaine*, by John Leland. London. EEBO.

Robynson, Ralph, trans. 1551. *Utopia*, by Thomas More. London. http://name .umdl.umich.edu/A07706.0001.001.

Rogers, Alfred. 1912. "Index." In *A Descriptive Catalogue of the Manuscripts in the Library of Corpus Christi College, Cambridge*, by M. R. James. Vol 2, 497–552. Cambridge: Cambridge University Press. Archive.org.

Rollo, David. 1998. *Historical Fabrication, Ethnic Fable and French Romance in Twelfth-Century England*. Lexington: French Forum.

"The Romance of the Holy Graal." 1861. Review of *The History of the Holy Graal*, by Henry Lovelich. *The Spectator*, December 28, 1861 (1748): 1425–26. ProQuest.

Romkey, John. 1988. "Nonstandard for Transmission of IP Datagrams over Serial Lines: SLIP." *Internet Engineering Task Force*, RFC 1055. https://datatracker.ietf .org/doc/rfc1055.

Rosser, Gervase. 2015. *The Art of Solidarity in the Middle Ages: Guilds in England 1250–1550*. Oxford: Oxford University Press.

Rothenberg, Jeff. 1995. "Ensuring the Longevity of Digital Documents." *Scientific American* 272 (1): 42–47. Revised 1999. www.clir.org/wp-content/uploads/ sites/6/ensuring.pdf.

Rubin, Miri. 1991. *Corpus Christi: The Eucharist in Late Medieval Culture*. Cambridge: Cambridge University Press.

Saintsbury, George. 1898. *A Short History of English Literature*. New York: Macmillan. HathiTrust.

———.1913. *The English Novel*. London: J. M. Dent and Sons. HathiTrust.

Sanderson, Robert, Paolo Ciccarese, and Benjamin Young, eds. 2017. "Web An-

notation Data Model." Accessed April 3, 2020. www.w3.org/TR/2017/REC
-annotation-model-20170223.

Santini, Monica. 2010. *The Impetus of Amateur Scholarship: Discussing and Editing Medieval Romances in Late-Eighteenth and Nineteenth-Century Britain*. Bern: Peter Lang.

Schmitt, Georg. 2018. "To Prevent a Digital Dark Age: World Economic Forum Launches Global Centre for Cybersecurity." Posted January 24, 2018. Accessed August 15, 2018. www.weforum.org/press/2018/01/to-prevent-a-digital-dark-age-world-economic-forum-launches-global-centre-for-cybersecurity.

Schneier, Joel, Timothy Stinson, and Matthew Davis. 2018. "BigDIVA and Networked Browsing: A Case for Generous Interfacing and Joyous Searching." *Digital Humanities Quarterly* 12 (2): www.digitalhumanities.org/dhq/vol/12/2/000376/000376.html.

Scott, Kathleen. 1980. *The Mirroure of the Worlde: MS Bodley 283 (England c. 1470–1480): The Physical Composition, Decoration, and Illustration*. Oxford: Roxburghe Club.

———.1996. *Later Gothic Manuscripts, 1390–1490*. 2 vols. London: Harvey Miller.

———.2014. "Past Ownership: Evidence of Book Ownership by English Merchants in the Later Middle Ages." In *Makers and Users of Medieval Books: Essays in Honor of A. S. G. Edwards*, edited by Carol M. Meale and Derek Pearsall, 150–77. Cambridge: D. S. Brewer.

Senchyne, Jonathan. 2019. *The Intimacy of Paper in Early and Nineteenth-Century American Literature*. Amherst: University of Massachusetts Press.

Shailor, Barbara. 1992. *Catalogue of Medieval and Renaissance Manuscripts in the Beinecke Rare Book and Manuscript Library, Yale University*. 3 vols. Binghamton: Medieval and Renaissance Texts and Studies.

Sharpe, Reginald, ed. 1899–1912. *Calendar of Letter-Books Preserved among the Archives of the Corporation of the City of London at Guildhall*. 11 vols. London: Corporation of London. British History Online.

Sherman, William. 2008. *Used Books: Marking Readers in Renaissance England*. Philadelphia: University of Pennsylvania Press.

Shermer, Michael. 2010. "Touching History." *Scepticblog* (blog). October 12, 2010. www.skepticblog.org/2010/10/12/touching-history, archived at https://perma.cc/XPE5-ZCZN.

Shetterly, Margot Lee. 2016. *Hidden Figures: The American Dream and the Untold Story of the Black Women Mathematicians Who Helped Win the Space Race*. New York: HarperCollins.

Shipton, Keith. 2015. "The Digital Dark Age Dilemma." *Photo Review* 64 (June-August): www.photoreview.com.au/tips/storage/the-digital-dark-age-dilemma.

Simpson, James and Sarah Peverley, eds. 2015. *Hardyng's Chronicle: Edited from British Library MS Lansdowne 204*. Kalamazoo: Medieval Institute Publications. http://d.lib.rochester.edu/teams/publication/simpson-pevereley-hardyng-chronicle.

Singleton, Antony. 2005. "The Early English Text Society in the Nineteenth Century: An Organizational History." *Review of English Studies*, n.s., 56 (223): 90–118. JSTOR.

Skeat, Walter, ed. 1865. *Lancelot of the Laik*. EETS OS 6. London: Trübner.

———, ed. 1867. *The Romance of William of Palerne*. EETS ES 1. London: Trübner.

———, ed. 1868. *The Lay of Havelok the Dane*. EETS ES 4. London: Trübner.

———, ed. 1871. *Joseph of Arimathie*. EETS OS 44. London: Trübner.

———. 1902a. "The Translator of 'The Graal.'" *The Athenaeum*, no. 3917 (November 22): 684. HathiTrust.

———. 1902b. "The Author of 'The Holy Grail.'" *The Athenaeum*, no. 3919 (December 6): 758. HathiTrust.

Smith, Sherry L. 2012. *Hippies, Indians, and the Fight for Red Power*. Oxford: Oxford University Press.

Smithies, James. 2017. *The Digital Humanities and the Digital Modern*. London: Palgrave Macmillan.

Smyly, Josiah Gilbart. 1919. "The Romance of Waldef." *Hermathena* 18:242–328.

Sommer, H. Oskar, ed. 1908–16. *The Vulgate Version of the Arthurian Romances*. 8 Vols. Washington: Carnegie Institution.

Spencer, Helen L. 2013. "The Early English Text Society 1930 to 1950: Wartime and Reconstruction." In *Probable Truth: Editing Medieval Texts from Britain in the Twenty-First Century*, edited by Vincent Gillespie and Anne Hudson, 15–35. Turnhout: Brepols.

———. 2015. "F. J. Furnivall's *Six of the Best: The Six-Text Canterbury Tales* and the Chaucer Society." *Review of English Studies* 66 (276): 601–23.

Sponsler, Claire. 1997. *Drama and Resistance: Bodies, Goods, and Theatricality in Late Medieval England*. Minneapolis: University of Minnesota Press.

———. 2014. *The Queen's Dumbshows: John Lydgate and the Making of Early Theater*. Philadelphia: University of Pennsylvania Press.

Srinivasan, Ramesh. 2017. *Whose Global Village? Rethinking How Technology Shapes Our World*. New York: New York University Press.

Stahuljak, Zrinka. 2004. "An Epistemology of Tension: Translation and Multiculturalism." *The Translator* 10 (1): 33–57. Taylor and Francis Online.

Staines, David. 1982. *Tennyson's Camelot: The Idylls of the King and Its Medieval Sources*. Waterloo: Wilfrid Laurier University Press.

Stanford, Emma. 2019. "Harry Potter and the Responsible Version Control of Digital Surrogates." *Shambandinel* (blog). January 31, 2019. https://shamban

dinel.wordpress.com/2019/01/31/harry-potter-and-the-problem-of-version
-controlling-digital-surrogates.

———. 2020. "A Field Guide to Digital Surrogates: Evaluating and Contextualizing a Rapidly Changing Resource." In *The Routledge Companion to Digital Humanities and Art History*, edited by Kathryn Brown, 203–14. London: Routledge.

[Stanley, William.] 1685. *A Discourse Concerning the Devotions of the Church of Rome*. London. EEBO.

———. 1688. *The Faith and Practice of a Church of England-Man*. London. EEBO.

———. 1722. *Catalogus librorum manuscriptorum in Bibliotheca Collegiis Corporis Christi in Cantabrigia: Quos legauit Matthaeus Parkerus Archiepiscopus Cantuariensis*. London. *ECCO: Eighteenth Century Collections Online*, Gale.com. Archive.org. Google.com.

Star, Susan Leigh. 1999. "The Ethnography of Infrastructure." *American Behavioral Scientist* 43 (3): 377–91. ProQuest.

Star, Susan Leigh, and Karen Ruhleder. 1996. "Steps toward an Ecology of Infrastructure: Design and Access for Large Information Spaces." *Information Systems Research* 7(1): 111–34. JSTOR.

Stead, William. 1894. *If Christ Came to Chicago! A Plea for the Union of All Who Love in the Service of All Who Suffer*. Chicago: Laird and Lee. Google Books.

Steeh, Judy. 2002. "Placque Honors Land Gift from Three Native American Tribes." *University Record Online*. November 18, 2002. www.ur.umich.edu/0102/Nov18_02/16.shtml.

Sterne, Jonathan. 2012. *MP3: The Meaning of a Format*. Durham, NC: Duke University Press.

———. 2015. "Compression: A Loose History." In *Signal Traffic: Critical Studies of Media Infrastructures*, edited by Lisa Parks and Nicole Starosielski, 31–52. Urbana: University of Illinois Press.

Stock, Brian. 1990. *Listening for the Text: On the Uses of the Past*. Baltimore: Johns Hopkins University Press.

Stokes, Henry P. 1898. *Corpus Christi*. London: F. E. Robinson. Archive.org.

Stokes, Peter. 2015. "Digital Approaches to Paleography and Book History: Some Challenges, Present and Future." *Frontiers in Digital Humanities* 2 (5): www.frontiersin.org/article/10.3389/fdigh.2015.00005.

Stones, M. Alison. 2000. "Seeing the Grail: Prolegomena to a Study of Grail Imagery in Arthurian Manuscripts." In *The Grail: A Casebook*, edited by Dhira Mahoney, 301–66. New York: Garland.

———. 2003. "'Mise en page' in the French *Lancelot-Grail*: The First 150 Years of the Illustrative Tradition." In Dover 2003, 125–44.

———. 2005. "Illustration and the Fortunes of Arthur." In *The Fortunes of King Arthur*, edited by Norris J. Lacy, 116–65. Cambridge: D. S. Brewer.

———.2010. "Two French Manuscripts: WLC/LM/6 and WLC/LM/7." In *The Wollaton Medieval Manuscripts: Texts, Owners, and Readers*, edited by Ralph Hanna and Thorlac Turville-Petre, 41–56. York: York Medieval Press.

———.2016. *The Lancelot-Grail Project: Chronological and Geographical Distribution of Lancelot-Grail Manuscripts*. www.lancelot-project.pitt.edu/LG-web/Arthur-LG-ChronGeog.html, archived at https://perma.cc/DQ57-2FDU.

Stow, John. 1598. *A Survay of London*. London. EEBO.

———.1633. *A Survey of London*. London. EEBO.

Straw, Will. 2007. "Embedded Memories." In *Residual Media*, edited by Charles Acland, 3–15. Minneapolis: University of Minnesota Press.

Streeter, Thomas. 2011. *The Net Effect: Romanticism, Capitalism, and the Internet*. New York: New York University Press. Project MUSE.

Strohm, Paul. 1998. *England's Empty Throne: Usurpation and Textual Legitimation, 1399–1422*. New Haven, CT: Yale University Press.

Summit, Jennifer. 2008. *Memory's Library: Medieval Books in Early Modern England*. Chicago: University of Chicago Press.

Sutton, Anne F. 2005. *The Mercery of London: Trade, Goods and People, 1130–1578*. Aldershot: Ashgate.

———.2013. "The Acquisition and Disposal of Books for Worship and Pleasure by Mercers of London in the Later Middle Ages." In *Manuscripts and Printed Books in Europe 1350–1550: Packaging, Presentation and Consumption*, edited by Emma Cayley and Susan Powell, 95–114. Liverpool: Liverpool University Press.

Sutton, Kenneth. 1992. "Gladys Krieble Delmas (July 3, 1913–November 20, 1991)." *Proceedings of the American Philosophical Society* 136 (2): 290–93. JSTOR.

Swinburn, Lilian, ed. 1917. *The Lanterne of Liȝt*. EETS OS 151. London: Kegan Paul, Trench, Trübner.

Swisher, Kara. 1996. "Anticipating the Internet." *Washington Post*, May 6, 1996. https://perma.cc/A5H5-TNLU.

Tarte, Ségolène. 2011a. "Digitizing the Act of Papyrological Interpretation: Negotiating Spurious Exactitude and Genuine Uncertainty." *Literary and Linguistic Computing* 26 (3): 349–58. Oxford Academic.

———.2011b. "'Şalmu' and the Nature of Digitized Artefacts." *Artefact to Meaning* (blog). June 5, 2011. https://charades.hypotheses.org/114.

Tatham, John. 1663. *Londinum Triumphans: Londons Triumphs*. London. EEBO.

Taube, Mortimer. 1961. *Computers and Common Sense: The Myth of Thinking Machines*. New York: Columbia University Press.

Taubman, Matthew. 1689. *Londons Great Jubilee*. London. EEBO.

Tennyson, Alfred. 1842. *Poems*. Vol 2. London: Edward Moxon. HathiTrust.

———.1859. *Idyls of the King*. London: Edward Moxon. HathiTrust.

Thrupp, Sylvia L. 1948. *The Merchant Class of Medieval London*. Ann Arbor: University of Michigan Press.

Thylstrup, Nanna Bonde. 2018. *The Politics of Mass Digitization*. Cambridge, MA: MIT Press.

Towler, Katherine. 2006. "History of Harkness: The Men behind the Plan." *Exeter Bulletin*, November 10, 2006. www.exeter.edu/news/history-harkness.

Treharne, Elaine. 2013. "Fleshing Out the Text: The Transcendent Manuscript in the Digital Age." *postmedieval* 4 (4): 465–78. ProQuest.

Trettien, Whitney. 2013. "A Deep History of Electronic Textuality: The Case of *English Reprints Jhon [sic] Milton Areopagitica*." *DHQ: Digital Humanities Quarterly* 7 (1): https://web.archive.org/web/20160723025659/http://digitalhumanities.org:8081/dhq/vol/7/1/000150/000150.html.

———. 2015. "Circuit-Bending History: Sketches toward a Digital Schematic." In *Between Humanities and the Digital*, edited by Patrick Svensson and David Theo Goldberg, 181–92. Cambridge, MA: MIT Press.

———. 2018. "Creative Destruction and the Digital Humanities." In *The Routledge Research Companion to Digital Medieval Literature and Culture*, edited by Jen Boyle and Helen Burgess, 47–60. London: Routledge.

Turner, Fred. 2006. *From Counterculture to Cyberculture: Stewart Brand, the Whole Earth Network, and the Rise of Digital Utopianism*. Chicago: University of Chicago Press.

Turner, Marion. 2007. *Chaucerian Conflict: Languages of Antagonism in Late Fourteenth-Century London*. Oxford: Oxford University Press.

Van Dussen, Michael. 2012. *From England to Bohemia: Heresy and Communication in the Later Middle Ages*. Cambridge: Cambridge University Press.

Van Zundert, Joris. 2018. "On Not Writing a Review about Mirador: Mirador, IIIF, and the Epistemological Gains of Distributed Digital Scholarly Resources." *Digital Medievalist* 11 (1): http://doi.org/10.16995/dm.78.

Vaughn, Richard, and John Fines. 1960. "A Handlist of Manuscripts in the Library of Corpus Christi College, Cambridge, Not Described by M. R. James." *Transactions of the Cambridge Bibliographical Society* 3 (2): 113–23. JSTOR.

Veale, Elspeth M. 1966. *The English Fur Trade in the Later Middle Ages*. Oxford: Clarendon Press.

Veeman, Kathryn. 2016. "John Shirley's Early Bureaucratic Career." *Studies in the Age of Chaucer* 38:255–63.

Vergil, Polydore. (1534) 1555. *Anglica Historia*, edited and translated by Dana F. Sutton. www.philological.bham.ac.uk/polverg.

Verhoeven, Deb. 2016. "As Luck Would Have It: Serendipity and Solace in Digital Research Infrastructure." *Feminist Media Histories* 2 (1): 7–28. http://fmh.ucpress.edu/content/2/1/7.

Vincent de Beauvais. 1591. *Speculum Historiale*. 4 vols. Venice. https://books .google.com/books?id=xq1o85WnSI4C.

Visser-Fuchs, Livia. 1998. "Edward IV's Only Romance? Cambridge, Corpus Christi College MS 91, *L'histoire des Seigneurs de Gavre*." *The Ricardian* 11: 278–87.

Vowel, Chelsea. 2016. "Beyond Territorial Acknowledgments." *Âpihtawikosisân: Law, Language, Culture* (blog). September 23, 2016. https://apihtawikosisan .com/2016/09/beyond-territorial-acknowledgments.

Wadmore, James. 1902. *Some Account of the Worshipful Company of Skinners of London, Being the Guild or Fraternity of Corpus Christi*. 2nd ed. London: Blades, East, and Blades. Archive.org.

Wallace, David. 1997. *Chaucerian Polity: Absolutist Lineages and Associational Forms in England and Italy*. Stanford: Stanford University Press.

Walter, Philippe, ed. 2001–9. *Le livre du graal*. 3 vols. Paris: Gallimard.

Ward, H. L., and J. A. Herbert. 1883–1910. *Catalogue of Romances in the Department of Manuscripts in the British Museum*. 3 vols. London: British Museum. Reprinted 1961–62. HathiTrust.

Warner, Lawrence. 2018. *Chaucer's Scribes: London Textual Production, 1384–1432*. Cambridge: Cambridge University Press.

Warnock, John. 1990. "The Camelot Project." https://planetpdf.com/planetpdf/ pdfs/warnock_camelot.pdf, archived at https://perma.cc/S3GM-PR76 and https://perma.cc/E9ZM-KSVU.

Warren, Michelle R. 2000. *History on the Edge: Excalibur and the Borders of Britain, 1100–1300*. Minneapolis: University of Minnesota Press.

———. 2003. "Post-Philology." In *Postcolonial Moves: Medieval through Modern*, edited by Patricia Clare Ingham and Michelle R. Warren, 19–45. New York: Palgrave Macmillan.

———. 2007. "Translation." In *Oxford Twenty-First Century Approaches to Literature: Middle English*, edited by Paul Strohm, 51–67. Oxford: Oxford University Press.

———. 2008. "Lydgate, Lovelich, and London Letters." In *Lydgate Matters: Poetry and Material Culture in the Fifteenth Century*, edited by Lisa Cooper and Andrea Denny-Brown, 113–38. New York: Palgrave Macmillan.

———. 2011. *Creole Medievalism: Colonial France and Joseph Bédier's Middle Ages*. Minneapolis: University of Minnesota Press.

———. 2015. "Philology in Ruins." *Florilegium* 32:59–76.

———. 2016. "On the Line of the Law: The London Skinners and the Biopolitics of Fur." In *The Politics of Ecology: Land, Life, and the Law in Medieval Britain*, edited by Randy Schiff and Joseph Taylor, 107–26. Columbus: Ohio State University Press.

———.2018a. "Good History, Bad Romance, and the Making of Literature." In *Thinking Medieval Romance*, edited by Nicola MacDonald and Katherine Little, 205–22. Oxford: Oxford University Press.

———.(@MichelleRWarren). 2018b. "hey digital mss friends, anyone have a clue about identifying 'the first digitized medieval manuscript'?" Twitter.com, September 18, 2018, 11:27 a.m. https://twitter.com/MichelleRWarren/status/1042072722023608321.

———.2020. "Making a Home for Medieval Manuscripts on the Internet." In Albritton, Henley, and Treharne 2020, 216–26.

Warren, Michelle R., Bay Lauris ByrneSim, and Laura Braunstein. 2018. "Remix the Medieval Manuscript: Experiments in Digital Infrastructure." *Archive Journal* (September): www.archivejournal.net/essays/remix-the-medieval-manuscript-experiments-with-digital-infrastructure.

Warton, Thomas. 1762. *Observations on the Fairy Queen of Spenser*. 2nd ed. London. HathiTrust.

———.1778. *The History of English Poetry, from the Close of the Eleventh to the Commencement of the Eighteenth Century*. Vol 2. London. HathiTrust.

Webster, John. 1624. *Monuments of Honor*. London. EEBO.

Wells, John. 1916. *A Manual of the Writings in Middle English, 1050–1400*. New Haven, CT: Yale University Press.

Weltevreden, Delano. 2019. "Deel van veelbesproken postkantoor Den Helder kan plat." *Noorhollands Dagblad* (December 3, 2019): www.noordhollandsdagblad.nl/cnt/dmf20191203_19679258.

———.2021. "Over het mediationtraject tussen de gemeente Den Helder en Rob Scholte wordt niets naar buiten gebracht." *Noordhollands Dagblad* (September 30, 2021): www.noordhollandsdagblad.nl/cnt/dmf20210929_40426491.

Werner, Sarah. 2018. "Early Digital Facsimiles." Pforzheimer Lecture, Harry Ransom Center, University of Texas, Austin. February 23, 2018. www.youtube.com/watch?v=g3XXRpO7bBg.

Whearty, Bridget. 2018. "Adam Scriveyn in Cyberspace: Loss, Labour, Ideology, and Infrastructure in Interoperable Reuse of Digital Manuscript Metadata." In *Meeting the Medieval in a Digital World*, edited by Matthew Evan Davis, Tamsyn Mahoney-Steel, and Ece Turnator, 157–201. Amsterdam: Amsterdam University Press.

———.Forthcoming. *Digital Codicology: Medieval Books and Modern Labor*. Stanford: Stanford University Press.

Wheatley, Henry, ed. 1865–69. *Merlin, or, The Early History of King Arthur: A Prose Romance*. EETS OS 10, 21, 36. London: Trübner.

White, Tom. 2020. "National Philology, Imperial Hierarchies, and the 'Defective'

Book of Sir John Mandeville." *Review of English Studies* 71:828–49. Oxford Academic.

"Why Was the Name Apache Chosen?" 2019. *The Apache Software Foundation.* Accessed November 24, 2019. www.apache.org/foundation/faq.html#name.

Wilder, Craig. 2013. *Ebony and Ivy: Race, Slavery, and the Troubled History of America's Universities.* New York: Bloomsbury.

Wilkins, Nigel. 1993. *Catalogue des manuscrits français de la bibliothèque Parker (Parker Library).* Typescript. Corpus Christi College, Cambridge: Parker Library. www.corpus.cam.ac.uk/sites/default/files/downloads/wilkins.pdf.

Williams, Moelwyn I. 1985. *A Directory of Rare Book and Special Collections in the United Kingdom and Republic of Ireland.* London: Library Association.

Willinsky, John. 1994. *Empire of Words: The Reign of the OED.* Princeton, NJ: Princeton University Press.

Willinsky, John, Alex Garnett, and Angela Pan Wong. 2012. "Refurbishing the Camelot of Scholarship: How to Improve the Digital Contribution of the PDF Research Article." *Journal of Electronic Publishing* 15 (1): https://quod.lib.umich.edu/j/jep/3336451.0015.102?view=text;rgn=main.

Wilson, William Jerome. 1942. "The Union Catalog of the Library of Congress." In *Symbols Used in the Union Catalog of the Library of Congress.* 4th ed., 3–7. Washington, DC: Library of Congress. HathiTrust.

———. 1943a. "Manuscripts in Microfilm: Problems of Librarian and Custodian." *Library Quarterly* 13 (3): 212–26. JSTOR.

———. 1943b. "Manuscripts in Microfilm: Problems of Cataloger and Bibliographer." *Library Quarterly* 13 (4): 293–309. JSTOR.

———. 1956. "Manuscript Cataloging." *Traditio* 12:457–555. JSTOR.

Wing, Donald. 1945–51. *Short-Title Catalogue of Books Printed in England, Scotland, Ireland, Wales, and British America, and of English Books Printed in Other Countries, 1641–1700.* New York: Index Society.

Winstanley, William. 1687. *The Honour of the Taylors, or, The Famous and Renowned History of Sir John Hawkwood, Knight.* London. EEBO.

Wogan-Browne, Jocelyn, Thelma Fenster, and Delbert Russell, eds. and trans. 2016. *Vernacular Literary Theory from the French of England: Texts and Translations, c.1120–c.1450.* Cambridge: D. S. Brewer.

Wooster, James Willet. 1949. *Edward Stephen Harkness, 1874–1940.* New York: William E. Rudge's Sons. Dartmouth College, Rauner Special Collections, Alumni W889e.

Wylie, James. 1914. *The Reign of Henry the Fifth.* Vol. 1. Cambridge: Cambridge University Press.

Young, Tyler A. 2018. "General Overview: OpenWayback." Accessed November 24, 2019. https://github.com/iipc/openwayback/wiki/General-overview.

Zeffiro, Andrea. 2019. "Digitizing Labor in the Google Books Project: Gloved Fingertips and Severed Hands." In *Humans at Work in the Digital Age: Forms of Digital Textual Labor*, edited by Shawna Ross and Andrew Pilsch, 133–53. New York: Routledge.

Zuroski, Eugenia. 2020. "Academic Land Acknowledgment for Settler Scholars." *American Society for Eighteenth Century Studies: Graduate Student Caucus* (blog). February 25, 2020. https://asecsgradcaucus.wordpress.com/2020/02/25/academic-land-acknowledgment-for-settler-scholars-a-guest-post-by-dr-eugenia-zuroski.

Bold page numbers refer to figures.

STANFORD
TEXT TECHNOLOGIES

Series Editors
Ruth Ahnert
Elaine Treharne

————

Blaine Greteman
Networking Print in Shakespeare's England: Influence,
Agency, and Revolutionary Change

Simon Reader
Notework: Victorian Literature and Nonlinear Style

Yohei Igarashi
The Connected Condition: Romanticism
and the Dream of Communication

Elaine Treharne and Claude Willan
Text Technologies: A History

CPSIA information can be obtained
at www.ICGtesting.com
Printed in the USA
JSHW031021300122
22400JS00002B/2